Juries *and the* Transformation *of* Criminal Justice *in* France

in the Nineteenth & Twentieth Centuries

JAMES M. DONOVAN

The University *of* North Carolina Press   Chapel Hill

© 2010
THE UNIVERSITY
OF NORTH CAROLINA
PRESS
Set in ITC Galliard by
Rebecca Evans
Manufactured in the
United States of America

The paper in this book meets the guidelines for
permanence and durability of the Committee on
Production Guidelines for Book Longevity of the
Council on Library Resources.

The University of North Carolina Press has been a
member of the Green Press Initiative since 2003.

Library of Congress Cataloging-in-Publication Data
Donovan, James M., professor
Juries and the transformation of criminal justice in
France in the nineteenth and twentieth centuries /
James M. Donovan.
p. cm. Includes bibliographical references and index.
ISBN 978-0-8078-3363-6 (cloth : alk. paper)
1. Jury—France—History. 2. Criminal procedure—
France—History. 3. Criminal justice, Administration
of—France—History. I. Title.
KJV8800.D66 2010
345.44'075—dc22 2009027710

14 13 12 11 10 5 4 3 2 1

CONTENTS

TABLES

ACKNOWLEDGMENTS

A number of individuals and institutions over the years have in some way contributed to or have helped to make possible the genesis and completion of this book. As a graduate student at New Mexico State University in the mid-1970s, I first became interested in the subject of criminality in nineteenth-century France when the late Edgar Leon Newman, my master's thesis advisor, suggested the topic of crime, revolution, and collective violence in France from 1825 through 1852. A few years later, when I was a doctoral student at Syracuse University, Cissie Fairchilds encouraged me to write an article on the behavior of French juries in the nineteenth century. As a consequence, by the early 1980s, my research agenda had come to focus on crime and justice in France in the nineteenth and twentieth centuries. After a series of papers and published articles, I became convinced of the importance of juries in changing the French penal system in the course of the nineteenth and twentieth centuries.

For this reason, I began work on the present book in 1998. Much of the research was done at the New York Public Library and at the Library of Congress. Penn State provided the necessary assistance through research grants and through the university's interlibrary loan system. I would also like to thank the College of the Liberal Arts at Penn State for providing financial support for the publication of the book.

As I approached completion of the first draft, Gregg Roeber, chair of Penn State's history department, suggested submitting the manuscript to the University of North Carolina Press Studies in Legal History series. I sent an abstract to Thomas Green, the Studies in Legal History editor responsible for non-American manuscripts. Tom's response was positive. It has been my good fortune to work with Tom, who has spent many hours making numerous excellent suggestions through a number of versions, which eventually resulted in a much better book. For this I am very grateful. Jim Whitman of the Yale Law School and Robert Allen of Stephen F. Austin State University both read the manuscript in its entirety and made many fine suggestions. Finally, I want to express my deep gratitude to my wife, Betty, for the support and encouragement she provided and for the sacrifices she made to help the book become a reality.

INTRODUCTION

The institution of trial by jury is intimately connected with democracy. It is based on the assumption that ordinary citizens are capable of administering justice, just as they are capable of choosing their political leaders. Juries, by virtue of their relative independence, have also often been important protectors of the people's liberties. In France, Britain, and the United States, they have frequently acquitted persons accused of political, press, or speech offenses, to the chagrin of the authorities.[1]

"Jury nullification"—being defined as the exercise of jury discretion in favor of a defendant whom the panel nevertheless believes committed the act for which he or she has been charged[2]—has also been at times applied to the far larger numbers of persons tried for nonpolitical (or "routine") felonies. This does not mean that juries necessarily disregard evidence. But in other cases, juries may react against the strict letter of the law. In political cases, jury nullification usually grows out of political motives (resistance to tyranny, defense of a free press, opposition to the regime in power, and the like). In the case of routine felonies, it usually arises from the jury's belief that the penalties prescribed by law for certain offenses are too severe or from the panel's sympathy with some types of offenders or with offenders in particular circumstances. Jury decisions in routine felony cases also embody changing moral and social norms.

The aim of this book is to combine a broad political-institutional approach to the subject of jury behavior with an "internalist" legal approach that focuses on the technicalities of jury trial. One is a necessary corrective to the other. Historians who have focused on the broad political-institutional aspects have often had a strong bias in favor of class-based explanations of jury behavior. For example, those who have studied jury trial in nineteenth-century France have frequently claimed that conviction rates for property crimes were much higher than for violent crimes because nearly all jurors were bourgeois and were therefore especially tough on those criminals who threatened property. These historians cite as evidence overall judicial statistics on conviction rates for property crimes and violent crimes and data on the occupations of jurors. But a more careful look at the judicial statistics and a close examination of contemporary legal sources show that there were other reasons as well for the differential having to do with legal issues, trial procedures, problems of evidence, and the subtle dynamics of jury trial. In fact, close study of these sources shows that bourgeois jurors were often surprisingly sympathetic to accused persons from the masses.

However, too great a focus on the legalistic internalist approach can also lead to distortions of perspective. For instance, contemporary jurists in nineteenth- and twentieth-century France usually saw "correctionalization"— that is, the downgrading of *crimes* (felonies), tried by the juries of the *cours d'assises* (courts of assizes), to *délits* (misdemeanors), which were tried by the three-judge panels of the *tribunaux correctionnels* (correctional courts)—as an administrative measure aimed at reducing the expense, cumbersomeness, and "incompetence" of jury trial in favor of a more rapid, streamlined, and efficacious procedure. But jurists paid little attention to the political reasons for correctionalization, especially under Napoleon III, who undermined jury trial in his pursuance of an authoritarian agenda.

A combination of broad political and internalist legal approaches is especially fruitful for understanding the behavior of juries in France since the Revolution. Until the middle of the twentieth century, the central dilemma there was the tendency of juries to acquit in cases where members of the legal profession believed it was appropriate to convict. In other instances, juries convicted persons on lesser charges than the most serious ones brought by the prosecution, again in cases where jurists thought that the evidence justified a different verdict. Something close to a consensus existed among legal writers (including officials of the Ministry of Justice) that juries were reacting against the harsh penalties prescribed by the Napoleonic *Code pénal*. It appears that in these cases, the panels were exercising a form of jury nullification.

But as Thomas A. Green notes, the term "jury nullification" needs to be carefully qualified.[3] It took various forms, though they were not always clearly distinguishable from each other. One form was rejection of the substantive law itself—that is, where the jury acquits an accused person because the panel believes the act he or she is accused of should not be defined by law as a crime. At least in France during the nineteenth and twentieth centuries, this form of nullification was mostly limited to political cases and usually grew out of resistance to laws seen as tyrannical or from defense of freedom of speech and press or opposition to the government. But far more common was sanction nullification, which was normally applicable to the much larger number of nonpolitical or "routine" felonies (homicide, infanticide, theft, rape, and the like). In sanction nullification, the jury does not reject the law the defendant is accused of violating but either acquits or—in what this book defines as jury devices for leniency—finds the defendant not guilty of the most serious offense charged but guilty of a lesser included offense. There are two kinds of sanction nullification. One is a systemic refusal to convict at a high level for certain kinds of offenses, and the other is rejection of sanctions in a given case due to specific considerations (for example, sympathy for a particular defendant) where juries are otherwise generally willing to convict.

It is with the general rejection of sanctions that this book is chiefly concerned. One caution is that sometimes it cannot be known when juries objected to the law itself or to the level of sanction or to both. For instance, in homicide cases before 1832, juries often seem to have opposed the sanction (the death penalty), but they might also have done so because they believed there had been extenuating circumstances that the law did not then recognize.

The preponderance of evidence shows that sanction nullification was the predominant form of jury nullification in France during the nineteenth and twentieth centuries. Certainly, that was what contemporary jurists believed. For two centuries, the authorities dealt with jury resistance to sanctions through a series of legal and administrative reforms that on one hand granted to juries more extensive legal powers in the imposition of punishment and on the other hand removed more cases from their purview and ultimately destroyed their independence. Yet the important point about the French example is that it shows how through nullification, juries can profoundly modify the operation of the criminal justice system in ways never originally intended.

This had been true in England—the birthplace of the modern jury system—from the time the criminal trial jury was introduced there following the church's decree in 1215 forbidding priests to bless trials by ordeal.[4] From the thirteenth century through the early nineteenth and beyond, juries in that country often engaged in nullification either through outright acquittals or through jury devices for leniency.[5]

Jury nullification remained a central feature of the English criminal justice system until the parliamentary reforms of the 1830–40 era abolished capital punishment for many of the less serious felonies. Thereafter, jury mitigation of penalties became a far less common practice, and it largely passed from public consciousness, save in celebrated cases.[6] Until modern times, it also largely passed from the consciousness of most historians, who, when they dealt with the concept of jury nullification at all, generally focused on its application to political cases, as examples of resistance to the authorities.[7]

In the last few decades, however, the rich history of jury discretion in England has been rediscovered by historians, and a considerable literature on it has been developed. Several historiographical trends have been responsible for this rediscovery. They include the rise since the late 1960s of social history, of "history from below," which among other things is concerned with what the actions of those who violated the criminal laws reveal about the wider society.[8] Then in the 1970s, "labeling" theory, borrowed from sociology, became influential. It held that an act was not "deviant" or criminal because of its own quality but rather because of the application by others of rules and penalties to the "offender."[9] Some social historians were influenced by British sociologists who revived Marxist theories of the state, with their "questions about how, why, and whether the state was the tool of a particular class."[10] Moreover, legal historians, who focus on changes in the law and in the legal system, began to do more research on the operation of the criminal justice system in the eighteenth century. All of these historiographical trends encouraged not only the study of crime but also the study of the machinery of justice.[11]

This included discretion in the imposition of punishment. Historians of the criminal justice system in England found that juries before the early nineteenth century often mitigated penalties through their verdicts. In the 1980s and after, scholars such as Thomas Green, J. M. Beattie, Peter King, and John H. Langbein have shown that juries in England from the Middle Ages through the eighteenth century repeatedly rendered verdicts that reflected social norms and popular conceptions of justice that were not always in agreement with the law. Jury devices for leniency were especially common during the eighteenth century, when many property crimes had become punishable by death. Jurors frequently convicted property offenders of lesser crimes than those for which they were tried in order to save the necks of prisoners they thought did not deserve to die. Rather than fight juries, authorities in England accommodated themselves to the panels' standards of justice, either through recommendations for leniency from the bench or through changes in the law.[12]

Yet just as jury mitigation of the law was becoming a relatively infrequent phenomenon in England, it was beginning to play a very important role in the criminal justice system of France. Green's statement that from the time the jury system was introduced in England, "both jury-based mitigation and a struggle to limit its reach were virtually inevitable"[13] was equally applicable to France after the jury was introduced there in 1791.[14]

Jury mitigation of punishment in France was facilitated by the fact that juries there answered a series of questions rather than rendered general verdicts. These questions included: Did the crime occur? Was the accused guilty of it? Did he or she intend to commit it? Were there aggravating circumstances or (after 1832) extenuating circumstances?[15] It would appear that since they answered a series of specific questions, jurors in France were less able than English ones to "bury" or conceal sanction nullification within a general verdict. But the answers to the specific questions were themselves sites for concealed sanction nullification, though the authorities were not fooled. For example, the Ministry of Justice claimed that in the early nineteenth century, juries often lightened penalties for the persons they convicted by answering "non" to the question of whether there were aggravating circumstances, even when these circumstances were very well proven.[16]

Again as in England, the authorities accommodated themselves to the juries' notions of justice through the bench's association with jury leniency in punishment and through statutes reducing penalties for certain crimes. But where in England the authorities eventually reduced jury recourse to extralegal mitigation of punishment by reforming sanctions, in France they sought to do so by granting to the panels a share in the power to determine penalties legally. An important act of 1832 allowed the panels to find legally mitigating circumstances (and therefore obliged the court to reduce the penalties) for persons found guilty of felonies. This reform was aimed at reducing acquittals and extralegal jury devices for leniency allegedly brought about by the panels' desire to spare culprits from the harsh and rigid punishments stipulated in the *Code pénal*. But the 1832 law did not require juries to give their reasoning,[17] and there is much evidence that they thereafter often used the law to practice sanction nullification through finding extenuating circumstances where they did not exist. In 1932, another law was passed giving to juries a direct and predominant share in determining the penalty. The result was that juries did much to replace an Enlightenment-inspired penal system of rigidly fixed punishments equally applicable to all offenders convicted of the same crime with a highly discretionary one that to some extent resembled that which had existed in England in the eighteenth century.

To American readers, a major means through which juries achieved this outcome—"partial verdicts"—may not seem a praiseworthy feature of the French justice system. They could be seen as providing lawyers with opportunities to manipulate juries for the defendants and are not a "norm" in the American justice system, in the sense that they are not openly encouraged in the courts. Certainly, to Anglo-American readers, the French system may appear perplexing. That partial verdicts were so common, open, and tolerated in France may seem surprising to them. But the key to understanding the French system is that its jury fact-finding procedure, with its series of questions rather than general verdicts, was designed to fit the level of punishment to what juries believed proved under French law. This gave the panels much leeway, especially after 1832 through the finding of legally mitigating circumstances. Such a system of fact-finding easily facilitated partial verdicts to achieve leniency in punishment. To some extent, the authorities tolerated this rather than reduced the severity of punishments through statutory law.

No systematic analysis of how juries did so much to create a highly discretionary penal system in France in the course of the nineteenth and twentieth centuries has been undertaken before. Certainly, articles and portions of books have appeared that have dealt with aspects of jury behavior in France during certain periods and with respect to certain crimes (for example, abortion, infanticide, violent crimes, theft, political and press offenses, and so on).[18] But no comprehensive study of the influence of juries on punishment or on the transformation of penal law in France during the nineteenth and early twentieth centuries has yet been published.[19] This book is such a study.

It should not, however, be assumed that juries were always or necessarily barometers of public opinion in France. Jury decisions were probably less representative of public mores in some cases than in others. The composition of the panels was very unrepresentative of the population as a whole, due at least in part to the fact that jury service in France was rarely acknowledged in theory as a right, and was almost never so in practice, until 1980, when jurors were finally designated by lot from electoral lists under a system of full suffrage.[20] It was usually regarded as a judicial function to be carried out not by all citizens but only by those who were "bons jurés" or assumed to be most "capable" of judging, and this meant that most jurors were bourgeois. During much of the nineteenth century, only wealthy or well-to-do men—the *notables*—served on juries. Even when the *notables* no longer dominated the panels after about 1880, male bourgeois property-owners continued to account for most jurors. Therefore, it can be argued that juries reflected the opinions of these elites only, the same elites that until 1848 monopolized the franchise.

Yet they were elites that, when they sat on juries, were often merciful to the generally lower-class people they tried. Upper- and middle-class jurors have not always been biased against or ferocious toward accused persons from the bottom levels of the social hierarchy, and they have often extended to them the benefits of sanction nullification. This is known from English experience. In England during the eighteenth century, property qualifications for jurors ensured that they came from at least the top half of the adult male population in terms of wealth, and much more likely from the top third or fourth.[21] Yet nearly all the people they tried came from segments of the population too poor to qualify for jury duty.[22] Jurors, however, often convicted defendants of lesser charges than the most serious ones brought by the prosecution for property crimes and thereby saved a significant number of lower-class defendants from the noose.

French jurors (at least before the end of the nineteenth century) came from an even more restricted group (less than 1 percent of the population during the era from 1815 through 1848). Yet they also delivered verdicts that mitigated the harshness of the law for many of the generally poor defendants.

Just why this was so is something of a mystery, especially in a country, such as France, where class conflict was so evident in the nineteenth century. Perhaps *notables* as jurors wanted to retain the goodwill of the masses in the provinces. Douglas Hay, writing of judges in eighteenth-century England, claims that they frequently granted pardons to persons condemned to death because popular opinion would not have tolerated the large number of executions that would have resulted from the strict application of the penal laws, and the "gentry were aware that their security depended on . . . belief in the justice of their rule."[23] Such a belief might have been behind certain jury decisions, too, in eighteenth-century England and nineteenth-century France.

But the analogy should not be taken too far. In nineteenth-century France, authority was much more contested than in eighteenth-century England. A more probable explanation for interclass jury sanction nullification in France is that *notables* as jurors were faced with the trials of individuals, not classes. Evidence from data on trial verdicts and the observations of contemporaries suggest that the *notables* who cheered the government's brutal suppression of the working-class insurrections in Paris and Lyon in 1831–34 and during the June Days uprising in Paris in 1848—rebellions that presumably so frightened the upper classes on the generalized political level—could be merciful as jurors when faced with individual defendants from the lower classes charged with routine felonies and whose particular circumstances rendered them worthy of mercy. For example, panels of *notables* found extenuating circumstances for the overwhelming majority of persons they convicted of theft by a servant, though jurors came from the classes that customarily employed servants and were most exposed to this potential danger within their homes. Perhaps not surprisingly, they may have felt a degree of mercy for a servant who was faced with at least five years' imprisonment (when extenuating circumstances were not found) for stealing something of trivial value from his or her employer.

Juries of *notables* also frequently were moved to mercy for the generally poor, unmarried, seduced, abandoned women accused of infanticide, who had so often been dismissed from their jobs, were usually without resources, whose options in dealing with illegitimate births were limited, and who were even prevented by law from getting any financial support from the fathers of their infants. Rarely did jurors, faced with these women as pitiable individuals, want to send them to the guillotine. Juries of *notables* in addition found first-time offenders accused of routine felonies in general often worthy of mercy.

Nor did governmental intrusion into the jury selection process significantly compromise the panels' independence from the authorities in the trials of political and press cases. The French were keenly aware of the political implications, and the potential for bias, when laws were proposed to change the qualifications of jurors or to change the officials who drew up the annual jury lists. This awareness was heightened by the fact that nearly every new regime changed the laws governing the selection of jurors to favor its supporters. Parliamentary debates of the nineteenth century clearly reflected this awareness. For instance, in the debate over the jury composition law of 1872, liberals in the National Assembly protested against the great authority the act gave to the judiciary in the drawing up of jury lists. This was because the liberals strongly distrusted a judiciary dominated by conservatives and assumed to be too much influenced by the prosecution and by the government.

Liberal fears of judicial bias against political and press defendants were not unfounded. A number of modern historians have claimed that the French judiciary of the nineteenth century was to a considerable degree politicized.[24] The judges of the bench were appointed by the minister of justice. Like most jurors (at least before the 1880s), most judges were well-to-do *notables*. They had to be. Both the *magistrature debout* (prosecutors and their assistants) and the *magistrature assise* (judges of the bench) were required to have law degrees and to have served for two years as *stagiaires* (trainees in a law office). Because study of the law was a lengthy process, scholarships were few, and *stagiaires* were usually unpaid, generally only well-to-do men could provide their sons with legal training. Moreover, lower-level judges received meager salaries. That meant they had to have considerable outside incomes in order to maintain the standard of living expected of magistrates.[25] Unlike prosecutors, who enjoyed no security of tenure, judges of the bench were supposed to be irremovable according to laws of 1810 and 1852.[26] However, their irremovability was compromised from time to time when new regimes came to power and sought to purge, at least to a limited extent, the partisans of the preceding regime from the magistrature.[27] Judges also had to be politically well-connected to secure promotion.[28] This meant that in political cases, judges (who were mostly conservatives before the 1880s) were not always impartial.[29] Judges of the bench, much more than jurors, tended to take the government's side in political and press cases.[30]

But judges found it especially difficult to control juries in political and press cases. It was also remarkable how little the repeated attempts by succeeding regimes to change jury selection rules and procedures altered the juries' proclivity to nullify in political and press cases. The panels were indeed the "palladium of liberty," for they constituted the chief guardians of freedom of expression in France. Whenever juries were allowed to try persons for crimes of opinion (*délits politiques et de presse*)—during most of the Revolution, 1819–22, 1830–51, and after 1870—they either acquitted most of the defendants or (after 1880) convicted a slim majority, but at a rate still well below that for ordinary felonies. Historians have tried to explain the frequent acquittals for political and press offenses, but they have done so only for separate periods, or for several adjoining ones. They have also tended to see the acquittals as manifestations of opposition to the regime in power, for the authorities who drew up jury lists were by no means able to always exclude government opponents from juries.[31]

But no explanation has been provided for the consistency of jury behavior in political and press cases through every regime that allowed jurors to try them. One reason for the persistence of frequent acquittals may have been the relatively high social status of many of the persons accused of *délits politiques et de presse*—journalists, editors, printers, writers.[32] These were not ordinary thugs, and the bourgeois jurors were often lenient to bourgeois defendants. Several other possible reasons for the persistence were interrelated—the often vague nature of the charges in political and press cases, the frequent changes of regime, and the lack of legitimacy of successive governments.

During the nineteenth century, juries in political and press cases were expected to rule on such charges as "inciting hatred and contempt of the gov-

Introduction

ernment," "inciting hatred and contempt of a class of persons," "provocation to disobedience of the laws," "attack against property," and the like. In
addition to these offenses, for which one could be charged throughout the
century, others were specific to certain regimes: "attack against the rights
and authority of the Chambers" (July Monarchy), "attack against the Constitution, the republican institutions, the rights of the Assembly" (Second
Republic), "attack against the National Assembly" (Third Republic), and
other political and press misdemeanors too numerous to mention. Such
broadly defined offenses could be stretched to include almost any criticisms
of the government, and juries must have been aware of this fact.

The charges not only were vague but also shifted with the political
winds. As several jurists of the late nineteenth and early twentieth centuries
observed, the definition of what constituted a political crime changed every
time a new regime came to power in France.[33] Not one of the republics or
monarchies established between 1789 and 1870 lasted for as long as twenty
years. The successive regimes in nineteenth-century France also lacked legitimacy—that is, there was no consensus among the French that they were
lawful or rightful governments, because each had come to power through
illegal or extralegal means. This (along with the sharp political divisions)
must have contributed to instability.

Because each regime was insecure, each resorted to repression against its
enemies, often in the form of political and press prosecutions. The fact that
with each change of regime the definition of what constituted a political
or press offense also changed could not help but breed a certain cynicism
among jurors who, often being well into middle age, had seen a number
of regimes come and go through illegal or extralegal means and whose
leaders sought to prosecute those who had once prosecuted them. The political criminal of yesterday was the government leader of today. And the
fact that each regime had come to power through other than legal means
must have made the hypocrisy of political and press prosecutions evident to
many jurors. Perhaps, too, jurors were simply more devoted to liberty than
governments.

Clearly, then, there were severe limits on the ability of the authorities
to control juries. But problematical for a study of the significance of jury
discretion in France is the fact that in that country, the history of the jury
is one of decline almost from the beginning. Scarcely had the institution
been introduced before it was sharply criticized by magistrates, political
authorities, and some jurists for alleged partiality, incompetence, and excessive leniency. Through the course of the nineteenth and early twentieth
centuries, the jury system was gradually reduced to a mere shadow of what

it had been in the Revolutionary period. It was distrusted by Napoleon, who significantly restricted its role in the justice system. Then, from the mid-nineteenth century onward, the magistrates who controlled the prosecution, investigation, and indictment process further undermined the jury system through the process of correctionalization.

It was true that correctionalization required the cooperation of the defendants, who could still insist on their right to jury trial. But they would have found it difficult to assert that right when they appeared before the *juge d'instruction* (examining magistrate), at least before 1897, when those accused at this investigatory stage were not informed of the charges against them.[34] However, when once brought before the *tribunal correctionnel*, the defendants, by pointing out the facts that would justify felony charges against them, could force the court to declare itself incompetent to try them. In fact, some American legal scholars have argued that the French practice of correctionalization in the nineteenth and twentieth centuries was a form of "tacit vertical charge bargain[ing]." The French legal system did not allow for "plea bargaining" as such, and there was still a trial, whether the case was bound for the *cour d'assises* or the *tribunal correctionnel*. There was no explicit trading of a lighter penalty for an admission of guilt. The accused's acquiescence in correctionalization was a sort of substitute. Defendants may have "cooperated" in not demanding a jury trial in exchange for receiving the lighter penalties imposed by the *tribunal correctionnel*.[35] But few defendants whose offenses were reclassified from felonies to misdemeanors protested, since it meant lighter penalties.[36]

Another critical stage in the decline of the jury system was reached in the early twentieth century when critics of the jury gained greater support from jurists, journalists, politicians, and the public due to a number of political, social, legal, and intellectual trends. By 1941, such critics had succeeded in replacing the independent jury system with the system of *échevinage*, in which the three judges of the *cours d'assises* deliberate and vote with the jurors in determining both the verdict and the penalty. By this time also, juries tried only a fraction of the number of cases they had tried a century earlier. The virtual abandonment of the jury system by French liberals, who in the nineteenth century had strongly defended it as the "palladium of liberty," dealt a crucial blow against the institution.

Yet before it was reduced to insignificance, the jury system in France played an important role in reforming the nation's legal system. It was true that the jurors were far from representative of the general population in socioeconomic and gender terms. Yet, members of an elite group can be divided about what constitutes justice, just as they can be divided on political issues. And more often than not, jurors have reflected public opinion more closely than have the state's appointed magistrates. The juries' refusal to convict many accused persons for fear they would be punished too harshly under the Revolutionary and Napoleonic penal codes resulted in a series of legal reforms. The juries' verdicts also expressed the changing norms of nineteenth- and early-twentieth-century France, even when these conflicted with the letter of the law.

Such verdicts were facilitated by the nature of trials in the *cours d'assises*, which appear to have often allowed jurors to decide in accordance with their personal sentiments. Much of this bias was due to the fact that juries often judged on the basis of the accused person's character; the trials were of personalities as much as they were of crimes. This was because of the ways in which evidence was presented, evidence that also appealed more to the emotions than to the reason of jurors. The *cours d'assises* were set up by Napoleon's Code of Criminal Procedure (*Code d'instruction criminelle*) in 1808 to try *crimes* (felonies). They were the only courts in France to use juries. There was one in each *département*. It was presided over by a *président* (chief justice) and two junior colleagues (four between 1808 and 1831) who voted with the *président* to determine the penalty. Questions of guilt or innocence were decided by twelve jurors. Trial proceedings in the *cours d'assises* were theatrical in nature,[37] and this, along with the active questioning of defendants and witnesses by the *président*, the lack of rules of evidence, and the requirement that jurors decide the questions put to them on the basis of their "intimate conviction" rather than by rigorous standards of proof, gave the panels many opportunities to render judgments that were not impartial.

The theatrical nature of the trial (whose procedure, following the flux of the Revolutionary era, was essentially fixed for a century and a half by Napoleon's Code of Criminal Procedure) was evident nearly from its start. First, the *président* asked the accused his or her name, age, occupation, residence, and place of birth. Then he administered an oath to the jurors as they stood: "Do you swear before man and God . . . that you will decide according to the charges and the evidence, following your conscience and intimate conviction, with the impartiality and firmness which becomes a free and upright man?" Each juror was called individually by the *président* and responded with his uplifted hand: "Je le jure" (I swear it).[38] Next, the *greffier* (court clerk) read to the court in a loud voice the *acte d'accusation* (bill of indictment), drawn up by the *procureur général* (public prosecutor) and summarizing the evidence against the accused. It was often long and denunciatory and included anything the public prosecutor wished to say against the accused. It was really a speech for the prosecution, "drawn with great literary skill."[39]

The accused then stepped to the witness box ("a moment of drama second only to the jury's announcement of the verdict"). The *président* of the court, armed with an extensive dossier of the accused drawn up by a *juge d'instruction*, which included not only the facts of the crime but also the defendant's whole past life, began his *interrogatoire* (interrogatory) of the defendant. The *interrogatoire* was based on the *président*'s authority to demand from either the accused or the witnesses any explanations or elucidations that the judge "believed necessary for the revelation of the truth."[40] The *interrogatoire* in important cases could last for several days, and again it included the accused's social and domestic life and any offenses he or she may have committed before and the facts relating thereto, "often to the evident and great prejudice of the prisoner."[41]

The court then heard the testimony of witnesses, who were also questioned by the *président*, following which the prosecution first and then the defense posed questions, not through direct cross-examination but through the mouth of the *président*. Not only were there no rules of evidence, but there were few rules regarding the competency of witnesses, who were free to say almost anything they pleased, including hearsay.[42] Opinion testimony was also allowed, and like the *interrogatoire*, it frequently dealt with the character, family situation, background, and criminal past (if there was one) of the accused person and even of the victim.[43] As the great jurist Henri Donnedieu de Vabres put it in the early twentieth century: "The juror has before him a man who defends himself. . . . His past, his attitude, his personality all have an effect, sometimes dangerous . . . on the verdict."[44] That the protagonist in Albert Camus's *The Stranger* was tried as much for his allegedly callous response to his mother's death as for the murder he committed later may have been literary invention, but it must have been conceivable enough in a trial to have any credibility with the author's French readers.

Following the hearing of the witnesses, first the prosecution (usually represented by an *avocat général*, or assistant public prosecutor) and then the defense presented their final arguments. The fact that the defense spoke last was a great advantage to the accused.[45] Often defense attorneys, faced with the results "of confessions confirmed beyond serious question by the fruits of the exhaustive pretrial research reflected in the *dossier*," refrained from contesting the defendant's guilt and instead elaborated "on the psychological, sociological, and economic factors which prompted the commission of the infraction."[46] These attorneys frequently delivered passionate pleas (*plaidoiries*) notable for their literary qualities, meant to be masterpieces of oratory, and designed very much to appeal to the emotions of "impressionable" jurors.[47] An advantage was also given to the defense by the fact that attorneys did not have to inform opposing counsel, or even the *président* of the court, before presenting new evidence during a trial. In their closing statements, defense attorneys often presented documents and exhibits unknown to the prosecution. Since the defense attorney's statement came at the end of the trial, prosecutors had no chance to question or "respond to the new evidence, however questionable it might be."[48]

Before 1881, the effect of defense *plaidoiries* could be neutralized to some extent by the *président's résumé* (summing-up of the case) at the very end of the trial.[49] But the *résumé*, like the *interrogatoire*, was often allegedly delivered in a manner that added to the impression of judicial unfairness, which some observers claimed created a degree of jury sympathy for accused persons.[50] It was no wonder that one juror of the early twentieth century wrote that the "spectacle" atmosphere of the *cour d'assises* created a "jurisdiction of impression."[51]

And it was on the basis of impression alone that the jurors decided their verdict (or rather answered a series of questions). Unanimity was not required for a conviction. During most of the era from 1808 to 1941, only a bare majority of seven of twelve votes in favor of the guilt of the defendant sufficed.[52] Once they retired to their chamber, the foreman of the jury read to the panel from a card instructing them not to judge based on rules regarding sufficiency of proof but rather in accordance with their "intimate conviction" only.[53] French legal writers in the nineteenth and early twentieth centuries repeatedly asserted that this system of "moral proofs" was largely responsible for the biased behavior of juries, for their "capricious and variable decisions," and for the tendency of jurors to "follow their personal sentiments," to even place themselves above the law.[54]

This system may have resulted in some regrettable verdicts, but it allowed juries to decide cases in accordance with their own sense of justice. By allowing them also to take into account the character of accused persons, the authorities enabled the panels to defy the Napoleonic *Code pénal*'s principle that only the crime should be judged. The saying, prevalent by the mid-twentieth century, that in French criminal proceedings "on juge l'homme, pas les faits" (one judges the man, not the facts)[55] had its origins, at least in part, in the way evidence was presented in trials. After hearing so much about the character of the accused and his or her past during the trial, jurors must have thought it relevant to determining their verdict. It had to be a major reason why, in the words of Raymond Saleilles, jurors became "so wholly absorbed in the impression of the individual that, time and again, in defiance of the law, they forget the crime."[56]

In fact, Saleilles, a Positivist criminologist who wrote in the years around 1900, theorized that juries behaved in a way that anticipated the concept of the "individualization of punishment," because where the Code pénal saw only crimes, juries saw individuals accused of those crimes and took into account their personal characteristics, chances for rehabilitation, and the motives for their offenses.[57] Nonetheless, a distinction should be made between the "individualization of punishment" proposed by the Positivist criminologists of the fin de siècle and jury-based individualization. The former was a "scientific" process that focused on the characteristics of individual offenders in order to understand their crimes and that devised the appropriate punishment (or treatment) to achieve what was necessary for the offenders' reform in light of their psychological or other problems. Jury-based individualization, on the other hand, was (as Saleilles admitted) an ad hoc and "unscientific" process derived from community-based ideas of justice and mercy, carried out in social and moral terms. It was mainly sanction nullification. For a jury to acquit a man because it felt that the punishment for the crime he was charged with was excessive, or to acquit a poor single woman charged with infanticide because the panel felt sorry for her, hardly constituted true individualization. Jury sanction nullification was at best a quasi-individualization based on social mores regarding such factors as "honor" or the reputation of the accused. Before the late nineteenth century, it was far from "scientific." However, by the end of the nineteenth century, the difference between jury sanction nullification and the Positivist concept of the individualization of punishment was not always hard and fast. There is some evidence that by then, juries began to be influenced by Positivist criminological ideas. But it should be clear that jury-based individualization was not by any means always identical with the scientific concept of the individualization of punishment.

Saleilles was not aware of it, but jury "defiance of the law" was facilitated by the fact that several features of the French criminal justice system, as set up by Napoleon, and which remained essentially intact for the next century and a half, worked at cross-purposes. On one hand, the Code pénal of 1810 embodied a "classical" system of justice that punished the crime and not the person. Everyone guilty of the same crime was to receive the same punishment. On the other hand, the Code of Criminal Procedure allowed for a procedure that inevitably led to the trial of personalities, whether this was intended or not. This goes a long ways toward explaining why almost from the beginning, jurors did not judge in the "objective" way they were supposed to judge, that is, by trying the crime rather than the criminal.

This history is one reason why the example of France in the nineteenth and twentieth centuries constitutes an excellent test case of the effects of jury trial on a legal system. Another is the abundant evidence available from that country for the period. This includes the Ministry of Justice's annual publication the *Compte général de l'administration de la justice criminelle*, which first appeared in 1825 and, except during World Wars I and II, continues to be published each year. It was the first complete published compilation of annual judicial statistics for any nation. Its vast data include total figures on the numbers of persons tried and what crimes they were tried for, with elaborate cross-tabulations showing convictions, acquittals, findings of extenuating circumstances, and punishments for each type of felony, and for felons according to gender, age, occupation, marital status, residence, geographical origin, and education. Moreover, each yearly volume of the *Compte général* includes an introduction by the minister of justice that analyzes the trends in the judicial statistics along with observations on the behavior of juries from the government's point of view. There are also vast archival and newspaper accounts of jury trials, as well as correspondence between government officials and magistrates on the juries. To this can be added the abundant literature concerning the juries penned by contemporary jurists.

The sources do, however, present problems of interpretation. For one thing, trends in jury verdicts were affected by changes in evidence-gathering, the presentation of prosecution cases, and the effectiveness of the police. For example, the very high acquittal rates of the early nineteenth century were apparently caused not only by jury nullification of sanctions but also by the fact that in this era, magistrates took a considerably larger proportion of reported cases to trial before both the *cours d'assises* and the *tribunaux correctionnels* than they would in the second half of the nineteenth century. This meant that more of the weaker cases were tried than in later periods.[58] Problems of proof also appear to have contributed to the especially high acquittal rates for certain crimes. For example, one evident reason for the high rates of exonerations for infanticide and abortion was that these crimes were harder to prove than many others. Moreover, the professionalization of policing may have contributed to the rise in conviction rates for crimes in general from the 1830s through the 1870s.[59] The fact that trials proceeded even when defendants admitted their guilt (which jurors were made aware of in every case where it occurred) also seemed to influence certain verdicts.[60]

Introduction

The most important problem with the sources, however, is that any explanations of jury behavior must remain speculative, since the panels were not required to give the reasoning for their verdicts and post-trial questioning of jurors by journalists was rare.[61] It cannot always be determined whether any form of nullification was applied in particular cases. For all the historian knows, a jury, rightly or wrongly, may have really believed a defendant was innocent or that there were legally extenuating circumstances or that the crime committed was actually a lesser one than the most serious charge in the indictment. This book therefore relies on aggregate percentages and what they suggest about the phenomenon of nullification as a general matter. Yet it is certain that nullification, mainly of sanctions, did occur often and that the authorities reacted to it. They were convinced that juries were practicing sanction nullification in many cases and sometimes nullification of the law itself (as in numerous political trials, homicides resulting from duels, feminine "crimes of passion," and perhaps abortion cases toward 1900). And though problems of proof and the effectiveness of prosecution cases must have affected verdicts, there was still much room for jury discretion. For example, the prosecution magistrates' increasing selectivity about what cases to take to trial and the growing professionalization of the police and of the criminal justice apparatus did not prevent a big rise in acquittal rates after 1880.

An analysis of the sources will therefore show how the jury system from 1791 to 1941 profoundly affected the criminal justice system in France, bringing it more into line with popular (or at least nongovernmental) notions of justice, especially regarding punishments. This book will track jury behavior toward both political cases and the nonpolitical "routine" felonies, such as theft and homicide. The former cases were very much tied to political events and struggles. But social and cultural norms and shifting ideas about criminal responsibility and appropriate punishment had much greater influence on jury verdicts for the far more numerous "routine" felonies (which have been divided into violent crimes, property crimes, white-collar offenses, crimes of sexual violence, and abortion and infanticide). Particularly sensitive to changes in social attitudes were offenses that were in some fashion related to sexuality and gender.

Infanticide and abortion are perhaps the clearest examples. Before 1832, jury resistance to the punishments provided by law seems to have been more applicable to infanticide than to any other felony. Then at the turn of the century, the acquittal rate for the crime rose sharply in response, it seems, to new ideas about women's diminished responsibility for their crimes, the mental state of the persons charged with infanticide, and a decline of the sexual "double standard." The acquittal rate for abortion also rose sharply at about the same time, evidently due both to the increasing gender bias in favor of women defendants and to the growing acceptance of abortion among the French.

Jury behavior toward these cases and toward nonpolitical felonies in general was also influenced by broad intellectual trends. For example, by the 1870s, the authorities, through various means, appeared to have brought juries under substantial control: acquittal rates had declined significantly since the 1830s. But there was a resurgence of jury sanction nullification after about 1880. The overall acquittal rate rose significantly, and by the years just before World War I, it had risen nearly to the level it had reached before the passage of the law on extenuating circumstances in 1832. Several factors seem to have been responsible for the trend, but evidently most important were popularizations of new Positivist criminological ideas holding that many criminals—because of hereditary degeneration, alcoholism, mental disorders, psychological and medical problems, and sociological factors— bore diminished responsibility for their violations of the law. Acquittal rates for women rose far more sharply than for men, however. This was because traditional male gallantry toward women was reinforced by new "scientific" ideas that females, because of their peculiar psychological and biological weaknesses, were less often responsible for their crimes than were men. Accused women were frequently seen as having acted from feminine emotions that were beyond their control, especially when they committed "crimes of passion."

Although social and cultural-intellectual factors profoundly influenced jurors in making their decisions, a general history of jury intervention in the law in France best follows the chronology of political events. This is because from its introduction during the Revolution, the jury system was a subject of considerable debate among various political factions. As Bernard Schnapper has put it, the history of the jury in France is that of a "long political conflict," and "few institutions have been criticized with so much vigor and tenacity."[62] The debates concerned issues such as the desirability of the jury system itself, which offenses it should be assigned to, how it should operate, how it should be reformed, what its role should be (if any) in punishment, which citizens should serve on juries, and who should select them.

The ideological positions of those involved in these debates played a key role. In general, liberals from the Revolution through the nineteenth century strongly favored the jury system. To them, it was the "palladium of liberty," a protector of the people's rights against the inroads of tyranny.

Conservatives, with their strong law-and-order outlook, tended to be more critical of juries, though few dared call for the outright abolition of what most French regarded as a sacred heritage of the Revolution. The Right saw juries as too lenient toward both ordinary criminals and radical political dissenters. Jurors were also too ignorant or incompetent to administer "bonne justice." These negative opinions of the jury system were shared by many magistrates, who would eventually find means of undermining it. Statistics on the severity or leniency of juries toward felonies in general and toward political offenses were repeatedly cited by one side or the other in support of its arguments.

Therefore, it was not surprising that changes in the jury system rather closely followed political events and changes in regime. When liberals were in power, they enacted reforms to strengthen the jury system (at least before the mid-twentieth century), giving jurors more power in the meting out of punishment, extending jury trial to political and press offenses, and further limiting the authority of the judges over the panels. They also tended to favor an expansion in the number of citizens eligible for jury duty, though within limits. Conservative or authoritarian regimes, on the other hand, favored reforms restricting the powers of juries, removing political and press offenses (and even many nonpolitical crimes) from their jurisdiction, granting more power to judges, and restricting participation on the panels to *notables* or to "bons jurés" committed to upholding law and order.

The ultimate outcome gave something to both sides. Through a series of reforms, particularly the laws of 1832 and 1932, juries were given a significant say in punishment. These reforms were aimed at combating jury sanction nullification allegedly brought about by the panels' desire to spare culprits from the harsh and rigid punishments stipulated in the *Code pénal*. As a consequence, by 1932 the juries' traditional authority to determine verdicts had been extended to include a predominant power in the imposition of punishments.

Yet, in another sense, the power of juries had been greatly reduced. By the mid-twentieth century, few criminal cases in France were still tried by juries; all but a very small number were now tried by the three-judge panels of the *tribunaux correctionnels*. This marked one important difference between the English and the French authorities in their response to jury sanction nullification. The French used the "lesser" criminal courts, composed solely of magistrates, to try misdemeanors and, through the manipulation of charges, eventually downgraded many felonies into misdemeanors, thereby taking them out of the juries' purview. In eighteenth-century England, however, juries tried both felonies and many misdemeanors.[63] The English more often than the French charged at a higher level, and it was left to juries to "down-charge," leading to transportation to a penal colony or whipping in place of death for persons convicted of capital property crimes.[64] After the early-nineteenth-century reform of sanctions, the English retained the jury for the trial of minor felonies and even misdemeanors.[65] Another major difference was that in England by the nineteenth century, judges, in order to control the jury and prevent what they perceived as jury errors following the rise of the "adversary" system and its removal of the judges from active comment on cases during trial, had developed strict rules of evidence.[66] The French did not develop such rules, and their eventual solution was to place the jury under the direct supervision of the judges in the system of *échevinage*, in which the three judges of the *cours d'assises* and the jury deliberated together on both verdict and penalty.

But this meant that the independence of jurors in the trials of those cases that remained under their jurisdiction was severely compromised. This outcome was made possible by the weakening in the twentieth century of the liberals' traditional defense of the jury system, a weakening brought about by several complex forces. These were to some extent related to the gradual rise since the mid-nineteenth century of the administrative state, in particular the bureaucratization and professionalization of the criminal justice apparatus. Here was a great paradox: on one hand, juries profoundly influenced the system of punishments, but on the other hand, most felonies were gradually removed from jury trial.

It is now necessary to describe the processes that brought about this outcome. Jury sanction nullification and the authorities' adjustment to it were constant factors during the century and a half that an independent jury system existed in France. But within this broad framework, there were changes over time. There were a number of distinct periods in which the particular forms or expressions of jury behavior altered along with the responses to them. These were related to ongoing changes in government and society and in the absorption of certain criminological ideas. With the full implementation of *échevinage* in 1941, jury sanction nullification finally ceased to be a significant phenomenon in France, and it will be instructive to briefly analyze how jury behavior thereafter differed from what it had been before. Whereas in England, jury nullification became much less common after the early-nineteenth-century reform of sanctions, the ultimate response of the French authorities was the near destruction of the jury.

Yet this was a lengthy and complex process. The road was not a straight one. There were brief periods when juries were strengthened. More important, those scholars who ignore one or the other of the major categories of

Introduction

forces—political, social-cultural, intellectual, or legal—will miss much of the story. Social historians who have tried in recent decades to analyze jury decisions in "routine" felony cases for what they reveal about social norms or public mores in France since the Revolution have tended to slight the very real impact of legal and political changes on those decisions. An exclusive focus on the political or legal aspects of jury trial also results in partial or distorted perspectives. What this book proposes to do in the following chapters is take the most comprehensive approach possible in order to understand more fully what juries did in France during the nineteenth and twentieth centuries.

chapter one

THE "PALLADIUM OF LIBERTY"

Juries, the Revolution, and Napoleon, 1791–1814

The eras of the French Revolution and Napoleon together composed the foundational period of trial by jury in France. During this time, the basic rules and machinery governing the jury were put into place for the next century and a half. The institution was introduced in a wave of Enlightenment-inspired enthusiasm and optimism about the capacity of citizen-judges (who expressed the sovereignty of the people) to judge on the basis of their common sense and on a sure knowledge of the "facts." This was the best guarantee of justice. Yet one of the most striking characteristics of the Revolutionary-Napoleonic era in respect to the jury was how this initial optimism about the institution soon turned into disillusionment among government officials and magistrates. The political turmoil of the Revolution negatively affected the jury system, and magistrates began to criticize jurors for bias and leniency. Napoleon then placed stricter limits on the jury system. But it still retained great powers, powers that it would use in unintended ways almost from the start.

The Constituent Assembly's introduction of the jury in 1791 marked a sharp break with French legal tradition. The jury was at the core of a fundamental overhaul of the nation's criminal justice system. In the preceding centuries, the inquisitorial or "romano-canonical" criminal procedure, in which accused persons and witnesses were examined in secret by professional judges only, had prevailed in France.

It was a system that had evolved as royal justice gradually supplanted feudal justice.[1] Before the thirteenth century, the use of laymen in courts was widespread in France, just as it had been in England. Assemblies of lay (or nonprofessional) judges drawn from the community meted out justice during the Carolingian era. With the disintegration of central authority in the ninth and tenth centuries, the courts became feudalized. But this did not mean the exclusion of laymen from judicial decision-making. In the feudal courts, the assembled vassals rendered judgments that required at most the concurrence of the lords.[2]

But lay participation in justice was gradually eliminated in France following the Fourth Lateran Council's condemnation of trial by ordeal and by battle in 1215. More rational means of proof had to be found. The French monarchy had to make a fundamental choice. Two alternative fact-finding methods were known in France. One was the group inquest, which had been developed in the Frankish empire and which was still widely used in the Norman courts. Royal or ducal authorities compelled selected groups of local people to answer under oath questions concerning fiscal and other matters. In England, forms of group testimony on oath, including lay verdicts on oath in the folk assemblies, had been known in Anglo-Saxon times. But it was the Norman rulers who introduced into England the royal use of inquests on a regularized basis.[3] The royal inquest would eventually be transformed into the common-law jury. The other fact-finding method was the Roman-canon law of evidence, first used in the church courts, in which individual witnesses were interrogated by professional judges who then made the findings of fact. When Louis IX issued an ordinance in 1258 abolishing the judicial duel, he decided to adopt this law of proof for the royal courts. According to John P. Dawson, the French monarchy chose the Roman-canon procedure in large part because royal officials could not compel groups of local inhabitants to answer questions under oath in the vast areas of the country still controlled in the thirteenth century by great territorial lords.[4]

Adoption of the Roman-canon law of evidence was in fact the response in most of continental Europe to the Fourth Lateran Council's decision of 1215. The outcome of trial by ordeal had been regarded as the judgment of God. Therefore, in order to make acceptable to the public the judgment by mere mortal judges in place of an infallible God, proof had to be complete and had to be obtained only under certain strict conditions in cases of serious crimes, that is, those punishable by death or severe physical maiming. The Roman-canon system of proof, based on "objective" criteria, was developed to provide the needed certainty. In capital cases, judges could not convict on circumstantial evidence. Conviction required two eyewitnesses to the crime or, failing this, the confession of the accused. Torture of the defendant was used in certain cases where there was neither the testimony of two eyewitnesses nor a voluntary confession from the accused. These were cases in which there was "half proof" against the defendant, meaning either one eyewitness or certain combinations of circumstantial evidence. For lesser crimes (*delicta levia*), judges could convict merely on the basis of the "subjective persuasion of the trier," so that the Roman-canon law of evidence and judicial torture were not used in these cases.[5]

The "Palladium of Liberty"

As the Roman-canon procedure evolved, French magistrates developed an elaborate and rigid system of legal proofs. The state initiated prosecutions, and the greatest part of the procedure was devoted to an extensive pretrial investigation (the *information*) conducted by an examining magistrate (the *lieutenant criminel*). He interrogated the witnesses and the accused in secret, without counsel for the defense, and evidence was based largely on written depositions. The accused was then tried by a panel of judges who interrogated him or her, again in the absence of counsel for the defense.[6]

There was no place for laymen in this system. As the power of the monarchy grew, the Roman-canon procedure was adopted throughout France. By about 1500, lay judges had almost disappeared. The adoption of the Roman-canon law of evidence did the same throughout most of continental Europe.[7] By the onset of modern times, "the Continent forgot all about the jury and enlightened opinion thought it an aberration to put the all-important question of guilt into the hands of an assembly of unlearned country-folk."[8]

But in England, the jury not only survived but was strengthened. Where in most of the European Continent the response to the church's condemnation of trial by ordeal was the adoption of the Roman-canon system of proof and trial by professional judges, in England it was the extension of trial by jury to criminal cases and conviction on the basis of circumstantial evidence alone.[9] Trial by jury was rooted in the "accusatory" system of justice developed in England. This evolved from customary Germanic precedents and was litigious in nature, with plaintiffs in criminal cases having to prove the guilt of defendants in a fashion not dissimilar to civil suits.[10] Trials were public, with laymen deciding on the question of fact based on oral testimony in court. They did not reach a verdict automatically on the basis of a certain combination of proofs but could interpret all admissible evidence in light of their own conscience or common sense. Nor did they have to explain their verdict. All of this meant that England's jury system was radically opposed to the Roman-canon or "inquisitorial" procedure.

The development of the jury system in England and its eventual adoption in France should be seen within a broad historical perspective concerning the participation of laymen in justice. "Juries" were used in classical Athens, although what they did was a far cry from modern lay judging. All citizens were eligible to serve on enormous panels of hundreds of men. Majority vote decided both the verdict and the punishment of the accused, without deliberating and following speeches by the defendant and his or her accusers (there were no district attorneys or professional lawyers).[11] The

Romans of the late Republic also used juries in criminal state trials. A body of jurors was drawn from annual lists prepared by a praetor and taken from one class—sometimes equestrian and at other times senatorial. Although a magistrate presided over the trial, the jurors by majority vote determined the guilt or innocence of an accused person.

Assemblies of laymen were also used in the courts of the early medieval Germanic peoples, including, as already noted, the Franks. By Charlemagne's time, *scabini* (persons known for their knowledge of the law) were appointed in each district by the central government. Panels of these permanent appointees met under the presidency of a count and gave judgment in the less important cases, though the general assemblies still met to decide more important ones. However, the juries or assemblies of lay judges among the ancient Athenians, Romans, and Germans all rendered judgment on both facts and law, whereas modern juries are normally called in by a court to determine only the former.[12]

The predecessor of the modern jury (which has been defined by Harry Kalven Jr. and Hans Zeisel as "a group of ad hoc assembled lay judges who, without participation of the learned judges, decide at least the question of guilt")[13] originated in England, where it was occasionally used by royal officials by the early twelfth century. The procedure was regularized by Henry II late in the century.[14] The jury grew out of the type of royal group inquest introduced by the Norman kings. Trial juries were first used in civil cases involving property disputes. A man who believed he had been unlawfully deprived of his land by another could obtain a writ commanding the sheriff to summon twelve freemen of the neighborhood assumed to know the most about the facts of the case in dispute, who then appeared in court and testified under oath as to rights of the parties. The judge ruled in accordance with their answer. Thus, the earliest English jurors were really sworn witnesses rather than men who decided a case based on testimony they heard at trial.[15] In criminal matters, juries were first used only at the presentment stage. In 1166, Henry II ordained, by the Assize of Clarendon, that twelve lawful men of each hundred (district) and four of each vill (township) should report under oath to the royal judge or sheriff any persons reputed to have committed certain serious crimes in their hundred or vill. Thus originated the grand jury, though for some time thereafter, criminal trial continued to be by ordeal.[16]

But of course the ordeal was condemned by the church in 1215, and trial by jury soon suggested itself as a ready substitute. By about 1220, the first criminal trial juries appeared in England, delivering verdicts of guilt or innocence before royal judges on circuit.[17] According to Dawson, the government came to rely on juries because the kings of England, unlike the kings of France, had the power throughout their realm to compel citizens to serve on the panels, the courts had never been feudalized in England, and the use of juries economized on the time of professional judges.[18] By the end of the Middle Ages, trial by jury in England had come to resemble what it is today. From 1220, jurors ("twelve good men and true") were not just sworn witnesses but were something like their later counterparts. Criminal trial jurors of the thirteenth century were self-informing, that is, were presumed to know the facts of the case before trial because they came from the locality where the alleged crime had been committed and in some instances had even served on the grand jury that presented the case. But jurors also gave their verdict based on their viewing of the confrontation between the defendant and the judge.[19] During the later Middle Ages, jurors gradually lost their self-informing role and became "passive triers" who, after hearing the evidence (including the testimony of witnesses) in an open trial, deliberated together and reached a verdict.[20]

For centuries, the use of the jury in Europe was restricted to England. Then in the eighteenth century, the Enlightenment *philosophes* called for its adoption on the Continent. This was connected to their condemnation of the Roman-canon procedure as authoritarian and secret. They especially criticized its use of torture.[21] In reality, according to John H. Langbein, judicial torture (formally abolished in France in 1780) was rarely resorted to by the eighteenth century because of the "revolution in the law of proof" that had occurred since the sixteenth century. After the adoption of the Roman-canon law of evidence, judges could still convict even in serious cases on the basis of partial proof so long as a noncapital penalty was imposed. In the course of the sixteenth and seventeenth centuries, capital punishment for serious crimes was increasingly replaced with various noncapital sanctions (in France, it was often condemnation to the galleys). In such cases, judges felt free to convict on the basis of what they considered compelling circumstantial evidence (meaning indirect evidence that the triers thought raised "a sufficient inference of guilt") or the "free judicial evaluation of the evidence" (in France, this became known as *l'intime conviction*). This meant that by the eighteenth century, the Roman-canon system of proofs remained in effect only for procedure against the worst offenders, for only they were still punished by death. Langbein maintains that historians have subscribed to a "fairy tale" that torture was abolished in Europe because of agitation from Enlightenment writers such as Voltaire and Cesare Beccaria. This is because historians have followed the eighteenth-century abolitionist writers, who had been unaware of the

The "Palladium of Liberty"

change that had already occurred before they launched their campaign against torture.[22]

The *philosophes* may have been ignorant of the degree to which the Roman-canon law of proof had been replaced by the "subjective persuasion of the trier," but their criticism of the former was one reason why some of them preferred trial by jury. Such major figures as Voltaire, Beccaria, Jean-Jacques Rousseau, and the baron de Montesquieu called for the introduction to continental Europe of the jury, seen by them as more just. Montesquieu, himself a magistrate, was particularly notable in this respect.[23] In fact, he laid down the rule that would govern how the French jury would arrive at its decisions: "The people are not jurists; all these restrictions and methods of arbitration are beyond their reach; they must have only one object and one single fact set before them; and then they have only to see whether they ought to condemn, to acquit, or to suspend their judgment."[24] The Enlightenment reformers may not have been primarily responsible for the abolition of torture, but the legal reforms they proposed, including the adoption of the jury system, were to be taken up by the leaders of the French Revolution.

It was not surprising, then, that many of the *cahiers* of 1789 demanded trial by jury in criminal cases.[25] In August 1789, the Constituent Assembly began to deal with the question of introducing the jury to France.[26] The majority in the assembly favored the adoption of the institution, whose growth in England was seen by them as associated with the growth of English liberty and which was a "true distinguishing mark of free countries."[27] As one scholar has written, "The jury fit easily into the normative universe of the French Revolution, for what could be more natural for a nation of *citoyens* than trial by one's peers?"[28]

However, the majority of deputies in the Constituent Assembly decided to limit jury trial to criminal cases. Nicolas Bergasse, deputy from Lyon, inspired by the examples of England and the American states, called for the adoption of that "sublime institution," the criminal jury. Yet other deputies wanted jury trial extended to civil cases as well. But Jacques-Guillaume Thouret persuaded the assembly to reject the civil jury, arguing that enlightened Englishmen criticized civil juries as too inexperienced for the kinds of cases they tried. Moreover, according to Thouret, it was impossible to separate law and fact in civil trials, and since jurors should deal only with questions of fact, civil trial was incompatible with jury trial.[29] Thus, the Constituent Assembly, by a decree of April 30, 1790, accepted the principle of the criminal jury but not the civil jury.[30]

It remained for the Constituent Assembly to draw up a law governing the jury. On November 27, 1790, Adrien Duport, on behalf of both the Committee on the Constitution and the Committee on Criminal Jurisprudence, introduced in the assembly a draft bill to institute procedure by jurors.[31] The debates of the Constituents in 1790–91 showed that most deputies were quite enthusiastic about the institution. Above all, the introduction of the jury system was the expression in the judicial sphere of the Revolution's transferal of sovereignty from the king to the nation. The jury would be the spokesman of the general will in the judicial realm, and the judge would be strictly confined to the role of servant of the law. This was in part a reaction against the power of the old *parlements* (royal appeals courts), whose judges had been independent by virtue of the purchase and inheritance of their offices and whose ability to refuse to register decrees and to protest against them had blocked reforms in the decades before the Revolution.

The Constituents put a stop to this: the judiciary had to be answerable to the nation. Law—which required absolute primacy—was the expression of the general will, and the jury would be its guardian. Each panel would help guarantee liberty by countering the power of a judiciary whose statist nature a portion of the deputies sensed could become oppressive.[32] The jury was based on the assumption that "the source of all justice is truly the people." Also in accordance with this philosophy, the Constituent Assembly introduced the election of judges.[33]

Adding to the Constituents' enthusiasm for the jury was the fact that it broke from the execrated penal justice of the Old Regime.[34] The jury was perceived as a counter to the presumably pro-conviction bias of the judges who, according to Thouret, were "inclined to see guilty people everywhere."[35]

Moreover, the deputies assumed that the common sense of citizen-judges was a better guarantee of justice than the learned and complicated system of legal proofs developed by the professional magistrates. The Revolution sought to "create a legal system accessible to the average citizen" and "exalted common sense over professional judgment."[36] As Adrien Duport, *rapporteur* for the law on the jury and himself a former judge of the *parlement* of Paris, put it in November 1790: "The pleasing element in the establishment of the jury is that, with it, everything is decided by force of honesty and good faith, a simplicity much preferable to that useless, melancholy mass of subtleties and forms, called, down to this day, justice."[37] The jury and the system of legal proofs were incompatible: laymen could not be expected to judge according to the complicated and meticulous rules of the system of legal proofs.[38] Jurors would judge on the basis of moral proofs alone, that is, according to their conscience or "intimate conviction," without any legal rules predetermining the value of the evidence and constraining their decision.[39] This was better than the system of legal proofs because jurors, "unlike judges[,] are not obliged . . . to decide as they are *supposed* to see things rather than as they *actually* see them; to go against their conscience and instead follow the false and absurd rules of probability."[40]

The system of moral proofs was written into the oath taken by jurors in the Code of Criminal Procedure of 1791: "Citizens, you swear and promise to examine with the most scrupulous attention the charges against . . . to betray neither the interest of the accused, nor those of the society which accuses him; to communicate with no one until after your verdict; to listen to neither hatred nor malice, neither fear nor affection; to give your decision according to the charges and pleas in defense, and following your intimate conviction with the impartiality and firmness proper in a free man."[41]

According to one modern scholar, to let the juror be guided only by his conscience reflected the Enlightenment's faith in the free man and the Revolutionaries' romantic belief that sentiment was less subject to error than the uncertain opinion of the learned man.[42] Yet though judgment by "intimate conviction" may have made it possible to decide according to sentiment, that was not the intent of the Constituent Assembly when it drew up the jurors' oath (which was repeated, almost verbatim, in the Napoleonic Code of Criminal Procedure). "Intimate conviction" really meant verdict by conscience, or by true belief, and resembled the American "reasonable doubt" standard.[43] The very wording of the oath seemed to warn against judging on the basis of "sentiment." The Constituents did not want jurors to decide according to vague "inclinations" or "opinions." Jurors had to be impartial and control their emotions, as was befitting free men.[44] The system of moral proofs meant simply that the juror was not to decide automatically on the basis of a certain combination of circumstances or proofs (as was the case in the Roman-canon system) but, after having heard all the evidence, "was entirely free to declare that he is convinced or not convinced."[45] The jury system therefore "rested on a faith in the virtues of the individual citizen — autonomous, responsible, and reflective."[46] What Langbein calls the "revolution in the law of proof," or the movement to replace the Roman-canon law of proof with one based on *l'intime conviction*, was completed in France with the introduction of the jury. Judgment on the basis of subjective persuasion was now the rule even in capital cases.

Jurors were capable of judging according to their "intimate conviction" because they were to concern themselves only with "fact," not "law." They would decide the "facts" (guilt or innocence), and the judges would apply the "law." In France, the latter meant, essentially, the punishment.[47] There were no rules of law regarding evidence for judges to use in guiding the jurors, nor were jurors instructed on the laws governing the specific cases they were to decide.[48] To judge the facts required no legal knowledge. As Maximilien Robespierre put it: "The facts are always the facts; even the most common of men can be the judge of them."[49] To facilitate this judgment on the basis of facts alone, the Constituent Assembly decided that jurors would not deliver general verdicts (as they normally do in Britain and the United States) but would vote separately on a series of questions. Here the assembly was influenced by Montesquieu's idea that jurors should be presented with only one fact at a time.[50] The committees of the Constituent Assembly that drew up the draft law on the jury in 1790 were aware that they were departing from the English common-law practice of general verdicts, but they hoped to simplify the jurors' task and make their determinations more precise by forcing them to answer several questions.[51] Jurors were required to vote yes or no to a series of written questions posed by the court: did the crime occur, was the accused guilty of it, did the accused intend to commit it, were there aggravating circumstances, and so on.[52] From the Revolution to the present, French jurors have continued to determine the facts in response to a series of questions.[53]

They did so after hearing strictly oral testimony in publicly conducted trials. This was another change from the old "inquisitorial" system, which had relied heavily on written depositions. The citizen-judges now also weighed the arguments of both prosecuting and defense attorneys, the latter being allowed for the first time. Therefore, jurors "would not be bound by lengthy and fossilized written statements but would weigh all the nuances of direct oral testimony and active cross-examination."[54] This further aided judgment on the basis of "intimate conviction" or "moral proofs."

In fact, the French took the system of "moral proofs" further than did the British and the Americans (though in the common-law system, the jury was not restricted to answering questions). From the Revolution through the twentieth century, there were almost no rules of evidence, not even simple ones, in French jury trials: there were few provisions regarding the relevance of testimony or the competency of witnesses, and hearsay testimony was allowed with few restrictions.[55] Since judges were not allowed to give jurors any guidance on the kinds of evidence they should consider, each juror had to decide himself which evidence was relevant, with no guide other than his conscience.[56] The jurors had to plow through the often contradictory, complicated, and impressionistic evidence as best they could.[57] Yet the system of "moral proofs" or "intimate conviction," and the fact that juries were not required to explain their verdicts, granted to the panels enormous (though unintended) power to transform the justice system.[58]

Nonetheless, a majority in the Constituent Assembly evidently did not believe that the common sense needed to judge according to intimate conviction extended very far down the social hierarchy. They did not agree with Robespierre that even "the most common of men" can be the judge of facts. Robespierre and fellow radical Jerome Pétion, both of whom held that every citizen should be eligible for jury service, fought without success the Constituent Assembly's proposal to extend the property qualifications it had approved for electors to jurors.[59] Robespierre questioned how trial by jury could be truly trial by one's peers when three-quarters of citizens were excluded from the juries. He also opposed the potential political abuse inherent in the proposal that the *procureur-syndic-général* (departmental executive officer) select two hundred names for the quarterly departmental jury list from all those eligible for jury duty.[60]

On the other hand, those on the Right claimed that "only propriétaires are true citizens." Their view prevailed. The assembly decided that jury service was an honor incompatible with the payment of any salary or compensation. It was not a right extended to the whole body of citizens but was restricted to those rich enough to serve without hardship.[61] Accordingly, the law of September 1791 organizing the jury system instituted property qualifications for jurors that were even higher than for the franchise. The Constitution of 1791 made a distinction between "active" and "passive" citizens. Only "active" citizens—those adult males twenty-five years or older paying taxes equal to three days' earnings of a common laborer—could vote. They in turn chose the *électeurs* who selected the deputies to the new Legislative Assembly and other officials. *Électeurs*, besides meeting the qualifications for "active citizens," had to own or rent property assessed on the tax rolls as worth at least one hundred to two hundred days of work, depending on where they lived, or be the tenant farmers or sharecroppers of lands worth at least four hundred days.[62] It was from among the *électeurs* that jurors had to be chosen. Moreover, among the jury lists there was a special section composed of notaries, bankers, and merchants who were to be chosen by preference when a trial involved matters presumably requiring a knowledge of business techniques, such as fraud, fraudulent bankruptcy, embezzlement of public monies, and the like—a provision that did not survive in later laws on the composition of juries.[63]

The issues raised by Robespierre in the debates over who should be jurors and what authorities should choose them would resonate down through the nineteenth and twentieth centuries. Here again, the Revolution set a controversial precedent. Succeeding regimes changed the qualifications for jury service and the authorities (prefects or other appointees of the central government, locally elected officials, judges) who drew up annual and session jury lists. Doubts would be expressed about the impartiality of all these officials.

The jury law of 1791 created an eight-man *jury d'accusation* (grand jury) in each *arrondissement* (district) and a twelve-man *jury de jugement* (trial jury) in each of the eighty-three departments. In every district, the *procureur-syndic* drew up a quarterly list of thirty jurors from among the *électeurs* for the *jury d'accusation*. Quarterly lists of two hundred names for the *jury de jugement* were drawn up by the departmental *procureur-syndic-général*, who, like the *procureur-syndic*, was an elected official.[64]

The operation of the *jurys d'accusation* showed just how far the new criminal justice system established by 1791 had deviated from the old "inquisitorial" procedure, even at the pretrial stage. The offices of public prosecutor and *lieutenant criminel* (or *juge d'instruction*) were eliminated. Either the police or private parties could bring complaints of criminal activities to a *juge de paix* (justice of the peace), established in each canton.[65] This magistrate interrogated the accused to determine whether grounds for prosecution existed. If so, he sent the case to the *directeur du jury*, a district civil court judge who served for six months on a rotating basis as the director of the *jury d'accusation*. He decided whether to dismiss the charges or, if he detained the accused, whether the case was a *délit*, punishable by no more than two years' imprisonment, or a *crime*, punishable by imprisonment of two years or more. If it was the former, the case went on to trial in the *tribunal de police correctionnelle*, one of which existed in each *arrondissement*, where the accused was tried by three judges without a jury.[66]

However, if the *directeur du jury* determined that the offense was a *crime*, he had to convoke the district's *jury d'accusation* to get an indictment.[67] The *directeur du jury* drew up an *acte d'accusation* summarizing the charges against the accused for presentation to the grand jury. After hearing the *directeur du jury*'s presentation (in the absence of the accused) and the witnesses, the grand jury by majority vote decided whether there were sufficient grounds to send the accused to trial by the *tribunal criminel*.[68]

There was one *tribunal criminel* in each department. It had four judges (the *président* of the court and three *assesseurs* or associate judges) and an *accusateur public* to argue the case against the accused; all were elected officeholders. The *accusateur public* was not a public prosecutor (that office, of course, had been abolished), for he did nothing until the prosecution had been decreed.[69]

The twelve-man *jury de jugement* decided guilt or innocence in these courts; the judges determined the punishment only. The jurors were, of course, chosen from the quarterly list of two hundred drawn up by the *procureur-syndic-général*. At the start of a trial, the *accusateur public* could peremptorily challenge twenty names. The rest of the names were then put into a box, and twelve jurors were drawn by lot. The accused person was then allowed to challenge those on this list, who were replaced by lot. He was allowed twenty peremptory challenges altogether. After that, he could still challenge other jurors, but only for cause and with the agreement of the judges.[70]

The twelve jurors having been selected, they proceeded to sit through a public trial conducted on the basis of oral testimony alone, including the arguments of the prosecution and the defense and the testimony of witnesses. After this, the jury deliberated in its own chamber. As already mentioned, the jurors were required to vote on a series of separate questions according to their "intimate conviction." Their verdict need not be unanimous: ten out of twelve were necessary to convict the accused. A lesser vote in favor of conviction meant acquittal.[71] The jury did not have to explain its verdict, which was "sovereign"—that is, it could not be appealed except on procedural grounds to the *tribunal de cassation* (the equivalent of a supreme court) in Paris.[72] If the jury voted in favor of conviction, the judges retired to deliberate on the penalty and then returned to announce the sentence.[73]

The first juries actually began operation in March 1792, and officials initially greeted the new institution with enthusiasm. The public evidently did so too, for audiences flocked to the earliest jury trials.[74] The panels were soon democratized: with the overthrow of the monarchy in August 1792, the original property qualifications for both voting and jury service were abolished. To make it more possible for poor men to serve on the panels, the National Convention in August 1793 enacted a law providing jurors with a daily stipend and payment for their travel expenses.[75] Jury service was no longer just a public function; it was a right. The years from 1792 to 1795 constituted one of the few periods when all adult male citizens were eligible for jury duty.

But official enthusiasm for the new jury system lasted only briefly. Scarcely had it been introduced before revolutionary governments began to undermine it. This would mark the beginning of many attempts by governments and magistrates to subvert the jury system in France. As Françoise

Lombard has observed, the history of the jury in France since the Revolution has been a history of the progressive elimination of its powers.[76]

For one thing, juries were put under great pressure by the events of 1792–99—the radicalization of the Revolution following the overthrow of the monarchy, counterrevolution, de-Christianization, the Jacobin Terror, and the anti-Jacobin reaction that followed. The major complaint of officials in the National Convention of 1792–95 against the juries was the unwillingness of the panels to convict many of those accused of political crimes or of crimes with political implications. Cases involving nonjuring priests, émigrés, and collective violence began to flood the courts in late 1792.[77] But many such cases ended in acquittal because the jurors either sympathized with the accused persons, or felt the punishments were too harsh, or did not share their government's unease with political opposition.[78]

In response to this leniency, the National Convention began to remove certain political cases from the jurisdiction of the juries and to devise rules to make it more possible for officials to stack the panels with government supporters. In March 1793, the convention created the Revolutionary Tribunal in Paris, and thereafter local revolutionary tribunals or extraordinary "commissions" were established by representatives-on-mission in a number of localities. The Revolutionary Tribunals tried persons accused of "treason" (which during the Terror was very broadly defined) in a summary fashion and without counsel for the defense. They used "jurors," but these were for all practical purposes government functionaries rather than true jurors, for they were permanent personnel of these courts, appointed directly by the National Convention. Moreover, the convention also allowed prosecutors to try political cases "a forme révolutionnaire" in the regular *tribunaux criminels*, that is, before the judges of the courts without the presence of juries.[79]

The National Convention next sought to change the law governing the selection of jurors in order to get more government supporters on the panels that tried the remaining cases. A law of December 1793 gave to the *agent national* (who had succeeded the *procureur-syndic* and was directly responsible to the central government) of each *arrondissement* the task of drawing up the jury lists (with one juror per thousand inhabitants) from among all those eligible to serve. He was to select the names based on his own personal knowledge and on that provided by the *agents nationaux* of the communes. Thus it was the executive power that chose the jurors, who could therefore not be independent in political cases. As the Terror of the Year II (1793–94) ran its course, the *agents nationaux* increasingly selected jurors in accordance with the wishes of Jacobin activists.[80] As this occurred, juries, where and when they were still allowed to try political offenses, showed more firmness toward accused persons than they had previously.[81]

The disinclination of jurors to convict persons accused of political offenses, the efforts by governments therefore to remove such cases from jury trial, and the attempts by officials to stack juries in favor of the government would all be repeated again and again in subsequent French history. Here once more, the Revolution set in place much of what was to come.

After the overthrow of the Jacobin dictatorship in July 1794, the tables were turned. In the Thermidorian Reaction, Jacobins were prosecuted and their enemies freed. The "White Terror" of 1794–99 followed, a mostly extralegal movement in which right-wing elements often attacked and murdered their former Jacobin tormentors. This was also accompanied by a "judicial reaction" on the part of both magistrates and juries. Many right-wing terrorists were neither indicted nor convicted. In the Midi—a center of the "White Terror"—most of the *juges de paix*, who were still elected to their offices, allegedly sympathized with violent anti-Jacobinism or were too intimidated by it to initiate procedures. When cases were taken to the *jurys d'accusation*, the jurors—allegedly influenced by elected *directeurs des jurys* infused with conservative sentiments—frequently refused to indict.[82]

When right-wing terrorists did go to trial (most political offenses were now again tried by the juries), the *jurys de jugement* often voted for acquittal, not just for anti-Jacobin terrorists but for many of the enemies of the government of the Directory of 1795–99 who had committed outrages and assaults. Frequently, they acquitted these persons on the basis of the *question intentionnelle*—that is, did the person intend to commit the crime? Even in departments such as the Vosges, Indre, Marne, Aisne, and Côte d'Or—departments far removed from the hotbeds of counterrevolutionary sentiment in the west and south—most political defendants were acquitted. The Directory's local agents complained bitterly about the frequency with which jurors acquitted "the most culpable enemies of the Republic."[83]

To be sure, not all such acquittals were due to right-wing bias. Robert Allen, in his study of jury verdicts in political cases in the Côte d'Or from 1792 to 1800, claims that jurors in that department were rather evenhanded; they acquitted most political defendants of either the Left or the Right. Even during the Terror of the Year II, less than half of all persons accused of political offenses were convicted (though a higher percentage were condemned in this year than in others). During the Thermidorian Reaction that followed, not only were most right-wing defendants acquitted, but so were most Jacobin terrorists charged with abuses of power they had committed when in office. Allen suggests that this may have been because many of the

The "Palladium of Liberty"

jurors in the Côte d'Or were not tightly bound up in the political struggles of the era, did not have a taste for the pursuit of political enemies, and did not share the anxiety of governments faced with political threats.[84]

The extent to which this was true in other departments is unclear. But Allen's contention is supported by the behavior of juries in political cases in later periods: throughout subsequent French history, whenever juries were allowed to try political and press offenses, both nonviolent and violent, they voted for acquittal in most instances, whatever the ideology of the accused persons and regardless of whether the government tried to rig the jury lists.

If there was a conservative bias among jurors outside the Côte d'Or (a bias that in part would have reflected the royalist sentiment of most Frenchmen following Thermidor), it was perhaps accentuated by the government's own reimposition of property qualifications for jury service as well as for voting. The Constitution of the Year III (1795) raised the age requirement for jurors from twenty-five to thirty and stipulated that persons included in the jury lists must be electors (that is, elected in the cantons by voters meeting the same qualifications as "active citizens" of 1791). Only the proprietors, usufructuaries, renters, and tenant farmers and sharecroppers of real estate worth between one hundred and two hundred days of work, depending on where they lived, could vote and be jurors. These men constituted a very narrow minority of the population. What is more, a law of 1797 limited the government payment of stipends and expenses only to jurors who needed to travel to try cases (a later law of 1811 was even more restrictive, maintaining government payment just for the transportation—and not for the food or lodging—of jurors who had to travel more than two kilometers. This was the only payment jurors could receive from this time until the enactment of laws of 1907–8). The jury lists were again drawn up by the administrative head of the department according to information provided by local administrations.[85]

Another major problem in the opinion of governments and magistrates was the frequency with which juries acquitted persons accused of ordinary crimes. No published nationwide statistics on acquittals and convictions by juries appeared until 1825. But data compiled for twenty-one of the departments show that in most of them, acquittal rates ranged between about 40 and 50 percent. In a few departments, they were even higher.[86]

A crisis point was reached during the years of the Directory. This period of political and economic chaos was accompanied by a serious revival of brigandage in the countryside, and France suffered what may well have been its worst outbreak of crime in modern times. Jurors were apparently intimidated by threats of retaliation from lawbreakers or their accomplices and acquitted many of them.[87] Therefore, the government held that juries bore a significant degree of responsibility for the situation of lawlessness.[88]

But the causes of jury leniency in the 1790s went well beyond fear of retaliation from lawbreakers, and these causes would remain long after the chaos of the Directory years passed. Already in the 1790s, some judges noted that juries showed what appeared to be pronounced biases in favor of persons accused of certain crimes, such as infanticide, violence against the agents of public authority, murders motivated by passion, and the like, along with a strong bias against persons accused of theft.[89] The reasons for these biases were complex and will be dealt with later. Suffice it to say that they contributed to high acquittal rates and would constitute a pattern that would hold into the nineteenth century.

Another alleged cause of the high acquittal rate was the jurors' interpretation of the *question intentionnelle*: being untrained in legal distinctions, they seem to have often confused intent (that is, did the accused act with criminal intent—did he or she have *mens rea*, a guilty mind—when committing the crime) with motivation (the motivating force or stimulus for the crime).[90] Jurors were also apparently confused by the lack of rules of evidence and the bewildering number of questions, which in complex cases involving several defendants could reach the hundreds.[91]

Perhaps the most important cause of the high acquittal rate already noticed by judges of the 1790s—and which was most often mentioned again by magistrates, jurists, and governments in the nineteenth and twentieth centuries—was the reluctance of jurors to convict because of the harsh penalties provided by the *Code pénal* of 1791 and the subsequent penal codes. According to Isser Woloch, the judicial legislation of the Revolution created an ambiguity that would plague the justice system well into the future. On one hand, the judicial reforms of the Revolution implemented important new rights for accused persons, including jury trial and the right to defense counsel. On the other hand, but also in accordance with Enlightenment thought, rigidly fixed punishments were implemented for the first time (whereas old regime judges were allowed discretion in punishment), and many of these punishments were seen as too severe by jurors who often evidently felt they had to acquit obviously guilty persons to save them from what they thought was an unjust but mandatory sentence.[92]

Faced with the breakdown of law and order and high acquittal rates for both politically and nonpolitically motivated crimes, the government of the Directory in the late 1790s responded as had the government of the Terror before it: by curtailing the jury system. The effort to do so began in

1797, and it was a part of the Directory's movement toward keeping power through illegal and undemocratic means. After royalists won most of the parliamentary and local elections of April 1797, a government fearful of a restoration of the monarchy annulled the election of 179 deputies and hundreds of departmental administrators and judges. This was followed by the scrapping of the jury lists in about half of the departments. The discovery that five well-known *chouans* (royalist guerrillas) had been included in a jury list in the Mayenne reinforced the government's determination to carry out this purge. Several times in the late 1790s, the justice minister sent circulars to the courts urging them to be more careful in the selection of jurors.[93]

The Directory more directly curtailed the juries by resorting to military tribunals to try certain types of accused civilians, beginning in 1797 with émigrés caught back in France and extending in the next two years to include all those accused of house burglary or armed robbery in groups of three or more.[94] Moreover, the number of jurors needed to convict in those cases they still tried was reduced to a simple majority of seven by a new law of 1797.[95]

The actions of the Directory set the stage for Napoleon Bonaparte, who did more than anyone else to curtail the jury system, and in ways still very evident in France. Following his coup of November 1799 overthrowing the Directory and establishing the Consulate, Napoleon set out to stamp out brigandage and reestablish law and order in the countryside through resolutely authoritarian means and with the support of a French public weary of chaos. The new dictator first increased the number of extraordinary military commissions to try brigands and political rebels in the Midi and in Brittany.[96] These were replaced in 1801 by the *cours spéciales*. Each was composed of eight persons—the president, two judges of the criminal court, three military men having the rank at least of captain, and two property-holding citizens with legal training—and no jury. The five non-magisterial members were appointed by Napoleon. The *cours spéciales* tried all persons accused of armed rebellion, armed smuggling, and counterfeiting; murders committed by mobs and assemblages; and any crimes committed by vagrants. A mere majority of five of eight sufficed for conviction, and there was no appeal from the court's verdict.[97] In the first six months of their operation, these special courts were set up in twenty-seven departments of the west and the Midi.[98]

The legislative debate over the creation of the *cours spéciales* was significant in that it was an early example of a controversy that would continue in France down through the twentieth century on the balance between the individual's right to jury trial and the need to maintain law and order, a law and order that juries were frequently accused of undermining. Liberals in the Tribunate and the Legislative Body opposed the establishment of the special courts because it was an unconstitutional abridgment of the rights of accused persons, unacceptable even in times of social disorder. The Constitution of the Year VIII, like those before it, had guaranteed trial by jury for *crimes*.[99]

But a majority in both houses accepted the law and order arguments of the partisans of the *cours spéciales*, who claimed that the jury system in the south and west had become "the safeguard of brigands."[100] In the end, the bill to establish the courts was passed in both the Tribunate and in the Legislative Body.[101] Historians have often regarded the legislative debate over the *cours spéciales* as a turning point in the relationship between Napoleon and the liberals. But as Howard G. Brown has pointed out, the special courts were actually a marked improvement over the extraordinary military commissions they replaced, for they followed more or less regular judicial procedure, though without juries or appeals.[102] They were kept throughout the remainder of the Napoleonic period, and even into the earliest years of the restored Bourbon monarchy.[103]

By 1804, Napoleon's *Conseil d'état* was debating the issue of whether the jury system should be maintained at all.[104] Many magistrates advised the council to eliminate juries. The experiences of the 1790s—the allegedly partisan nature of many verdicts for political or politically inspired crimes, the juries' biases in many other cases, the high rates of acquittals, the supposed incompetence and ignorance of jurors, their susceptibility to eloquent defense attorneys, their gullibility and impressionability—had left a sour taste in the mouths of many judges.[105] In fact, according to late-nineteenth-century legal historian Adhemar Esmein, the attacks on juries originated among magistrates, who considered the jury system wrongheaded: "They could not understand why the evanescent oral testimony should be preferred to the written record, ignorance to knowledge, irresolution to experience and to the professional sentiment of duty."[106]

The hostility of a large portion of the judiciary to the jury system became quite evident when the *Conseil d'état*, in the years XII and XIII, launched an inquiry asking judges for their opinions on proposed revisions to the criminal code. According to Esmein's analysis of the results of the inquiry, the judges of the *tribunaux criminels* were evenly split on the question of the jury: of the seventy-five of these courts that responded, twenty-three did not clearly state whether they opposed or favored the retention of the jury system, twenty-six favored keeping it, and twenty-six called for its abolition. The *tribunaux d'appel* came out more strongly against the jury system. Of

The "Palladium of Liberty"

the twenty-two appeals courts that responded, twelve opposed the jury, five gave no opinion, and only five favored its retention.[107]

Some of the complaints of the *tribunaux d'appel* would be echoed by later magistrates. Principal among these claims: juries were incompetent and excessively lenient, often acquitting obviously guilty persons.[108] In addition, jurors were too ignorant, too impressionable, and too biased to judge cases wisely. Other complaints were peculiar to the period and reflected the experiences of the Revolution and the Anglophobia produced by the wars against England: a dangerous spirit of party determined decisions among juries of the Revolutionary era, and trial by jury, because it was of English origin, was not suitable to the French character and customs.[109] In 1791, the English jury had been regarded very positively as the "palladium of liberty" among most members of the Constituent Assembly. By the beginning of the nineteenth century, however, it was seen by many French magistrates as an undesirable import.

Despite the magistrates' advice, Napoleon kept the jury system. But he severely curtailed it in the 1808 Code of Criminal Procedure. Trial by jury was retained for persons who had committed *crimes* punishable by death, hard labor, or at least five years' imprisonment. This by itself did not significantly reduce the role of the jury, for although the penal code of 1791 guaranteed trial by jury for persons accused of offenses punishable by at least two years' imprisonment, under Napoleon's new code the penalties for many misdemeanors were increased beyond this former threshold. Persons charged with *délits* (now defined as offenses punishable by no more than five years' imprisonment) were to be tried by the three-judge panels of the *tribunaux correctionnels*, one of which existed in each *arrondissement*.[110]

In other ways, however, Napoleon restricted the role of juries. For one thing, his Code of Criminal Procedure introduced several articles that allowed trial judges to second-guess juries and thereby limit the "sovereignty" of the latter. Article 351 (repealed in 1831) stipulated that if the jury convicted the accused of the principal charge by a vote of seven to five, the judges were to be polled on the verdict. If four of the five judges accepted the opinion of the minority of the jury, the accused was then acquitted by a vote of nine to eight. Article 352 stated that even when the jury voted for conviction by a majority greater than seven, if the judges were unanimously convinced that there had been a miscarriage of justice, they could suspend the verdict and send the case to trial in the next court session, to be submitted to a new jury, from which all those who first tried the case were excluded. Both articles concerned only convictions; acquittals could not be overturned. These articles were, however, rarely invoked. Otherwise, conviction by a jury could

The "Palladium of Liberty"

be overturned only by the *cour de cassation*, or supreme court. But this court decided only on errors of law, not fact. It ruled merely on whether the jury's decision was legal, that is, whether all the provisions of the law regarding the trial had "been observed and properly applied." If not, the court quashed the verdict and sent the case back for retrial.[111]

More important was the fact that while the code maintained the jury system for the trial stage of felony prosecutions, it restored most of the elements of the old inquisitorial system for the pretrial phase. Already, laws of the years VIII and IX (1800–1801) replaced elected judges (except justices of the peace and judges of the Tribunal of Cassation) with ones appointed for life by the central government, and the Ancien Régime offices of *procureurs* (public prosecutors) and *juges d'instruction* (examining magistrates) were restored, along with the secret preliminary examination of accused persons. Napoleon's Code of Criminal Procedure carried the process further by eliminating the *jurys d'accusation*.[112] This came following the harsh criticisms of these panels by magistrates and by Napoleon himself because of their frequent refusals to indict and their presumed incompetence at deciding whether there was the "beginning of proof" against an accused person, something investigators felt they were better able to determine.[113]

Therefore, the code now granted to professional magistrates a complete monopoly over the investigation and indictment process. Only the *procureurs*, not citizens or elected justices of the peace, could initiate prosecutions. Felony cases were then sent to the *juges d'instruction*, one of whom existed in each *arrondissement* (cases the *procureurs* determined to be *délits* could go directly to trial before a *tribunal correctionnel*). These magistrates determined whether there was sufficient evidence to try a suspect. The powers of the *juge d'instruction* were very broad. He interrogated the suspect in his chamber, in secret, virtually without check, and (before 1897) without the presence of counsel for the accused. Granted nearly unlimited powers of search and seizure, the *juge d'instruction* carried out a thorough and searching examination of the suspect, often to the point of covering his or her whole life history.[114] The *juge d'instruction* was therefore very much the successor of the *lieutenant criminel* of the Old Regime.

The *juge d'instruction* and two judges from the nearest lower tribunal then reviewed the case in the *chambre du conseil* (eventually abolished in 1856), where the examining magistrate's findings were rarely challenged by the two other magistrates.[115] If this panel (and after 1856, the *juge d'instruction* alone) decided that there was enough evidence that a felony had been committed (again, *délits* might go straight to trial in the *tribunaux correctionnels*), the case went to a *chambre des mises en accusation* (indictment

The "Palladium of Liberty"

court) composed entirely of judges (five altogether) taken from the *cours d'appel*.[116] As one modern scholar summed it up, proceedings before trial "were to be secret, written, and weighted toward the prosecution."[117] Even though the accused was considered innocent until proven guilty, the exhaustive preliminary investigation by magistrates and the voluminous dossier that accompanied the accused to trial weighed heavily against him or her.[118]

If the *chambre des mises en accusation* formally indicted an accused person for a felony, the case went to trial in a *cour d'assises*—the successor to the *tribunal criminel*. These courts held quarterly sessions. They were headed by a presiding judge (*président*), who was an appeals court judge on circuit selected by the minister of justice, and four (after 1831, two) junior colleagues (*assesseurs*), also taken from the *cour d'appel* if the *cour d'assises* met in the same town as the appeals court, or from the nearest civil court if it met elsewhere. In these courts, the questions of guilt or innocence were determined by twelve jurors, with seven necessary (as had been the case since 1797) to convict.[119] Here, the procedure was radically different from that of the pretrial phase: all was public and oral, the accused was defended by counsel, and the decision of guilt or innocence was made by citizen-magistrates.

But Napoleon restricted the pool of these citizen-magistrates to a narrow elite hand-picked by his prefects. He had agreed to retain the jury only "if it is possible to insure its proper composition."[120] In the nine years preceding the publication of the Code of Criminal Procedure, magistrates and government officials complained about what they perceived as the low "niveau intellectuel" of the jury due to the fact that the Constitution of the Year VIII (1799) had done away with property qualifications for voting and therefore also for jury service. The elected *juges de paix* every three months drew up preliminary cantonal jury lists triple the cantonal quota of jurors, which was then progressively reduced to the actual quota by the subprefect and the prefect. This allegedly led to the selection of many illiterate and poorly educated jurors, especially in rural areas where few people were educated.[121]

The emperor agreed with this negative assessment of the democratically composed juries. He wanted panels of *notables* committed to law, order, and the protection of property. His Code of Criminal Procedure stipulated that jurors were to be men from the social and intellectual elites only. Inclusion in the jury lists was limited to the members of the electoral colleges; the three hundred most heavily taxed persons in the department; administrative officeholders appointed by the emperor; doctors and graduates of one or more of the four faculties of law, medicine, sciences, and belles lettres; members and correspondents of the Institute of France and of the other learned societies recognized by the government; and notaries. Also included were bankers, stockbrokers, merchants paying a *patente* (license fee) of one of the first two classes, and civil servants with salaries of at least four thousand francs.[122] Napoleon's government claimed that jurors such as these would best maintain law and order because they had the strongest interest in doing so.[123]

Napoleon also sought to ensure the political reliability of the jurors by making the drawing up of jury lists the responsibility of the prefects, the central government's chief appointees in the departments. According to his code, at least fifteen days before each quarterly session of the *cour d'assises*, the prefect drew up from the general list of all persons eligible for jury duty a session list of sixty jurors, which was then reduced to thirty-six by the *président* of the *cour d'assises*.[124] This meant that during sessions, jurors often heard many cases, especially during the early nineteenth century when trials in the *cours d'assises* were far more numerous than they were to become in the late nineteenth and twentieth centuries. For example, in the department of the Côtes-du-Nord from 1811 to 1832, some sessions of the *cours d'assises* lasted for nearly two months; those that lasted for no longer than a week (which was about the maximum for sessions in France by the twentieth century) were rare.[125] French jurors of the era were in this respect rather like the English ones of the eighteenth century, who also heard many cases. Some English historians have seen this as resulting in the semi-professionalization of jury service.[126] Something similar could be said of jury service in France, at least during the early nineteenth century.

At the start of a trial, the names of those on the reduced session list of thirty-six were placed in an urn, and as each name was pulled out of the urn, the accused first and then the *procureur général* had the right peremptorily to challenge an equal number of jurors until the list was subtracted to twelve names, who then made up the trial jury.[127] Therefore, the *président* of the *cour d'assises*, the defense, and the prosecution all had a hand in the selection of jurors. But those who served could come only from the list drawn up by the prefect. Gordon Wright has claimed that Napoleon's willingness to keep the jury system rested in part "on his expectation . . . that the selection of jurors would henceforth be carefully controlled by the prefects."[128] Napoleon's system of trial by *notables* drawn from lists prepared by the prefects survived into the two succeeding regimes of the Bourbon Restoration and the July Monarchy.[129]

But the other major element of the Napoleonic compromise in respect to the jury—the restoration of the inquisitorial system in the pretrial phase and the retention of the accusatory system in the trial phase of felonies—

remained intact throughout the nineteenth and twentieth centuries, with minor revisions. It was to be an uneasy compromise. Whereas the inquisitorial system was weighted heavily against defendants, juries acquitted many of them. Governments and magistrates would find it hard to control juries, especially in political cases and despite laws giving government authorities the power to hand-pick jurors. Accused persons retained their right to defense counsel, and the jury did not have to explain its verdict, which it still gave in response to a series of questions and which could be appealed to the *cour de cassation* only on procedural grounds (the *cours d'appel* just reviewed cases from the civil and correctional tribunals).

Yet the writers of Napoleon's codes exerted perhaps the most important influence on the future behavior of the juries by retaining two other fundamental principles from the Revolutionary legal reforms. These were the system of "moral proofs"[130] and the concept (though later modified) of fixed punishments. The former was embodied in Article 342 of the 1808 Code of Criminal Procedure, which contained two paragraphs of instructions that the foreman was required to read to the jury at the beginning of its deliberations, instructions that were also posted in large letters in the most visible part of the panel's chamber. The first paragraph enjoined jurors to judge according to "moral proofs" in the following terms:

> The law does not ask jurors to account for the means by which they are convinced; it prescribes no rules by which they must particularly base the fullness or sufficiency of a proof: it enjoins them to ask themselves, in silence and meditation, and seek in the sincerity of their conscience, what impression the proofs against the accused, and those for the defense, have made on their reason. The law does not say to them: "You shall take as true every fact attested by such or such a number of witnesses"; nor does it say: "You shall regard as not sufficiently established every proof which shall not consist of such a report, such documents, such testimony, or such evidence"; it asks them only this question, which contains the full extent of their duties: "Have you an intimate conviction?"[131]

The instruction meant that jurors were to find fact with their reason unconstrained by some preset formula in regard to the proofs but in accord with their common sense as persons morally dedicated to finding a true assessment of fact alone. Where the Roman-canon system of legal proofs required judges to convict (at least in capital cases) on the basis of a certain combination of proofs, jurors were free to judge according to their consciences without any rule predetermining the value of proofs; they could acquit or convict no matter how strong or weak the evidence.[132]

The "Palladium of Liberty"

The wording of the instruction did not imply that jurors had rights that extended beyond fact-finding. Yet according to some observers in the nineteenth and twentieth centuries, the decision by the writers of Napoleon's Code of Criminal Procedure to keep the Revolution's principle of judgment by "moral proofs" made it possible for jurors often to judge merely on the basis of their emotions, biases, or impressions, or in accordance with customs that conflicted with the letter of the law, rather than on the basis of reason. Jurors in effect often placed themselves above the law,[133] though this was inconsistent with the above instruction. That juries did not have to explain their verdicts made this all the more possible. As early as 1791, during the Constituent Assembly's debates on instituting the jury, the deputy Louis Prugnon sensed the danger implied by the arbitrariness of assessment of fact by those not trained to set aside any possible bias in that process of assessment: "If legal proofs are no longer necessary to establish the guilt of the accused, everything must become conjectural, and the life and honor of the citizens are brought before a court of conjectures. . . . [T]he proof will lie in the individual perception of each juror."[134]

This criticism would be repeated more than two centuries later when American legal historian William Savitt wrote that "the French approach appeals rather to the juror's impressions and instincts than to reason and sober weighing of evidence."[135] This, in addition to uncertainty brought about by the lack of rules of evidence, the often bewildering number of questions jurors had to answer, the resistance of jurors to an inquisitorial system perceived as very much stacked against accused persons, and the theatrical nature of trials in the *cours d'assises*, allegedly led to many acquittals.

But juries presumably acquitted even more defendants in reaction against the second principle, that of fixed punishments, punishments the panels often felt were too harsh.[136] They did so in defiance of the second paragraph of Article 342, which instructed them to ignore the penal consequences of their verdicts; they were to judge only "fact," not "law" (again, the latter meant punishment, not law in the more general sense): "It is essential not to forget that the jury are to concern themselves solely with facts; and they fail to do their duty when they take into consideration the penal consequences which follow upon their verdict. Their mission has for its object neither the prosecution nor the punishment of offenses; they are called upon only to decide whether the accused is or is not guilty of the crime with which he is charged."[137]

In practice, it was not possible for juries to clearly separate "fact" from "law." The Code of Criminal Procedure left it to the judges to decide the law in the general sense: after a jury handed down a guilty verdict, the public prosecutor asked the court to apply the law. If the court determined that the act that the accused was found guilty of was indeed forbidden by penal law, the judges then applied the penalty established by the law (Articles 362–65). Yet it appears that Article 342's stipulation that jurors were called upon to decide whether the accused was or was not "guilty of the crime" he or she was charged with may have required some sort of legal judgment to determine the "facts." Considerations of guilt and punishment may have interacted. The first principle of Article 342 permitted jurors to assess fact in accordance with "their reason" and "intimate conviction." Jurors were thereby given room to accept (in light of their own nonlegal notions) the defendant's excuse or justification and at the same time felt it was appropriate because the penalty was not deserved.

The juries' defiance of the instruction not to take into consideration the penal consequences of their verdicts was related to their rebellion against the "classical" system of penology put into place by the Revolution. This would remain a major theme in the history of the jury in France until the mid-twentieth century. The Revolutionary *Code pénal* of 1791, and in a somewhat modified form the Napoleonic *Code pénal* of 1810, embodied the "classical" view of punishment, which gradually became the basis for criminal codes throughout Europe. Classical penology had been formulated in the eighteenth century by thinkers such as Cesare Beccaria and Jeremy Bentham, and it was based on the assumption that criminals were rational persons generally possessed of sufficient free will to be deemed responsible for their crimes.[138] Accordingly, the Revolutionary and Napoleonic codes punished the crime rather than the criminal and operated on Beccaria's notion that the punishment must fit the crime and be equally applicable to all individuals who committed it, regardless of pity, the character of the individual, or the circumstances that led one to commit the offense.[139]

Therefore, penalties had to be rigidly fixed by law—an idea all the more appealing to Revolutionary legislators in that it eliminated the "arbitrary" or discretionary sentencing powers that had been wielded by Old Regime judges. This was yet another blow against Old Regime judicial despotism. Equality of justice under the law would now be guaranteed in the *Code pénal* by the fixation of penalties in advance for every crime.[140]

Juries, on the other hand, often did not accept this rigid framework, even from the beginning. Faced with the choice between harsh, fixed punishments or outright acquittal for certain criminals they tried who were obviously guilty but whose responsibility for their crimes was perceived as diminished, juries often chose the latter option.

In fact, Napoleon's government was the first to recognize the need to ameliorate penalties in order to obtain more convictions, for its *Code pénal* of 1810 broke somewhat from the fixed punishments of the Revolutionary penal code. In the new code, both minimum and maximum penalties were provided for many crimes. This reform was explicitly aimed at getting juries to convict more often as a consequence of their knowledge that judges could moderate the penalties.[141] Thus, for the first time, juries had a major impact on French criminal law. In the course of the nineteenth and twentieth centuries, French governments would continue to react to jury verdicts in their revisions of penal laws.

They and their magistrates would also react by taking a number of actions that ultimately destroyed the importance and independence of the jury in the justice system. This was a complex and lengthy process, and many of the factors that contributed to the decline of the jury system in France did not play a role in this process until well after the Revolutionary and Napoleonic periods. Yet it was during these periods that much of the machinery was put into place that made it possible for juries to influence greatly the evolution of the French criminal justice system; in addition, much had also been introduced that (as we shall see) ultimately made possible the near extinction of the jury.

chapter two

THE "JURYS CENSITAIRES," 1815–1848

The periods of the Bourbon Restoration (1815–30) and the July Monarchy (1830–48) together marked the era of the "Jurys Censitaires," when the panels were composed almost exclusively of *notables*. In addition, at least two major developments distinguished the era. One was that liberal support for the jury as the "palladium of liberty" now reached its peak. Perhaps in no other era was there such a strong consciousness of the political role of the jury, a consciousness heightened by the sharp political controversies of the era. The other major development was the significant expansion of jury-based mitigation of penalties through the law of 1832 on extenuating circumstances. Acquittal rates were quite high during the early years of the period, especially for violent crimes. Moreover, a large proportion of those persons who were convicted were found guilty of lesser charges than the most serious ones brought by the prosecution. Governments of the period, reasoning that such verdicts were often the consequence of jurors' unwillingness to impose the punishments provided by law, responded primarily through reforms enabling judges and juries to legally reduce penalties for persons found guilty in the *cours d'assises*. The reform of 1832 (the most important) did little to reduce the overall acquittal rate through the remainder of the period, but it did result in a sharp decline in extralegal jury devices for leniency, which before had been the only means by which juries could ameliorate the penalties of persons they convicted.

Yet it was in this era that the great paradox in the history of the jury system in France first became evident, though only in retrospect. On one hand, and with much notice, a series of measures was enacted to strengthen the jury system, especially during the early years of the July Monarchy. On the other hand, and with much less notice, several forces began to operate that would eventually contribute significantly to the decline of the jury system in France. Massive correctionalization as a response to jury sanction nullification belonged to later eras, but during the Bourbon Restoration and July Monarchy, the practice had its modest beginnings.

Correctionalization was initiated by conservative magistrates and governments despite the fact that throughout the Bourbon Restoration and

July Monarchy eras, jurors were still almost all *notables* chosen from lists drawn up by the prefects. Napoleon's system of selecting most jurors from the electoral colleges was kept,[1] which meant that the citizen-judges were ordinarily "censitaires," men who had to meet the stiff property qualifications for voting. The Constitutional Charter of 1814 limited the franchise to males at least thirty years old who paid three hundred francs or more in direct taxes.[2] Such men accounted for only about 90,000 to 100,000 people in all of France.[3] In 1831, the new regime of the July Monarchy enacted a law that reduced the taxation requirement for electors from three hundred to two hundred francs and the age requirement from thirty to twenty-five years. But even with the resulting increase in the number of electors, they still accounted for less than 1 percent of the population.[4]

Yet electors accounted for 90.5 percent of all persons inscribed in the annual jury lists for the years 1828 (when the Ministry of Justice began to publish the composition of the lists in the annual *Compte général de l'administration de la justice criminelle*) through 1848.[5] They were often wealthy landowners.[6] Although the Ministry of Justice's published jury lists for the nation as a whole did not mention the occupations of jurors until 1849, several local studies have shown that during the Restoration and the July Monarchy, a large proportion of jurymen were *propriétaires* and *rentiers*. The proportion of these men varied from one-third of all jurors in the Nord department[7] to half or more in the Herault,[8] Deux-Sevres, Indre, and Sarthe.[9]

The apparent conservatism of such jurors was reinforced by the fact that many of them were well into middle age. Even though the electoral law of 1831 reduced the age requirement for voting to twenty-five, the minimum age for jury duty remained at thirty.[10] But whether it was due to choice by the prefects or to the time it took to accumulate or inherit enough wealth to qualify for jury duty, the average juror of the Restoration and July Monarchy eras was about fifty years old, if the results of several local studies are representative of the nation.[11]

Despite the elite status and maturity of most jurors, judges continued to criticize the incompetence of many of them. Not all the rural *notables* were well-educated by any means, and in some departments the *présidents* of the *cours d'assises* complained to the justice minister of jurors who were illiterate or did not even speak French.[12] In a number of instances, they felt compelled to ask the prefects to exclude from the annual jury lists illiterates, men without intelligence, those who did not speak French, less wealthy electors, ex-convicts, and drunks.[13] The judges' emphasis on what they saw as the incompetence of jurors would continue and grow even more pronounced as juries became more democratized in subsequent periods.

The "Jurys Censitaires"

Yet however restricted the jury pool of the era from 1815 to 1848 was, the panels of *notables* certainly did not always behave in a fashion one would presumably expect from propertied and middle-aged men chosen from lists drawn up by government appointees. Instead of being the tools of the governments that selected them and the consistent upholders of law and order that Napoleon had hoped for when he restricted jury duty to *notables*, juries acted in a very independent fashion. Above all, as in the 1790s, they continued to acquit many persons accused of both political and nonpolitical crimes.

The leniency of juries angered conservatives, who believed that the panels did not sufficiently uphold law and order. But liberals, who more than ever saw the jury system as the "palladium of liberty," sought to strengthen it through a series of reforms. They gradually made progress in this effort, especially after the overthrow of the reactionary Charles X in 1830. The liberal program of jury reform centered on four proposals: (1) a restraining of the authority of the prefects in the selection of jurors; (2) the transferal of jurisdiction over *délits politiques et de presse* (political and press misdemeanors) from the judges of the *tribunaux correctionnels* to the juries of the *cours d'assises*; (3) a strengthening of the jury at the expense of the judges of the *cours d'assises*; and, related to this, (4) the enactment of a law, finally passed in 1832, giving to juries the authority to find extenuating circumstances for the persons they convicted.

In respect to the first part of their program of jury reform—restraining the power of prefects in the selection of jurors—the liberals accomplished rather little. They charged that prefects drew up jury session lists according to the dictates of the government and prosecutors, especially in political cases. There was some evidence to support this accusation. For example, in the Marne department in 1820, the name of each juror was annotated. In one instance, an *avocat général* was tactless enough to speak of "his jury" during a trial. The Ministry of Justice managed to get enough intelligence on the manner with which jurors fulfilled their functions to permit it to express its satisfaction to those who showed "a laudable zeal." The ministry also encouraged prefects to choose jurors who were the most "enlightened," which probably meant those most attached to the social order and to the government.[14]

In 1821, liberal members of the Chamber of Deputies issued an unsuccessful petition protesting the role of prefects in the establishment of jury lists. The clamor of the liberals for a reform was such that by late 1826, even the reactionary government of Charles X and his prime minister the comte de Villèle felt compelled to introduce a bill reforming the mode of

The "Jurys Censitaires"

jury selection.[15] The bill was passed to become the law of May 2, 1827. In reality, it only slightly modified the system of prefectoral selection of jurors. No longer was the prefect to draw up a session list of sixty jurors fifteen days before the meeting of the department's *cour d'assises*. Instead, each fall he was to compose an annual jury list for the following year consisting of one-fourth of the names from the general list of all persons eligible for jury duty, provided that the selected number did not exceed three hundred for any department, except the Seine, where it was fixed at fifteen hundred. Ten days before the opening of a session of the *cour d'assises*, the premier president of the *cour royale* (appeals court) chose by lot a session list of thirty-six jurors from the annual list prepared by the prefect.[16]

Since the prefect could no longer draw up a list of only sixty names before the opening of the *cour d'assises*, the authors of the new law hoped that it would answer the criticisms of those who claimed that the old law had given the prefects too much power in choosing jurors.[17] After all, it is harder to investigate the political opinions of three hundred men than it is of sixty. However, by giving to the prefects alone the responsibility of drawing up the annual jury lists, the 1827 law maintained much of the influence of these officials in the selection of jurors.

The law also revealed the limitations of the liberals' program of jury reform. It retained Napoleon's system of selecting most jurors from persons wealthy enough to be members of the electoral colleges.[18] The liberals, who themselves believed in a restricted franchise, had no objection to the choosing of jurors among the *notables*; they objected only to their being chosen by the administration. No one, at least according to the surviving evidence, proposed that jurors be paid for their lodging and lost wages.[19]

Moreover, after liberals took over control of the government in the July Revolution of 1830, they did nothing to change the mode of jury selection, except indirectly through the electoral law of 1831, which lowered the taxation requirement for voting, and therefore also for jury service, from three hundred to two hundred francs. The law of 1827 was not modified in any way during the July Monarchy. The major difference now was that Orleanist rather than Bourbon Ultra-royalist or Legitimist prefects got to draw up the jury lists.

Like their predecessors, Orleanist prefects evidently felt no compunction about trying to stack juries in the government's favor. Although it must have been a rather daunting task to investigate the political opinions of all the men eligible for jury duty in a department and each year draw up a list of three hundred politically reliable potential jurors, the prefects did have some help in keeping undesirables (such as Legitimists and Republicans) out of the jury pool (although by no means could this always be done).[20] Françoise Lombard has studied the electoral lists drawn up by the sub-prefects of the *arrondissements* of Douai, Avesnes, and Valenciennes (all in the Nord) for the years 1841 (in the first case) and 1842 (in the latter two cases). These *arrondissement* electoral lists were used by the prefect to compose the departmental jury list of three hundred men. They included not only the names and professions of the electors but also comments made by the sub-prefects regarding many individuals on the lists. The comments were sometimes political, mentioning such information as whether a certain voter was a supporter of the government or was a Legitimist and the like. Therefore, as Lombard noted, "these observations formulated by the sub-prefects allow one to presume that the choice of jurors was not neutral."[21]

The evident attempts by July Monarchy officials to keep political opponents off juries were very much tied to the regime's political culture. The July Monarchy was a particularly fragile regime. Its right to rule was based on neither hereditary succession nor on popular sovereignty (no election—not even a rigged one—was ever held to confirm Louis Philippe's revolutionary accession to the throne). As one scholar puts it, "The essential character of the July regime was the absence of political and moral legitimacy. It was its principal weakness, which it would never overcome."[22] Republicans charged that the July Revolution of 1830 had been hijacked from the marquis de Lafayette and his Republican supporters by Orleanist constitutional monarchists. Legitimist supporters of the overthrown Bourbons regarded Louis Philippe as a usurper. These two groups were irreconcilable. Moreover, liberals who had supported the 1830 revolution became increasingly disillusioned with a regime that, following a few early reforms, became more and more conservative and authoritarian as the party of "resistance" soon clearly gained the upper hand over the party of "movement" in the councils of government.[23]

Officials of the July Monarchy therefore saw control of elections as important for keeping the regime in power. A major task of the prefects and sub-prefects—who were very much political appointees—was to secure the election of official candidates, and they practiced "every form of chicanery possible" to do so. Prefects were also expected to report to the government on the activities of Legitimists and Republicans.[24] The electoral lists, with their comments about individual electors made by the sub-prefects, were thus part of this system.

Control of juries along with control of elections were seen as essential by the regime because liberals in 1830 had succeeded in enacting the reform they had insisted on most—a guarantee of trial by jury for persons accused of *délits politiques et de presse*. The idea of the jury as the "palladium of liberty" had its most obvious application in the trial of political and press offenses. Jury trial for such cases was a very contentious issue during the Restoration and July Monarchy. To understand why first requires an understanding of the three different categories of political and quasi-political offenses.

Two of these categories were always (except from 1815 to 1818) tried by juries because they were classified by the *Code pénal* as *crimes* punishable by *peines afflictives et infamantes*, such as death, hard labor, or more than five years' imprisonment. The first was *crimes politiques* (political felonies), which were defined as acts against either the external or internal security of the state (such as plotting to overthrow the government or to assassinate the head of state and the like).[25] A second kind of felony was not strictly a political offense, but it often had political implications. This was *rébellion*. It was defined in the *Code pénal* (Article 209) as "any attack, any resistance with violence and assault" against government officials or law enforcement officers carrying out their orders or official duties. *Rébellion* constituted a *crime* or *délit*, depending on the circumstances. If it was an individual act (such as resisting arrest), it was only a *délit*. But to be serious enough to constitute a *crime* and therefore to be tried by a jury, it had to be committed by at least three armed persons or more than twenty unarmed ones. These were therefore acts of collective violence against either public officials or law enforcement officers. Contemporaries did not, however, strictly regard *rébellion* as a *crime politique*, because it applied only to those who, in a "local and instantaneous" way, violently resisted the "isolated" acts of the agents of public authority, without the intention of destroying or changing the government.[26] Even so, any act by an armed group of men or by a crowd against the enforcement of the laws challenged the government's authority.

It was over the issue of who should try the third category of offenses— *délits politiques et de presse*—that liberals clashed with the government of the Restoration. Since these were misdemeanors, they were punishable by fines or no more than five years' imprisonment. They constituted generally what one could call crimes of opinion in speech and press (yelling seditious slogans, defaming public officials, inciting hatred or contempt of the government, and so on). Napoleon's *Code pénal* placed them along with other *délits* under the jurisdiction of the *tribunaux correctionnels*. Liberals of the Restoration era, however, believed that an exception should be made for the political and press cases and that their trials should be transferred to the juries, since the panels were much more independent of the government and presumed to be less biased against the accused persons than the appointed professional judges of the *tribunaux correctionnels*.

The controversy over the trials of these offenses was intimately connected with political events. The Constitutional Charter of 1814 guaranteed trial by jury but made several exceptions: "Changes which experience may cause to be deemed necessary in connection therewith [i.e., juries] may be effected only by law," and provost courts could be created "if their reestablishment is deemed necessary."[27] The government soon made use of these exceptions. Napoleon's return and final downfall in the Hundred Days of 1815 were followed by a period of extreme reaction, manifested in a new White Terror and in the election of the Ultra-royalist *Chambre introuvable*. This body took strong measures against the enemies of the Bourbons and at the same time felt the need to control the disorders of the White Terror.

The result was the creation, in December 1815, of the *cours prévôtales*, the successors to Napoleon's *cours spéciales*.[28] There was to be one such court in each department, and it was to be composed of a president, four judges taken from the *tribunal de première instance* of the place where the *cour prévôtale* sat, and a military officer aged thirty or over and having the rank of at least colonel to serve as *prévôt*.[29] It summarily tried a large number of offenses, many of which were *crimes* normally tried by the juries—armed or seditious rebellion, premeditated homicide, armed robbery, acts of violence committed on the highways, pillage by soldiers on active duty, and, from April 1816, cases of contraband. It also tried certain *délits* of opinion: carrying a flag other than the white flag of the Bourbons; seditious cries in the royal palace or on the route of the king; the posting, distribution, or selling of writings threatening the person of the king or other members of the royal family; calling for the king's overthrow or for changing the succession to the throne or shouting in public these same sentiments.[30]

However, following Louis XVIII's dissolution of the *Chambre introuvable* in 1816 and its succession by a Chamber of Deputies dominated by moderate, constitutional royalists, the government restored trial by jury for all persons accused of *crimes*. The *cours prévôtales* were abolished in 1818.[31]

But this did not satisfy liberals, who wanted jury trial extended to misdemeanors of the press. They soon had their way. In the elections of 1818, liberals increased their representation in the Chamber of Deputies, and this was followed by the formation of a ministry headed by Élie Decazes, who was more liberal than his predecessor, the duc de Richelieu. In May 1819, the Decazes government secured the passage of a new press law granting jury trial to persons accused of *délits de presse*.[32]

This law could not, however, survive long into the period of reaction following the assassination in 1820 of the duc de Berry, the only member of the royal family who it was hoped could sire future Bourbons.[33] In March 1822, a new act was passed that abolished jury trial for *délits de presse* and returned jurisdiction over these cases to the judges of the *tribunaux correctionnels*.[34] Liberals, of course, opposed this measure. Hence it was that after they came to power in the July Revolution of 1830, the charter of the new regime guaranteed trial by jury for persons accused of *délits politiques et de presse*.[35]

Liberals were also successful in their legislative efforts to reduce the power of judges and to expand those of the jury in ordinary criminal matters. Heirs of the revolutionary tradition of 1789, they distrusted the judiciary and sought to expand the powers of the jury at its expense. In March 1831, the Parliament passed a law that "affirmed the superiority of the jury." The number of judges in the *cour d'assises* was reduced from five to three so that they were no longer such an intimidating presence before the jurors. Moreover, the number of jurors needed to obtain a conviction was raised from seven to eight. The law also repealed the *Code d'instruction criminelle*'s provision that had stipulated that conviction by a mere majority vote of seven of twelve jurors had to be confirmed by the assent of at least four of the five judges. This procedure had rarely been employed, but it was still seen as a "certificate of stupidity delivered to the jury." Henceforth, the judges could only refuse to pronounce the conviction and suspend the case to the next session of the *cour d'assises* if a majority of them believed there had been a miscarriage of justice.[36]

A much more important measure augmenting the power of the jury at the expense of the judiciary was the law of 1832 that transferred from the judges of the *cours d'assises* to their juries the power (which the judges had exercised since 1824) to rule on extenuating circumstances for persons found guilty of *crimes*. In this fashion, juries for the first time gained significant legal power in determining the punishment of those they convicted, a power previously exercised by judges only. Of all the jury reforms enacted during the July Monarchy, this would prove to be the most consequential for the future, for it was a major step toward a gradation of sanctions by jurors that would profoundly alter the French penal system.

It was a reform spurred on by the verdicts of juries. Restoration juries balked at the stern and rigid penalties stipulated by the Napoleonic *Code pénal*.[37] The panels resisted them through several means. One was a frequent recourse to jury devices for leniency for convicted persons, which in most instances reduced the charges to mere misdemeanors. Juries sometimes did this by voting negatively on the principal accusation but affirma-

The "Jurys Censitaires"

tively on a "subsidiary question" or lesser charge. But more commonly it was done by responding negatively to the question of whether there were aggravating circumstances in the original charge, even when the evidence clearly showed aggravation. To the Ministry of Justice, this "was a means of flagrant falsehoods" meant to lighten the penalty.[38]

The allegation by contemporary Ministry of Justice officials that juries reduced the charges against convicted persons in disregard of the truth in order to mitigate penalties had also been made by jurists in eighteenth-century England. In the latter country, the value of objects stolen distinguished capital from noncapital larceny. English juries therefore often intentionally downgraded the value of goods stolen in order to convict thieves of noncapital larceny and thereby save the necks of defendants the jurors thought did not deserve to die. The great jurist William Blackstone labeled this "pious perjury."[39] In French criminal law, the circumstances of the crime determined the level of punishment. This was why juries in France before 1832 often rejected prosecution charges of aggravating circumstances in order to reduce the severity of punishment.

According to some modern scholars, the panels went even beyond jury devices for leniency and, as in the 1790s, resisted sanctions through outright acquittals.[40] They were especially loath to convict persons who faced the death penalty. Napoleon's *Code pénal* had prescribed the ultimate penalty for no less than thirty-six crimes, including homicides and arsons of inhabited dwellings, but also thefts accompanied by certain aggravating circumstances and counterfeiting.[41] Yet less than half of persons accused of capital crimes from 1825 through 1831 were found guilty.[42]

Modern historians (and at least one contemporary when citing the case of infanticide) have noted that the government hoped to reduce acquittals of mercy by enacting the first law of extenuating circumstances in 1824. It was modest in scope. The measure gave to the judges of the *cours d'assises* the authority to reduce the penalty for a limited number of offenses (infanticide by the mother but not by her accomplice, serious wounding, and certain aggravated thefts) below the minimum provided by the law. Jurors would presumably convict more people if they knew that the judges could reduce the penalties.[43]

But the law did not reduce acquittals. Since the judges alone could find extenuating circumstances, jurors were not assured that the penalties for persons they convicted would be reduced to what they thought reasonable.[44] From 1825 (when published national judicial statistics first became available in the annual *Compte général de l'administration de la justice criminelle*) through 1831, French juries acquitted about two-fifths of all the

The "Jurys Censitaires"

TABLE 2.1. Convictions and Acquittals in the *Cours d'Assises*, by Period

Years	Convicted	Acquitted	Total
1825–31	30,432 (60.3%)	20,056 (39.7%)	50,488
1832–35	17,450 (58.7%)	12,277 (41.3%)	29,727
1836–47	59,857 (66.1%)	30,700 (33.9%)	90,557
1848	4,304 (58.5%)	3,048 (41.5)%	7,352
1849–53	23,610 (66.2%)	12,059 (33.8%)	35,669
1854–70	64,479 (75.8%)	20,600 (24.2%)	85,079
1871–72	7,526 (74.8%)	2,532 (25.2%)	10,058
1873–79	26,256 (79.4%)	6,803 (20.6%)	33,059
1880–93	43,068 (72.1%)	16,681 (27.9%)	59,749
1894–1908	34,030 (68.3%)	15,817 (31.7%)	49,847
1909–13	10,029 (64.2%)	5,599 (35.8%)	15,628
1914–18	5,991 (65.3%)	3,181 (34.7%)	9,172
1919–31	18,656 (65.7%)	9,743 (34.3%)	28,399
1932–38[a]	7,989 (73.9%)	2,824 (26.1%)	10,813
1940–41	1,209 (75.8%)	385 (24.2%)	1,594
1942–44	2,324 (91.2%)	225 (8.8%)	2,549
1945–52[b]	14,202 (89.7%)	1,631 (10.3%)	15,833
1957–58	2,152 (92.1%)	185 (7.9%)	2,337
1959–63[c]	5,139 (87.5%)	733 (12.5%)	5,872

Sources: *Compte général*, 1825–60, Table 2, p. 3; 1861–1909, Table 2, p. 5; 1910–13 and 1919–23, Table 2, p. 7; 1924–31, Table 1, p. 7; 1914–18, 1932–38, 1940–52, and 1957–63, Ministère de l'Economie et des Finances, *Annuaire statistique*, 162–63.

[a] The judicial statistics for 1939 were never published.
[b] The *Compte général*'s figures for the years 1953–56 refer only to those convicted of crimes, and therefore it is impossible to calculate conviction and acquittal rates for those years.
[c] The figures for the years after 1963 again refer only to those convicted of crimes.

persons they tried (see Table 2.1)—more than double the acquittal rate among persons tried by U.S. federal juries in the 1980s and 1990s.[45] The very high acquittal rates in the *cours d'assises* were not solely the result of jury sanction nullification: in this era, magistrates took a considerably larger proportion of reported cases to trial before both the *cours d'assises* and the *tribunaux correctionnels* than they would in the second half of the nineteenth century. This meant that more of the weaker cases were tried than in later periods.[46] Nonetheless, this does not explain why the acquittal rate in the *cours d'assises* was more than two and a half times higher than the contemporaneous acquittal rate of about one-seventh of accused persons in the magistrate-only *tribunaux correctionnels* (see Table 2.2). The presence or absence of defense attorneys does not appear to have been a significant cause of the differential: defense counsel was required for all persons charged with offenses that could result in a prison sentence, whether tried by the *tribunaux correctionnels* or the *cours d'assises*.[47] Perhaps many *délits* were simpler to try than were *crimes* and the evidence was therefore clearer. But this factor can hardly appear to account for the huge differential in acquittal rates between persons tried in the *tribunaux correctionnels* and those tried in the *cours d'assises*. Jury resistance to sanctions was the primary reason for the high acquittal rate in the *cours d'assises*.

It was again in order to reduce acquittals that the Parliament enacted the much more important and sweeping second law on extenuating circumstances in 1832, passed as part of a revision of the *Code pénal*. As already mentioned, this law transferred from the judges of the *cours d'assises* to their juries the authority to find extenuating circumstances for convicted persons and now made it applicable to all felonies. Whenever a jury found extenuating circumstances for someone it convicted, the judges were obligated to lower the penalty by at least one degree below the minimum prescribed by law.[48] Judges were also given the discretionary power to lower the penalty by an additional degree when extenuating circumstances were found for a crime punishable by death or hard labor.[49] For a person convicted of premeditated homicide with extenuating circumstances, for instance, the law required the judges to lower the penalty from death to hard labor for life. But they could choose to lower it still more to five to twenty years' hard labor.

The law of 1832 was later seen by the Ministry of Justice and by a number of scholars as a reform of fundamental importance that "transformed the face of our penal law."[50] It struck a serious blow against the "immutable rigors of the law," or the classical penal concept of fixed punishments.[51] Juries could now take into account the personal characteristics, chances

TABLE 2.2. Convictions and Acquittals in the
Tribunaux Correctionnels, by Period

Years	Convicted	Acquitted	Total
1826–31	977,763 (85.4%)	167,079 (14.6%)	1,144,842
1832–35	652,266 (85.7%)	109,031 (14.3%)	761,297
1836–47	2,083,314 (87.4%)	300,011 (12.6%)	2,383,325
1848	189,669 (87.9%)	26,150 (12.1%)	215,819
1849–53	1,042,871 (88.4%)	136,310 (11.6%)	1,179,181
1854–70	2,904,931 (90.2%)	316,126 (9.8%)	3,221,057
1871–72	317,201 (90.6%)	32,793 (9.4%)	349,994
1873–79	1,269,210 (92.2%)	107,846 (7.8%)	1,377,056
1880–93	2,895,696 (92.5%)	235,843 (7.5%)	3,131,539
1894–1908	3,010,786 (91.9%)	265,398 (8.1%)	3,276,184
1909–13	1,052,963 (91.0%)	104,012 (9.0%)	1,156,975
1914–18	619,299 (88.6%)	79,461 (11.4%)	698,760
1919–31	2,749,027 (90.3%)	295,270 (9.7%)	3,044,297
1932–38[a]	1,573,266 (89.5%)	183,649 (10.5%)	1,756,915
1940–41	563,108 (87.9%)	77,423 (12.1%)	640,531
1942–44	1,025,735 (87.9%)	141,656 (12.1%)	1,167,391
1945–52[b]	2,218,382 (88.5%)	288,379 (11.5%)	2,506,761

Sources: Compte général, 1826, Table 74, p. 111; 1827, Table 82, p. 121; 1828, Table 91, p. 139; 1829, Table 92, p. 141; 1830, Table 68, p. 115; 1831, Table 65, p. 105; 1832, Table 68, p. 109; 1833, Table 73, p. 117; 1834, Table 70, p. 113; 1835–36, Table 76, p. 119; 1837–51, Table 75, p. 117; 1852, Table 73, p. 113; 1853, Table 72, p. 111; 1854–57, Table 74, p. 113; 1858–59, Table 72, p. 111; 1860, Table 70, p. 109; 1861–63, Table 70, p. 111; 1864–69, Table 67, p. 109; 1870, Table 62, p. 101; 1871, Table 60, p. 101; 1872–73, Table 64, p. 107; 1874, Table 38, p. 87; 1875–78, Table 35, p. 81; 1879–85, Table 35, p. 85; 1886–88, Table 30, p. 61; 1889–1909, Table 29, p. 57; 1910–13, Table 29, p. 59; 1919–20, Table 28, p. 67; 1921–23, Table 24, p. 61; 1924–31, Table 19, p. 53; 1914–18, 1932–38, and 1940–52, Ministère de l'Economie et des Finances, *Annuaire statistique*, 164–65.

[a] The judicial statistics for 1939 were never published.

[b] From 1953, the judicial statistics on persons tried in the *tribunaux correctionnels* refer only to those who were convicted, thereby making it impossible to calculate acquittal and conviction rates for the years after 1952.

for rehabilitation, and motives of the criminals they convicted in deciding whether or not to find extenuating circumstances. The law also made it more possible for jurors to judge the mental state of defendants. Already, Article 64 of the *Code pénal* of 1810 allowed for the insanity defense, declaring that an accused person could not be found criminally responsible for a crime he or she committed in a "state of dementia."[52] This opened the way for the use of expert psychiatric testimony in trials. The 1832 law broadened the use of psychiatric experts to testify on the mental state of defendants. Unlike in many other penal codes, the French law on extenuating circumstances did not specify the mental states (or indeed any other states) that were qualified as extenuating. But this very fact gave French judges wide discretion to allow psychiatric testimony during trials. After 1832, presiding judges gradually permitted more psychiatric experts into the courtroom to provide the needed guidance for deliberations on mental illness and extenuating circumstances.[53] From 1832 on, a jury's verdict was no longer just a judgment of guilt or innocence but also included an assessment of the offender's potential to conform to society's standards of "desirable" behavior.[54]

The adoption of the concept of extenuating circumstances by French criminal law was in striking contrast to developments in penal philosophy in England by the 1830s. There, a new emphasis on the character rather than on the acts of the criminal had a very different result. Between 1830 and 1840, a major reform of sanctions occurred in England when Parliament removed the death penalty for many of the less serious crimes.[55] The reform of sanctions supported a new penal regime that assumed criminals were fully responsible for their actions, but they were punished in all but a very few cases with a number of years in prison. England's early Victorian penal reformers believed that law should aid the mass development of a new ideal personality type characterized by self-discipline, rationality, and the calculation of one's long-term self-interest. Therefore, a "crucial supposition underlying early Victorian efforts at law reform was that the most desirable way of making people self-governing was to hold them, sternly and unblinkingly, responsible for the consequences of their actions." This meant that the "power of circumstances external to the will had to be played down." Early and mid-Victorian penal reformers replaced the flexibility and inequality of eighteenth-century justice with greater uniformity of incarcerative punishment, and judges increasingly rejected pleas for leniency based on defendants' claims that they had acted out of impulse.[56] Moreover, where in France the insanity defense was allowed if those accused could merely prove that they had been in a "state of dementia" at the time they committed their crimes, in England under the McNaughten rules of 1843,

The "Jurys Censitaires"

they could plead insanity only if they were incapable of knowing that their acts were illegal when they committed them.[57] Not until the late nineteenth century did less voluntaristic notions of criminality begin to make headway in England.

Therefore, the verdicts of juries had brought about one of the most fundamental changes in French criminal law since the construction of the Revolutionary and Napoleonic codes. The Ministry of Justice itself pointed out that the 1832 law was made necessary by the "tendencies of the jury" and "consecrated and regularized" the jurors' previous tactic of often lessening penalties by refusing to vote in the affirmative on the question of aggravating circumstances. The ministry added: "The verdicts of the jury were scarcely less lenient before this law [the one on extenuating circumstances] . . . since the jurors often dismissed the best established aggravating circumstances in order to attenuate the penalties incurred by the accused persons; while today [1850], they attain the same end without so gravely undermining the truth."[58]

The judicial statistics on jury devices for leniency provided some evidence to support the ministry's contention. From 1826 (when data on jury devices for leniency were first included in the *Compte général*) through 1831, juries entirely accepted prosecution charges against all or at least one of the defendants in only slightly more than half of the cases that resulted in conviction. In about one-tenth of cases, they condemned the culprits on lesser felony charges. But in more than a third, the convicts were found guilty of misdemeanors only.[59]

Following the enactment of the law on extenuating circumstances, these figures changed significantly. From 1832 through 1847, juries fully accepted prosecution charges in 67.0 percent of convictions. The proportion found guilty of lesser felony charges rose somewhat, but misdemeanor convictions dropped sharply.[60] This indeed suggests that before 1832, juries often resorted to such convictions in order to reduce punishments to what they considered reasonable levels. After 1832, they could achieve the same objective by voting in favor of extenuating circumstances rather than by rejecting the original felony charges.

Yet in respect to its original primary objective—the reduction of acquittals—the law of 1832 had little immediate impact.[61] To be sure, the 1831 law raising the majority of jurors necessary to convict from seven to eight seems to have initially counteracted the effect of the law on extenuating circumstances, for the conviction rate actually declined slightly from the period 1825–31 to 1832–35. But one of the "September Laws" of 1835 restored the rule of the seven-vote majority.[62] Thereafter, in the years from 1836 through 1847, the conviction rate rose only modestly from what it had been in 1825–31 (see Table 2.1). According to some legal scholars, the rise was not greater because the juries still thought punishments for many crimes were too severe even with extenuating circumstances.[63]

Nonetheless, the law on extenuating circumstances did allow juries to exert a major influence on punishments. From 1834 (when tables on the number of findings for extenuating circumstances in the *cours d'assises* first became available in the *Compte général*) through 1847, juries found extenuating circumstances—and thus reduced the sentences—for 68.8 percent of persons they convicted of *crimes*[64] (those the panels found guilty of misdemeanors only and juveniles sentenced to houses of correction until the age of twenty-one were excluded from the calculation because they were not eligible for findings of extenuating circumstances by vote of the jury).[65] The figure would rise even higher in subsequent periods.

The impact on penalties was indeed significant. Among persons convicted in the *cours d'assises*, the proportions sentenced to hard labor terms of life and less and to more than five years' imprisonment declined substantially following the passage of the 1832 law. The proportion sentenced to mere misdemeanor prison terms, however, rose sharply. As a consequence, such penalties were handed out to nearly three-fifths of all persons convicted in the *cours d'assises* from 1832 through 1847 (see Table 2.3). Of course, some of these convicts had in fact been found guilty only of misdemeanors. But more than two-thirds were convicted of felonies with extenuating circumstances.[66]

This did not mean that juries alone were responsible for the trend toward leniency in punishment. The sentencing practices of judges contributed also. In about two-thirds of the cases in which the judges of the *cours d'assises* were allowed to lower the penalty by two degrees for persons convicted with extenuating circumstances, they did in fact do so.[67] This is evidence that French judges of the nineteenth century shared the juries' notions of leniency in punishment, if not in the finding of guilt, just as judges in eighteenth-century England often issued reprieves and recommendations for pardon for persons convicted of capital crimes.[68] But since in France after 1832 the justices could hand down sentences reduced by two degrees only after juries had found extenuating circumstances, juries played the primary role in the movement toward lesser penalties (though it can be argued that in England, judges might have recommended leniency in order to induce jury convictions, and thereby juries indirectly influenced judges in this regard).[69]

The French juries' important role in reducing penalties after 1832 was

TABLE 2.3. Punishments of People Convicted in the *Cours d'Assises*, by Period

Years	Death	Hard Labor —Life[a]	Hard Labor —Less Than Life[b]	5+ Years Prison	5 Years or Less Prison	Other	Total
1825–31	838	1,969	7,569	8,159	11,506	391	30,432
	(2.8%)	(6.5%)	(24.9%)	(26.8%)	(37.8%)	(1.3%)	
1832–47	773	2,962	14,071	13,470	45,359	672	77,307
	(1.0%)	(3.8%)	(18.2%)	(17.4%)	(58.7%)	(0.9%)	
1848	36	162	782	714	2,555	55	4,304
	(0.8%)	(3.8%)	(18.2%)	(16.6%)	(59.4%)	(1.3%)	
1849–53	234	1,126	5,156	4,444	12,442	228	23,610
	(1.0%)	(4.8%)	(21.8%)	(18.8%)	(52.6%)	(1.0%)	
1854–70	550	2,811	14,574	13,879	32,166	499	64,479
	(0.9%)	(4.8%)	(22.6%)	(21.5%)	(49.9%)	(0.8%)	
1871–72	47	276	1,617	1,464	4,022	100	7,526
	(0.6%)	(3.7%)	(21.5%)	(19.5%)	(53.4%)	(1.3%)	
1873–79	202	1,003	6,477	5,665	12,719	180	26,246
	(0.8%)	(3.8%)	(24.7%)	(21.6%)	(48.5%)	(0.7%)	
1880–93	417	1,605	10,819	8,416	21,595	216	43,068
	(1.0%)	(3.7%)	(25.1%)	(19.5%)	(50.1%)	(0.5%)	
1894–1908	336	1,299	7,528	6,745	17,853	264	34,025
	(1.0%)	(3.8%)	(22.1%)	(19.8%)	(52.5%)	(0.8%)	
1909–13[c]	136	450	1,870	2,047	5,325	201	10,029
	(1.4%)	(4.5%)	(18.6%)	(20.4%)	(53.1%)	(2.0%)	
1919–31	419	939	3,115	4,028	9,908	247	18,656
	(2.2%)	(5.0%)	(16.7%)	(21.6%)	(53.1%)	(1.3%)	
1932–38	138	299	1,141	1,789	4,622	0	7,989
	(1.7%)	(3.7%)	(14.3%)	(22.4%)	(57.9%)		
1945–52	395	726	3,308	3,048	6,725	0	14,202
	(2.8%)	(5.1%)	(23.3%)	(21.5%)	(47.4%)		
1953–64	140	480	1,664	4,166	6,900	0	13,350
	(1.0%)	(3.6%)	(12.5%)	(31.2%)	(51.7%)		

Sources: *Compte général*, 1825–60, Table 2, p. 3; 1861–1909 and 1910–13, Table 2, p. 5; 1919–23, Table 2, p. 7; 1924–31, Table 1, p. 7; 1932–64, Ministère de l'Economie et des Finances, *Annuaire statistique*, 163.

[a] The punishment of hard labor for life was abolished in 1960 and was replaced by life imprisonment.
[b] The punishment of hard labor for less than life was abolished in 1960, and the penalty henceforth substituted was more than five years' imprisonment.
[c] Published data on punishments for the years 1914–18 are unavailable.

most clearly evident in respect to the death penalty. From 1825 through 1831, the judges of the *cours d'assises* imposed the death penalty on an average of about 120 convicted persons each year. From 1832 through 1847, however, the juries imposed the death sentence on an average of only 48 convicted persons each year.[70]

Part of the decline was no doubt due to the reduction in the number of capital offenses from thirty-six to twenty-two in the revised penal code of 1832.[71] Yet this was a much less important factor than the law on extenuating circumstances. The principal offenses for which capital punishment had been abolished in the revised code—counterfeiting, theft with aggravating circumstances, and arson of uninhabited edifices—accounted for only a small proportion of the death sentences handed down during the period from 1825 through 1831.[72] Most of the persons sentenced to the guillotine had been found guilty of a half-dozen offenses—premeditated homicide, unpremeditated homicide accompanied by another crime, poisoning, parricide, infanticide, and arson of inhabited edifices—which remained punishable by death after 1832. Juries invoked the law on extenuating circumstances to save from the guillotine more than four-fifths of the persons they convicted of capital crimes from 1834 through 1847.[73]

In sending so few persons to the guillotine, juries appear to have reflected changing attitudes toward capital punishment in France. In the early and mid-nineteenth century, the movement to abolish—or at least to severely limit—the death penalty was gaining strength. The campaign against the scaffold began to make headway in the second half of the eighteenth century when the *philosophes*, in particular Beccaria and his followers, launched an attack on capital punishment on humanitarian grounds, from a belief in the rehabilitation of criminals, and from utilitarian considerations: the death penalty did not deter crime and if inflicted should be resorted to only in exceptional cases. These ideas influenced the men of the Revolution: France's *Code pénal* of 1791 reduced the number of crimes punishable by death from 119 to 32.[74]

But in the first half of the nineteenth century, the movement against capital punishment began to have a greater impact on public opinion because of the influence of a number of romantic writers and playwrights who came out in support of abolition. They included not only important figures such as Victor Hugo and Alphonse de Lamartine but also a host of minor writers and playwrights who expressed opinions against the death penalty in the popular theater and in serialized novels. As one modern scholar has noted, the abolitionist movement was therefore no longer restricted to the councils of government and to the circles of *philosophes*: it now spread to the boule-

The "Jurys Censitaires"

vards.[75] Abolitionists continued to attack capital punishment on utilitarian and humanitarian grounds. But now a number of important Catholic writers (Félicité Robert de Lamennais, François René de Chateaubriand, and the like) attacked the death penalty in the name of divine mercy and from a belief that only God can take life. Socialists also criticized the death penalty because of their belief that crime was caused by social conditions. However, the strongest argument against capital punishment in the nineteenth century was one that appealed to the public's increased respect for human rights: the justice system could err and send innocent people to the guillotine. When a person was wrongly executed, the harm was irreparable.[76]

The reduction in the number of capital crimes and the law on extenuating circumstances together made up what one modern scholar has labeled "the compromise of 1832" between abolitionists and those who favored the retention of the death penalty. It was a compromise that left it principally to juries—the representatives of public opinion (or at least of the electorate as it was then constituted)—to decide on life or death for persons found guilty of capital crimes.[77]

The result seems to have been fewer acquittals of mercy in capital cases. This is suggested by the fact that after 1832, the conviction rate for capital crimes increased more sharply than for crimes in general. The conviction rate for the former rose nearly thirteen percentage points, from 49.8 percent in 1825–31 to 62.5 percent in 1836–47,[78] whereas the rate for all crimes rose less than six points, from 60.3 percent to 66.1 percent (see Table 2.1). Here is evidence that indeed suggests that juries before 1832 acquitted a significant number of persons they evidently recognized as guilty of capital crimes in order to save them from the guillotine. After 1832, this was no longer necessary, and juries were able to reserve the guillotine only for those criminals they thought the most cold-blooded, dangerous, and reprehensible.

Moreover, the law on extenuating circumstances allowed juries to make distinctions among capital offenders according to the perceived seriousness or dangerousness of their crimes, their circumstances and motivations, and the prevailing social norms. The fact that from 1834 through 1847, juries least often found extenuating circumstances (at a rate of 64.1 percent) for persons they convicted of parricide may well have reflected the special revulsion felt toward this crime in the patriarchal France of the nineteenth century.[79] Extenuating circumstances were found for a slightly higher 68.2 percent of those convicted of premeditated homicide. Juries were significantly more lenient toward those they convicted of unpremeditated murder accompanied by another crime, for they found extenuating circumstances for 75.8 percent of them. The figure was about 85 percent for persons convicted of both poisoning (though the *Compte général*'s tables on findings of extenuating circumstances did not distinguish between poisoning resulting in death and attempted poisoning, both of which were punished the same)[80] and of the arson of inhabited structures.[81]

But findings of extenuating circumstances were most common for persons convicted of infanticide. There was no better example of the influence of the penalty on jury verdicts in capital cases in nineteenth-century France. The Napoleonic *Code pénal*, which defined the crime as "the murder of a newborn infant," provided only one penalty for it: death.[82] Yet juries were loath to send the accused women to the guillotine. The panels were sympathetic to many of the defendants. Most of the persons tried for the crime were unmarried, the residents of rural communes, and, in more than one-third of cases, servants.[83] Such women, if they bore infants, would almost certainly lose their jobs and fail to find employment. The situation was made worse for these women by the Napoleonic *Code civil*'s ban on any *recherches de la paternité* (paternity suits) aimed at identifying the fathers of illegitimate children and compelling them to support their offspring,[84] as had been the case during the Ancien Régime.[85] The plight of the unwed mothers was further worsened by the government's gradual suppression after 1833 of the *tours*—the revolving boxes at the entrances to the foundling hospices that had allowed such women to abandon their unwanted babies anonymously.[86] Moreover, since female workers in nineteenth-century France were very poorly paid,[87] most unwed mothers must have found it impossible to support their illegitimate offspring.

Defendants in infanticide cases were especially the objects of jury sympathy when the defense called upon witnesses who could attest to the accused woman's "good conduct"—that she was a hard worker, had had only one lover, was from an "honest" family, was promised marriage, and then was abandoned by her lover when she became pregnant.[88] Several forensic doctors familiar with the juries' treatment of infanticide cases contended that many of the accused women were acquitted because the jurors felt that it was unfair that the females alone should bear responsibility for the crimes. This was because the men who had impregnated the women (and jurors often felt that the accused persons had been seduced) frequently abandoned them and bore no legal responsibility for the consequences of their lust.[89]

Moreover, the fact that the victims of infanticide were mostly illegitimate babies might have lessened the jurors' valuation of their lives. One possible reason for the jurymen's relative lack of compassion for murdered newborns was a belief that bastards, resulting from "vice" and born outside paternal authority, were potential juvenile delinquents destined to become criminals, rioters, and prostitutes. The leniency of juries toward the defendants may even have been founded on the defense of the legitimate family and its exclusive place for procreation.[90]

But by no means were jurors always sympathetic to women accused of infanticide: defendants who had killed their infants in a brutal or especially violent fashion or who had a reputation for "loose morality" faced likely conviction. However, in many other instances, "sentiments of pity for the poor, seduced, abandoned, and desperately lonely women outweighed jurors' sentiments for the newborn infant."[91]

Despite this sympathy, the acquittal rate (47.7 percent) for persons tried for infanticide from 1825 through 1831, though high, was slightly below the rate for all other intentional homicides.[92] The rate of exonerations for infanticide probably would have been even lower were it not for the fact that the murder of newborns was harder to prove than the murder of adults.[93]

Figures on outright acquittals are, however, only a partial measurement of jury "indulgence" toward persons accused of infanticide before 1832. Between the extremes of sending guilty women to the guillotine and acquitting them lay the alternative of convicting of a lesser crime. The Ministry of Justice, troubled by the high acquittal rate for infanticide, encouraged the *présidents* of the *cours d'assises* to let the juries consider, whenever possible, the charge of negligent homicide of a newborn, a misdemeanor punishable by only two years' imprisonment.[94] Juries often responded to this "subsidiary" question with a guilty verdict: more than two-thirds of all persons found guilty in infanticide trials from 1826 through 1831 were convicted of a lesser crime. In most such instances, the lesser crime was almost certainly negligent homicide of a newborn.[95] This was the preferred option to save the culprits from the guillotine: the law of 1824 included infanticide among the crimes for which judges were allowed to find extenuating circumstances, but jurors could not be certain that the magistrates would so rule when the defendants were convicted of the original charge.[96] Here, French and English penal practices were similar in the early nineteenth century. In 1803, the British parliament, aware that juries were reluctant to convict women accused of a crime that carried the death penalty, created the alternative offense of concealment of birth, punishable by up to two years' imprisonment. This soon became the preferred charge against women who had killed their infants.[97]

In France, the Ministry of Justice's assertion that juries used devices for leniency for the persons they convicted in order to ameliorate punishments before 1832 was more applicable to infanticide than to any other crime. Largely as a consequence of the fact that so many persons tried for infanti-

The "Jurys Censitaires"

cide were convicted of lesser crimes, only 5 percent of the convicts from 1825 through 1831 were sentenced to death, and about two-thirds were sentenced to mere *peines correctionnelles* of imprisonment of five years or less.[98]

The thesis that punishment had an important influence on jury verdicts in infanticide cases is further supported by the data from the years following the passage of the 1832 law on extenuating circumstances. Once juries could find extenuating circumstances for the persons they convicted, both acquittals and convictions on reduced charges for infanticide declined significantly, especially the latter. Findings of guilty on lesser charges dropped to less than half among those convicted from 1832 through 1847.[99] Juries could now use extenuating circumstances in place of convictions for lesser crimes to achieve the objective of mercy in punishment: from 1834 through 1847, the panels found extenuating circumstances for 96.4 percent of the persons they convicted of infanticide itself and thereby saved them from the guillotine.[100] Largely as a consequence, the proportion of death sentences dropped sharply.[101]

The proclivity of juries to use the law on extenuating circumstances to reduce penalties they evidently felt were too harsh was hardly limited to infanticide or to other capital crimes, however. Several noncapital offenses were often the objects of jury leniency in punishment. One was *vol domestique*, or theft by a servant. The *Code pénal* imposed a harsher punishment for this crime than for other thefts since it implied treachery.[102] Yet juries appear to have regarded it as too harsh in most circumstances. The conviction rate for *vol domestique* was slightly lower than for other thefts.[103] Much more striking, however, was the fact that juries found extenuating circumstances for more than eight of every ten persons convicted of theft by a servant from 1834 through 1847, far above the figure of six in ten among persons convicted of all other aggravated thefts.[104]

Perhaps jurors went easy on the culprits in order to make the punishment proportionate to the crime. Theft by a servant was a felony no matter how low the value of the money or goods stolen.[105] The judicial statistics do not provide figures on the size of thefts in such cases, but they must have often been small or even trivial. To punish servants guilty of petty thievery with prison or hard labor terms of more than five years must have seemed excessive to many jurors. Perhaps the authorities preserved the "black letter" of the law for its "exhortatory" and deterrent effect and expected, or even welcomed, jury mitigation of the penalty in such cases.

The juries' leniency toward the persons they convicted of *vol domestique* appears somewhat surprising considering the fact that nearly all jurors of the era were *notables* who ordinarily employed servants. Presumably, they would have felt particularly threatened by the potential danger of thieving servants within their own households. The fact that jurors frequently responded to this threat with leniency has important implications for the oft-repeated thesis that in the nineteenth century, juries were much more biased against persons accused of property crimes (mainly theft) than they were toward those accused of violent crimes. This thesis is mainly based on analyses of judicial statistics that show that conviction rates for the former were substantially higher than for the latter. Contemporaries often claimed that the bias was due to the fact that jurors were generally bourgeois property-owners and were therefore more concerned with the protection of property than with the protection of persons.[106] In the late twentieth century, a number of historians repeated this thesis, which had become a sort of orthodoxy.[107]

In the 1990s, however, one scholar, William Savitt, broke from this orthodoxy. In his article "Villainous Verdicts? Rethinking the Nineteenth-Century French Jury," Savitt claims that a careful analysis of court dossiers, rather than a reliance on the published judicial statistics, shows that there is actually little evidence to support the notion that jurors were biased against persons charged with property crimes. Savitt uses archival sources to show that in the *cour d'assises* of the Côte d'Or from 1830 to 1865, the conviction rate for theft was indeed much higher than the conviction rate for violent crimes, but this was not primarily due to the bias of propertied jurors. Rather, it was much more the result of the nature of the evidence. Most important, thieves far more often confessed to their crimes than did defendants accused of acts of violence. During the investigation stage of cases, magistrates frequently encouraged confessions, for they "represented the ideal proof . . . moreover, they were regarded as a healthy sign of contrition." The magistrates tempted the defendants by holding out the prospect of a more lenient sentence should they confess, and many did so.[108]

But most confessions were made by thieves, and violent criminals much more often contested the charges against them in court. According to Savitt, nearly four of every ten thieves tried in the *cour d'assises* of the Côte d'Or from 1830 to 1865 confessed to their crimes, whereas less than five of every hundred persons tried for violent crimes did so. Therefore, "confessions in court left no real choice to jurors but to convict regularly for theft charges." When one eliminates the numbers of criminals who confessed to their crimes and looks at the data only for those who contested the charges against them, the difference in acquittal rates for those accused of violent crimes narrowed from 17 percent to 7 percent. If one excludes assault and battery (which had an exceptionally high acquittal rate) and looks at the

The "Jurys Censitaires"

figures for the other violent crimes—homicide, rape, and indecent assault—acquittal rates for persons accused of these offenses and who contested the charges against them were almost as low as the acquittal rate for thieves who refused to confess. Moreover, when property crimes other than theft (arson and vandalism) are factored in, the total acquittal rate for all persons accused of crimes against property who contested the charges against them was less than four percentage points below the overall acquittal rate for violent crimes. Therefore, according to Savitt, "the conventional wisdom that juries were harsh on property crimes but soft on violent crime must be discarded."[109]

Savitt states that perhaps the most important reason why thieves much more often confessed than did violent criminals was the more solid evidence typically found against the former. Most persons accused of theft were either arrested in *flagrant délit* or "found with recently stolen goods and no reasonable explanation." Therefore, knowing the overwhelming evidence against them and hoping for lenient sentences, it made sense for many thieves to confess. The charges against violent criminals, on the other hand, were much more often supported by only uncertain evidence, and there was frequently more "moral ambiguity" involved in such cases. Defendants accused of violent acts often admitted they had committed them but denied they were criminal in nature because they had acted in self-defense or to protect their honor or were the results of accidents or misunderstandings. "Assaults and homicides often emerged from cabaret brawls of obscure origin or from complex squabbles, and though prosecutions typically revealed the author of the wounding-blow, the question of who caused an incident, or which party merited real punishment, or whether the whole episode was an unfortunate accident, could be opaque indeed." Therefore, violent defendants often refused to confess because even when they admitted to their acts, they denied they were responsible for them. Savitt concludes that attentive consideration of the evidence, not the class or personal characteristics of jurors, generally decided verdicts.[110]

To test Savitt's thesis on the national level would be a very difficult task indeed. The published statistics in the *Compte général* do not indicate which accused persons confessed or the nature of the evidence against them. To look into the actual court dossiers for all of France, as Savitt has done for the Côte d'Or alone, would be a daunting, near-impossible task involving a close examination of many thousands of cases. Studies such as Savitt's are practicable only on the local level, and perhaps in the future other historians, through analyses of court dossiers in other departments, will reach similar conclusions. Yet even an examination of the published national judicial

The "Jurys Censitaires"

statistics during the era of 1825 through 1847, when most jurors were drawn from the ranks of the wealthiest men in the country, provides evidence that at least suggests some modification of the often-repeated charge that juries in nineteenth-century France were biased against property crimes because of the bourgeois composition of the panels.

The statistics do show wide gaps between conviction rates for theft and two types of violent crime: felony assault of a non-parent (defined before 1863 as assault resulting in the victim's incapacity to work for more than twenty days) and manslaughter. In the eras 1825–31 and 1832–47, conviction rates for theft were about twenty to twenty-five percentage points higher than for the two violent crimes (see Table 2.4). The pattern of greater leniency toward persons accused of assault and manslaughter was also reflected in findings of extenuating circumstances for those persons the juries did convict. From 1834 through 1847, juries answered affirmatively to the question of whether extenuating circumstances existed for 64.8 percent of the persons they found guilty of theft. The figure was 77.9 percent in cases of assault resulting in the victim's incapacity to work for more than twenty days and 72.6 percent in cases of manslaughter.[111] But the gap in conviction rates between theft and intentional homicides (excluding infanticide, a form of murder that received special treatment from the juries) was much narrower, at least after 1832. Opposition to imposing the death penalty for many murderers seems to explain why from 1825 through 1831 the conviction rate for murder (51.9 percent) was 17.5 percentage points below the rate for theft. However, the passage of the law on extenuating circumstances, as already shown, had a significant effect: from 1832 through 1847, the gap between theft and intentional homicides narrowed considerably to 8.1 percentage points, as convictions for the latter rose to 65.4 percent.[112] When the data are divided by types of intentional homicide, they show that the gap was narrowest between theft and premeditated murder (*assassinat*): it was 10.7 percentage points in the years 1825–31 and only 4.6 points in 1832–47 (see Table 2.5).

The judicial statistics therefore provide evidence to suggest that, although class bias against property crimes cannot be discounted, a more important reason why conviction rates for theft were significantly higher than for most violent crimes was the impulsivity with which culprits often committed the latter offenses. The Ministry of Justice in the nineteenth century and Savitt in his recent article agree on the "moral ambiguity" and "passionate" nature of many violent crimes, which often grew out of "brawls of obscure origin" and "unthinking sentiments of hatred or vengeance deriving from personal relations."[113] The fact that conviction rates for violent crimes varied

TABLE 2.4. Convictions and Acquittals in the *Cours d'Assises* for Theft, Assault of a Non-Parent, and Manslaughter, by Period

Years	THEFT[a]			ASSAULT			MANSLAUGHTER[b]		
	Convicted	Acquitted	Total	Convicted	Acquitted	Total	Convicted	Acquitted	Total
1825–31	21,818 (69.4%)	9,616 (30.6%)	31,434	1,098 (44.4%)	1,373 (55.6%)	2,471	—	—	—
1832–47	48,650 (73.5%)	17,525 (26.5%)	66,175	2,211 (48.2%)	2,372 (51.8%)	4,583	1,225 (49.4%)	1,256 (50.6%)	2,418
1848	2,132 (74.9%)	716 (25.1%)	2,848	80 (42.8%)	107 (57.2%)	187	81 (49.4%)	83 (50.6%)	164
1849–53	12,466 (77.1%)	3,696 (22.9%)	16,162	450 (46.6%)	516 (53.4%)	966	402 (51.6%)	377 (48.4%)	779
1854–62	18,416 (83.6%)	3,613 (16.4%)	22,029	415 (62.3%)	251 (37.7%)	666	537 (63.6%)	308 (36.4%)	845
1863–70	11,180 (85.1%)	1,952 (14.9%)	13,132	98 (61.3%)	62 (38.8%)	160	653 (62.0%)	400 (38.0%)	1,053
1871–72	4,008 (82.7%)	841 (17.3%)	4,849	23 (47.9%)	25 (52.1%)	48	158 (56.4%)	122 (43.6%)	280
1873–79	11,818 (85.7%)	1,974 (14.3%)	13,792	75 (54.3%)	63 (45.7%)	138	508 (62.5%)	305 (37.5%)	813
1880–93	19,978 (81.7%)	4,489 (18.3%)	24,467	177 (48.5%)	188 (51.5%)	365	1,028 (56.0%)	808 (44.0%)	1,836
1894–1908	15,945 (79.1%)	4,217 (20.9%)	20,162	184 (40.6%)	269 (59.4%)	453	1,217 (52.8%)	1,088 (47.2%)	2,305
1909–13[c]	4,069 (73.8%)	1,444 (26.2%)	5,513	85 (49.7%)	86 (50.3%)	171	401 (52.3%)	366 (47.7%)	767
1919–31	5,933 (73.8%)	2,104 (26.2%)	8,037	230 (51.8%)	214 (48.2%)	444	879 (56.7%)	671 (43.3%)	1,550

Source: Compte général, 1825–60, Tables 1 and 2, pp. 2–3; 1861–1909, Tables 1 and 2, pp. 4–5; 1910–13 and 1919–23, Tables 1 and 2, pp. 6–7; 1924–31, Table 1, pp. 6–7.

[a] Includes abuse of confidence.

[b] Figures for this crime are from 1833.

[c] Published data on convictions and acquittals for specific crimes for the years 1914–18 are unavailable.

TABLE 2.5. Convictions and Acquittals in the *Cours d'Assises* for Unpremeditated Murder and Premeditated Murder, by Period

Years	UNPREMEDITATED MURDER			PREMEDITATED MURDER		
	Convicted	*Acquitted*	*Total*	*Convicted*	*Acquitted*	*Total*
1825–31	1,036 (48.2%)	1,112 (51.8%)	2,148	1,042 (58.7%)	732 (41.3%)	1,774
1832–47	2,064 (62.1%)	1,258 (37.9%)	3,322	3,276 (68.9%)	1,479 (31.1%)	4,755
1848	167 (69.9%)	72 (30.1%)	239	217 (62.5%)	130 (37.5%)	347
1849–53	788 (62.5%)	472 (37.5%)	1,260	1,140 (69.9%)	492 (30.1%)	1,632
1854–62	778 (76.9%)	234 (23.1%)	1,012	1,724 (80.9%)	408 (19.1%)	2,132
1863–70	802 (74.3%)	278 (25.7%)	1,080	1,441 (79.5%)	372 (20.5%)	1,813
1871–72	320 (71.7%)	126 (28.3%)	446	402 (76.9%)	121 (23.1%)	523
1873–79	849 (74.4%)	292 (25.6%)	1,141	1,404 (83.7%)	273 (16.3%)	1,677
1880–93	2,071 (69.7%)	900 (30.3%)	2,971	2,871 (76.1%)	902 (23.9%)	3,773
1894–1908	2,689 (67.1%)	1,319 (32.9%)	4,008	2,487 (75.1%)	824 (24.9%)	3,311
1909–13[a]	1,168 (62.9%)	688 (37.1%)	1,856	800 (72.5%)	304 (27.5%)	1,104
1919–31	2,973 (67.7%)	1,420 (32.3%)	4,393	1,949 (79.7%)	497 (20.3%)	2,446

Source: *Compte général*, 1825–60, Table 1, p. 2; 1861–1909, Table 1, p. 4; 1910–13 and 1919–31, Table 1, p. 6.

[a] Published data on convictions and acquittals for specific crimes for the years 1914–18 are unavailable.

according to the degree of intentionality and premeditation with which they were committed seems to support this assertion. The conviction rate for assault, which often seems to have occurred in a brawl and in which the victim was left alive but seriously injured, was the lowest among violent felonies. Only slightly higher was the conviction rate for manslaughter, in which the assailant killed the victim but did not intend to do so. Significantly higher was the conviction rate for *meurtre*, in which the culprit intentionally killed the victim, but not with premeditation. Most often found guilty were those tried for *assassinat*, in which the murderer killed the victim with premeditation. Here the defendants were least able to claim they had acted out of uncontrollable impulse or "passion," self-defense, or "moral ambiguity."

There was, however, one type of intentional homicide that juries always forgave: murders resulting from duels. Here the accused persons could plead that they had acted to protect their honor, a kind of plea jurors were very sympathetic to and which thieves could never make. When it came to the custom of dueling and government efforts to suppress it, juries consistently came down on the side of custom. The number of dueling cases tried in the *cours d'assises* was too small to have had a significant impact on the differential in conviction rates between property crimes and violent crimes, but in no other cases (save those of self-defense) was jury acceptance of justification for violence so evident. This was not quite nullification of the law, since dueling itself was not illegal under the Napoleonic *Code pénal*, and it was far from clear in the code that deaths resulting from duels were criminal homicides.[114]

Nonetheless, in the 1830s, the government began to take serious steps to suppress the duel, and this helped to touch off a considerable debate on the custom. By this time the duel, which had been part of the aristocratic code of honor, had spread to the French bourgeoisie, who had embraced that code in part because in the first decades of the nineteenth century, "the social and political amalgamation of the old nobility and the bourgeoisie was cemented." All *notables* were now men of honor. To the opponents of the duel, it was a barbaric relic. To its defenders, it was necessary for the maintenance of civility and good manners among *notables*.[115]

The defenders' arguments did not sway Louis Philippe's chief prosecutor, André-Marie Dupin, who in 1836 announced a new policy of treating deaths resulting from duels as criminal homicides. He cautioned prosecutors to be careful, however, in deciding which duelists to bring to justice. They were to consider the motives, seriousness, and conditions of the duel (for example, had one duelist provoked the other, was one much more experienced in arms than the other, and so on).[116]

The "Jurys Censitaires"

But this policy yielded no convictions. From 1837 through 1847, 124 duelists were tried in the *cours d'assises* for either premeditated or unpremeditated murder. Most had participated in duels that the Ministry of Justice characterized as "frivolous" in origin. Whether the disputes merited this characterization or not, juries acquitted every duelist they tried.[117] When no less a figure than François Guizot, de facto prime minister from 1840 to 1847 and the de jure one from 1847 to 1848, differed from the policy of his own government's chief prosecutor and praised the civilized and French nature of the duel before the Parliament,[118] one could have hardly expected jurors to find duelists guilty of murder.

If juries upheld the *notables'* code of honor by acquitting duelists, they also upheld patriarchy by convicting persons who assaulted their parents. The exclusively male, mostly middle-aged jurors, the majority of whom must have been fathers, evidently made a distinction between assaults that threatened family order or patriarchal authority and other assaults. From 1825 through 1831, 50.1 percent of persons tried for assault and wounding of a parent or guardian were convicted. However, this figure rose to 62.7 percent in 1832–47, or 14.7 points higher than for other assaults.[119] Hence, the gap between conviction rates for theft and assault narrowed considerably in this instance.

Very low conviction rates for property crimes other than theft add more evidence to the thesis that juries of *notables* handed down verdicts motivated by something else than just the protection of property. Conviction rates for arson, destruction of property, and pillaging were even lower than for assault. Most persons charged with these crimes were acquitted. Of course, arson was a crime very difficult to prove, especially considering the state of forensic knowledge in the early nineteenth century. But that is just the point: in arson cases, jurors appear to have been swayed much more by evidentiary considerations than by a bias against property crimes. Evidentiary problems may also have contributed to the low conviction rate for destruction of property.[120]

Pillaging was a special case. Most of the accused persons were charged with the pillaging of grains or of harvests.[121] The great majority of these incidents occurred during periods of hunger and sharply rising bread prices (1828–32, 1839–40, and above all 1846–47).[122] Sympathy for persons whose crimes were motivated by hunger, along with the difficulty of proving the guilt of accused individuals who had acted in the confusion of crowd situations, may very well have contributed to the very low conviction rate for such crimes.[123] Whatever the reasons, the fact remains that wealthy and propertied jurors acquitted the overwhelming majority of persons they tried for pillaging. Other considerations outweighed a pro-property bias. This pattern of behavior among upper-class jurors was hardly unique to France during the Bourbon Restoration and July Monarchy eras. Grand juries in Sussex County in England in the eighteenth century, although dominated by the gentry—the rough equivalent to the French *notabilité* of the nineteenth century—more often refused to indict the rural poor for property crimes during years of poor harvests than during years of good harvests.[124]

Therefore, the evidence on convictions and acquittals for property crimes and violent crimes, added to the evidence of frequent jury leniency in punishment for persons convicted of theft by a servant, suggests that biases of propertied jurors were more complicated than the traditional class justice theory leads one to believe. At the least, jury bias against thieves was tempered by mercy and by some sense of appropriateness in punishment. Persons accused of theft were proportionately more often convicted than those accused of violent crimes. But jurors found extenuating circumstances for nearly two-thirds of all persons they convicted of theft from 1834 through 1847. Of course, the figure was four-fifths for persons convicted of *vol domestique*—higher than the figures for assault and manslaughter and equal to that for persons found guilty of capital crimes. If the "jurys censitaires" were motivated entirely by a desire to punish people who threatened property, especially within the very homes of those who employed servants, these figures presumably would have been quite different. The behavior of the propertied French jurors of the 1825–47 period seems not dissimilar to the behavior of propertied jurors in the county of Surrey in England in the eighteenth century who acquitted a considerable proportion of prisoners they tried for certain crimes—forgery, fraud, and malicious damage—which threatened men of property (although English trial jurors of the eighteenth century were mostly minor property-owners of the "middling sort"—farmers, artisans, tradesmen, and the like—rather than men from the top of the social scale).[125]

There was, however, one category of crimes in which the class bias of bourgeois jurors in France perhaps did play a role. These were what can be loosely labeled "white-collar crimes" (fraud, fraudulent bankruptcy, extortion of titles and signatures, counterfeiting, and cases of official corruption). Though the *Compte général*'s tables classified these felonies among "crimes against property," they need to be distinguished from such offenses as theft and arson because of their "clever" nature and by the fact that they were

The "Jurys Censitaires"

more often committed by the bourgeoisie than was the case with other crimes.[126] White-collar felonies were in some fashion related to commerce, finance, business, or bureaucracy (private or governmental).

As with infanticide and *vol domestique*, jury verdicts in such cases seem to have been strongly influenced by considerations of punishment. But the evidence suggests that jurors felt a particular aversion to sentencing the often well-off defendants to the hard labor terms stipulated for most white-collar felonies.[127] For juries of *notables*, such sentences for high-status offenders would have seemed not only harsh but unacceptably degrading. In eighteenth-century France, imprisonment had been seen as an "honorable" punishment for persons of high social standing, while forced labor (where one labored under the whip of another) was an "infaming," "dishonorable," or "degrading" punishment appropriate only for lower-status convicts. This reflected the hierarchical nature of Ancien Régime society. Hard labor punishments were abolished in 1791 but were reinstituted in the Napoleonic *Code pénal* of 1810, complete with ball and chain. Although France was now a society of legal equality, bourgeois Frenchmen still saw hard labor as a degrading punishment inappropriate for high-status offenders. It was abolished for political prisoners in 1834[128] but remained in effect for most white-collar felonies.

However, after 1832, juries were able to spare the overwhelming majority (about eight to nine of every ten) of the persons they convicted of white-collar crimes from the degradation of hard labor punishments by finding extenuating circumstances. They did so even though in no other category of crimes were genuine extenuating circumstances seemingly more rare. White-collar crimes were committed out of cold calculation for financial or material motives. Acquittal rates for these felonies were also high, though this may have been due in part to difficulties in proving guilt in such complicated cases. Nonetheless, the juries' decisions in white-collar cases provide the clearest evidence that the law on extenuating circumstances had not ended a frequent recourse to jury sanction nullification.

This was evident in every category of white-collar crime. Jury verdicts for fraud (which accounted for most white-collar felonies and were divided into fraud in a commercial document, fraud in an official public document, and fraud in a private document),[129] fraudulent bankruptcy, and extortion of titles and signatures were quite similar. Acquittal rates for these offenses were high,[130] and extenuating circumstances were found for about four-fifths of the persons convicted of each of them from 1834 through 1847.[131] As a consequence, few of those found guilty were still sentenced to hard labor terms. In most instances, these were replaced by mere misdemeanor penalties.[132] That juries found extenuating circumstances for about equal proportions of persons convicted of both extortion and fraudulent bankruptcy is particularly telling evidence of how the panels used the 1832 law for purposes of sanction nullification. Genuine extenuating circumstances were probably even rarer in cases of extortion than in cases of fraudulent bankruptcy. Some of the persons accused of the latter crime could have been trying to avoid genuine bankruptcy and the loss of all property. The same could not be said of those found guilty of blackmail or of "obtaining property or consent from someone through the use of actual or threatened violence or fear."[133]

But it was in counterfeiting cases more than in any others (save, perhaps, infanticide) that juror resistance to imposing the penalty provided by law was most evident. No other crime presumably required more skill and premeditation. Yet from 1825 through 1831, the acquittal rate for *fausse monnaie* was very high—63.1 percent, higher than for fraud, infanticide, or fraudulent bankruptcy.[134] Moreover, about four of every ten persons convicted in counterfeiting cases from 1826 through 1831 were found guilty of a lesser crime.[135] Such verdicts seem to have been largely the consequence of the juries' reluctance to condemn the culprits to the guillotine: before 1832, counterfeiting was one of the few nonfatal crimes punishable by death.[136]

Strong circumstantial evidence in support of this conclusion can be found in the fact that after the abolition of the death penalty for counterfeiting in 1832, the conviction rate for the crime rose sharply.[137] Even so, in all but a few cases, juries balked at imposing the penalty of hard labor for life, which the reform of 1832 had substituted for the death sentence in most cases of counterfeiting. From 1834 through 1847, extenuating circumstances were found for more than eight of every ten persons convicted of counterfeiting.[138] Consequently, only about 13 percent of persons found guilty of counterfeiting from 1832 through 1847 were sentenced to life at hard labor. The majority, in fact, were not punished with hard labor terms at all but rather with imprisonment.[139] Meanwhile, convictions on lesser charges had become proportionately far less common than they had been before 1832.[140]

Juries also ameliorated the penalty for the overwhelming majority of the corrupt civil servants they convicted. Nearly all crimes of official corruption (embezzlement by a public official, fraudulent withholding of official deeds and records by public officials, thefts of valuables from the mails by postal employees, and smuggling by a customs agent) were punishable by sentences of five to twenty years of hard labor in the absence of extenuating circumstances. Bribery and the acceptance of bribes by public officials

The "Jurys Censitaires"

were punished more leniently with imprisonment exceeding five years and *dégradation civique* (loss of civil rights) in the absence of extenuating circumstances. But jury verdicts ensured that very few public officials charged with any of these crimes suffered the penalties provided by the *Code pénal*. From 1825 through 1853 (because of the relatively small number of persons tried for crimes of official corruption, the data for them have been lumped together into longer periods than for other crimes), more than half of all persons tried for felonies of official corruption punishable by hard labor were acquitted.[141] Extenuating circumstances were found for more than four-fifths of those who were convicted from 1834 through 1853.[142] Few of those found guilty during the entire period from 1825 through 1853 were sentenced to hard labor. Most (nearly two-thirds) received misdemeanor punishments.[143]

The panels were most lenient toward the persons they tried for offering or accepting bribes. The number charged with these crimes was small, yet the conviction rate for them was among the lowest for all felonies: about one-fifth of all those tried from 1825 through 1847.[144] And after 1832, it was rare for the few persons convicted of offering and accepting bribes to receive the felony punishments provided by the *Code pénal*,[145] for extenuating circumstances were found for nine of every ten, with the result that a similar proportion were sentenced to misdemeanor penalties only.[146]

The law on extenuating circumstances of 1832 therefore seemed to greatly strengthen the juries by granting to them a powerful new tool to mitigate penalties. That they appear to have often used this tool to reduce penalties they thought too harsh was most evident when it came to certain crimes — capital crimes generally (but above all infanticide), theft by a servant, and white-collar offenses. Yet it was very shortly after 1832 that certain forces began to appear that would considerably weaken the juries in the long term and whose significance would be understood only later.

One of these forces actually grew out of the second law of extenuating circumstances. This legislation, by formally granting to juries for the first time some say in the punishment of those they convicted, constituted the first breach in the wall between "fact," previously the exclusive concern of juries, and "law" (again, this essentially meant the penalty), previously the exclusive concern of judges.[147] It marked the beginning of a movement that would eventually, by the mid-twentieth century, result in the merging of the jury with the judges in the system of *échevinage*, in which the jurymen and magistrates deliberated together in determining both verdict and penalty. This would destroy the independence of the juries. The law of 1832 was certainly not the only factor that contributed to this eventual outcome, but it constituted an important precedent for it, and in the twentieth century the champions of *échevinage* sought to extend its logic.

The jury system was eventually undermined most by correctionalization, though at first it affected few cases. This process of downgrading *crimes* to *délits* was begun by governments and magistrates of the Bourbon Restoration and July Monarchy eras for a number of reasons. Among them were the victim's provocation of or misdeeds toward the accused, the slightness of the injuries, the culprit's drunkenness, the low value of the objects or money stolen (even though in France it was circumstance, not the value of stolen objects, that legally determined whether a theft was a felony or a misdemeanor), the accused's restitution to the victim or return of stolen objects, the culprit's age and antecedents, and the desire for speedy justice and assurance that the *cours d'assises* would not be overloaded with cases that were not really serious.[148]

But contemporary legal scholars and interpreters of the judicial statistics most often claimed that the primary reason for the correctionalization movement was the magistrates' desire to remove cases from "indulgent" juries in order to ensure more convictions, since acquittals were far rarer in the judges-only *tribunaux correctionnels* than in the *cours d'assises*. The Ministry of Justice agreed with this explanation.[149] Magistrates were therefore willing to accept a lighter penalty in exchange for a much greater certainty of punishment.[150]

Correctionalization was carried out through two means. One was legal: the passage of a series of laws in the course of the nineteenth and twentieth centuries formally reducing a number of *crimes* to *délits*. The first such law was passed in 1824. It correctionalized certain crimes committed by minors aged sixteen and under as well as thefts in fields and inns.[151] It marked the modest beginning of a movement that in time would deprive the juries of much of their power in the criminal justice system.

The other means was extralegal: magistrates at the pretrial stage reclassified as misdemeanors those offenses whose circumstances really gave them the character of felonies.[152] They commonly did this by dismissing from the charges the aggravating circumstances that in France set felonies apart. Thus, cases of infanticide (a *crime*) were sometimes tried as negligent homicide of a newborn (a *délit*) or (from 1863) as concealment of birth, another misdemeanor. Aggravated theft (*vol qualifié*), again a *crime*, could be prosecuted as simple theft, a *délit*. Indecent assault (*attentat à la pudeur*), another felony, could be reduced to the misdemeanor of public indecency (*outrage public à la pudeur*), and so on.[153]

Procedurally, extralegal correctionalization could occur at any one of the

The "Jurys Censitaires"

three stages that preceded trial in the *cour d'assises*. The *procureur* first decided whether a reported criminal case was to be filed away or acted upon and, if the latter, whether it was to be classified as a *crime* or *délit*. In some cases, the *procureurs* chose to ignore the circumstances that made an offense a *crime* and labeled it a *délit* instead. The case was then sent directly to trial in the *tribunal correctionnel*. If, however, the *procureur* still labeled the offense a *crime*, it had to be sent to the *juge d'instruction* for investigation. This magistrate might decide, through either an evaluation of the actual facts or through ignoring the circumstances that indicated it was a felony, that it was a *délit* and send it to trial in the *tribunal correctionnel*. If the charge still remained a felony, it then of course went to the *Chambre des mises en accusation* for formal indictment. This panel also had the authority to reclassify a *crime* as a *délit*, but it rarely did so. Correctionalization was therefore generally carried out by either the *procureur* or by the *juge d'instruction*.[154] As already mentioned, many defendants appear to have cooperated in the correctionalization of their offenses. This cooperation may have been encouraged by the magistrates' tactic of holding out the prospect of leniency to defendants who confessed to their crimes.

It was, in fact, principally through extralegal means that correctionalization was carried out from the mid-nineteenth century onward. Before the 1840s, however, magistrates appear to have resorted to the procedure only rarely. It is true that judges of the Bourbon Restoration and July Monarchy, like their predecessors of the Revolutionary and Napoleonic eras, continued to express considerable displeasure with juries. They often criticized juror incompetence, of course, but they also complained about the leniency and apparent bias of many of the panels. Juries frequently pronounced "acquittements scandaleux" and were politically unreliable, acquitting most persons accused of political and press offenses.[155]

Yet at this stage, the magistrates did not practice correctionalization on a significant scale. Despite their misgivings, they accepted the fact that they had to work within the jury system.[156] They really had no choice, since liberals of the period strongly supported the jury system.[157] Even the Bourbon Restoration governments at their most reactionary dared not eliminate it, and of course the July Monarchy regime strengthened juries in its first years. The political climate was therefore not yet propitious for attacks on the jury system.

The magistrates' movement to correctionalize felonies did not really start until after the July Monarchy government began to lose its early enthusiasm for the institution of the jury. This was connected to several factors that were not altogether unrelated: political events, the government's frustration with many jury verdicts, and its desire for cheap and quick justice.

The July Monarchy regime soon learned to regret the new powers it had granted to juries in the early 1830s. Scarcely had it come to power when it was challenged by the plots and uprisings of its Legitimist, Republican, and Bonapartist enemies, as well as by working-class rebellions, above all those in Lyon in 1831 and 1834. The government was particularly fearful of the power of the opposition press, perhaps because it was well aware that Louis Philippe himself had become king because of a revolution begun by newspapers.[158]

In this situation, the regime turned to repression, enforcing a host of laws limiting freedom of speech and press it had inherited from previous governments and enacting new ones. In the year 1831 alone, more than a thousand persons were tried for *délits politiques et de presse*.[159] Indeed, if one is to judge by the number of prosecutions, the "liberal" July Monarchy was more repressive than the reactionary Bourbon Restoration that preceded it. From 1826 through 1830, an average of about 344 persons were tried each year for *délits politiques et de presse*. This figure nearly doubled to 641 from 1831 through 1835.[160] Some of the rise in repression might have been more apparent than real: the Constitutional Charter of 1830 had abolished the prior censorship exercised by the authorities under the Bourbon Restoration,[161] so that the new regime could only silence its opposition through prosecutions following the publication or expression of the antigovernment sentiments.

But juries would not cooperate with the government in its program of repression. Despite the considerable authority the government's representatives exercised in selecting the men who served on the juries and the fact that jurymen belonged to the *"pays légal* whose members were the prop and stay of the July Monarchy,"[162] the panels from 1831 through 1835 acquitted 72 percent of all persons they tried for *délits politiques et de presse*. This was far higher than the acquittal rate of 39 percent from 1826 through 1830, when the three-judge panels of the *tribunaux correctionnels* tried these offenses.[163] Moreover, juries went well beyond exonerating merely the persons accused of nonviolent crimes of opinion: they also acquitted most of those charged with *crimes politiques* and *rébellion* during the early turbulent period of the July Monarchy's existence.[164]

This leniency was even extended to persons from across the political spectrum. Such was the case in 1832, when the regime was threatened by Republican and Legitimist uprisings. Among those tried for *crimes politiques* in that year, juries exonerated the majority of those tried for their participation in the Legitimist uprisings in the west and in the rue des Prouvaires in Paris in February, along with most of those accused of participating in the Republican insurrection in the capital city in June and in the November 1831 uprising of the Lyons silk workers.[165] It was not unknown, in fact, for Legitimist and Republican jurors to combine to secure acquittals in political and press cases, and the government alleged that jurymen who might be favorable to its cause were intimidated by the supporters of the accused persons (there was as yet no secret voting by jurors) or would have their names or addresses published in the newspapers.[166]

The even-handedness of the juries' leniency in political and press cases during the early July Monarchy recalls the similar behavior of jurors in the Côte d'Or in the 1790s or of those in the Côtes-du-Nord during the Restoration who acquitted most persons of all political persuasions accused of political or politically inspired felonies and *délits de presse* (when the *cours d'assises* had jurisdiction over these offenses from 1819 to 1822), even though a majority of the men on the panels were royalists and Catholics.[167] The frequency with which juries acquitted political and press offenders of all political persuasions does indeed suggest that they were the "palladium of liberty."

But the threatened government was not pleased with the proclivity of juries to live up to this role. The insurrections of 1831–34 and the frequency with which juries acquitted political defendants led the government to rein in the panels. The first step was taken in 1834, with the passage of a law that declared illegal all associations of more than twenty persons and which removed from the jurisdiction of juries all crimes connected with associations. If these were crimes against the state (conspiracy to attempt an assassination, attacks against the Charter, offenses against the king), the Chambre des Pairs (the upper house of the Parliament) would judge. Less serious cases would be tried by the *tribunaux correctionnels*.[168]

The famous attempted assassination of Louis Philippe by Giuseppe Fieschi in July 1835 led the government of the duc de Broglie to take further and more extensive action against juries. The outcome was the passage of the repressive "September Laws" of 1835, aimed at making convictions easier in jury trials.[169] The number of votes needed to convict an accused person was once again reduced from eight to seven. Moreover, jurors were to vote by secret ballot.[170] The theory behind this was that they would thereby be protected from threats made by the regime's enemies.[171] In addition, if all three judges of the *cour d'assises* agreed that there had been a miscarriage of justice, they could order a retrial.[172]

The "Jurys Censitaires"

The acts also allowed for the removal of additional political and press cases from the jurisdiction of juries. Incitement to hatred of the king or contempt for his person or his constitutional authority and incitement to the overthrow of the form of government established by the Charter of 1830 were declared crimes against the security of the state and could be tried by the Chambre des Pairs rather than by the juries of the *cours d'assises*.[173]

But the September Laws had very little effect on juries in respect to the cases that they continued to try. The acquittal rate for *délits politiques et de presse* declined only marginally following their passage.[174] The percentage of acquittals among persons accused of *crimes politiques* and *rébellion* also dropped only modestly, and juries continued to exonerate most of those they tried for these crimes.[175] The government's apparent assumption that there was a "silent majority" of jurors who would vote for conviction if only they were allowed secret ballots turned out to be incorrect. Nor did lowering the number of votes needed to convict do much good for the government's cause.

Faced with continued jury leniency in political and press cases, the government tried a new tactic. In the 1840s, it prosecuted many opposition newspapers for petty offenses (defamation of an official, publishing a political journal without depositing "caution money," and the like) that were tried by the *tribunaux correctionnels*, rather than prosecuting them for seditious libel, which was tried by the *cours d'assises*.[176]

This method of combating jury leniency by reclassifying and thereby transferring cases from the *cours d'assises* to the *tribunaux correctionnels* was soon applied to nonpolitical crimes as well, although budgetary considerations also played a role. A circular of August 16, 1842, issued by Minister of Justice N. Martin (du Nord) and addressed to the *procureurs généraux*, authorized and even encouraged the practice of correctionalization. The minister, mentioning the growing costs of the justice system, brought to the prosecutors' attention the fact that juries had "fairly often" tried cases where the aggravating circumstances that distinguished felonies from misdemeanors were not well proven. Such cases should therefore be correctionalized to avoid acquittals and reduce the considerable expense associated with jury trials.[177] A number of historians have claimed that this circular either marked the beginning of the correctionalization movement or at least gave it considerable momentum.[178] From the mid-1830s on, the government of the July Monarchy had worked to undermine the jury system in political and press cases; by the early 1840s, it had begun to do so in nonpolitical cases.

However, the circular of 1842 had little immediate effect. According to

The "Jurys Censitaires"

TABLE 2.6. Number of People Tried in the *Cours d'Assises*,
Total and Annual Average, by Period

Years	Total	Annual Average
1825–41	127,101	7,477
1842–47	43,670	7,279
1848–54	50,577	7,225
1855–62	43,198	5,400
1863–70	34,325	4,291
1871–78	38,760	4,845
1879–93	64,096	4,273
1894–1913	65,474	3,274
1914–18	9,172	1,834
1919–31	28,399	2,185
1932–38	10,813	1,545
1940–44	4,143	829
1945–52	15,833	1,979
1957–63	8,209	1,173

Sources: *Compte général*, 1825–60, Table 2, p. 3; 1861–1909, Table 2, p. 5;
1910–13 and 1919–23, Table 2, p. 7; 1924–31, Table 1, p. 7; 1914–18
and 1932–63, Ministère de l'Economie et des Finances, *Annuaire
statistique*, 162–63.

André Toulemon, extralegal correctionalization was practiced at first tim-
idly and quietly by the magistrates, who were urged by the Ministry of
Justice to resort to it only with prudence and reserve.[179] The annual average
number of persons tried in the *cours d'assises* dropped very slightly during
the remaining years of the July Monarchy (see Table 2.6). Extralegal correctionalization did not become a wholesale procedure until the 1850s, during
the Second Empire. But the July Monarchy had set a precedent. The reduction of penalties and correctionalization were the two principal responses
of governments and magistrates to high acquittal rates. Both undermined
the jury system in ways that liberals of the period did not foresee.

chapter three

THE GREAT TURNING POINT

The Juries of the Second Republic and Second Empire, 1848–1870

The eras of the Second Republic (1848–52) and Second Empire (1852–70) witnessed the most important turning point in the history of the jury in France from the Revolution to World War II. Whereas the primary response of the authorities to jury sanction nullification during the preceding period was to grant to juries the power to rule on extenuating circumstances, the governments of the 1848–70 era (especially that of the Second Empire) responded primarily through wholesale correctionalization. Rising conviction rates for the offenses the panels continued to try were another distinctive feature of the period, brought about by a combination of increasing recidivism (which now became a major concern among public officials) and reforms that placed the panels under greater government control. Where the government of the July Monarchy strengthened juries, the administration of Louis-Napoleon Bonaparte did more than any other between that of the great Napoleon and Vichy to weaken them. This was connected with the drift toward authoritarianism characteristic of the era.

Napoleon III's government took a number of actions to undermine or "tame" the juries. But what the regime did more than anything else to weaken the jury system was to build upon the precedent established by the July Monarchy and initiate the wholesale correctionalization of felonies. Most of the regime's other actions against the juries were wholly or partially reversed during the Third Republic. Yet large-scale correctionalization became a permanent phenomenon. It was carried even further by succeeding governments until the jury system was reduced to insignificance in France. On the other hand, even in its decline, the jury system continued to have an important effect on the evolution of punishment.

The Second Empire's actions against the juries followed those that had already been taken during the Second Republic. An initial flurry of reforms to strengthen the panels in the aftermath of the revolution of February 1848 was soon followed by efforts to curb them in response to rebellion and the jurors' lack of cooperation in the work of repression. The same process had occurred during the July Monarchy. Yet it was now repeated much more quickly and in a more extreme fashion.

The provisional government of the Second Republic, established following the overthrow of the July Monarchy in February 1848, was characterized in its first months by a spirit of liberal legal reform. Within only a few days of its installation, the provisional government issued a decree abolishing the death penalty for political crimes. The way for this reform was prepared by the arguments against political executions written during the preceding decades by important liberals such as Benjamin Constant, François Guizot, and Alphonse de Lamartine (one of the leaders of the Revolution of 1848). One of the arguments was that the execution of leaders of rebellions was futile in an era when revolutionary doctrines spread rapidly throughout the nation. Moreover, according to Guizot, the public was increasingly opposed to such executions because the immorality of political felonies was not evident when the definition of what constituted *crimes politiques* changed so often in this era of frequent revolutions. The memory of the excesses of the Jacobin Terror of 1793–94 also played a role.[1] One measure of public opposition to the death penalty for political felonies was the refusal of juries to impose it in any such cases since 1836.[2]

In the same spirit of legal reform, the provisional government enacted two decrees in March that embodied the liberal desires to strengthen the "palladium of liberty," eliminate the role of the prefects in the selection of jurors, and democratize the composition of the panels. One decree repealed the September Laws and raised the number of jurors needed to convict from seven to nine.[3] The other decree stated that with the introduction of universal manhood suffrage, "all citizens are electors, and every elector is a juror, and that the jury would be drawn in the future from the electoral list."[4] Jury duty was now the right of all citizens.

But following the election of the conservative National Assembly in April and the June Days insurrection that panicked conservatives and moderates, the government retreated from this principle. The same reaction that led to the repression of left-wing radicals and the limitation of democracy brought about a return to a restricted jury selection process, though it remained more democratic than it had been during the July Monarchy. The result was the law of August 7, 1848, voted in following discussions in which the June Days had been very much on the minds of the deputies.[5] It meant a return to the principle of excluding certain groups from the juries. E. Leroux, *rapporteur* (spokesman) for the committee that drew up the new law, justified it in the following terms: "To society *en masse* belongs the right to judge all crimes. If it could exercise this right directly, the exclusions, the choices, would not be necessary; the majority of upright, honest, and capable men would right the immoral or incapable, and therefore dangerous, minority. But the people can only judge by delegation, this delegation must be made with discernment, unless one wishes to lead society to its ruin. . . . At the moment when we are changing the form of government, should we leave justice to the hands of chance?"[6]

As before, jurors had to be at least thirty years old. They had to be in possession of civil and political rights and could not be servants (because of their "lack of independence"), illiterates, bankrupts, priests, public functionaries, national schoolmasters, state officers, or persons convicted of crimes for which they had been sentenced to more than one year in prison. Moreover, commissions composed almost entirely of elected officials chose from among the eligible persons those who were to be inscribed on the annual jury lists, with the prefects reduced to the role of merely collating the registers. Communal lists of jurors were drawn up by the mayors of the communes. The prefect combined these lists to form the cantonal list, which was then revised by a cantonal commission consisting of a *conseiller général* as president, a justice of the peace as vice president, and two members of the municipal council of each commune in the canton. All were elected officials except the *juge de paix*. The commission was to select one juror for every two hundred inhabitants of the canton. The prefect then collated the lists drawn up by the cantonal commissions to form the annual departmental list.[7]

Several provisions of the law made it very difficult if not impossible for poor men to serve on juries and may have reflected the government's fear of the working classes following the June Days insurrection. These included the exclusions of servants, illiterates, and bankrupts. But more important was a provision that allowed workingmen who lived by their daily labor to be excused from jury duty upon their request if they could prove that it would impose too much of a hardship upon them.[8] In most cases, they could prove this was true, since jurors continued to serve without any sort of pay, even for travel and lodging expenses, save for the payment for the transportation of jurors who had to journey more than two kilometers to the *cour d'assises*.[9] So long as jurors were not paid, the opening up of the panels to poor men was much more theoretical than real, especially when sessions of the *cours d'assises* normally lasted from two to three weeks. Yet the idea of paying jurors scarcely occurred to even most democrats or radicals of the time: only one petition calling for the compensation of jurors has survived from the democratic clubs of the Second Republic.[10]

As a result, the juries of the Second Republic, although somewhat more

The Great Turning Point

democratic in composition than those of the July Monarchy, were still heavily weighted with *notables*. Through most of 1848, the annual jury lists of *notables* drawn up in the fall of the preceding year continued to be used pending the passage of a definitive new law on the juries. This meant that the decree of March opening up the juries to all enfranchised citizens never went into effect. Moreover, because of the time it took to put into operation the machinery of the law of August 7, in some departments the old lists continued to be used down through the end of the year.[11]

Following the full implementation of the new law at the beginning of 1849, the proportion of *notables* on the annual jury lists was reduced, though not enough to erase their dominance. From 1849 through 1853—the period in which the law of August 7, 1848, regulated the selection of jurors—only 8 percent of the persons included in the annual jury lists nationwide were workers or artisans (though this was certainly much higher than their almost total absence during the Restoration and July Monarchy) and 14 percent were peasants. The rest were bourgeois: 8 percent were civil servants, 18 percent were merchants and manufacturers, 11 percent belonged to the liberal professions, and a significant 41 percent were *propriétaires* and *rentiers* living from incomes provided by their properties or investments.[12] Bernard Schnapper's analysis of the jury session lists in the Sarthe, Deux-Sevres, and Indre roughly confirms the national figures.[13] However, like the prefects before them, the commissions that drew up the annual jury lists appear to have had a preference for selecting men well into middle age: according to local studies, the average juror during the Second Republic was in his late forties, only slightly younger than during the July Monarchy.[14]

The second act of the National Assembly to retreat from the democratic jury reforms of March 1848 was a law of October 18, 1848, reducing the number of jurors needed to convict from nine to eight. Unlike the law of August 7, this proposal touched off much debate in the assembly. But the government strongly supported it, and even Adolphe Cremieux, the former minister of justice who authored the law of nine votes in March and who by this time had been succeeded by the more conservative Pierre Marie, repudiated his reform under pressure from the presidents of the *cours d'assises*, who had noted a sharp increase in acquittal rates since the spring.[15] Their concern was not entirely unfounded: although month-to-month figures on verdicts are not available in the *Compte général*, the acquittal rate in the *cours d'assises* had risen from 33.0 percent in 1847 to 41.5 percent in 1848.[16]

Perhaps what really concerned the judges and the government—just as it had earlier regimes—was the high acquittal rate for political and press offenses. Following the June Days insurrection, the provisional government led by Godfroy Cavaignac engaged in a campaign of repression against left-wing radicals, reimposing censorship and initiating numerous prosecutions against the leftist Montagnard newspapers on such vague charges as "inciting civil war," "inciting hatred and contempt of the republican government," "inciting hatred and contempt of a class of citizens," "inciting disobedience of the laws," "apology for criminal acts," and the like.[17] But juries, as so often before, refused to cooperate in the work of repression: most of the persons they tried in 1848 for *délits politiques et de presse*, *crimes politiques*, and *rébellion* were acquitted.[18]

However, the law of October 18, 1848, like the September Laws before it, scarcely made a dent in the high acquittal rates for political offenders. The election of Louis-Napoleon Bonaparte to the presidency in December 1848, the growing hysteria of the "party of order" concerning the presumed threat to the social order posed by the "red peril," and a new press law of 1849 creating still more offenses led to even more government repression of the Left.[19] As a result, in the years 1849–50, the number of persons tried for *délits politiques et de presse* rose sharply to the highest level it had ever been from 1831 through 1851.[20] Yet again, juries nullified most of the government's repressive efforts in the courts: almost two-thirds of persons tried for *délits politiques et de presse* in the years 1849 and 1850 were acquitted, as were even higher proportions of those accused of *crimes politiques* and *rébellion*.[21] Evidently many of the jurors, even if they were still often middle-aged *notables*, did not share what Howard Machin has called the "neurotic anxiety of the party of order."[22]

Several actions taken by the government in 1850 should have ensured that more men belonging to the "party of order" were placed on juries. On May 31, a law was passed that, by limiting the franchise to those who had lived in their communes for at least three years, took the vote away from many urban working-class men.[23] This also meant that these persons were no longer inscribed on the electoral lists from which the annual jury lists were drawn.[24] Moreover, in the same year, the government sharply stepped up its purge of mayors and municipal councils, mostly for political reasons.[25] Therefore, many mayors and municipal councillors belonging to the Montagnard party must have been eliminated from the commissions that in the fall of 1850 drew up the annual jury lists for the following year.

But these actions did not lead to significantly more convictions in political and press cases. The acquittal rate for *délits politiques et de presse* remained virtually unchanged in 1851, although there were minor decreases in rates

The Great Turning Point

of exonerations for *crimes politiques* and *rébellion*.[26] No matter what it tried, the government could not get juries to convict the majority of political and press offenders.

The government's actions—particularly the law of October 18, 1848—appear to have been somewhat more successful in raising the proportion of guilty verdicts for ordinary felonies. The total conviction rate for persons tried for *crimes* in the *cours d'assises* rose steadily, though by no means sharply, from 1848 through 1851.[27]

The rise in the conviction rate was evidently not sharp enough to please the government, which was moreover very displeased by jury verdicts in political and press cases. The result was further action by the political authorities against the juries. In December 1850, the Ministry of Justice launched an *enquête* (survey) among the *présidents* of the *cours d'assises* to gather their opinions about the functioning of the jury system. As in the Napoleonic era, most of the judges expressed opinions highly critical of the juries, though they did not generally call for their outright abolition. According to Schnapper's analysis of the survey, the majority of *présidents* held that the democratization of the panels (modest though it was) had gone too far and threatened the "moral order." It had led to more jury incompetence and weakness. Judges in certain rural departments claimed that too many jurors were ignorant peasants incapable of judging intelligently. Once again, the *présidents* complained of jurors who were illiterate, or did not speak French, or were drunk, and were too lenient. Some of the *présidents* deplored what they saw as the politicization of the juries by the elected officials of the cantonal commissions, by that really meaning the inclusion of men of the extreme Left on the panels.[28]

The *présidents* proposed a number of reforms to rid juries of such "defects." These included the elimination of the municipal councillors from the cantonal commissions, giving the judicial element a predominant role on the commissions, a reduction in the number of jurors per department, and a return to a simple majority vote for conviction in order to reduce the number of "shocking acquittals." Some of the judges suggested that juries be deprived of their authority to grant extenuating circumstances. Others suggested the further correctionalization of felonies: too many small infractions were being sent to the *cours d'assises* with the aggravating circumstances not sufficiently proven. The *chambres des mises en accusation* should refer such cases to the *tribunaux correctionnels* when harm or injury to the victim of the crime was not great, or some crimes could be correctionalized through a revision of the penal code.[29]

Indeed, according to Schnapper, the *présidents'* responses in the *enquête*

The Great Turning Point

of 1850–52 showed that "nothing seems to have changed much since the beginning of the century. These [the *présidents* of the *cours d'assises*] are repressive magistrates for whom a good jury is that which obediently convicts the accused persons. In fact, how can people without training see more clearly than the *juges d'instruction*, the *chambres du conseil*, the *chambres des mises en accusation* who had sent the suspects to the *assises*? It is the attitude of men of order and of *techniciens de droit* in the face of the vulgar."[30]

The leaders of the Second Republic, in its late "période autoritaire," took one of the judges' suggestions to heart: like the officials of the July Monarchy before them, they encouraged magistrates to resort to correctionalization. On September 13, 1851, the minister of justice issued a new circular recommending the correctionalization of felonies in even stronger terms than in the document of 1842: "It is necessary to avoid, in the interest of justice and of the Treasury, pronouncements by jurors in cases in which the accusation is not supported by positive proofs or the aggravating circumstances are not perfectly established; whenever cases of this nature can be sent to correctional jurisdiction, magistrates must seize the occasion with assiduity: they do not have, in fact, any chance of success before the jury and often the only outcome is a scandalous acquittal."[31]

It is not clear why an acquittal was "scandalous" when the charge was "not supported by positive proofs." In any event, soon after this circular was issued, Louis-Napoleon Bonaparte carried out his coup d'état of December 2, 1851, and established his dictatorship. His Second Empire regime engaged in a much more concerted attack on the juries, an attack that began almost immediately after the coup. Louis-Napoleon distrusted juries, especially when it came to trying political and press cases. Like his uncle before him, he did not eliminate the panels, because it was politically impossible to do so in a country where jury trial was regarded as an essential right inherited from the Revolution. But he significantly reduced their powers, their independence from government control, and the number of offenses they tried.

The process began with a series of laws and decrees from 1851 to 1853. As can be expected, the first step was the elimination of jury trial for persons accused of *délits politiques et de presse*. On December 31, 1851—less than a month after the coup d'état—a decree returned jurisdiction over political and press misdemeanors to the judges of the *tribunaux correctionnels*, who were much more reliable when it came to convicting enemies of the regime. The decree was confirmed by the press law of February 17, 1852.[32]

Those persons accused of participating in the insurrections that broke out in December 1851 in reaction against the coup d'état were also deprived of jury trial. As had occurred in France before, exceptional tribunals were created. A circular of February 3, 1852, established the *commissions mixtes*—each consisting of a prefect, a *procureur*, and a general, but no jury nor even a judge of the bench—to summarily try the insurgents. Perhaps judges of the bench were excluded because they were (at least in theory) irremovable magistrates who, though politicized to some degree, were still independent enough and legalistic enough to protest the use of commissions that were of questionable legality because they were created not by law but only by an administrative directive soon after "validated" by a decree of Louis-Napoleon Bonaparte.[33] According to one modern historian, even some of the *procureurs* were "embarrassed" by the "irregular procedure and excessive powers" of the *commissions mixtes*.[34] Within weeks, the commissions convicted 25,000 persons.[35]

The regime then enacted several measures to ensure more convictions by juries in the nonpolitical cases they still tried and to increase government control over the panels. A law of June 9, 1853, restored the pre-1848 rule of conviction by a simple majority of seven votes.[36]

But the most far-reaching jury legislation of the Second Empire was the law on the formation of the jury of June 4, 1853. It significantly increased government influence in the selection of jurors and further narrowed the socioeconomic and political bases of the panels. These outcomes were achieved first of all by replacing the commissions made up mostly of locally elected officials with new ones composed entirely of appointees of the central government: the *juges de paix* (who unlike the judges of the bench could be removed from office), prefects, sub-prefects, and mayors (mayors had been elected during the Second Republic, but under Napoleon III they were all state appointees).[37]

The new commissions were provided with abundant opportunities to be selective in the choice of jurors, especially at the *arrondissement* level. The number of jurors per population was reduced from one per two hundred to one per six hundred.[38] First, a cantonal commission consisting of the *juge de paix* as president and all the mayors of the canton drew up a list of names triple the number fixed as the canton's quota. Then an *arrondissement* commission, composed of the prefect or sub-prefect as president and all the *juges de paix* of the *arrondissement*, chose one-third of the names from the cantonal lists to make up the quota set for the *arrondissement*. The commission could reduce the number of names from one canton and add to another, so long as the reduction or augmentation did not exceed one-fourth of the cantonal quota and did not affect the *arrondissement* quota. The *arrondissement* lists, which had to be completed by November 15, were

The Great Turning Point

then sent to the *secretariat général* of the prefecture and put together to form the annual departmental list.[39]

The 1853 law contained yet other provisions to exclude from the jury lists persons the regime thought undesirable. All who had been convicted of felonies and misdemeanors for which they had been sentenced to at least three months in prison were permanently excluded from juries, a category that included ordinary criminals but certain political and press offenders as well. Those who had been condemned to at least one month in prison were to be excluded from juries for five years following the expiration of their penalty, a category that again included some political and press offenders. Moreover, persons who had been convicted of "outrage to public and religious morality [a vaguely defined offense separate from public indecency but encompassing cases of public expression in speech or press deemed immoral and which could include certain statements and publications with political implications], attack against the principle of property and the rights of the family" were permanently barred from jury duty.[40]

Jurors would also come largely from the propertied classes that supported the emperor and law and order. All those ever imprisoned for vagabondage or mendicity (no matter how light their sentence) were forbidden to serve on juries. The exclusion from juries of illiterates, bankrupts, and servants was continued. Moreover, Article 5 of the law declared *dispenses* (exempted) from jury service all "those who need their daily and manual labor in order to live."[41] This went beyond the law of August 7, 1848, which excused such persons from jury duty only if they could prove it imposed too much of a hardship upon them. Now workingmen were granted an automatic exemption whenever they asked for it.[42]

As a result, the law restored the *notables* to a level of dominance on the juries almost equal to that of the July Monarchy, and the modest democratization of the panels initiated by the Second Republic was virtually erased.[43] On the national level, the percentage of persons listed as workers or artisans on the annual jury lists dropped sharply from 8 percent for the years 1849–53 to a meager 2 percent for 1854–70. The percentage of peasants also declined substantially from 14 percent to 7 percent. *Rentiers* and *propriétaires* living from the incomes provided by their properties or investments, on the other hand, saw their representation increase from 41 percent to 47 percent, or almost half of the total. Civil servants also increased their representation on the jury lists somewhat from 8 percent to 13 percent, while merchants, manufacturers, and members of the liberal professions maintained roughly the same proportions in 1854–70 as they did in 1849–53.[44] In fact, the national statistics on the composition of the annual jury lists may underestimate the

The Great Turning Point

changes wrought by the law of 1853, for several local studies show an even sharper increase in *notables* selected for the actual trial panels.[45]

The Ministry of Justice sought additional guarantees of securing "bons jurés" by issuing circulars to its magistrates instructing them on how to choose jurors who the regime thought desirable. A circular of 1853 informed prosecutors that they must summarily challenge "those jurors who, imbued with false systems or too weak in character, are disposed to deny, or to leave the social law without sanction."[46] As Schnapper has suggested, this was almost certain to mean the exclusion of known opponents of the government.[47]

The Ministry of Justice also ordered prosecutors to provide direction to the jury commissions on which men should be inscribed on their lists. This was the explicit purpose of an 1857 circular that recommended that prosecutors gather information on jurors from the *présidents* of the *cours d'assises* in order to inform the jury commissions which men should be excluded from the annual lists. Since the intelligence on jurors provided by the *présidents* was so crucial to this process, the circular recommended to these judges that they study with care the behavior and composition of juries, which was of "great interest in order to know the categories of citizens who offer the best guarantees of a firm and enlightened justice, and who, consequently, must be recommended to the choice of the cantonal and *arrondissement* commissions."[48]

Indeed, Christian Soulas has summed up the jury selection process during the Second Empire as follows: "Certain official writings mark with clarity the desire to make a single and rather narrowly limited class the essential source of jurors. Urban dwellers were preferred to country folk, the rich to the poor, *intellectuels* to *manuels*."[49] The *juges de paix* on the *arrondissement* jury commissions, who were lowly magistrates without security of tenure and who were subordinate to the *procureurs*,[50] were in no position to deny the wishes of the prosecutors.

The laws of 1853 and the central government's interference in the selection of jurors evidently worked in empanelling juries more committed to law and order than those of the past. The conviction rate for all felonies rose substantially from 66.2 percent in 1849–53 to 75.8 percent in 1854–70—the highest conviction rate since the first publication of the judicial statistics in 1825 and the second highest of the entire era between 1825 and 1940 (see Table 2.1). More than any of its predecessors since 1815, the government of the Second Empire had mastered the art of hand-picking juries to reflect its will. This was not so much from a strictly political point of view, since

most political and press offenses had been removed from the juries' jurisdiction. But Napoleon III's regime, like authoritarian regimes in general,
had a strong law-and-order bias, and it was reflected in the behavior of
the juries chosen during this period. Indeed, the Ministry of Justice of the
Second Empire alluded to the relationship when it claimed that three of the
four reasons for the rise in the conviction rate were "the strengthening of
the principles of order and authority so strongly shaken by the revolution
of 1848," "a greater solicitude taken by the administration in the composition of the general jury lists," and "a better appreciation by the jurors of the
importance of their mission."[51]

But these were not the only reasons for the proportionate increase in
guilty verdicts: the fourth was "an intensification of the care with which
the prosecution and the examining magistrates have gathered the proofs of
cases submitted to the jury, and to take hold only of those facts whose criminal character is well-established."[52] If one judges by the rise in the number
of cases abandoned before trial, this movement had already begun during
the July Monarchy and progressed further during the Second Empire. The
proportion of all reported criminal cases filed by the *parquets* (public prosecutors' offices) without proceeding to prosecution rose continuously from
an annual average of only 13.1 percent in 1831–35 to about two-fifths or more
in the 1860s.[53] This suggests that more of the weaker cases that would have
ended in acquittal were abandoned before trial.

The preparation of stronger prosecution cases was probably assisted
by improvements in policing and evidence-gathering during the mid-
nineteenth century, especially during the Second Empire. The qualifications
of magistrates did not change, but the size and professionalism of police
forces increased considerably. In the towns, the *commissaires de police* (police
superintendents), who gathered proof of alleged crimes and misdemeanors
and reported on them to the *procureurs*, were hired and fired by the Ministry of the Interior (upon recommendation by the prefects) increasingly on
the basis of competence and efficiency, whereas almost exclusively political
considerations prevailed during the earliest years of the Restoration. The
number of *commissaires* was increased sharply during the Second Empire.
So was the number of uniformed *gendarmes*, who belonged technically to a
military corps under the minister of war but who performed civilian police
duties in the countryside. These policemen, considered the most professional in France, increasingly replaced the much less competent and poorly
paid *gardes champêtres* (field guards) in rural areas. In Paris, the number
of detectives who worked for the Sûreté (the agency which in the capital

investigated crimes) grew sharply during the July Monarchy and Second Empire.[54] Magistrates could provide better proofs to juries in part because there were now more professional police to gather those proofs.

There was, however, a fifth—and significant—reason for the proportionate increase in guilty verdicts, which the Ministry of Justice did not explicitly mention. This was the big rise in the percentage of recidivists (by that meaning all persons who had been previously convicted of a felony or misdemeanor) tried in the *cours d'assises*. By the middle of the nineteenth century, government officials and others were expressing concern about this rise, and the belief was growing that "habitual" criminals were responsible for most crimes.[55] Analysis of the *Compte général* indicates that the proportion of repeat offenders among all persons tried in the *cours d'assises* had already begun to increase before about 1850, from 15.8 percent in the years 1826–31 to 22.5 percent in 1832–47. But thereafter, the increase accelerated, to 30.3 percent in the years 1849–53 to 37.4 percent in 1854–70.[56]

Some of the rise was apparent rather than real, however. During the 1850s and through the first half of the 1860s, the Ministry of Justice repeatedly maintained that much of the increase in recidivism after 1850 was due to the introduction of the *casiers judiciaires*, or "rap sheets." These made it much easier for prosecutors to verify the criminal records of persons newly charged with crimes. A circular of 1850 required the establishment in the clerks' offices of the *tribunal civil* of every *arrondissement* in France of a *casier judiciaire* for every individual ever convicted of a felony or misdemeanor since 1830. All convictions were recorded immediately in their *casiers*, which were kept in their *arrondissement* of birth. The prosecutors' offices only needed to know the place of an accused person's birth to obtain easily, within anywhere from two to five days, a complete record of his or her previous convictions.[57]

This was very relevant to jury verdicts because judges regularly drew upon information from the *casiers judiciaires*, or any other information about the accused person's prior criminal record, in their *interrogatoires*.[58] The result was to prejudice strongly the jury against the accused recidivist, who in certain instances may have been convicted for having a bad character rather than for the facts of his or her most recent crime. Indeed, at least before 1870,[59] the strongest bias of juries was against accused persons with prior criminal records. The conviction rate for recidivists, which rose from 80 percent in 1826–31 to 88.5 percent in 1863–70, was (except in 1848 when the differential was even wider) about twenty to twenty-five percentage points higher than the conviction rate for first-time offenders, which rose from 55.9 percent in 1826–31 to 68.5 percent in 1863–70) (see Table 3.1). It seems that in

The Great Turning Point

TABLE 3.1. Convictions and Acquittals in the *Cours d'Assises* of Recidivists and Nonrecidivists, by Period

	RECIDIVISTS			NONRECIDIVISTS		
Years	Convicted	Acquitted	Total	Convicted	Acquitted	Total
1826–31	5,462	1,369	6,831	20,376	16,047	36,423
	(80.0%)	(20.0%)		(55.9%)	(44.1%)	
1832–47	22,712	4,357	27,069	54,569	38,620	93,189
	(83.9%)	(16.1%)		(58.6%)	(41.4%)	
1848	1,426	299	1,725	2,878	2,749	5,627
	(82.7%)	(17.3%)		(51.1%)	(48.9%)	
1849–53	9,002	1,822	10,824	14,608	10,237	24,845
	(83.2%)	(16.8%)		(58.8%)	(41.2%)	
1854–62	15,839	2,231	18,070	22,372	10,312	32,684
	(87.7%)	(12.3%)		(68.4%)	(31.6%)	
1863–70	12,174	1,582	13,756	14,094	6,475	20,569
	(88.5%)	(11.5%)		(68.5%)	(31.5%)	

Source: *Compte général*, 1826, Table 2, p. 3, and Tables 69–71, pp. 100–102; 1827, Table 2, p. 3, and Table 70, p. 98; 1828, Table 2, p. 3, and Table 76, p. 112; 1829, Table 2, p. 3, and Table 77, p. 114; 1830, Table 2, p. 3, and Table 69, p. 94; 1831, Table 2, p. 3, and Table 94, p. 157; 1832, Table 2, p. 3, and Table 96, p. 161; 1833, Table 2, p. 3, and Table 101, p. 169; 1834, Table 2, p. 3, and Table 98, p. 165; 1835, Table 2, p. 3, and Table 102, p. 171; 1836, Table 2, p. 3, and Table 111, pp. 182–83; 1837–38, Table 2, p. 3, and Table 103, p. 169; 1839–48, Table 2, p. 3, and Table 105, p. 171; 1849–50, Table 2, p. 3, and Table 106, p. 167; 1851, Table 2, p. 3, and Table 107, p. 167; 1852, Table 2, p. 3, and Table 109, p. 167; 1853, Table 2, p. 3, and Table 108, p. 169; 1854, Table 2, p. 3, and Table 110, p. 171; 1855, Table 2, p. 3, and Table 110, p. 174; 1856, Table 2, p. 3, and Table 110, p. 173; 1857, Table 2, p. 3, and Table 111, p. 174; 1858–59, Table 2, p. 3, and Table 109, p. 172; 1860, Table 2, p. 3, and Table 105, p. 168; 1861–62, Table 2, p. 5, and Table 105, p. 170; 1863, Table 2, p. 5, and Table 107, p. 173; 1864–69, Table 2, p. 5, and Table 104, p. 171; 1870, Table 2, p. 5, and Table 72, p. 139.

nineteenth-century France, as in eighteenth-century England, the character of the accused person often had a significant influence on the jury verdict, though in England the prior record of the defendant was not introduced during trial.[60] It is hard to believe that such a high proportion of recidivists were really guilty and that such a high proportion of nonrecidivists were really innocent.

The big increase in the percentage of recidivists among accused persons therefore contributed to the rise in overall convictions. A statistical analysis that takes into account the increase in the conviction rate for all persons tried in the *cours d'assises* and the increase in the proportion of recidivists among them and among all those convicted shows that about four-tenths of the rise in the conviction rate from 1832–47 to 1854–70 was due to the increase in recidivism.[61]

One effect of recidivism that the Ministry of Justice did mention explicitly had to do with the differential between conviction rates for theft and violent crimes. By the 1860s, the ministry had developed an alternative to the class bias explanation for this differential. Among the defendants tried in the *cours d'assises*, a significantly higher proportion of those charged with theft had previously been convicted of a felony or misdemeanor than was the case with those charged with violent crimes.[62] Repeatedly, down into the early 1900s, the ministry insisted that this was the major reason why conviction rates for theft were considerably higher than conviction rates for violent crimes.[63] The ministry's explanation for the gap was that jurors tended to see thieves as "habitual" criminals, whereas violent crimes were frequently impulsive acts committed by otherwise law-abiding people who were deserving of greater leniency.[64]

The recidivism thesis of the Ministry of Justice appears to offer a logical alternative to the class bias theory of jury behavior in nineteenth-century France. Yet in general it is scarcely supported by the evidence. Recidivists had much higher conviction rates than nonrecidivists, but the increase was roughly proportionate for every type of crime. Therefore, when recidivists are excluded from the figures, the differentials between conviction rates for theft and conviction rates for most violent crimes narrowed only slightly (by a few percentage points) from the overall conviction rates (see Table 3.2).

Of some significance, however, was the fact that by the Second Empire era, this narrowing was enough almost to erase the difference in conviction rates between theft and unpremeditated murder and entirely erase it between theft and *assassinat*. From 1826 through 1831, the differential between conviction rates for nonrecidivists accused of theft and nonrecidivists accused of *meurtre* was quite large (20.4 percentage points). But again, the law on extenuating circumstances appears to have made a real difference: by 1854–62, the gap had declined to 3.2 points. The conviction rate for nonrecidivists accused of *assassinat* from 1826 through 1831 was 8.3 percentage points lower than for nonrecidivists accused of theft, but by 1854–62, first-time offenders accused of theft and premeditated murder for the first time had identical conviction rates. From 1863 through 1870, the rate was actually slightly higher for *assassinat* than for *vol qualifié* (see Table 3.2).

In addition to recidivists and premeditated murderers, juries had become increasingly tough on child molesters by the Second Empire period. Conviction rates for persons accused of sex crimes against children almost

The Great Turning Point

equaled conviction rates for recidivists. In fact, jury verdicts for crimes of sexual violence reflected both changes in social mores and the persistence of older attitudes. In child molestation cases, jurors and the authorities shared in a new consensus on the need to be tough, at least when it came to convicting the alleged culprits. On the other hand, older attitudes of blaming the victim still remained quite prevalent in the trial of crimes of sexual violence against adults.

By the middle of the nineteenth century, the authorities in France had abandoned the relative indifference toward child molestation that had prevailed in the eighteenth century and in the first decades of the nineteenth.[65] The new attitude appears to have been connected to a growing movement to protect children—now seen as helpless and vulnerable beings with special needs rather than as miniature adults—from exploitation and abuse.[66] In the Napoleonic criminal code of 1810, the rape and violent indecent assault of children (defined as persons under the age of fifteen) was more harshly punished than the rape and indecent assault of adults.[67] But it was not until 1832 that the Parliament revised the *Code pénal* to criminalize all nonviolent sexual encounters with children under a certain age, in this case eleven. In 1863, the law was toughened to include all children under the age of thirteen.[68]

The crackdown on child sexual abuse—especially the new laws of 1832 and 1863—appears to have been primarily responsible for the huge rise in the number of persons tried for the rape and indecent assault of minors under the age of fifteen, from an annual average of 133 (or 4.2 per million population) in the years 1825–30 to 766 (or 20.5 per million population) from 1861 through 1865.[69] In fact, prosecutions for child molestation reached their maximum between 1850 and 1880.[70] The conservatives and clericals who dominated the regimes of the Second Empire and the early Third Republic governments of 1871–79 were especially concerned with child prostitution and with the need to protect children from this scourge.[71] In such an atmosphere, the *procureurs* must have felt increased pressure to bring cases of child molestation to justice.

Juries of the Second Empire era appear to have strongly endorsed the authorities' increasingly vigorous repression of child molestation, perhaps in part because so many jurors were *notables* and chosen, as much as possible, because they appeared sympathetic to the government's moral and law-and-order priorities. The conviction rate for the rape and indecent assault of minors (violent and nonviolent cases combined) rose from 62.6 percent in the era from 1825 through 1831 to 83.5 percent in the years 1855–62.[72] From 1855 (when the *Compte général*'s tables first distinguished nonviolent

TABLE 3.2. Convictions and Acquittals in the *Cours d'Assises* of All People and Nonrecidivists for Theft and Violent Crimes, by Period

1826–31

Crime	ALL PERSONS			NONRECIDIVISTS		
	Convicted	*Acquitted*	*Total*	*Convicted*	*Acquitted*	*Total*
Theft	18,754 (69.1%)	8,406 (30.9%)	27,160	14,123 (65.4%)	7,476 (34.6%)	21,599
Unpremeditated murder	824 (46.9%)	934 (53.1%)	1,758	740 (45.0%)	904 (55.0%)	1,644
Premeditated murder	900 (58.8%)	630 (41.2%)	1,530	803 (57.1%)	603 (42.9%)	1,406
Assaults	1,130 (44.7%)	1,397 (55.3%)	2,527	974 (42.3%)	1,329 (57.7%)	2,303

1832–47

Crime	ALL PERSONS			NONRECIDIVISTS		
	Convicted	*Acquitted*	*Total*	*Convicted*	*Acquitted*	*Total*
Theft	48,650 (73.5%)	17,525 (26.5%)	66,175	31,101 (67.4%)	15,050 (32.6%)	46,151
Unpremeditated murder	2,064 (62.1%)	1,258 (37.9%)	3,322	1,730 (59.6%)	1,173 (40.4%)	2,903
Premeditated murder	3,276 (68.9%)	1,479 (31.1%)	4,755	2,526 (65.3%)	1,343 (34.7%)	3,869
Manslaughter[a]	1,225 (49.4%)	1,256 (50.6%)	2,418	1,081 (47.6%)	1,189 (52.4%)	2,270
Assaults	3,060 (51.5%)	2,876 (48.5%)	5,936	2,412 (47.7%)	2,640 (52.3%)	5,052

1848–53

Crime	ALL PERSONS			NONRECIDIVISTS		
	Convicted	*Acquitted*	*Total*	*Convicted*	*Acquitted*	*Total*
Theft	14,598 (76.8%)	4,412 (23.2%)	19,010	7,756 (68.2%)	3,619 (31.8%)	11,375
Unpremeditated murder	955 (63.7%)	544 (36.3%)	1,499	715 (63.8%)	405 (36.2%)	1,120
Premeditated murder	1,357 (68.6%)	622 (31.4%)	1,979	924 (62.6%)	553 (37.4%)	1,477
Manslaughter	483 (51.2%)	460 (48.8%)	943	401 (48.1%)	433 (51.9%)	834
Assaults	991 (52.8%)	886 (47.2%)	1,877	706 (49.4%)	722 (50.6%)	1,428

Crime	ALL PERSONS			NONRECIDIVISTS		
	Convicted	Acquitted	Total	Convicted	Acquitted	Total
Theft	18,416	3,613	22,029	8,698	2,754	11,452
	(83.6%)	(16.4%)		(76.0%)	(24.0%)	
Unpremeditated murder	778	234	1,012	507	189	696
	(76.9%)	(23.1%)		(72.8%)	(27.2%)	
Premeditated murder	1,724	408	2,132	995	315	1,310
	(80.9%)	(19.1%)		(76.0%)	(24.0%)	
Manslaughter	537	308	845	406	274	680
	(63.6%)	(36.4%)		(59.7%)	(40.3%)	
Assaults	804	365	1,169	506	301	807
	(68.8%)	(31.2%)		(62.7%)	(37.3%)	

1863–70

Crime	ALL PERSONS			NONRECIDIVISTS		
	Convicted	Acquitted	Total	Convicted	Acquitted	Total
Theft	11,180	1,952	13,132	4,218	1,447	5,665
	(85.1%)	(14.9%)		(74.5%)	(25.5%)	
Unpremeditated murder	802	278	1,080	466	220	686
	(74.3%)	(25.7%)		(67.9%)	(32.1%)	
Premeditated murder	1,441	372	1,813	838	283	1,121
	(79.5%)	(20.5%)		(74.8%)	(25.2%)	
Manslaughter	653	400	1,053	475	352	827
	(62.0%)	(38.0%)		(57.4%)	(42.6%)	
Assaults	380	141	521	190	107	297
	(72.9%)	(27.1%)		(64.0%)	(36.0%)	

Source: *Compte général*, 1826, Tables 1–2, pp. 2–3, and Tables 69–71, pp. 100–102; 1827, Tables 1–2, pp. 2–3, and Tables 72–75, pp. 104–7; 1828, Tables 1–2, pp. 2–3, and Tables 87–89, pp. 130–32; 1829, Tables 1–2, pp. 2–3, and Tables 88–90, pp. 133–35; 1830, Tables 1–2, pp. 2–3, and Table 66, pp. 108–9; 1831, Tables 1–2, pp. 2–3, and Table 101, pp. 168–69; 1832, Tables 1–2, pp. 2–3, and Table 103, pp. 172–73; 1833, Tables 1–2, pp. 2–3, and Table 108, pp. 180–81; 1834, Tables 1–2, pp. 2–3, and Table 105, pp. 176–77; 1835, Tables 1–2, pp. 2–3, and Table 109, pp. 182–83; 1836, Tables 1–2, pp. 2–3, and Table 111, pp. 182–83; 1837–38, Tables 1–2, pp. 2–3, and Table 110, pp. 180–81; 1839–48, Tables 1–2, pp. 2–3, and Table 112, pp. 182–83; 1849–50, Tables 1–2, pp. 2–3, and Table 113, pp. 176–77; 1851, Tables 1–2, pp. 2–3, and Table 114, pp. 176–77; 1852–53, Tables 1–2, pp. 2–3, and Table 109, pp. 170–73; 1854, Tables 1–2, pp. 2–3, and Table 111, pp. 172–75; 1855, Tables 1–2, pp. 2–3, and Table 109, pp. 170–73; 1856–57, Tables 1–2, pp. 2–3, and Table 110, pp. 170–73; 1858–59, Tables 1–2, pp. 2–3, and Table 108, pp. 168–71; 1860, Tables 1–2, pp. 2–3, and Table 104, pp. 164–67; 1861–62, Tables 1–2, pp. 4–5, and Table 104, pp. 166–69; 1863, Tables 1–2, pp. 4–5, and Table 107, pp. 172–73; 1864–69, Tables 1–2, pp. 4–5, and Table 104, pp. 170–71; 1870, Tables 1–2, pp. 4–5, and Table 72, pp. 138–39.

[a] Before 1832, manslaughter was classed with unpremeditated murder.

indecent assault of children from the violent cases) to 1870, about 85 percent of all persons tried for the violent or aggravated rape and indecent assault of children were convicted, and an only slightly smaller percentage of those charged with nonviolent molestation were found guilty.[73] In fact, from 1832 on, and down through the early twentieth century, conviction rates for the violent or aggravated rape and indecent assault of children under the age of fifteen about equaled or slightly exceeded conviction rates for theft. Prosecutors and jurymen appear to have shared in a consensus harshly condemning child molestation.

But attitudes toward crimes of sexual violence against adults changed much more slowly. Far fewer such cases were brought to trial, and although the conviction rate rose after 1832, in the Second Empire period it remained approximately twenty percentage points lower than the rate for the violent or aggravated indecent assault of children under the age of fifteen.[74] What is more, extenuating circumstances were found for a significantly higher percentage of persons convicted of crimes of sexual violence against adults than was the case with condemned violent child molesters.[75] Jurors remained suspicious of the adult victims of sex crimes, and prosecution after prosecution foundered on the issue of consent. Actual violence, not just lack of consent, had to be proven in adult rape cases. Moreover, for a reasonable chance of conviction in cases of the rape of adults, the criminal acts had to occur in public and in the presence of witnesses; otherwise, juries were likely to acquit, even when confronted by proof of violence. Jurors frequently doubted the victims, who were often suspected of having consented. This attitude was supplemented by an old belief, still common in the nineteenth century even among experts of legal medicine, that one man acting alone cannot succeed in raping a woman. In other instances, jurors suspected the victims because they appeared to have been too "free" sexually. The few cases brought to trial of the rape of adult women committed in private generally ended in acquittal. As one scholar puts it, "There was a gulf between the letter of the law and the strength of custom."[76]

In fact, juries were still seen by the government as not strict enough in enforcing the letter of the law when it came to convicting persons tried for crimes in general, however tough they may have become on recidivists, assassins, and child molesters. The overall acquittal rate for persons tried in the *cours d'assises* (24.2 percent from 1854 through 1870), though lower than in the past, still far exceeded the acquittal rate of less than 10 percent for all persons tried (the *Compte général's* figures made no distinction between true misdemeanors and serious offenses removed from jury trial) in the *tribunaux correctionnels* (see Tables 2.1 and 2.2). Moreover, juries became

The Great Turning Point

more lenient toward those they found guilty: findings of extenuating circumstances among all persons convicted of *crimes* rose from 69.3 percent in 1849–53 to 73.3 percent in 1854–70.[77] Therefore, the panels still exhibited a degree of independence from the government: in about one-fourth of the cases they tried, juries did not buy the arguments for conviction presented by the public prosecutors. What is more, the panels continued to push the justice system toward greater and greater leniency in punishment.

The government of the Second Empire responded to the continued "indulgence" of the juries by resorting to correctionalization on a greater scale than had any previous regime. The practice also furthered the regime's goal of increasing the powers of magistrates at the expense of juries.[78] As a consequence, for the first time, correctionalization had a significant effect on the number of jury trials, which declined more sharply during the Second Empire than in any other period. This meant many more convictions, though at the price of still lesser punishments.[79]

The resort to correctionalization was facilitated by the law of July 17, 1856, which abolished the *chambre du conseil*, the three-member panel that included two judges from the nearest lower tribunal who, along with the *juge d'instruction*, had to agree with the latter's findings before a case was sent on to the *chambre des mises en accusation*. Henceforth, the *juge d'instruction* alone exercised the powers formerly reserved to the chamber.[80]

The mid-1850s marked the turning point in the correctionalization movement. From 1825 through 1854, the *cours d'assises* tried an average of more than 7,000 persons each year. But from 1855 through 1862, the figure dropped to 5,400 (see Table 2.6). Contemporaries claimed the decline was due primarily to correctionalization and not to a decrease in serious crimes.[81]

The Ministry of Justice justified correctionalization by noting that the juries themselves, either through finding extenuating circumstances or through convicting defendants accused of felonies of misdemeanors only, had punished many persons tried for *crimes* with mere *peines correctionnelles*.[82] As already noted, such sentences increased sharply following the passage of the 1832 law on extenuating circumstances. It is true that the trend was slightly reversed after the Revolution of 1848, despite the continued rise in findings of extenuating circumstances (see Table 2.3). This can be explained by the fact that the proportion of misdemeanor verdicts among all cases resulting in convictions in the *cours d'assises* continued to decline sharply.[83] But the magistrates probably contributed to this trend by removing from the *cours d'assises* more of the cases likely to result in jury downcharging.

The Great Turning Point

As the less serious felonies were removed from trial in the *cours d'assises*, findings of extenuating circumstances increasingly benefited those convicted of the most harshly punished crimes. Despite the abolition of the death penalty for political felonies in 1848, juries continued to find extenuating circumstances for an increasing proportion of persons they convicted of capital crimes. The partial correctionalization of infanticide in 1863 did not stop the rise, which, in fact, accelerated: from that date through 1870, juries found extenuating circumstances for 95.0 percent of all persons they convicted of capital crimes.[84] Largely as a result, the number of death sentences dropped significantly from an average of forty-eight per year in 1832–47 to sixteen in 1863–70.[85] The jurors of the Second Empire may have been more conservative than those of the Second Republic, but they were even less disposed to impose the death penalty. This may, in fact, have had something to do with the rise in the conviction rate for capital crimes, which might have left more residual doubts among jurors about the guilt of the persons they convicted; they perhaps drew back at the thought of sending to the guillotine people who could have been innocent. Here the fear of wrongful execution, which became so strong in the nineteenth century, must have influenced jurors.

For persons convicted of infanticide, whether their guilt was doubtful or not, the death penalty was no longer carried out at all after 1860. Jury verdicts were not the only reason, however. The trend toward finding extenuating circumstances in place of acquittals and misdemeanor verdicts in order to achieve mercy in punishment for persons charged with infanticide continued after the July Monarchy. By the Second Empire period, extenuating circumstances were found for nearly all persons (98 to almost 100 percent) convicted of infanticide proper—the highest rate among all capital crimes.[86] But the government's executive branch went even further by commuting the sentence of every person condemned to death for infanticide after 1860, though formal abolition of the death penalty for the crime did not occur until 1901.[87] It is not clear whether jurymen were aware of the commutations, but the fact that juries could now guarantee the lives of persons convicted of infanticide by finding extenuating circumstances seems to have contributed significantly to the rise in the conviction rate for the crime, from barely half of those tried in 1825–31 to more than two-thirds in 1854–70.[88]

Yet it had become very evident by the Second Empire era that the 1832 law on extenuating circumstances had had a paradoxical effect on punishments for infanticide. It meant a sharp decline in the most severe sentences of death and hard labor for life, but also a sharp decline in the most lenient sentences of five years' imprisonment or less. This was no doubt due mainly to the fact that persons tried for infanticide were now much less often convicted of lesser crimes. Juries in infanticide cases were no longer confronted with the stark choices between death with an uncertain chance of hard labor for life on one hand and a mere misdemeanor penalty or outright acquittal on the other. The result was to push punishments for infanticide into a middle range. This was five to twenty years of hard labor. Before 1832, it was not an option for infanticide convictions, but by the Second Empire era, it had become the penalty for the overwhelming majority of persons found guilty in trials for the crime.[89]

These figures also show that when it came to punishment for infanticide, the judges were in most instances even more lenient than the juries. The law of 1832 required the judges to lower the penalty by one degree when a jury found extenuating circumstances. For infanticide convictions, this meant hard labor for life in place of the death penalty. But for most infanticide convictions, the judges of the *cours d'assises* exercised their option of lowering the penalty by two degrees, to a term of five to twenty years of hard labor. It is possible, however, that this penalty was often imposed after secret or unofficial discussions between the *présidents* of the *cours d'assises* and the juries regarding punishments. In any case, for several decades (the trend continued into the 1870s), a midlevel standard of punishment for persons convicted of infanticide arose from the decisions of juries and judges.

But the sharp decline in misdemeanor penalties for infanticide was exceptional: by the Second Empire era, nearly half of all persons convicted in the *cours d'assises* still received *peines correctionnelles*. This provided the authorities with evidence to argue in favor of the further correctionalization of felonies. As the Ministry of Justice pointed out several times, misdemeanor penalties were handed down for heavy majorities of persons convicted of assault resulting in the incapacity of the victim to work for more than twenty days, *rébellion*, misappropriation of public funds, bribery, perjury, and subornation and for those cases of theft and indecent assault that would have been punished by *réclusion* (more than five years' imprisonment) had the juries rejected extenuating circumstances. Since the panels of citizen-judges had determined that such crimes should in most instances be punished as misdemeanors, the ministry maintained that it would be more advantageous or fitting that they be tried in the *tribunaux correctionnels*.[90] Therefore, magistrates who correctionalized these crimes had shown a "wise foresight," so long as the procedure was carried out with "great reserve."[91] To the government, it made sense to correctionalize such crimes; since they were in most cases punished by misdemeanor penalties, much time and expense (and chances of acquittal) could be avoided by having them tried in the *tribunaux correctionnels* rather than in the *cours d'assises*.

The regime's magistrates were especially keen on using the process of extralegal correctionalization to remove from the juries' jurisdiction most cases of violence against the agents of public authority, cases that had frequently ended in acquittal and that were rarely punished other than by *peines correctionnelles*.[92] Therefore, the number of persons tried for crimes against public order (*rébellion* and assaults resulting in the shedding of the blood of state officials or agents of public authority) dropped precipitously between 1842 and 1862.[93]

Extralegal correctionalization by magistrates was also frequently carried out in cases of aggravated theft. This again occurred following a sharp increase in *peines correctionnelles* for persons convicted of this crime in the *cours d'assises*. From 1825 through 1831, just under two-fifths of persons convicted of theft by the juries received punishments of five years or less in prison. The figure rose very considerably to more than three-fifths in 1832–47.[94] Magistrates responded by trying many such cases in the *tribunaux correctionnels*. Largely as a result, the number of persons tried for theft in the *cours d'assises* dropped from an average of well over four thousand per year before 1842 to only a little more than two thousand in 1855–62.[95]

According to the Ministry of Justice, this decrease was due to some extent to a decline in thefts carried out with violence, but it was also due to correctionalization, an "incontestable" cause of the decline at a time when theft, as measured by the number of cases tried in the *tribunaux correctionnels*, was actually increasing sharply in France. The ministry applauded the correctionalization of theft cases as a "proof of the prudent reserve of the magistrates."[96] Probably as a result of the removal of less serious thefts from the jurisdiction of the *cours d'assises*, the proportion of thieves convicted in these courts who were punished by *peines correctionnelles* declined to 50.4 percent in 1854–62.[97]

The correctionalization of crimes following lenient jury verdicts was most evident in cases of assault resulting in the incapacity of the victim to work for more than twenty days. More than half of those tried for this offense in the *cours d'assises* were acquitted outright from 1832 through 1853.[98] Among those found guilty, most either benefited from findings of extenuating circumstances or were convicted of misdemeanors. As a result, nine-tenths of the convicts received only *peines correctionnelles*.[99] From 1854 through 1862, the acquittal rate for the crime dropped to 37.7 percent but still remained well above the acquittal rate for all felonies. The proportion of those convicted who were sentenced to *peines correctionnelles* declined only slightly.[100]

Before 1863, magistrates reacted to this situation by engaging in the extralegal correctionalization of the crime. Here, they were in fact following the precedent established by juries themselves. From 1827 through 1831, in seven of every ten cases resulting in conviction, juries reduced the charge of felony assault to misdemeanor assault. This figure declined to less than one-third in 1854–63 but still remained substantial.[101] The decrease was no doubt in part due to the law on extenuating circumstances, but it was also evidently due to the magistrates' decisions to remove more and more of the less serious felony assault cases from jury trial and transfer them to the *tribunaux correctionnels*. They were therefore able to avoid the time and expense of jury trial (and the higher chances of acquittal) for cases that frequently ended in conviction on misdemeanor charges anyway or in misdemeanor punishments. This was probably the primary reason why the number of persons tried in the *cours d'assises* for assault resulting in the victim's incapacity to work for more than twenty days dropped dramatically after 1842.[102]

In 1863, Minister of Justice Claude Delangle finally sought to legalize what juries and magistrates had already done in respect to this crime and to certain others by introducing a bill officially reducing a number of *crimes* to *délits*. After again noting that those convicted of certain felonies were almost always punished with misdemeanor penalties, he stated: "These outcomes must have my special attention; they prove that to the eyes of the jury these criminal acts have lost the character of *crimes* and merit classification among the simple *délits*. In response to this information . . . I have prepared a bill, now under consideration in the *Corps législatif*, which will submit these crimes to correctional jurisdiction in place of the *cours d'assises*. The repression will thus be more lenient and more rapid."[103] Delangle's proposal became the law of May 13, 1863. It downgraded from *crimes* to *délits* several types of offenses: assault resulting in the victim's incapacity to work for more than twenty days (henceforth only attacks on parents and attacks resulting in the victim's permanent disability remained felonies), several types of official corruption, perjury in correctional cases, and threats. The same law facilitated the legal correctionalization of some infanticide cases by creating the new misdemeanor of *suppression d'enfant* (concealment of birth), which allowed prosecutors and *juges d'instruction* to defer to the *tribunaux correctionnels* infanticide accusations when it could not be proven clearly that the infants had been born alive.[104] The passage of the 1863 correctionalization law was followed by a further drop in the number of persons tried in the *cours d'assises* (see Table 2.6).

This period thus witnessed an important step forward in the restriction of the right of jury trial for accused persons. The significant new power over punishment granted to juries by the 1832 law on extenuating circumstances eventually proved to be a double-edged sword. The juries' verdicts after the passage of the law resulted in a considerable reduction of penalties. However, the fact that, largely as a result, so many persons tried for certain crimes in the *cours d'assises* received only misdemeanor sentences provided the government with justification for removing such crimes from jury trial. Once again, the juries had a significant effect on punishment, and the law was eventually rewritten to accommodate their ideas of appropriate punishment, as had occurred in 1810, 1824, and 1832. But the reform of 1863 also took away some of the power of the juries by officially removing certain crimes from their jurisdiction, and it thus further restricted the right of jury trial for accused persons. The succeeding, more democratic Third Republic regime, far from reversing this process, would take it even further.

chapter four

THE JURIES OF THE REPUBLIC, 1870–1914

Between the proclamation of the Third Republic in 1870 and the outbreak of World War I in 1914, a crucial shift began in regard to liberal support of the jury system. During the earliest years of the Third Republic, liberals sought to defend and strengthen the jury as a counter to a conservative judiciary they distrusted. Once Republicans gained control of the nation's justice system following their purge of the judiciary in the years around 1880, the long trend toward higher conviction rates was reversed. For a variety of reasons—structural, political, cultural, and above all intellectual—acquittals by Republican-dominated juries increased markedly. A more professional but still politicized magistrature responded to this trend by engaging in a new and intensified round of criticism of the jury system and by doing more than ever to undermine it. Ironically, new criminological theories that appear to have influenced juries to become more lenient were used against the panels by its critics in favor of a more "scientific" fact-finding process. For this reason and others, Republicans began to weaken in their defense of the jury system. The result was a crisis of the jury that would not be resolved until after 1914.

Liberal defense of the jury system was still very evident during the first years of the Third Republic. This was closely connected to the political controversies of an era when Republicans were engaged in a bitter struggle with monarchists. The liberals' old distrust of the judiciary had been intensified by Louis-Napoleon Bonaparte's success in making the magistracy an instrument of his authoritarian rule. To restore to the juries the degree of independence, power, and relatively democratic composition they had had before the Second Empire was therefore seen as necessary to counter the power of the judiciary.

This Republicans quickly moved to do following Napoleon III's defeat at Sedan and his overthrow in September 1870. Toward the end of the Second Empire, men of the Republican Left and of the liberal center called for the restoration of the right of trial by jury for those accused of political and press offenses.[1] They got their way when the provisional Government of National Defense enacted a decree returning jurisdiction over *délits politiques et de presse* to the juries, a decree confirmed by a law of April 1871.[2]

The provisional government also, in October 1870, issued a decree repealing the Second Empire's law of June 4, 1853, on the composition of the jury because it was "not in harmony with the principles of republican government," and the relatively democratic law of August 7, 1848, was reinstated.[3] The new regime sought further to strengthen the juries when its justice minister, the Jacobin Adolphe Cremieux, in January 1871 issued an injunction against correctionalization.[4]

But the election of a conservative National Assembly in February 1871 was followed by actions to weaken the juries again. In April 1871, Cremieux's successor as minister of justice, Jules Dufaure, overturned his predecessor's injunction against correctionalization and gave an order that finally and permanently authorized the practice.[5]

The experiences of the Paris Commune of 1871, which further embittered divisions between Left and Right, were followed by at least one other significant conservative move against the jury system. The anxiety of the men of order about the menace of radicalism played a major role in the passage in 1872 of a new, more restrictive law on the composition of the juries. The proposed law was introduced in the National Assembly on May 30, 1872, by Minister of Justice Dufaure, who explicitly rejected the principle that jury duty was a right of the citizen. Rather, it was a public function that should be confined to those with "an absolute independence and a sufficient intelligence."[6] Such jurors could be picked by giving the judiciary a much greater role in the selection of persons to be inscribed on the annual jury lists. In place of the existing system of jury list formation by elected officials almost exclusively, the task was now to be divided between politicians and judges, with the latter being given a significant veto power over the choices of the former.

This was to be done by creating two jury commissions in place of one. The cantonal commissions would continue to be dominated by the mayors of the communes, who from 1871 on were elected officials. But above these, new *arrondissement* commissions dominated by judges (the *président* of the *tribunal civil* and the *arrondissement's juges de paix*, who would have a one-vote majority over elected *conseillers* from every canton) would revise the primary jury lists drawn up by the cantonal commissions. The second commissions would thereby correct the "errors" of the first and see to it that the political preferences of the elected officials did not influence the formation of the jury lists. Moreover, according to restrictions reintroduced from the law of 1853, the jurors selected could never include persons who had ever been condemned to imprisonment for "outrage to public and religious morality, attack against the principle of property and the rights of the family." Those imprisoned for other *délits politiques et de presse* would be excluded for five years. The completed *arrondissement* lists were then collated by the premier president of the *cour d'appel* or the president of the *tribunal chef-lieu d'assises* (the civil tribunal that met in the same town as the departmental *cour d'assises*) to form the departmental list of one juror per five hundred inhabitants.[7]

The introduction of the proposed law touched off a sharp debate in the National Assembly. It was a debate that perhaps illustrated better than any other of the nineteenth century the differences between liberals and conservatives over the issues of who should serve on juries and who should choose the jurors. The bill had the strong support of conservatives. Their arguments in its favor were essentially summarized by Albert Desjardins, who presented to the National Assembly the report of the commission charged with examining the proposed law. Desjardins claimed that the resurrected law of 1848 had resulted in a more defective administration of justice. It had led to an increase in the number of jurors who were unenlightened and lacking in firmness. This decline in the quality of jurors grew out of the "unfortunate" principle, embodied in the law of 1848, that jury duty was the right of every Frenchman, "aged thirty, enjoying civil and political rights."[8] Rather, in the interest of the best possible administration of justice, Desjardins declared, jury duty should be restricted only to those who by their intelligence and firmness are capable of fulfilling their functions. One commission would repair the errors of the other "to obtain a good jury."[9] Desjardins made his contentions in spite of the fact that the reinstatement of the law of August 7, 1848, had resulted in only a slight democratization of the juries[10] and hardly any less firmness on their part toward accused persons, at least as measured by conviction rates for felonies (see Table 2.1).

These facts were pointed out by the liberals who opposed the proposed law. Their criticisms were focused on two points: (1) the bill would give too much power in the drawing up of the jury lists to a conservative judiciary the liberals distrusted as biased and whose behavior during the Second Empire seemed to prove this bias, and (2) it was too restrictive in respect to the number of citizens who could serve on juries and in its exclusion of political offenders from the panels. The Right spoke as if the judiciary was impartial and nonpolitical. The Left held that this assumption was wrong.

Several of the liberal deputies pointed out, for instance, that the *juges de paix*, who would now have a much larger role on the jury commissions, were removable magistrates whose advancement to higher judicial offices was dependent on the *présidents* of the *tribunaux civils* and the *procureurs de la République* (district attorneys). They were therefore the "docile" instruments of the prosecution magistrates, and the latter would thereby gain control over the formation of the jury lists, as they had done during the Second Empire. The preponderance of removable magistrates on the jury commissions would create the suspicion that the juries were under government control, and the panels would therefore lose popular support whenever they convicted political offenders.[11]

When Dufaure responded to these criticisms by pointing out that in England and Belgium, magistrates (the sheriffs in the former country and the presidents of the tribunals in the latter) drew up jury lists without encountering suspicion,[12] M. Lepère countered by claiming that their situation could not be compared to the situation of magistrates in France. In England and Belgium, political trials scarcely occurred, and the press was free. Therefore, magistrates were not preoccupied by political considerations when they formed the jury lists. But in France, juries tried political offenders, and most magistrates were conservatives who would interpret the proposed law in such a way as to ensure that only members of the *classes dirigeantes* (ruling classes) would be placed on juries.[13]

This concern was related to the other major criticism by deputies opposed to the bill—that it was too restrictive in respect to those who might serve on juries. Several deputies favored retention of the law of 1848 because jury service was a right and juries must reflect "the judgment of the country" free from the prejudices of one class.[14] Some deputies objected to the exclusion of political offenders from the panels. According to Charles Boysset, the stipulation that persons convicted of *délits politiques et de presse* be barred from jury service for five years following the expiration of their penalty would have resulted in the temporary exclusion of Chateaubriand, Armand Carrel, Lamennais, and other great writers. In addition, Boysset opposed the permanent exclusion of those convicted of "outrage to public and religious morality," for this was really a political crime and was vaguely defined.[15] Other deputies added that the government proposed the new law for political reasons, for while the reinstatement of the law of 1848 had resulted in almost no lowering of the conviction rate for ordinary crimes, the majority of political offenders had been acquitted.[16]

Liberals also protested that the proposed law restricted jury service to a tiny elite. This was because so few citizens (one per five hundred people as opposed to one per two hundred under the law of 1848) would be placed on the annual jury lists. Many men capable of jury service would be excluded, and magistrates would have plenty of opportunities to keep out those whose opinions were suspect.[17] The deputies on the Right answered these objections by repeating their contention that many citizens were too ignorant or too incapable of being jurors and that the law of 1848 had allowed political influences to intrude in the formation of the jury lists.[18] The conservatives prevailed, for on November 21, 1872, the proposed jury law was approved by the National Assembly.[19]

The liberals in the National Assembly had argued strenuously against the new law, for they saw it as an attempt to pack the juries with supporters of the conservative government. When Dufaure consulted the presidents of the *cours d'assises* and the *procureurs généraux* before introducing his proposal, he was not communicating with a disinterested party: the magistrates informed him of the "abuses" in the formation of the jury lists under the restored law of 1848.[20] The Left's traditional distrust of the magistrates who would now play such an important role in the inscription of persons on the jury lists was greatly reinforced by the still fresh memories of the Second Empire, when the government used the judiciary to establish authoritarian rule and select jurors favorable to the regime. Many of the Second Empire's magistrates were still at their posts, and liberals were skeptical of conservative claims that they would select jurors on an impartial basis.

But the liberals' protests against the undemocratic provisions of the jury law of 1872 were really limited in scope. The deputies of the Left protested the exclusion of men from the juries for primarily political reasons, not for reasons of social class. Of concern to them was the fact that the new law would prevent a Chateaubriand or a Lamennais from serving, not that it continued the virtual exclusion of the poor from jury duty.[21]

The liberals were right, however, to express concern that the law of 1872 would result in the central government's interference in the selection of jurors. On November 24, 1872—only four days after the National Assembly's passage of the law—the Ministry of Justice issued to the *juges de paix* a circular reminiscent of those of the Second Empire: "I count on you, M. Juge de Paix, to make the commission meeting under your presidency understand how important it is to inscribe, even on the preparatory list, only citizens who, by a proven morality, an independent and firm character, and a sufficiently developed intelligence, are capable of properly fulfilling the high mission of justice which society confides in them."[22]

During the period from 1873 through 1879, when the conservative government of "moral order" controlled the judiciary, such instructions seem to have had some modest impact. The conviction rate for felonies rose from 74.8 percent in 1871–72 to 79.4 percent in 1873–79. The latter was the highest rate ever recorded before the 1940s (see Table 2.1). The Ministry of Justice

The Juries of the Republic

expressed satisfaction with the "intelligent firmness" of the juries of the period and attributed at least part of it to the law of 1872.[23]

But despite the apparent fears of the liberals, the law of 1872 brought about almost no decline in the acquittal rate for persons tried by juries for *délits politiques et de presse*.[24] Once again, changes in the rules governing the selection of jurors scarcely altered their proclivity to acquit persons accused of political and press offenses.

The government of "moral order" responded to this proclivity by doing what regimes before it had done: removing certain cases from jury trial. In 1875, the Parliament passed a law making important exceptions to the act of 1871 guaranteeing jury trial for persons accused of *délits politiques et de presse*. Those charged with offenses against the president or either chamber of the Parliament or with verbal defamation of a civil servant were now to be tried in the *tribunaux correctionnels*.[25] The law was followed by a sharp drop in the number of persons tried by the *cours d'assises* for *délits politiques et de presse*, though the acquittal rate for the small number of cases still heard by juries remained virtually the same.[26]

However, the resignation of the conservative president Marshal Mac-Mahon in January 1879 inaugurated a new era in the history of the French justice system. The Republicans, who had already gained control of both houses of the Parliament, now began to construct a liberal democratic regime.[27] As in the past, this meant a strengthening of the jury system, at least during the first years of the "république aux républicains." The law of 1881 on the liberty of the press restored to the *cours d'assises* jurisdiction over all *délits politiques et de presse*, except some infractions relative to administrative regulation, outrages against good morals through designs, the defamation of private individuals, and the publication of penal proceedings.[28] In the same year, the Parliament passed a law abolishing the *résumé*, or summing up of the case by the *président* of the *cour d'assises* at the end of the trial, because it gave the judge too much of an opportunity to express his opinions and sway the jury.[29] According to Françoise Lombard, however, this law was motivated more by the desire of Republicans to limit the influence of a judiciary they distrusted than by a desire to affirm the power and independence of juries.[30]

Defense of the jury system was particularly strong among the deputies of the Republican Left, who still saw it as a great democratic institution.[31] In 1881, Léon Gambetta delivered an electoral speech in which he protested against correctionalization and called for its reversal.[32] Gambetta, a lawyer and one of the founders of the Third Republic, gave this speech at a time when Republicans were consolidating their recently acquired power but still encountered a judiciary dominated by conservatives. In this political context, not only the personnel of the judiciary but also its power were at issue.[33] A protest against correctionalization was a good way for Gambetta, a strong champion of democracy, to defend the jury system.

Other politicians advocated an actual extension of the jury system. In 1872, Odilon Barrot demanded jury trials for civil cases. Between 1877 and 1904, left-wing deputies in the Parliament presented a number of proposals to extend trial by jury to certain *délits*, at least to those punishable by a year in prison and a one-thousand-franc fine.[34]

Nothing came of these proposals to extend jury trial. Nonetheless, the Republican takeover was followed by significant changes in the composition and behavior of juries. One thing it did not change was the politicization of the French justice system. Liberals at the beginning of the Third Republic protested against the politicization of the judiciary and its lack of independence. But once Republicans got control of the government, they would compromise this independence even more.[35] Republicans of both moderate and left-wing tendencies combined to remake the political complexion of the judiciary. In the process, they also altered, at least somewhat, the composition of the juries. They did not repeal the jury law of 1872, which remained in effect until the end of the Third Republic. Rather, they used the machinery of the law to serve their own purposes.

Of great significance here was the "révolution judiciaire" of 1879–83, when the Republicans engaged in a massive purge of the conservative magistrates, some of whom did not hesitate to make their anti-Republican sentiments known and many of whom refused to enforce new anti-clerical laws.[36] The purge of the judiciary was almost complete: it resulted in the removal not only of most members of the *magistrature debout* but also of many judges of the bench, whose *inamovibilité* was suspended for three months by an 1883 law. They were replaced by men "dedicated to republican institutions."[37]

This meant that henceforth, the jury commissions were controlled by Republican magistrates and elected officials. Although the evidence is somewhat scattered (after 1872, the *Compte général* no longer published national compilations of the annual jury lists), it appears that they replaced many of the *notables* on juries with men belonging to the "nouvelles couches sociales" of petits bourgeois and landowning peasants. By the 1890s, according to evidence gathered by a number of contemporary jurists and jurors, men belonging to the commercial and professional bourgeoisie, together with farmers, outnumbered the *rentiers*, *propriétaires*, and *négociants notables* who had previously dominated the panels.[38]

Whether by design or by accident, the jury commissions, by selecting so many men belonging to the "nouvelles couches sociales" and excluding both the old *notables* and the workers, were able to pack the panels with men who tended to come from groups that strongly supported the Republic. Although the modern historian cannot be sure, people of the time thought the jury commissions were not totally impartial in selecting qualified jurors. In 1890, former magistrate Louis Loubet complained that the mayors who accounted for nearly all of the members of the cantonal jury commissions "seek above all to exclude from the list those who do not share their political opinions." Most often, this meant the exclusion of conservatives from the juries.[39] André Gide, who served on a jury shortly before World War I, was convinced he would not have been chosen for jury duty had he not insisted that the mayor of his district inscribe him on the jury list.[40] So long as commissions of judges and politicians decided who was most "capable" of serving on juries, the politicization of the panels was perhaps inevitable.

The jury commissions may well have picked men of the "nouvelles couches sociales" in order to stack the juries in the government's favor in political cases. In the 1880s, prosecutions of political and press offenses shifted to the Republic's enemies on the Right. Some monarchist journals were prosecuted. In the late 1880s, there was a wave of trials of journals favorable to General Georges Boulanger, an authoritarian "man on horseback" backed by royalists and Bonapartists and whose political activities threatened the Republic until he fled France in 1889. Then in the early 1890s, the focus of political and press prosecutions began to shift to a new threat from the Far Left—anarchists.[41] Republican magistrates were more successful than their conservative and monarchist predecessors at getting juries to convict in political and press cases. From 1881 through 1893, juries for the first time convicted a slim majority of the political and press defendants they tried, though the rate of exonerations in such cases remained above the rate for nonpolitical crimes.[42]

The juries remained almost entirely bourgeois, however, for it was still impractical for the poor to serve on the panels. Working-class men were not formally barred from jury duty: the law of 1872 simply granted, upon their request, an automatic exemption to those who had need of their daily and manual labor in order to live. The great majority of workers called to jury duty invoked their right to a peremptory exemption. As a consequence, the jury commissions, hoping to avoid the problem of too many jurors being excused when called to duty, refused to inscribe workers on the annual jury lists save in rare instances.[43]

In 1908, pressure from the Left finally forced the commissions to abandon this practice. In the early 1900s, the Socialists demanded the democratization of juries.[44] In January 1908, Aristide Briand, the Socialist justice minister in the government of the "Bloc des gauches," issued a circular ordering the commissions drawing up jury lists to inscribe workers so as to create a "more democratic jury."[45] This order was given practical effect by laws of 1907 and 1908 that, for the first time since the Revolution, compensated jurors for their lost wages and for their lodging expenses.[46] The result, according to a report issued by the Directeur des affaires criminelles et des graces, was that the proportion of *ouvriers* (workers) on the annual jury lists rose from less than 1 percent in 1908 to more than 10 percent in 1909; *employés* rose from less than 3 percent to more than 6 percent.[47] Certainly the lower classes remained underrepresented: the compensation granted to jurors was rather meager, and workers retained the right to demand exemption from jury duty if it imposed too much of a financial hardship.[48] The circular of 1908 thus seems not to have greatly altered the juries' bourgeois character.[49]

However, it may have altered the composition of the juries enough to have led to some narrowing of the gap in conviction rates between theft and violent crimes, a change that seems to support the class-bias theory of jury behavior. The Republican middle-class panels of 1880–1908 appear to have been even slightly more biased against thieves relative to violent criminals than had been the case with their *notable*-dominated predecessors of the eras 1825–47, 1854–70, and 1873–79 (see Tables 2.4 and 2.5). Most jurors were still property-owners, and small shopkeepers had perhaps more to fear from thieves than did large landowners.

But after 1908, the bias became less evident. Most notable was the decline in the differential in conviction rates between theft and assault from 38.5 percentage points in 1894–1908 to 24.1 points in 1909–13. More modest was the narrowing of the gaps between theft and manslaughter (26.3 to 21.5 points) and theft and unpremeditated murder (12 to 10.9 points). The decline in the gap between theft and premeditated murder (from 4 percentage points in 1894–1908 to 1.3 points in 1909–13) was also modest, but it meant that by the latter period, the differential between conviction rates for the two crimes had almost disappeared (see Tables 2.4 and 2.5). Except for theft versus assault, the change was not very noticeable before World War I. But after the war, the differentials in conviction rates between theft and violent crimes would narrow still further.

Much more important before the war was the fact that the changes in jury composition that began around 1880 were accompanied by a significant reversal of the slow general rise in the overall conviction rate that had occurred from the 1830s through the 1870s. The first annual jury lists to be composed when the Republicans were firmly in control of the government were drawn up in the fall of 1879 for use in 1880. It marked a turning point. Whereas from 1873 through 1879 only 20.6 percent of persons tried in the *cours d'assises* were acquitted, the figure rose to 27.9 percent from 1880 through 1893. The stepping-up in the rate of correctionalization from the mid-1890s on did not stop the trend: 31.7 percent of accused persons were acquitted from 1894 through 1908. Once workingmen began to serve on juries, the acquittal rate rose higher yet, to 35.8 percent in 1909–13 (see Table 2.1).

It is uncertain to what extent the changes in jury composition affected the acquittal rate. Jurors selected by Republican magistrates and locally elected officials may not have been as biased in favor of conviction in nonpolitical cases as their more conservative predecessors had been. Conservatism was associated with a firm defense of law and order,[50] whereas Republican or Republican-selected jurors probably believed more strongly in the rights of accused persons and were more inclined to see them as innocent in the absence of convincing proof of guilt.

Yet if this was a factor, it was hardly the only one. The reasons for the significant rise in acquittal rates after about 1880 were really quite complex and not always clear-cut. They converged to create growing doubt about the guilt or criminal responsibility of many accused persons and the justice of the punishments to which they were exposed.

Weaker prosecution cases were not responsible for the trend. To the contrary, prosecutors became more careful than before about which cases to take to trial. After 1880, the long-term rise in the pretrial abandonment of cases by magistrates continued until it reached three-fifths of all reports of suspected criminal activity in 1901–13, either because they were filed away by the public prosecutors without further action or were dismissed by the *juges d'instruction*. One modern scholar suggests these magistrates became ever more selective about which cases to pursue according to the criteria of seriousness and proof because the enormous rise in reported crimes during the period increasingly exceeded the capacity of the police to arrest criminals and the courts to try them.[51] This may have been related to trends in policing and administration. In this era, the continued expansion of policing and the beginnings of scientific detection in France (which also helped pretrial magistrates to be increasingly selective about which cases to take to trial) must have contributed to the big rise in reported crimes.[52] But the number of judges and prosecutors remained relatively constant between 1883 and 1914.[53]

Greater selectivity in the prosecution of cases was outweighed, however, by the forces that converged to produce higher acquittal rates after 1880. These included a key procedural reform—the abolition in 1881 of the *résumé*, or summing up of the case, by the *président* of the *cour d'assises* at the end of the trial. This was the one reform in late-nineteenth-century France meant to address the problem of judicial bias. Contemporaries had claimed that through the *résumé*, the *présidents* were able to prejudice jurors against defendants.[54] Its abolition appears to have resulted in more acquittals for at least two reasons.

One was that because the *président's interrogatoire* of the accused during trial was retained, the elimination of the *résumé* had the ironical result of intensifying jurors' perception of judicial unfairness. In the early twentieth century, American jurist James W. Garner pointed out several reasons why French judges never had the reputation for impartiality that English judges had by the nineteenth century.[55] One was that in England by this period, judges were more insulated from political pressures than were French judges, whose selection and promotion were highly politicized.[56] Also, whereas English judges had no prior familiarity with the evidence, the French *président* of the *cour d'assises* came to trial armed with the results of a thorough, official pretrial investigation contained in the defendant's dossier.[57] But Garner maintained that the most important reason for the difference in attitudes was the French judges' very active questioning of defendants, which in England and in the United States was done by counsel.[58] As the "adversary" system of trial developed in England in the course of the eighteenth century, judges there gradually withdrew from their once very active questioning of defendants.[59] In the United States, from the 1780s on, laws and state constitutional provisions were enacted to forbid judges to comment on the evidence.[60]

But in France, judicial questioning of defendants became even more extensive after 1881 because the *présidents* of the *cours d'assises* often began inserting into their *interrogatoires* (which before had frequently been kept within "reasonable limits") opinions that they had formerly reserved for their *résumés*. As a result, by the early twentieth century, interrogatories were sometimes "carried to lengths . . . so manifestly unfair to the accused that it provokes spirited protests from the bar." The post-1881 *interrogatoires* were even more prejudicial to defendants than the old *résumés* because whereas the latter came at the end of trials, the former (which followed the reading of the *acte d'accusation*) preceded the presentation of the defense case and the hearing of the witnesses. Juries evidently reacted against this unfairness: by the early twentieth century, according to some contemporary jurists, the lengthy, searching, and sometimes harsh *interrogatoires* of the

The Juries of the Republic

présidents made jurors doubt the judges' impartiality and created sympathy for the accused that often led to acquittals despite evidence of guilt.[61]

The second reason why the *résumé*'s abolition may have resulted in more acquittals was that it made it more difficult for jurors to evaluate the evidence. Before 1881, the *résumé* provided them with their only guidance in respect to the evidence.[62] Since rules of evidence were almost absent in the French *cours d'assises*, jurors must have faced difficulties in assessing the weight and validity of confusing and contradictory evidence. For this reason, early-twentieth-century Lyon *procureur général* William Loubat regretted the abolition of the *résumé*, which he claimed had been very useful as an analysis of sometimes quite confusing trial proceedings. Following the closing speeches for the prosecution and the defense, many juries understood a case less than before. But: "The *résumé* restored calm and clarity to minds; it had the immense advantage of not letting the jury leave for its deliberation room so soon after the last words of the attorney. An eloquent reply has a stunning effect: it shakes convictions, it dispels hesitations, it wins the verdict. It is the *résumé* of the defense. The *résumé* of the president checks the carrying away, cools down the enthusiasms like an ice-cold shower."[63]

Since with the elimination of the *résumé* the defense now truly had the last word,[64] more acquittals might very well have resulted. Even if no judges had used the *résumé* to prejudice jurors against accused persons, its abolition must have led to less certainty in the minds of jurors concerning the guilt of defendants.

A more important cause of the rise in acquittals after about 1880, in the opinion of contemporaries, was the juries' growing reluctance to impose the stern punishments specified in the *Code pénal*. In the late nineteenth and early twentieth centuries, some jurists, including magistrates, as well as the Ministry of Justice continued to assert that many defendants were acquitted because juries thought they would be too harshly punished, even when their sentences had been reduced for extenuating circumstances.[65] One of the few pieces of direct evidence that supports this assertion is a letter written in February 1907 by the jury of the *cour d'assises* of the Seine, addressed to the judges of the court and the assistant public prosecutor. The jury stated that "sometimes fearing a penalty too severe and disproportionate with the act committed, we have been led to render six verdicts of acquittal out of the twelve which have already been judged."[66]

Such acquittals occurred in spite of the fact that by the late nineteenth century, it was possible for the jury to bargain with the *président* of the *cour d'assises* concerning the sentencing of criminals. The custom had become established that allowed a jury, when it had retired to its chamber to deliberate, to ask the *président* to enter the jury room (and he could do so only at the panel's request) to give explanations on doubtful points of law, or even to discuss the penalty in light of a possible conviction.[67] The result was often negotiations between judges and juries concerning penalties.[68] Before 1908, this was known as an "extra-legal secret confab" or "secret communication," which appeared to technically violate the Code of Criminal Procedure's Article 342 forbidding jurors from taking into consideration the penal consequences of their verdicts.[69] The practice was finally legalized by a law of 1908 that, however, stipulated that the *président* could enter the jury room only when summoned by the foreman and was accompanied by the accused's defense attorney, the state's attorney, and the court clerk. But whether in extralegal or legal form, the negotiations between *président* and jury often did not end in agreement. This was because the *président*'s promises were not binding on the two assistant judges—men who were forbidden to enter the jury room but who could outvote their superior colleague on the question of punishment. Some observers claimed that a jury often responded by acquitting the defendant to make sure he did not suffer a penalty the panel thought excessive.[70]

Jury verdicts in cases of nonviolent child molestation provided a good example of the growing tendency of jurors in this era to resist a penalty they thought "too severe and disproportionate with the act committed." After 1880, the trend toward toughness in such cases was reversed. The conviction rate for nonviolent or non-aggravated child molestation declined significantly. Juries found extenuating circumstances for more than four-fifths of those they did convict from 1894 through 1913, who were thereby sentenced to misdemeanor punishments.[71] In many instances, jurors must have thought that the acts covered under the law were not serious enough to receive a felony-level punishment.

This did not mean that the era after 1880 marked a return to the days of legal indifference toward the sexual abuse and exploitation of children. It is true that the number of prosecutions for child molestation declined sharply following its peak in 1876–80.[72] But the best explanation for the decline was the increasing resort to the correctionalization of such offenses.[73] Moreover, the trend toward leniency was mostly limited to the nonviolent cases. Certainly it was not absent when it came to the violent rape and indecent assault of children: both findings of extenuating circumstances and misdemeanor punishments for these crimes rose between the eras 1873–79 and 1909–13.[74] But the conviction rate for violent child molestation declined much less than had been the case for nonviolent molestation.[75] It also declined much less than the conviction rate for felonies in general. As a consequence, by the

The Juries of the Republic

early twentieth century, the proportion of guilty verdicts in violent or aggravated child molestation cases well exceeded the aggregate rate for all other crimes. The differential reached nearly sixteen points in the era 1909–13.[76]

That the French had not become "soft" on child sexual abuse after 1880 is further demonstrated by the rise of a movement whose traces largely escape the *Compte général*'s judicial statistics. This was the crusade to abolish the police registration of underage prostitutes led by moralists, proponents of child welfare, persons who wanted either to reform or to abolish the system of regulated prostitution, and feminists. The campaign's efforts led to the passage in 1908 of an act outlawing the police registration of prostitutes aged eighteen and under.[77] However, the evidence does suggest that, more often than before, after 1880 juries found the punishment for nonviolent child molestation too severe.

The same trend seems to have affected verdicts for the rape and indecent assault of adults. As already shown, juries had always been less tough on those who committed sexual assaults on adults than on those who had committed such assaults on children. Nonetheless, the conviction rate for sex crimes against adults had slowly risen from the 1830s through the 1870s. But after it reached its peak of 73.8 percent in 1873–79, it dropped to 63.1 percent in 1894–1908, before rising slightly again in the years just before World War I.[78] As before 1880, juries continued to find extenuating circumstances for about eight-tenths of those they convicted.[79] However, the proportion punished with imprisonment of five years or less rose from 52.9 percent in 1873–79 to 63.3 percent in 1880–93, though the figure decreased very slightly in the remaining years before World War I.[80] Meanwhile, the number of persons brought to trial before the *cours d'assises* for the rape and indecent assault of adults dropped sharply after 1880.[81] As with the child molestation cases, the decline in prosecutions was probably in large part due to correctionalization.[82] But it meant that more rapists were receiving misdemeanor punishments. In this regard, magistrates again seem to have been following the lead of juries.

In general, to state that juries after 1880 acquitted more of the persons they tried because they found unacceptable the penalties that potentially would be imposed when they convicted, even with extenuating circumstances, does not answer the question of *why* penalties that were seen as reasonable before were now seen as too harsh. Jury reluctance to impose the punishments specified by the *Code pénal* was a traditional reason for acquittals. Through giving jurors a say in punishments, the state and its magistrates had succeeded in reducing acquittal rates in the *cours d'assises* from the

1830s through the 1870s. But the rise in not guilty verdicts thereafter shows that this official strategy of jury control worked less well after 1880.

The most important reason for the trend seems to have been the appearance in the late nineteenth century of a major new force that, according to contemporary Paris *avocat général* Jean Cruppi and several historians since, created growing doubt among jurors concerning the guilt of accused persons. This was the development and popularization of new theories that suggested that certain criminals bore diminished or even no responsibility for their offenses.[83] To Edward Berenson, Robespierre's idea that jurors could always judge on the basis of self-evident facts was naive to begin with, and it became even more naive by the end of the nineteenth century, "when the bewildering array of new psychological and sociological theories—all widely disseminated in the press—made it difficult for jurors to know what the facts were, much less how to interpret them."[84]

These theories were an outgrowth of the rise of scientific criminology. This meant some movement away from the notion, formulated by the "classical" penologists of the eighteenth century such as Cesare Beccaria and Jeremy Bentham, that criminals were rational persons generally possessed of free will and were therefore wholly responsible for their crimes.[85] This very presumption was embodied in France's own *Code pénal*.[86] Yet already, in the early and mid-nineteenth century, such French psychiatric thinkers as Dr. J. E. D. Esquirol and Benoit Augustin Morel developed theories purporting to show that some criminals, including murderers, suffered from partial insanity or were driven to crime by hereditary mental, moral, or physical degeneracy.[87]

Then in the late nineteenth century, a growing number of social scientists and doctors created new theories that stated that at least some criminals were deprived of part or all of their volition because they had been impelled to commit their offenses because of insanity, psychological weaknesses, or biological inferiorities.[88] The ascent of the new discipline of criminology—the scientific study of crime's medical, psychiatric, psychological, and sociological causes—began essentially with the 1876 publication of Cesare Lombroso's *Uomo delinquente*. Although Lombroso's concept of "born criminals" as evolutionary throwbacks, descended from earlier stages of human evolution, found little support in France, theories linking crime to insanity, alcoholism, and hereditary degeneration, as well as to various sociological factors, gained increasing acceptance among the country's jurists in the late nineteenth and early twentieth centuries. The "science" of criminology flourished in France during the *fin de siècle*, when men such as

Gabriel de Tarde, Raymond Saleilles, Henri Joly, Emile Garçon, and others made major contributions to the field. It was part of what has been called France's "medicalization of criminal deviance" during this era.[89]

The influence of the new ideas was not confined to France but also extended to England and the United States. In England, criminological science undermined the extremely voluntaristic notions of criminal responsibility that had been prevalent in the early and mid-Victorian eras. Martin J. Wiener has linked the rise of the science of criminology to broad developments in the natural and social sciences that, along with the increasing complexity of modern society, appeared to diminish the autonomy of individuals by the late nineteenth century and made them more the product of physical, psychological, and social forces extrinsic to their will. By the end of the nineteenth century in England as in France, many lawbreakers were seen in the literature on crime not as criminals entirely or primarily by choice but as persons who had been impelled to commit their acts by their weaknesses. These weaknesses lay either in their hereditary mental or biological constitutions or were due to the impersonal forces of the environment or social conditions. Such ideas eventually led to a movement for greater leniency in punishment in England.[90]

In the United States, among behavioral scientists who specialized in criminological and penological issues, the new deterministic ideas had become "dominant" in the *fin de siècle* era. These ideas had an impact on Progressive Era penal reforms. But Americans, by and large, rejected strict determinism as incompatible with human liberty and arrived at a middle position that preserved the notions of free will and criminal guilt: Progressive Era penology aimed at rehabilitating the criminal through "a process of strengthening the will of persons who, by reason of one social influence or another, had been unable to resist the temptation to break the law."[91]

In France, jurors were quite evidently influenced by the new criminological theories, and they therefore became even less certain of the facts and less certain of the guilt of criminal defendants than in earlier periods. Many jurors had become acquainted with popularizations of these theories, which appeared in widely read newspapers of the turn of the century.[92] An increasing resort to expert psychiatric testimony (again, the law of extenuating circumstances of 1832 allowed for a wider use of such testimony than in Anglo-American common law) must also have helped to acquaint jurors with new theories of diminished criminal responsibility.[93] By the late 1890s, Cruppi could write: "As things stand today, with the tangle of systems, with vulgarized theories disseminated everywhere—theories of atavistic inevitability, of determinism, of the corrupting influence of certain social milieux—who can confidently declare a man guilty without emotion or any doubt whatever? . . . The school, the barracks, the book, the newspaper—all have acted on people's minds [even the most limited ones], disturbing their straightforward and absolute notions with latent psychological doubts, doubts that the words of the lawyer and the expert will bring to consciousness."[94]

The new theories affected jurors' views of defendants in general. The tendency in France to judge the person and not the facts, which originally grew out of the way evidence was presented in trials before the *cours d'assises*, was intensified by the influence exerted by the new criminal anthropology. But the theories were applied especially to women. The acquittal rate for women rose much more sharply than the acquittal rate for men in the era when the new theories came into vogue. A larger proportion of female than of male defendants had been acquitted ever since the national judicial statistics were first published in the *Compte général*. However, before the 1850s, the gap between male and female acquittal rates was rather narrow. It widened significantly thereafter, but most sharply from 1880. From 1894 on, actual majorities of accused women were exonerated. By the years 1909–13, the female acquittal rate was more than double the male acquittal rate. Altogether, a 3.3 percentage point difference in favor of female defendants in the years 1826–1831 had widened enormously to a 31.4 percentage point difference in the five years preceding the outbreak of World War I (see Table 4.1).

The sharp increase in acquittals of women defendants was therefore certainly a cause of the overall rise in exonerations in the *cours d'assises* from about 1880 on. It cannot account for most of the rise, since women made up only 15.2 percent of all defendants from 1873 through 1913.[95] Yet there is no doubt that more female acquittals contributed significantly to the overall increase in exonerations. As already shown, the acquittal rate for all defendants rose 15.2 points from 1873–79 to 1909–13. Women's acquittal rate rose 30.8 points. If we multiply that figure by the female ratio among all accused persons (.152), it means that the rise in female acquittals contributed 4.7 points, or just under one-third (30.9 percent), to the total increase. Of course, more than two-thirds of the rise in acquittals from 1873–79 to 1909–13 was caused by factors other than the increase in female exonerations. But the rise in female acquittals, though it did not account for most of the rise in overall acquittals, was the one factor that contributed to it in a way that is actually quantifiable. Moreover, since the new criminological and psychological theories of diminished responsibility were applied more thoroughly to women's crimes than to those of men, the impact of such theories on verdicts can be seen most clearly through an analysis of jury

The Juries of the Republic

TABLE 4.1. Convictions and Acquittals in the *Cours d'Assises*,
by Gender and Period

Years	MALES			FEMALES		
	Convicted	Acquitted	Total	Convicted	Acquitted	Total
1826–31[a]	21,277	13,981	35,258	4,561	3,435	7,996
	(60.3%)	(39.7%)		(57.0%)	(43.0%)	
1832–47	65,123	34,497	99,620	12,184	8,480	20,664
	(65.4%)	(34.6%)		(59.0%)	(41.0%)	
1848	3,777	2,561	6,338	527	487	1,014
	(59.6%)	(40.4%)		(52.0%)	(48.0%)	
1849–53	20,029	9,658	29,687	3,581	2,401	5,982
	(67.5%)	(32.5%)		(59.9%)	(40.1%)	
1854–70	54,947	15,656	70,603	9,532	4,944	14,476
	(77.8%)	(22.2%)		(65.8%)	(34.2%)	
1871–72	6,429	1,944	8,373	1,097	588	1,685
	(76.8%)	(23.2%)		(65.1%)	(34.9%)	
1873–79	22,588	5,140	27,728	3,658	1,663	5,321
	(81.5%)	(18.5%)		(68.7%)	(31.3%)	
1880–93	38,314	12,533	50,847	4,754	4,148	8,902
	(75.4%)	(24.6%)		(53.4%)	(46.6%)	
1894–1908	30,728	11,882	42,610	3,302	3,935	7,237
	(72.1%)	(27.9%)		(45.6%)	(54.4%)	
1909–13	9,052	4,001	13,053	977	1,598	2,575
	(69.3%)	(30.7%)		(37.9%)	(62.1%)	

Source: *Compte général*, 1826–27, Table 7, p. 14; 1828–31, Table 12, p. 22; 1832, Table 12, p. 24;
1833, Table 14, p. 28; 1834–35, Table 15, p. 30; 1836–60, Table 15, p. 28; 1861–70, Table 15,
p. 30; 1871–73, Table 15, p. 34; 1874, Table 16, p. 42; 1875–78, Table 16, p. 40; 1879–85, Table
18, p. 42; 1886–89, Table 15, pp. 30–31; 1890–1909, Table 13, p. 27; 1910–13, Table 13, p. 29.

[a] The *Compte général* began to divide accused persons by gender in 1826.

behavior toward women defendants. Therefore, while many French jurists and social scientists tended to stress the social causes of male crime (such as urbanization, industrialization, and migration) and thereby maintained that male offenders still possessed some degree of free will, however modified, they tended to stress the much more deterministic psychological and biological causes of female criminality.[96] Women's supposed inferiorities to men[97] were such that they rendered them less responsible for their crimes than males were for their offenses.

To be sure, jurors after 1880 continued to acquit women more often than men for some traditional reasons. These included the difficulty of proving such predominantly female crimes as abortion, infanticide, and poisoning; sympathy for women who committed them; and the gallantry of the all-male juries. There were indeed sharp increases in acquittal rates for abortion and infanticide after 1880. But in the late nineteenth century, these crimes were no harder to prove than before. More important, the big rise in female acquittals extended to every category of crime. Even in cases of theft and fraud, female acquittal rates had come to far exceed the rates for men.[98] The new criminology appears to have made the difference.

In France at the end of the nineteenth century and at the beginning of the twentieth, the traditional notion that women were the "weaker sex" was reinforced and magnified by a proliferation of medical and scientific theories that claimed to prove both the physical and psychological inferiority of women. A growing body of literature was produced that purported to show that many women who committed crimes did so because of psychological and biological weaknesses that were either peculiar to their gender or were much more widespread among them than among males.[99] Some criminologists of the period also maintained that grown females were mentally and morally akin to children.[100] Hence, it was assumed that women's crimes were frequently due to irresistible impulses over which the defendants had little or no control. Women had less free will than men and were therefore less responsible for their breaches of the law.[101]

In fact, women criminals of all types were often seen as afflicted with hysteria. The late nineteenth century witnessed the invention of this new form of mental illness, and women were regarded as especially susceptible to it.[102] G. Macé, a former section head of the Sûreté Nationale, asserted rather hyperbolically that by the 1880s, women criminals were all seen as hysterics.[103] Nonetheless, when accused females were examined by doctors during their pretrial detentions, it was generally to determine whether they were suffering from hysteria.[104]

The criminological literature of the *fin de siècle* also frequently claimed that women were driven to both violent crimes and property crimes by mental troubles caused by feminine bodily functions such as menstruation, menopause, pregnancy, childbirth, and lactation.[105] Moreover, psychiatrists by the end of the nineteenth century saw women as much more prone than men to kleptomania, or an irresistible tendency to steal without apparent reason.[106]

But the new criminological theories of women's irresponsibility were most strongly applied to two types of predominantly female crimes: "crimes of passion" and infanticide. These accounted for only a minority of female felonies,[107] yet they deserve special mention because they appear to illustrate better than any other examples the influence of the new "scientific" criminology on the verdicts of juries.

"Crimes of passion" were narrowly defined as violent acts of vengeance committed by women either against their unfaithful husbands or lovers or against the mistresses or rivals for the affection of these men. Journalists, criminologists, and jurists of the late nineteenth century asserted with increasing frequency that such women acted from irresistible impulses or from passionate feminine emotions over which they had little or no control.[108] What is more, by the early years of the twentieth century, it appeared that the term *crime passionnel* had acquired a broader meaning. According to Patricia O'Brien, many of the serious crimes committed by women were seen as crimes of passion, whether the circumstances bore this out or not.[109] Henri Bergson, who had himself served on a jury, made no reference to the gender of accused persons when in 1914 he went so far as to state that to juries, "any crime is *passionnel* when it is not motivated by theft."[110] Nonetheless, according to the estimation of one modern historian, in Paris between 1880 and 1910, a far larger proportion of female murder defendants than male ones claimed to have committed crimes of passion.[111]

Although jurors often acquitted women accused of "crimes of passion,"[112] it is difficult to know just how much they were influenced by theories that stressed women's irresponsibility when they committed these crimes. However, there is some evidence that magistrates who accepted the new ideas swayed jurors to be lenient toward the women defendants. Judge Louis Proal referred to sentencing and not to the question of guilt when he wrote at the beginning of the twentieth century that "clemency towards women accused of crimes of passion is also obligatory in the majority of cases for physiological and psychical reasons."[113] Yet a number of instances can be cited in which juries actually acquitted women following statements during trials by magistrates who expressed similar ideas. This was true in the 1897 murder trial of Madame Charmillon, who successfully based her defense plea on temporary insanity brought on by pregnancy. She was accused of having murdered her child with a hatchet and of having attempted to do the same to her husband. At her trial, a court-appointed psychiatrist pleaded for mercy for the accused, because "her pregnancy may have produced that particular state of excitability and impressionability that one observes in women at such times." The judge himself seemed to agree with this conclusion, and evidently so did the jury, which acquitted Mme. Charmillon.[114]

In several other cases, juries acquitted women apparently because the latter were afflicted with hysteria. One such case was that of Marguerite Pascal, who was tried for the murders of both her husband and his aunt by the *cour d'assises* of the Seine in 1912. Despite the apparent cold-bloodedness and premeditation with which she committed her crimes, the prosecution asked that Mme. Pascal be convicted with extenuating circumstances because she was a hysteric. The jury went further and simply acquitted the accused.[115]

Vera Gelo also used the hysteria defense, which the *président* of the court seemed to accept. Mademoiselle Gelo was a twenty-year-old student from Russia who in 1901 attempted to murder a professor at the College de France but who accidentally killed her friend and compatriot Zelenine Alexandrine instead.[116] In this instance, the *président* of the court sought to find a psychiatric reason for the crime and stressed the irrationality of the accused, asking psychiatric expert witness Paul Garnier, "Wasn't there in this instance a kind of auto-suggestion?" To this, Garnier replied in the affirmative, and the jury acquitted Mlle. Gelo.[117]

In infanticide cases, new psychiatric theories stressing female irresponsibility added to jurors' traditional sympathy for the accused women. In this era, defense attorneys in some infanticide cases began to plead their clients' innocence on the basis of temporary insanity (*folie passagère*). By the end of the nineteenth century, some medical men and criminologists were claiming that pregnancy and childbirth could bring on mental abnormalities, or a *folie puerperal*, under whose influence a mother might commit infanticide.[118] In certain infanticide trials where the acts of accusation revealed that the murdered infants' bodies had been especially mutilated, the defense attorneys pleaded that the accused person had fallen victim to a *fureur maniaque* or *folie passagère* due to the atrocious pains of the last moments of labor, when the defendants had killed their newborns without being conscious of their acts, for which they later expressed bitter regret. Some doctors were moving toward a diagnosis of what today we call "postpartum psychosis," and consideration for *l'état morbide* of the mother was one justification for the abolition of the death penalty for infanticide in 1901.[119] Often the accused woman claimed, "I lost my head." An infanticide defendant by 1900 could argue not only that she was "a victim of society; but she might also have been a victim of her body—of her biology and sex."[120] One might presume juror receptiveness to this kind of plea may have at least contributed to the sharp and continuous rise in the acquittal rate for infanticide, from a low of 23.4 percent in the years 1873–79 to 60.3 percent in 1909–13.[121] The notion that infanticidal women were mentally ill had gained at least as much, if not more, acceptance in England, where "by the close of the Victorian era bureaucrats, judges, and juries all considered the killing of newborn infants . . . as prima facie evidence of mental illness."[122]

In France, the juries' increasing bias in favor of acquitting female defendants, no doubt due largely to the influence of new "scientific" criminological theories, led some observers by the opening years of the twentieth century to suggest legal reforms imposing lighter penalties for women than for men convicted of the same crimes. Juries were in rebellion against the *Code pénal*'s principle of gender equality in punishments.[123]

The new criminological theories were evidently the most important— but not the only—cause of the dramatically increased jury leniency toward women defendants. Changes in social norms or cultural attitudes appear to have benefited women accused of infanticide, "crimes of passion," and abortion. The trend toward absolving women accused of infanticide seems especially important, for after 1880, females (at least outside of Paris) continued to be much more often tried for this crime than for other intentional homicides.[124] This did not necessarily mean that the new theories on infanticide had no impact on the authorities: the number of prosecutions for the crime dropped steeply after 1880.[125] Rather, it was a reflection of the fact that so few other murders were committed by women. A sharply rising proportion of persons accused of infanticide were acquitted in part, it seems, because of the juries' greater insistence on relatively light sentences for the crime. Jurors with increasing frequency found that even the standard punishment of the era from about 1850 to 1880—five to twenty years' hard labor—was unacceptably harsh. During the period from 1891 through 1901, extenuating circumstances were found for every person convicted of infanticide proper, which explains why there were no more death sentences for the crime. The penalty of hard labor for life had also become a dead letter. Meanwhile, a sharp increase in convictions on lesser charges for persons tried for infanticide resulted in a big rise in misdemeanor penalties.[126]

It was in order to reduce acquittals, and to formalize in law what the juries had already done in a de facto fashion, that the Parliament on November 21, 1901, abolished the death penalty for infanticide. This was a belated move. The authorities had for years allowed juries to mitigate the penalty for infanticide. Now the authorities decided to take more direct control over the penalty by formally changing it. The maximum punishment was lowered to hard labor for life, a penalty that could henceforth be reduced to *réclusion* (at least five years' imprisonment) when the jury found extenuating circumstances.[127]

The law did not, however, do anything to reverse the trend toward higher acquittal rates for infanticide.[128] Moreover, despite the abolition of capital punishment for the crime, juries continued to find extenuating circumstances for nearly all the persons they convicted between 1902 and 1913.[129] During that time, only about 2 percent of convicts received sentences of five to twenty years of hard labor, about 8 percent were sentenced to more than five years in prison, and nearly nine of ten received *peines correctionnelles* of five years or less in prison.[130]

Increased jury leniency for women charged with infanticide may have been linked in part to changes in sexual attitudes. There is significant evidence that by the opening of the twentieth century, the sexual exploitation of women, the "double standard," and male irresponsibility for illegitimate pregnancies and births—all factors often encountered in infanticide cases— were seen as less acceptable by the French than they had been in the early and mid-nineteenth century. The persons accused of this offense appear to have benefited from two rather contrary trends: a very nonfeminist gallantry of male jurors toward female defendants, and a feminist-influenced campaign against the unequal treatment of women in the sphere of sexuality, a campaign that accelerated during the *fin de siècle*.[131]

From the 1870s on, feminists in France vigorously crusaded against the "double standard" of sexuality, which punished women much more severely than men for their sexual misconduct (and for its consequences). Hence, feminists campaigned against those provisions of the French law on adultery that punished wives much more harshly than husbands.[132] Feminists also fought against the system of legal prostitution in France, a system that implied that male extramarital sex was acceptable (or at least was not a grave matter) as long as regulations were in place to prevent the spread of venereal diseases.[133]

A movement to legalize paternity suits was part of this feminist crusade. Women's rights leaders in France attacked the male sexual irresponsibility allowed by the ban on *recherche de la paternité*.[134] The ban not only deprived unwed mothers of needed financial assistance for the support of their illegitimate offspring but also reinforced the sexual double standard by forcing the women alone to carry the burdens resulting from their sexual liaisons.

By the end of the nineteenth century, feminists were beginning to exert

The Juries of the Republic

some influence in French society, particularly as a result of their attacks on the double standard and on male sexual irresponsibility. There were political reasons for this. In the 1870s, French feminists were allied to the liberal Republicans in their struggle against the monarchist Right.[135] After the Republicans acquired complete control of the government in 1879, several acts favorable to women were passed by the Parliament.[136] These included an 1884 law legalizing divorce in France for the first time since 1816. The divorce law partially reduced the double standard by allowing wives as well as husbands to sue for divorce on the grounds of adultery.[137] The decline of the double standard was also perhaps a factor in the juries' frequent acquittals from the 1870s on of women accused of "crimes of passion"—acts that cuckolded husbands alone had by law been allowed to commit (according to the *Code pénal*, a husband could legally kill his adulterous wife or her lover if he caught them having sex in the conjugal home).[138] Moreover, by the late nineteenth century, judges began to hand out increasingly lenient sentences to women convicted of the misdemeanor of adultery.[139]

During the same period, a number of politicians introduced proposals in the Parliament to allow *recherche de la paternité*,[140] and some jurists also called for the legalization of paternity suits.[141] Finally, in 1912 a law was enacted that accomplished this.[142] It is impossible to demonstrate how much the movement to legalize paternity suits influenced jurors, but the feeling was evidently widespread among them that the accused women—most of whom were unmarried—were "taking the rap" when their seducers were at least partly responsible. In England, too, infanticide by the Victorian era was blamed increasingly on bad men who had seduced and abandoned naive and poor unmarried women.[143]

One reason for jury leniency toward women accused of infanticide in France was, however, missing in England. This was an apparently heightened sensitivity to feminine honor by the *fin de siècle*. In the late nineteenth century, Frenchmen became even more concerned than before with the protection of their personal honor. The spread of this once largely aristocratic concept to the bourgeoisie, already evident by the early nineteenth century, became yet more apparent during the Third Republic. Duels still frequently occurred, but duelists were now rarely prosecuted. Dueling was, of course, part of the code of masculine honor.[144] But women also had their honor to protect, though it was of a primarily sexual nature. It has been argued that one reason for the increasing acquittal rate for women accused of "crimes of passion" in late-nineteenth- and early-twentieth-century France was that juries believed that many such defendants, by killing their unfaithful husbands or husbands' mistresses, had committed somehow justifiable homicides because they had acted to protect their wounded honor.[145] Similarly, according to Ruth Harris, mothers accused of infanticide were treated leniently by juries when they could convince them that they were young, seduced innocents who had killed their illegitimate infants because of a sense of shame and to protect their honor.[146] Therefore, the growing emphasis on honor in *fin de siècle* France might very well have contributed to the rising rate of exonerations for infanticide.

The evident French tolerance for killings motivated by honor was in strong contrast to the increasing intolerance for such killings in England by the late nineteenth century. By then, the duel had disappeared in England. Moreover, where in France, juries became increasingly lenient toward persons accused of "crimes of passion," English juries became much tougher. Unlike in France, in England almost all persons tried for murdering an adulterous or allegedly adulterous spouse from 1841 through 1900 were men. But after 1872, not one of them was acquitted. British newspapers of the era deplored the frequency with which French juries acquitted persons accused of "crimes of passion" and noted with satisfaction how much more "civilized" Britons were in not forgiving such crimes. Englishness had become identified with self-control and a resistance to violent impulses. Violence in general became less and less acceptable and excusable in England in the course of the nineteenth century. In England, as in France, women who committed infanticide continued to be viewed sympathetically by jurors and were often either acquitted outright or convicted of a lesser charge, but not because of "honor."[147] The differences between English and French juries in their behavior toward killings motivated by honor once again reveal the importance of culture and of changing social norms in influencing the verdicts of jurors.

Changes in social norms also largely contributed to a big rise in the acquittal rate for abortion in France, though before 1911 the number of persons tried for this crime remained far below the number tried for infanticide and did not even exceed an annual average of one hundred until the years 1891–95.[148] In the opinion of some contemporaries, and of some historians since, many persons were acquitted of abortion for the same reason many were acquitted of infanticide: the jurors' sympathy for defendants who were single, young, poor, and seduced; who were forbidden to launch paternity suits; and who were increasingly deprived of the alternative of anonymously depositing their babies at the *tours* because of the government's gradual suppression of these between 1833 and 1889.[149] It seems safe to assume that

The Juries of the Republic

this sympathy was a factor in some exonerations, for a slim majority of all persons tried for the crime between 1825 and 1913 were unmarried (though the statistics did not show conviction rates by marital status).[150]

But sympathy for single girls in trouble appears to have been much less often a reason for acquittals in abortion cases than it was in infanticide cases. For one thing, a far larger proportion (nearly half) of all persons tried for abortion were married than was true among those tried for infanticide (less than one-sixth).[151] Perhaps most surprisingly, when it came to punishment, jury leniency toward abortionists about equaled or surpassed the leniency toward *avortées*. The statistics on convictions and acquittals did not distinguish between the *avortées* (the presumed objects of so much jury sympathy) and those who performed the operations. But from 1873 on, the *Compte général*'s tables on findings of extenuating circumstances for convicted persons did distinguish abortionists from *avortées*, and they show that extenuating circumstances were found for the former at about the same rate (three-fourths from 1873 through 1879 and nine-tenths from 1880 through 1913) as for the latter.[152] Perhaps juries so often found extenuating circumstances for abortionists (most of whom were midwives) because the punishment for performing the operation without extenuating circumstances (five to twenty years of hard labor) was so severe, whereas the punishment for *avortées* without extenuating circumstances was five to ten years' imprisonment.[153] Because of the juries' findings of extenuating circumstances, very few of the abortionists convicted from 1880 through 1913 received penalties of hard labor.[154]

Yet though a smaller proportion of abortion defendants than infanticide ones received the sympathy for young girls in trouble, the acquittal rate for the former crime rose even more sharply, from 37.7 percent in 1873–79 to a high of 72.0 percent from 1902 through 1908, before dropping slightly thereafter.[155] In part, this was because of the even greater difficulty of proving guilt in abortion cases. However, the evidentiary problems were no greater than they were in the early and mid-nineteenth century.[156] According to contemporaries, one reason for the rise in the acquittal rate for abortion, as in the rise in the rate for infanticide, was sentiment among jurors by the early twentieth century that the penalties for the crime were too harsh.[157] It is impossible to prove how many acquittals were due to this consideration, but evidence for it can be found in the significant increase in findings of extenuating circumstances for those persons who were convicted of the crime, from roughly seven of ten convictions between 1849 and 1879 to nine of ten between 1891 and 1913.[158] As a consequence, by the years 1902–13, nearly nine of every ten persons convicted of abortion received misdemeanor punishments of imprisonment of five years or less.[159] Jurors viewed abortion as a lesser offense than did the law. This did not, however, preclude the possibility that the authorities preferred leaving the matter to jurors and preserved the "black letter" of the law in order to maintain its "deterrent" effect.

Indeed, it appears that the most important reason for the rise in the acquittal rate for abortion in the late nineteenth and early twentieth centuries was an increasingly tolerant attitude among the French public. A decline in the influence of the Catholic church, which accelerated after the secular-minded and anticlerical Republicans took effective control of the government in the late 1870s, must have contributed to the trend.[160] Perhaps it was not coincidental that the acquittal rate for abortion began to rise sharply—much more sharply than for all other crimes, even infanticide—in 1880, the year jurors selected by Republican politicians and magistrates began to dominate in the jury boxes of the *cours d'assises*.

A related explanation for the growing acceptance of the act has been provided by Angus McLaren. According to McLaren, the increasing tolerance of abortion and also a probable rise in their number were due to the growing use of birth control in the course of the nineteenth century.[161] The French appear to have resorted to contraceptive practices on a widespread scale at an earlier date than did other Western peoples. In the course of the nineteenth century, the French birthrate declined significantly, and by about 1900 it had fallen well below that of the other major European powers.[162] Contemporaries offered a number of reasons for the decline of French fertility. These included the influence of Thomas Malthus (a classical economist who claimed that population growth would eventually exceed the food supply), de-Christianization, the love of luxury, urbanization, a growing spirit of prudence, a desire to maintain rising living standards, and the wish of many Frenchmen—especially peasants—to avoid the subdivision of their family properties when confronted by the *Code civil*'s requirement that property be divided equally among heirs.[163]

Whatever the reasons for the drop in the French birthrate, McLaren contends that the desire to limit family size led to an increase in abortions. He reasons that since there were definite limitations to the effectiveness of the contraceptive techniques available in the nineteenth century, a growing number of Frenchwomen found abortion necessary as a backup method of birth control. By the end of the nineteenth century, it had become a common practice among married as well as unmarried women. Estimates of the annual number by the late nineteenth and early twentieth centuries ranged from 150,000 to 500,000.[164] It was even alleged that abortions exceeded

The Juries of the Republic

births in the nation's great centers of population.[165] The sharp increase in the number reported to the police (though not in the number prosecuted) from the 1830s to the early twentieth century[166] might very well have echoed a real increase in the incidence of the crime. Contemporaries apparently believed this to have been the case.[167] Thus, it is not surprising that by the late nineteenth and early twentieth centuries, a number of contemporaries were contending that many ordinary French citizens no longer viewed abortion as a crime.[168] The juries appear to have ratified this sentiment. As Maurice Ajam put it in 1899, "The jury is Malthusian."[169]

Perhaps jurors were "Malthusian" because they were middle-class. It has generally been assumed that the desire to limit family size began among the upper and middle classes, and then spread gradually to lower orders.[170] In nineteenth-century France, the birthrate of the bourgeoisie was apparently below that of the poorer classes.[171] Since the middle classes were the most likely to use contraception, they were perhaps also the most likely to be sympathetic to those accused of abortion—even if many of the latter were apparently lower-class women.[172] However, after the admission of working-class men to juries in 1908, there was no significant change in the acquittal rate.[173] This probably reflected the fact that by the beginning of the twentieth century, there was no compelling reason why the lower classes should have been less lenient than the bourgeoisie toward persons accused of the crime. While the birthrate of the former remained higher than that of the latter, abortion was evidently more widespread among the poor (who also outnumbered the bourgeoisie) than among the better-off classes, who were more knowledgeable about effective contraceptive practices.[174]

Therefore, for a variety of reasons, juries became significantly more lenient toward criminal defendants in the decades following 1880. There was one exception, however, and that was in respect to the punishment of capital crimes. The conviction rate for capital crimes declined significantly after 1879.[175] But juries became increasingly willing to impose the death penalty on those they did convict of these crimes. To be sure, the panels continued to find extenuating circumstances for the great majority of persons they found guilty of capital crimes, but the proportion slowly decreased after 1870.[176] The annual average number of death sentences rose from sixteen in 1863–70, to twenty-nine in 1873–79, to thirty in 1880–93, down somewhat to twenty-two in 1894–1908, and up again to twenty-seven in 1909–13.[177] The long-term movement of juries away from capital punishment from 1832 through 1870 was slowly reversed.

Several factors can explain this trend. The rise in acquittals for "crimes of passion" from the 1870s on meant the exoneration of a number of accused persons who probably would have been convicted in earlier eras, but with extenuating circumstances. Perhaps, too, with the decline in the conviction rate, juries were more convinced of the guilt of those persons they did convict, and hence they felt more certain that they were not sending innocent persons to the guillotine.

One other factor appears to have contributed to the increased willingness of juries to impose the death penalty in the years shortly after 1900: the strong reaction of the panels against the proposal to abolish capital punishment, debated in the Parliament in 1906–8. Both Robert A. Nye and Gordon Wright have mentioned the fact that juries in many departments inundated Paris with petitions opposing the bill.[178] Wright claims that jury opinion in this instance reflected "a violent and emotional public reaction" against the abolition proposal (which was defeated in 1908), touched off in part by a "deep social fear" heightened by a rise in crime statistics after 1902 and in part by the propaganda campaign of those who favored retention of capital punishment and of "certain mass-circulation newspapers, which seized upon a few dramatic and bloody crimes as evidence that the lives and property of Frenchmen were gravely threatened." As a consequence, juries "turned tough" and handed down more death sentences.[179]

The statistics on jury decisions in capital punishment cases appear to lend some support to Wright's contention. From 1906 through 1913, the movement to impose more death sentences accelerated markedly.[180] The effect of the juries on the death sentence debate of 1906–8 again shows how the panels significantly influenced laws on punishment, though in this case it was in favor of toughness rather than leniency.

Yet there certainly remained limits to this toughness. The juries still saved from the guillotine four-fifths of the capital offenders they convicted. The panels had gradually arrived at a consensus that only the most heinous, dispassionate, and premeditated murders, and murders motivated by the desire for material gain, should be punished by the guillotine. By this period, they reserved the guillotine almost solely for persons convicted of premeditated murder, unpremeditated homicide accompanied by other crimes, and parricide.[181] Most convicted murderers who were sentenced to the guillotine had killed to steal. The juries drew a sharp distinction between these killers and those who had acted out of "passion," most of whom were either convicted with extenuating circumstances or were acquitted outright.[182] In this regard, late-nineteenth-century French jurors behaved much like those of eighteenth-century England, who, along with the judges, for the most part agreed on the justice of the execution of persons who killed in cold blood.[183]

The Juries of the Republic

But in France after 1880, the toughness of juries toward persons who killed in cold blood was overshadowed by the big increase in the rate of acquittals for crimes in general. A major historical reversal occurred. From the 1830s through the 1870s, the authorities appeared to have had some success in their fight against jury sanction nullification. But after 1880, the tactics employed to bring about this success—such as granting to jurors the right to find extenuating circumstances and better prosecution cases—no longer seemed to work. The rise in acquittal rates touched off a wave of angry public criticism of juries. The anti-jury campaign was led by magistrates. They were exasperated by the fact that the existing means of fighting jury nullification did not prevent the rise in acquittals. The magistrates and their allies thereafter developed a new program of jury reform that would ultimately destroy the independence of the panels.

chapter five

THE CAMPAIGN AGAINST THE JURIES,
CIRCA 1890–1914

It was not long before magistrates began to respond to the increased jury nullification of the era after 1880 by renewing their attacks on the jury system. But the new criticisms were different from those of the past, and they entailed a major irony. The rise of "scientific" criminology was the most important contributor to increased jury-based leniency, and in that sense the state and its magistrates found it more difficult to control jurors. But the magistrates and their allies soon discovered that science could be used against the jury. The new criminological ideas seemed to call for a justice by experts in place of a justice by jurors. What is more, magisterial criticisms of the juries were now more often seconded by other jurists, the press, criminologists, politicians, and a new group—repopulationists—who were angered by the many acquittals for abortion. Moreover, from the mid-1890s, Republican magistrates responded to increased jury leniency by taking the process of correctionalization even further than had their Bonapartist-monarchist predecessors. In general, the attack on the jury system that would ultimately result in the destruction of its independence and the further reduction of its role in the justice system began in earnest during the approximate quarter-century preceding the outbreak of World War I. At the same time, and for several reasons, liberal, Republican politicians—even some left-wing ones—began to waver in their defense of the jury system.

At least one of these reasons was political rather than criminological: the fearful reaction of Republican politicians to the wave of anarchist violence that France experienced in the early and mid-1890s. The government responded with the repressive *lois scélérates* (villainous laws) of 1893–94. In December 1893, one anarchist, Auguste Vaillant, threw a bomb in the Chamber of Deputies, wounding several of the lawmakers.[1] The Parliament quickly responded by strengthening an existing law against "*apologie* [praise or vindication] for criminal acts" in order to repress anarchist propaganda or "any *entente* [understanding or agreement] with the goal of preparing or committing crimes against persons or properties" and stipulated that those found guilty be punished with hard labor.[2]

However, more than half of the persons tried by juries in 1894 for violating the revised law were acquitted.[3] Then in July 1894, following the assassination of President Sadi Carnot by an anarchist, the Parliament passed a new law transferring trials of persons accused of anarchist activities from the *cours d'assises* to the *tribunaux correctionnels*.[4] Evidently, this measure was aimed more against the slowness of procedures in the *cours d'assises* than it was a fear of jury "indulgence."[5] The Radical Republicans protested against the act but did not repeal it when they came to power.[6]

Even before this, in March 1893, a law had been enacted transferring from the *cours d'assises* to the *tribunaux correctionnels* trials for persons accused of "outrages by means of the press against chiefs of state or their ambassadors."[7] In subsequent years, the *cour de cassation* handed down a number of decisions embodying legal interpretations that whittled away still more of the jurisdiction of the juries in press cases.[8]

Evidently, these *cour de cassation* opinions, and the laws of 1893–94, were largely responsible for the decline in the number of persons tried by juries for *délits politiques et de presse* from the mid-1890s on. In 1879 and 1880, when the restrictive law of 1875 was still in effect, only a tiny number (five in the first year, two in the second) of persons were tried by juries for *délits politiques et de presse*. The law of 1881 restoring most trials for political and press offenses to juries was followed by a big increase, to an average of 61 per year. In 1894, the number rose sharply, to 263, mostly due to prosecutions under the anti-anarchist law of December 1893.[9] From 1895 through 1913, however, an average of only 46 persons per year were tried for *délits politiques et de presse* in the *cours d'assises*. If one excludes the figures for 1896 and 1907, years in which abnormally high numbers of people (172 in the first year and 109 in the second) were tried by juries, the annual average came to only 35. Nearly half of all persons tried for political and press misdemeanors by juries from 1895 through 1913 were acquitted.[10]

A much more serious factor undermining jury trial from the mid-1890s on was the resumption of significant progress in the correctionalization of nonpolitical crimes, now carried out by Republican magistrates with the blessing of the Republican government. Since the inauguration of the Third Republic, there had been an apparent leveling off of the correctionalization rate. However, the average annual number of persons tried each year for felonies in the *cours d'assises* then dropped substantially from 4,273 from 1879 through 1893 to 3,274 from 1894 though 1913. This was well under half the figure recorded for the years 1825–54 (see Table 2.6). By 1894–1913, juries

The Campaign against the Juries

tried only 1.5 percent of criminal defendants in France, compared to 3.8 percent in 1826–41 (see Table 5.1). The trend was evidently not due to a rise in misdemeanors.[11] *Fin de siècle* jurists and observers of the criminal justice system, like their predecessors, claimed the decline was due principally to correctionalization.[12] Jean Cruppi was right to state in 1898 that the juries were being dispossessed, that the *cours d'assises*, originally conceived as the country's "general and ordinary" criminal courts, had gradually become "exceptional" tribunals.[13]

Contemporary legal writers and criminologists asserted that the Republican magistrates of the 1890s and after resorted to correctionalization for the same reason as their Bonapartist-monarchist predecessors had: to avoid acquittals by juries.[14] But the leaders of the Republican governments defended correctionalization on several other grounds as well. One was that, as in the past, magistrates were in part merely following jury decisions reducing certain felonies to misdemeanors, and therefore it made sense to try such cases in the *tribunaux correctionnels*, where justice proceeded more expeditiously and cheaply. The Ministry of Justice, in its introductory report to the *Compte général* for 1894, noted that there had been an increase since the 1870s in the proportion of convictions in the *cours d'assises* in which juries rejected the felony accusations and found the culprits guilty of misdemeanors instead. For crimes against persons, the figure had risen from 5.4 percent in 1874 to 7.9 percent in 1894, and for crimes against property, it rose from 4.5 percent to 7.3 percent. The ministry concluded from these figures that "the jury itself, like the *Parquet*, has entered and progressed on the road to correctionalization."[15]

The proportion of convictions downgraded to misdemeanors by juries continued to rise after 1894, reaching 13.3 percent in 1909–13.[16] Moreover, the fact that slightly more than half of all persons convicted in the *cours d'assises* from 1880 through 1913 still received only *peines correctionnelles* provided further justification for correctionalization(see Table 2.3). More often than the judges, juries for all practical purposes decided these lesser sentences through findings of extenuating circumstances for persons they convicted of felonies and through finding other persons they tried guilty of misdemeanors only.[17] The crimes that by the turn of the twentieth century were most often punished in the *cours d'assises* with misdemeanor sentences—theft, abuse of confidence, fraud, indecent assault, and infanticide—were also the crimes that were most frequently correctionalized.[18]

The process was particularly evident when it came to white-collar crimes. After 1880, findings of extenuating circumstances for white-collar felonies became proportionately even more common than before. The result was

TABLE 5.1. Number of All Criminal Defendants Tried by the
Cours d'Assises and *Tribunaux Correctionnels*, by Period

Years	Cours d'Assises	Tribunaux Correctionnels	Total
1826–41	119,867 (3.8%)	3,052,855 (96.2%)	3,172,722
1842–47	43,670 (3.4%)	1,236,609 (96.6%)	1,280,279
1848–54	50,577 (3.0%)	1,651,670 (97.0%)	1,702,247
1855–62	43,198 (2.6%)	1,628,328 (97.4%)	1,671,526
1863–70	34,325 (2.5%)	1,336,059 (97.5%)	1,370,384
1871–78	38,760 (2.5%)	1,530,994 (97.5%)	1,569,754
1879–93	64,096 (1.9%)	3,327,595 (98.1%)	3,391,691
1894–1913	65,474 (1.5%)	4,433,159 (98.5%)	4,498,633
1914–18	9,172 (1.3%)	698,760 (98.7%)	707,932
1919–31	28,399 (0.9%)	3,044,297 (99.1%)	3,072,696
1932–38	10,813 (0.6%)	1,756,915 (99.4%)	1,767,728
1940–44	4,143 (0.2%)	1,807,822 (99.8%)	1,811,965
1945–52	15,833 (0.6%)	2,506,761 (99.4%)	2,522,594

Sources: Compte général, 1826, Table 2, p. 3, and Table 74, p. 111; 1827, Table 2, p. 3, and Table
82, p. 121; 1828, Table 2, p. 3, and Table 91, p. 139; 1829, Table 2, p. 3, and Table 92, p. 141;
1830, Table 2, p. 3, and Table 68, p. 115; 1831, Table 2, p. 3, and Table 65, p. 105; 1832, Table
2, p. 3, and Table 68, p. 109; 1833, Table 2, p. 3, and Table 73, p. 117; 1834, Table 2, p. 3, and
Table 70, p. 113; 1835–36, Table 2, p. 3, and Table 76, p. 119; 1837–51, Table 2, p. 3, and Table
75, p. 117; 1852, Table 2, p. 3, and Table 73, p. 113; 1853, Table 2, p. 3, and Table 72, p. 111;
1854–57, Table 2, p. 3, and Table 74, p. 113; 1858–59, Table 2, p. 3, and Table 72, p. 111; 1860,
Table 2, p. 3, and Table 70, p. 109; 1861–63, Table 2, p. 5, and Table 70, p. 111; 1864–69,
Table 2, p. 5, and Table 67, p. 109; 1870, Table 2, p. 5, and Table 62, p. 101; 1871, Table 2,
p. 5, and Table 60, p. 101; 1872–73, Table 2, p. 5, and Table 64, p. 107; 1874, Table 2, p. 5,
and Table 38, p. 87; 1875–78, Table 2, p. 5, and Table 35, p. 81; 1879–85, Table 2, p. 5, and
Table 35, p. 85; 1886–88, Table 2, p. 5, and Table 30, p. 61; 1889–1909, Table 2, p. 5, and
Table 29, p. 57; 1910–13, Table 2, p. 7, and Table 29, p. 59; 1919–20, Table 2, p. 7, and Table
28, p. 67; 1921–23, Table 2, p. 7, and Table 24, p. 61; 1924–31, Table 1, p. 7, and Table 19,
p. 53; 1914–18 and 1932–52, Ministère de l'Economie et des Finances, *Annuaire statistique*,
162–65.

that juries had turned most of these crimes into de facto misdemeanors. Conviction rates for most white-collar felonies (especially fraud, fraudulent bankruptcy, and cases of official corruption other than offering and accepting bribes) declined significantly.[19] Findings of extenuating circumstances for those who were convicted of the original felony charges and not of *délits* had risen, though not dramatically, from about eight of every ten in the 1832–47 period to about nine of every ten (save for those found guilty of offering or accepting bribes) from 1880 through 1913.[20] Except for counterfeiting (which was sternly punished by the *Code pénal*), about eight to nine of every ten persons found guilty of all white-collar crimes in the *cours d'assises* from 1880 to 1913 were sentenced to misdemeanor punishments.[21]

Therefore, it made sense for magistrates to save on the time and expense of jury trial by correctionalizing crimes that in the overwhelming majority of cases were punished with misdemeanor sentences. The average annual numbers of persons tried in the *cours d'assises* for most white-collar crimes dropped sharply from the middle years of the nineteenth century through the early years of the twentieth.[22] A big decline in fraud cases accounted for most of the decrease in white-collar trials in the *cours d'assises*, and the Ministry of Justice explicitly linked this to correctionalization following the lead of juries that regarded felony punishments as too harsh for most persons guilty of fraud.[23] This evidently contributed to a corresponding rise in trials for misdemeanor fraud (*escroquerie*) in the *tribunaux correctionnels*.[24]

Republican government leaders also justified correctionalization for these and other crimes on the grounds that it led to more humane punishment. The *fin de siècle* was an era of penal reform in France, when advocates of a new "individualization of punishment" school of penology were able to secure the passage of laws on parole (1885) and suspended sentences (1891) aimed at the rehabilitation rather than the punishment of first-time offenders.[25] In this atmosphere, Republican magistrates appointed by liberal politicians in some instances may not have just sought to avoid jury trials but rather charged accused persons who committed apparent felonies with misdemeanors in order to obtain leniency in punishment. If this was done, it was in an extralegal fashion, for between 1863 and the 1920s, no laws were passed formally reclassifying *crimes* into *délits*. However, by the opening of the twentieth century, merciful extralegal correctionalization had the approval of even Left-liberal governmental leaders. In 1904, Ernest Valle, justice minister in the Radical government of Emile Combes, defended the correctionalization of some crimes as a humane measure "in the interests even of the people charged, because, when it is not a question of *crimes passionnels*, the *cour d'assises* is much more severe than the *tribunaux correctionnels*."[26]

Significantly, Valle mentioned the fact that the accused persons retained the right to demand trial in the *cour d'assises*.[27] It seemed that magistrates could not have resorted to correctionalization in such an increasing number of cases from the mid-1890s on without the approval or acquiescence of the Republican leaders who appointed and promoted them and the defendants who appear to have engaged in a form of "tacit vertical charge bar[gaining]."

The weakening of the liberals' traditional support of the jury could not have come at a worse time for the institution, for by the turn of the century, juries were being subjected to a growing and intense barrage of criticism from several quarters. Few demanded the actual abolition of the jury system, but critics of the institution called for reforms that would weaken it even more through the further correctionalization of felonies or through the imposition of greater judicial control over the "incompetent" panels.

These critics included a new group: repopulationists, who sought to speed up France's slow population growth and who were unhappy with most jury verdicts in abortion cases. Repopulationism arose as a major movement after the French had been defeated in the Franco-Prussian War of 1870–71. The movement soon attracted many doctors, social scientists, and politicians who had come to see France's declining birthrate (which by about 1900 had dropped below replacement level) as a threat to the nation's great-power status, to successful *revanche* (revenge) against the rapidly reproducing Germans, and to future economic growth. By the early twentieth century, the repopulationists were beginning to influence France's political leaders.[28]

Although the repopulationist movement seemed to have the verbal support of many intellectuals, doctors, politicians, and officials, one trend still disturbed them: the majority of the people continued to act, though not necessarily speak, in a "Malthusian" fashion. Contraception and abortion remained widespread practices.[29] The latter was of special concern to the repopulationists: they attributed much of the decline in the birthrate to the crime.[30] The suppression of abortion, therefore, became a major part of the repopulationist program.

Yet juries refused to cooperate in the movement to stamp out abortion. Not only were few abortionists and their clients brought to justice, but only a minority of these were convicted. In fact, as already shown, jury decisions were moving in a direction opposite from that called for by repopulationists, with the proportion of acquittals among all persons tried for abortion

The Campaign against the Juries

in the *cours d'assises* rising sharply from nearly two-fifths from 1873 through 1879 to nearly three-fourths from 1902 through 1908. Repopulationists bitterly denounced the panels' tendency to acquit abortionists and their clients. In 1911, Felix Allemane complained of the "regrettable and complacent leniency of the jury with regard to crimes of abortion . . . completely scandalous from the moral point of view." In 1917, H. Berthélemy stated that in abortion cases, "we can reproach the jury for its deplorable weakness. . . . Some celebrated acquittals have created a scandal to the point, we think, of discouraging prosecutions."[31]

Therefore, although the pro-natalists proposed a variety of measures aimed at discouraging abortion,[32] at the heart of their program to combat it was a proposal to correctionalize the crime and thereby take it out of the hands of lenient juries.[33] The punishment would be lesser but more certain.[34] This was because the movement evidently believed that the magistrate-only *tribunaux correctionnels* would be less swayed by public sympathy for persons accused of the crime than were the juries of the *cours d'assises*, since the judges were appointed officials and were more likely to convict offenders in general.

The proposal to correctionalize abortion did not, however, enjoy immediate success. It was introduced in the Parliament several times between 1891 and 1917 but was not enacted.[35] One reason may have been the resistance in the Parliament to a further weakening of the jury system before World War I. Another may have been the fact that many politicians—like many people in general—were pro-populationist in their statements but "Malthusian" in practice.[36] Not until 1923 did the Parliament pass a law to reclassify abortion from a *crime* to a *délit*.

Indeed, the repopulationist campaign against abortion was only a modest threat to the jury system, for the movement proposed to take only one crime out of the hands of jurors, a crime that was by no means the most often tried among those brought before the *cours d'assises* (though the number of abortion cases presented to juries increased sharply in the few years before World War I).[37] Far more threatening to the system was a renewed and intensified campaign against the citizen-judges carried out by magistrates and their allies among other jurists and the press. Their objections to the jury system as it then functioned in France were much more fundamental and involved much broader issues than those raised by the repopulationists. The magistrates had always been critical of the juries as too lenient, incompetent, biased, and impressionable. But in the years from about 1890 to 1914, they made these criticisms much more publicly and vigorously than before through numerous publications.

The Campaign against the Juries

Several of their charges echoed those of earlier eras. The rise in acquittal rates after 1880, especially for abortion, infanticide, "crimes of passion," and women defendants in general, led to renewed criticisms of jury "indulgence." An outpouring of literature critical of juries appeared (from about 1890 to 1941) condemning jurors' biases and their tendency to acquit persons whom the writers thought were obviously guilty. Many of these critiques were written by magistrates.[38] Few called for the complete abolition of juries, but several magistrates did suggest that even more crimes should be correctionalized and thus removed from the jurisdiction of the *cours d'assises*.[39]

Another traditional magisterial criticism of juries—that they were ignorant and incompetent—was sharpened by the judges' reactions to the changing social composition of the panels during the *fin de siècle*. Some magistrates saw the partial democratization of juries carried out in the course of the late nineteenth and early twentieth centuries as going too far. They complained that the more democratically composed juries were even less competent than their elite predecessors. They were less educated, less intelligent, more easily persuaded by eloquent defense attorneys, more impressionable, and often influenced by melodramatic novels and plays that made heroes of those who committed *crimes passionnels*.[40] The magisterial protests against jurors' supposed incapacity and low intellectual level (including the familiar allegations of illiteracy) intensified following the admission of workingmen to the panels in 1908.[41]

There is reason to believe, however, that the magisterial critics of the jury exaggerated the number of ignorant, illiterate, or lower-class jurors, perhaps because they disliked many of their verdicts. The law of 1872 on the jury, in effect until the end of the Third Republic in 1940, excluded illiterates from jury duty.[42] Moreover, as already mentioned, even after 1908, most jurors remained bourgeois. The situation was analogous to what it had been in eighteenth-century England, where many of the critics of the juries also charged that the panels were made up largely of "illiterates" and "plebeians." Yet as P. J. R. King points out, the property qualifications for jury service in England at the time ensured that jurors were drawn exclusively from the top half of the spectrum in terms of wealth and social status, and most were able to read.[43] "Plebeian" was a relative term—most jurors were "middling men" (tradesmen, artisans, farmers, and the like), between the gentry and the poor.[44] King claims that those who attacked juries were mainly wealthy members of the eighteenth-century elite who made their charges that the panels were composed of "ignorant" and "illiterate" people because they did not like many of their decisions (for example, frequent acquittals and jury down-charging for persons accused of major property crimes).[45] The same prejudice may have influenced French magistrates of the 1890–1914 period, most of whom continued to be drawn from the class of wealthy and well-to-do *notables*[46] but who were now faced with juries composed largely of "middling men" who often handed down verdicts the jury critics thought too lenient.

Perhaps the magistrates also exaggerated jurors' incompetence because they did not like what they perceived as a politicized selection process. They argued that although the 1872 law regulating the drawing up of jury lists gave judges much more say in selecting jurors, it placed too much power in the hands of politicians. Some magistrates alleged that the local elected officials on jury commissions excluded systematically from the lists capable men who belonged to opposing parties or factions. The magistrates, who were political appointees, could not buck the will of men elected by universal suffrage.[47]

In fact, the judges' protests against the 1872 law, and their anti-jury campaign, were related to the political struggle between magistrates and politicians that occurred between about 1880 and World War I. This involved two closely connected phenomena: the conflict between magistrates and politicians that began with the advent of the "république aux républicains," and the professionalization of the magistrature. According to Françoise Lombard, the magistrates' attack on juries in the late nineteenth and early twentieth centuries, including correctionalization and the movement toward *échevinage*, was part of an effort by the magistrature to free itself from political control and become a body of professional civil servants—true *fonctionnaires* (or "techniciens de droit")—whose appointments would be based strictly on merit rather than on political considerations. As part of this movement toward professionalization, the magistrature sought to reconquer its "professional space" through the progressive elimination or neutralization of the jury.[48]

That it was easier to campaign against juries than to confront politicians directly had something to do with this. Although each candidate for the magistrature had to fulfill a few professional requirements—a law degree and two years' service as an *avocat stagiaire* (trainee in a law office)—appointment and promotion by the Ministry of Justice depended largely on political patronage.[49] Moreover, magistrates were under the close scrutiny of prefects.[50] The *magistrature debout* (the prosecutors and their assistants) enjoyed no security of tenure, and despite 1810 and 1852 laws protecting the *inamovibilité* of the judges of the bench (*magistrature assise*), succeeding re-gimes repeatedly purged their ranks (although these purges were relatively modest from 1815 through the earliest years of the Third Republic).[51]

However, the 1879 declaration of the "république aux républicains" touched off a period of intense conflict between a conservative judiciary and Republican politicians. The resulting purge of magistrates in the "révo-lution judiciaire" of 1879–83 left the judiciary in a state of shock. The judges responded by seeking to free themselves from political control. An effort in this direction was made in 1906, when the government issued the "dé-cret Sarrien" establishing a *concours* for candidates for the magistrature. This competitive examination was abandoned in 1908 after many politicians, es-pecially those on the Left, protested that it interfered with the Republic's duty to ensure that its magistrates were Republicans. Not until 1958 was a *concours* reestablished.[52]

During the remainder of the Third Republic, therefore, magistrates could do little to stop politicians from interfering in their appointment and pro-motion. But they could do something about jurors: correctionalization was a handy tool for reducing the influence of these nonprofessionals, whose selection was at least partly the work of politicians. Judges thus stressed their own professional competence and their role as upholders of the "gen-eral interest" in contrast to juries' "incompetence."[53] Magistrates could gain some degree of independence, and at least partially free themselves from political influence, by shaking off citizen-magistrates and the limitations they imposed on a judge's power.

In their campaign against the juries, the magistrates also found allies in the press. Some contemporary jurists claimed that the press—which became increasingly influential from the late nineteenth century on—did much to turn "public opinion" against juries, a contention that has been repeated by some historians. This "public opinion" is not clearly defined, but it seems to mean respectable, bourgeois opinion as expressed in the newspapers. Bernard Schnapper has noted that a "veritable campagne de presse" began in the 1880s, with many newspaper attacks on juries' partiality, especially their tendency to acquit defendants accused of *crimes passionnels*. By the 1890s, according to Fernand Gineste, accounts in the daily newspapers of juries' "infinite mercy" in many of their verdicts were arousing the public's ire. "Infinite mercy" was something of an overstatement, however, since it did not extend to theft, the only crime that another contemporary, Ga-briel de Tarde, claimed juries felt "the need of punishing." In the years just before World War I, several journals—*Le Temps, La Revue judiciaire, L'Opi-nion*—opened their columns to jurists who called for *échevinage*. By 1913,

The Campaign against the Juries

criticism of the jury system had become so common that André Gide could write, "One cannot deny that the machinery of justice occasionally creaks. But people seem to believe now that the only creakings are caused by the jury."[54]

On the intellectual level, the campaign against juries found powerful new ammunition in the ideas of criminal anthropology. The science was a double-edged sword in regard to juries. On one hand, it influenced the panels to acquit more defendants. On the other, the alleged lowering in the intellectual capacity of juries occurred at the very time when the rise of scientific criminology resulted in a growing call for a justice by experts. The magistrates' traditional charge, that jurors were incompetent, was now bolstered by the arguments of criminologists. By the end of the nineteenth century, juries had come to be seen as outmoded and unscientific within juristic and criminological circles. The new theories seemed to undermine the notion that the common sense of the citizen-magistrate was sufficient guide in determining guilt or innocence. Some criminologists and magistrates argued that jurors—who were generally not learned persons—were incapable of understanding the sophisticated new science of criminology, deemed necessary for judging. This was the contention of Cesare Lombroso's followers, who constituted the Italian "Positivist" school of criminology. Most important were the arguments of Enrico Ferri and Rafaele Garafalo, both of whom called for the jury system's abolition. According to these two men, those who tried criminals had to be versed in the arduous new science, for which jurors generally lacked both aptitude and training.[55]

By the 1890s, Ferri's and Garafalo's ideas had spread to France,[56] where their arguments were taken up by a number of magistrates. The most notable was Tarde, a former *juge d'instruction*, who rejected Lombroso's concept of the "born criminal" but accepted the Italian Positivist critique of the jury system. Juries were too easily impressed by the eloquence of defense attorneys, and they were ignorant and unscientific in arriving at their verdicts because they could not properly evaluate forensic and psychiatric evidence. They were also often biased, acquitting when they ought to convict and convicting when they ought to acquit. "In one way or another, science will prevail over ignorance. . . . Such is the new power, increasing every day, before which the jury is bound to disappear." Tarde's reasoning was echoed by another *juge d'instruction*, H. Pinon, who wrote in 1910 that the admission of workingmen to the juries two years before had added to the problem of jury incompetence, for workers are "little capable of understanding all the psychological nuances which can sometimes aggravate, more often extenuate, sometimes even justify an action contrary to the laws."[57]

The Campaign against the Juries

For this reason, argued Raymond Saleilles, the "individualization of punishment" should not be decided by ordinary jurors but by panels of experts. Saleilles was in fact the chief theoretician of a new penology, inspired by criminal anthropology, which sought to replace jury nullification of sanctions with a "scientific" individualization of punishment. He was a disciple of Tarde, who in the years around 1900 was professor of comparative law at the University of Paris and in the College of Social Sciences.[58] Saleilles admitted that juries were the first to practice a sort of ad hoc individualization, "prompted by a sense of popular and sentimental justice." But the panels applied this policy poorly, in ways that were casual, inopportune, sometimes emotional, and sometimes unjust. They rendered "wholly inconsistent verdicts," the "injustice of which is well-nigh scandalous; for there is no rule, no uniform standard of judgment." Each jury has "its own standards of justice," resulting almost in "a justice of chance."[59]

Therefore, according to Saleilles, the "empirical" form of individualization long practiced by juries needed to be replaced by one based "upon a truly scientific criterion." Saleilles maintained that possibly the best solution was to associate with the judges a "second jury of experts appointed to determine the punishment." The "ordinary jury, drawn by lot," would still determine the facts. But the second "technical jury," composed mainly of "physicians, directors of reformatory institutions, professional educators, and others qualified by their calling to judge and deal with men," would "become a jury of individualization" and with the judges would determine the penalty.[60]

Saleilles's proposal never became law, but several penal reforms were enacted toward the end of the nineteenth century that sought to create some kind of rational and legal system for the individualization of punishment in place of the old jury-based quasi-individualization. Here, the double-edged sword of criminal anthropology was again apparent. French penal reformers were influenced by the Italian school to take a very "harsh" approach toward "incorrigibles," who must be permanently excluded from society, and a "merciful" approach toward first-time offenders (or at least those criminals who could be rehabilitated).[61] As already shown, juries had for a long time in a "crude" way drawn a sharp distinction between recidivists and nonrecidivists by convicting the former at a much higher rate than the latter.

The first reform, the Relegation Law of 1885, embodied the "harsh" approach toward recidivists. A widespread and growing fear of "habitual criminals" among "honest folk" resulted in the Parliament's passage of the act by an overwhelming margin. The Relegation Law provided for the automatic transportation to the penal colonies for life of recidivists convicted of certain crimes, including some misdemeanors.[62] French treatment of recidivists was in fact becoming tougher just at the time when it was becoming more lenient in England. There, penal reformers, bureaucrats, and judges with increasing frequency saw many recidivists as weak rather than strong, as mentally unfit social misfits. This was accompanied by increasing criticism of the cumulative sentences that had often been handed out to repeat offenders, and such sentences became less common in the 1880s and 1890s.[63]

However, the French made a sharp distinction between recidivists and first-time offenders, and the stern Relegation Law was soon followed by other reforms that manifested the merciful character of the new penology for nonrecidivists. Immediately after the passage of the Relegation Law, the Parliament passed an act establishing what was then the most liberal parole law in Europe. Within a stipulated maximum and minimum, the penitentiary administration determined the length of incarceration, and the criterion for this was not the nature of the crime but the criminal's potential for rehabilitation.[64] This was followed by another act in 1891 that authorized judges to hand down suspended sentences to first-time offenders.[65]

These reforms to some extent put the individualization of punishment into the hands of experts (judges and prison administrators), although juries still decided the verdicts and found extenuating circumstances. The new penology in France presaged a similar movement to rationalize the individualization of punishment in the United States carried out by Progressive reformers in the era from about 1900 to 1920. They too were influenced by criminal anthropology and sought to replace fixed sentences with probation, parole, and indeterminate sentences according to the offenders' needs, characteristics, and chances for rehabilitation.[66] This meant some modernization of the courts, including the professionalization of the judiciary and the creation of specialized courts where judges assigned to them would be experts for specific kinds of cases (for example, domestic relations, morals, juveniles), and the "root social causes" of crime would be taken into account in the adjudication of cases. Progressives called too for the creation of criminological clinics for the mental testing of offenders and for the expansion of summary justice (trial by judges only) in misdemeanor and quasi-criminal cases.[67]

Progressive penal reformers in the United States also criticized jury-based individualization in terms similar to those used by Positivists in France. In 1909, many of the American reformers met at the First National Conference on Criminal Law and Criminology in Chicago. The conference led to the formation of the American Institute of Criminal Law and Criminology (AICLC) and to the founding of the *Journal of Criminal Law and Criminology*. The legal scholars and practitioners who met at Chicago in 1909 were very much aware of European criminology, and the First National Conference resolved that the AICLC sponsor the translation of European criminological texts. The AICLC called for a penology of individualization but wanted it placed on a "scientific" basis. Progressive penal reformers therefore often criticized jury-based individualization for its ad hoc, emotional, and accidental character.[68]

In 1911, the AICLC sponsored a translation into English of Saleilles's *The Individualization of Punishment*. In his "Introduction to the English Version," the great Progressive jurist Roscoe Pound criticized American juries in terms very similar to those Saleilles applied to the French panels. In some states, in order to get juries to convict in homicide cases, the penalty was left to the panels. But Pound claimed the choice of penalty depended "very largely on the temper of particular juries. . . . [T]he crude individualization achieved by our juries . . . involves quite as much inequality and injustice as the mechanical applications of the law by a magistrate."[69] Pound was not the only American jurist of the twentieth century to criticize juries in such terms.[70] In fact, another Progressive jurist associated with the AICLC, James W. Garner, in 1916 published an article on "Criminal Procedure in France" in the *Yale Law Journal*, in which he pointed out there was in the United States, as in France, "much complaint of the results of trial by jury."[71] As the examples of Pound and Garner made clear, American Progressive penal reformers (or at least some of them) were very much aware of the criticisms made of trial by jury by their Positivist counterparts in France and shared the latter's concerns about the competence of juries in determining punishment. Progressive penal reforms gave new powers to criminal justice experts—judges, prison wardens, parole boards, probation officers, and the like—to carry out the individualization of punishment (though in the United States in the 1970s and 1980s, there was a return to relatively fixed sentences).[72] In both France and the United States around 1900, penal reformers hoped to replace the "crude individualization" of juries with a more professional approach.

In fact, this was related to a broader theme in both nations: the rise of a modern administrative state run by experts or trained administrators, the kind of state called for by American Progressives. This included the bureaucratization and professionalization of criminal justice systems along "scientific" lines. In France, the beginnings of the trend can be dated back to the middle of the nineteenth century, with the professionalization of

The Campaign against the Juries

policing, the better preparation of prosecution cases, and the trial of more criminal defendants by judges in place of juries as a result of correctionalization. In the late nineteenth century, the movement accelerated with the rise of scientific detection, the professionalization of the magistrature, and the development of criminal anthropology. In both France and the United States, the professionalization of criminal justice systems and the Positivist call for a "scientific" individualization of punishment meant some reduction of the role of the jury.

But the abolition of the jury was not suggested in the United States. Even the Progressive penal reformers were not consistent in their criticisms of juries. Pound, among others, at times held that jurors in some instances, though in a "crude" and "half-grasped" way, exhibited modern, progressive thinking in their verdicts. Pound, in particular, shifted back and forth in his attitude toward jurors. He and other Progressive penal reformers maintained that trial by jury had to be kept to preserve political liberty. Progressives, along with most Americans, believed that the jury should still decide on the questions of guilt and innocence.[73] In America, there was great attachment to the idea of trial by jury as a constitutional right; the jury had deep historical roots and was viewed with "reverence and respect"; it had become deeply ingrained in the American political tradition as a protector of the people's liberties (particularly in political cases); and Americans believed that "the sovereign power of judgment ought to be vested directly in the people."[74]

In France, however, the jury was a relatively recent innovation. Authoritarian traditions were stronger in France, along with the idea that only "capable" men should judge. And the judiciary in France—which for centuries monopolized the justice system in that country—was much more hostile to jury trial than was the judiciary in the United States. Therefore, although criminal anthropology influenced jurists in both France and the United States, it was more subversive of jury trial in the former country.

Yet even in France, mounting criticism of juries during the *fin de siècle* did not mean that most citizens were prepared to discard the jury system altogether. The outright abolition of a system seen by them as an important gain of the Revolution was not politically possible. Those unhappy with juries could only suggest reforms.

The principal reform proposed by the critics of the jury system in the years around 1900 was the implementation of *échevinage*, or the collaboration between judges and jury, first introduced in the French Parliament in 1882.[75] Its aim was twofold—to reduce acquittals and to place jurors, who were assumed to be too incompetent to render justice without strict

The Campaign against the Juries

supervision, more closely under the guidance of magistrates.[76] According to Lombard, the magistrature saw *échevinage* as a means of neutralizing the jury system without completely destroying it.[77]

There were several versions of *échevinage*. One version, proposed in 1898 by Cruppi, called for judges and jury to deliberate together on the verdict.[78] Corentin Guyho, another *avocat général* at the Paris *cour d'appel*, in 1908 proposed a system in which the jurors alone decided both verdict and penalty. After a jury had convicted a person, the jurors, along with the prosecution attorney, defense attorney, court clerk, and judges, would retire to the jury chamber to discuss the penalty. The judges would act only in a consultative capacity. The jury would then proceed to vote on the penalty.[79]

But the version most popular in the early years of the twentieth century called for the jury to continue to decide questions of guilt and innocence and then for the three judges and the jury to vote together on the penalty. This reform would give juries a direct and predominant role in imposing punishment. It was based on the assumption that if the jurors themselves were allowed to impose a penalty they thought reasonable, they would be more willing to convict.[80] The proposal appealed to the men of the Republican Left, for it seemed to expand the power of juries. In 1908, it was proposed by the Socialist justice minister Aristide Briand.[81] In 1910, Briand's successor, Louis Barthou, also took up the proposal, and he presented to Parliament a bill to abrogate Article 342 of the Code of Criminal Procedure.[82] The idea moreover had the support of Henri Robert, one of the most prominent defense attorneys of the era.[83]

The proposal that judges and jury vote together on punishment did not become law until 1932. This reform would have a paradoxical result. Though it increased the power of juries to determine the penalty, it paved the way for the implementation of another system of *échevinage* in 1941 that destroyed the independence of the jury by requiring that judges and jurors vote together on *both* verdict and punishment.

Yet neither form of *échevinage* could succeed in the political climate that existed before World War I. Liberal defense of the jury system had not weakened enough to permit its implementation. The jury still had many defenders, particularly in the Republican Left, where it continued to be seen as a great democratic institution.[84] As already shown, left-wing deputies in the Parliament during the *fin de siècle* presented a number of proposals to extend trial by jury. Other champions of the jury system during the pre–World War I period argued that it accorded penal justice with popular notions of right and wrong, changing social norms, and evolving conceptions of what constituted just punishment.[85] How far France still had to go in adopting *échevinage* was reflected in the 1908 law that barred the *président* from the jury room unless he had been summoned by the foreman and was accompanied by the accused's defense attorney, the state's attorney, and the court clerk. This law, according to Lombard, reflected the continuing mistrust of the judiciary among Republican politicians.[86] As long as this mistrust persisted, Parliament was not about to give judges greater control over juries. Even though the juries' defenders could not stop correctionalization or get their proposals to extend trial by citizen-magistrates enacted into law, they did restrain efforts to weaken the jury system.

But the political landscape would change after World War I. The jury system's defenders were further weakened, and the movement to introduce *échevinage* finally triumphed in the 1930s and 1940s. It is now necessary to describe the final convergence of forces that after 1919 made it possible to destroy the independent jury system in France and thereby break with a century and a half of tradition.

chapter six

THE TRIUMPH OF EXPERTS OVER JURORS

Justice in France since World War I

The Positivists of the pre–World War I era laid the intellectual foundations for the destruction of the independent jury system in France. By 1941, the opponents of that system had finally gathered the strength to destroy it. Several powerful political forces combined with intellectual ones to bring about this outcome. For one thing, an intensification in the 1920s and 1930s of the wave of bad press concerning juries that began before World War I suggested an erosion of public support for the panels. Particularly crucial was the liberals' abandonment of their traditional support of an independent jury system. The abandonment was a major reason why the system of *échevinage* instituted by the Vichy government in 1941 was kept by France's post–World War II regimes. This was related to an even broader theme: the triumph of *fonctionnaires* over democracy by the mid-twentieth century. The rise of government by experts—by trained, professional administrators— was already noticeable during the interwar years,[1] and it became still more evident later. Within this context, *échevinage* was seen by many jurists (especially magistrates), criminologists, and politicians as a means by which juries would be guided by judges, the experts of the criminal justice system. The victory of magistrates over jurors seems to have meant the end of jury sanction nullification as a significant factor in the justice rendered in the *cours d'assises*.

A major irony occurred, however, in how the destruction of the independent jury system was carried out. Jury sanction nullification in the post–World War I years was first combated by the passage of a law in 1932 giving jurors a predominant share in determining the punishment. But this increased authority, along with the continuation of high acquittal rates, led to a successful push by jury reformers to extend the joint determination of juries and judges to the question of guilt with the full implementation of *échevinage* in 1941.

This crucial shift occurred during an era in the history of crime and criminology in France little examined by current scholars. Whereas a considerable historical literature on the subject exists for the two centuries from about 1700 to 1913, few historians have studied the interwar period.[2] This has much to do with the fact that among the French of the era—very much unlike their predecessors of the nineteenth century and of the first years of the twentieth—there was a "shriveling of interest in criminological ques- tions." According to Gordon Wright, French criminology, so vital during the *fin de siècle*, sank into "intellectual stagnancy" after World War I. Even the *Compte général* lost much of its old luster; its volumes became shorter, its data and tables more summary and less informative than those of the era before World War I. Wright claims that the major reason for the decline of interest in crime was that there was simply less of it than before: following a brief postwar rise in 1920–21, the crime rate dropped sharply. For most French citizens, crime was no longer a serious problem demanding their attention.[3]

However, the decrease in crime rates—as measured by the numbers of cases brought to trial—was perhaps deceptive. What really occurred was a decline in prosecutions, not in total cases reported. From 1921 through 1925, the number of cases reported to the public prosecutors' offices decreased, but thereafter, it rose to higher levels than ever before. The prosecution magistrates, however, took a smaller percentage of reported cases to trial, perhaps because, as André Davidovitch has suggested, the "judicial machinery" had reached the limit in the number of prosecutions it could handle.[4] Whatever the reality, Wright maintains that the perception among the French was that crime was on the decrease.[5]

But though interest in crime itself had declined in France, interest in the jury system and in its reform remained very much alive, at least among magistrates, jurists, journalists, and politicians. Before 1932, the jury reformers' immediate objective was the passage of a law allowing juries to vote with the judges in determining the punishment. Again, it was a reform aimed at reducing acquittals of mercy by allowing jurors a direct and predominant role in handing down the penalty.[6]

The champions of the proposal were able to point to judicial statistics showing that jury leniency was still very evident after World War I: from 1919 through 1931, the acquittal rate in the *cours d'assises* remained virtually the same as it had been since 1894 (see Table 2.1), as had the proportion of convicts granted extenuating circumstances.[7] Again, more than half of all convicted persons received misdemeanor penalties (see Table 2.3).

One exception to this leniency was the continuation of the resurgence of capital punishment that began during the great debate of 1906–8. The proportion of all persons convicted of capital crimes who were sentenced to death rose somewhat from 20.1 percent in 1909–13 to 29.3 percent from 1919 through 1923—the highest it had ever been since the *Compte général* began to publish statistics on findings of extenuating circumstances in the *cours d'assises* (it cannot be precisely calculated which guilty verdicts for *crimes* after 1923 included findings of extenuating circumstances).[8]

Another trend begun during the years just before World War I—the lessening of jury bias against theft relative to violent crimes—also made further progress after the war. The differential between conviction rates for theft and assault was still high, but it declined to 22 percentage points in 1919–31, and between theft and manslaughter it was now 17.1 points. The differential in conviction rates between theft and unpremeditated murder, which was about eleven points in 1909–13, dropped to about six points in the 1919–31 era. Moreover, by this era the conviction rate for premeditated homicide actually *exceeded* the rate for theft by nearly six percentage points (see Tables 2.4 and 2.5). There is perhaps no better evidence of the change in the pattern of jury behavior after 1908.

Certainly, the evident bias against thieves relevant to violent criminals had by no means disappeared: the gaps between conviction rates for theft and the two violent crimes of assault and manslaughter remained wide. Moreover, factors other than the change in the class composition of juries may have contributed to the narrowing of the gap between conviction rates for theft and violent crimes: perhaps prosecutors and examining magistrates had become more careful about which cases of violence to take to juries. But it is at least suggestive that a significant lessening of the apparent bias against theft relative to violent crimes did not occur until after the admission of workers to juries in 1908. Some contemporaries and historians may have overstated the antitheft bias of the propertied jurors of the nineteenth century, but here is evidence to suggest that the bias was not altogether absent.

Governments and magistrates of the post–World War I era continued to respond to jury leniency through the correctionalization of felonies. For one thing, repopulationist pressure finally resulted in the reclassification of abortion from a *crime* to a *délit* in 1923. World War I made this outcome possible. In terms of human lives, France suffered very heavy losses in the war. Had it not been for the reannexation of Alsace-Lorraine, the nation would have sustained a net population loss of more than 2 million people (in 1921 there were 37,000,000 inhabitants in the prewar territory of France, compared to 39,602,000 in 1911). Even with the reannexation of Alsace-Lorraine, France had fewer people than it had in 1911.[9]

These figures increased the urgency of the repopulationists' crusade and

The Triumph of Experts over Jurors

added clout to their propaganda. Perhaps as a result, prosecutors took many more abortion cases to trial: the average annual number of persons brought before the *cours d'assises* for the crime more than doubled from 73 in 1906–10 to 154 in 1911–13 and then nearly doubled again to 299 in the years 1919–23.[10] But juries still did not cooperate in the repression of the crime: the acquittal rate dropped only slightly after the war.[11] The panels seemed immune to repopulationist pressure.

However, politicians now became sufficiently alarmed at the prospect of depopulation to write pro-natalist proposals into law.[12] Although the repopulationists had supporters from across the political spectrum, their movement was probably helped by the election in 1919 of the highly nationalistic and conservative Bloc National.[13] The Parliament passed a law in 1920 banning propaganda in favor of contraception and abortion; anyone culpable of disseminating contraception propaganda was guilty of a misdemeanor and was to be punished by one to six months in prison and by fines of 100 to 5,000 francs. Furthermore, those convicted of recommending abortion were to receive prison sentences of six months to three years and fines of 100 to 3,000 francs. This was followed by another law in 1923 that finally changed the offense from a felony to a misdemeanor punishable by imprisonment of six months to five years and by fines of 100 to 10,000 francs.[14] The law resulted in a significant decrease in the number of cases tried by jury, for more than one-tenth of all persons brought before the *cours d'assises* from 1919 to 1923 had been charged with abortion.[15]

The extralegal correctionalization of other felonies by magistrates also continued to contribute to a decline in the number of jury trials, though, as was the case with abortion,[16] they were still careful to limit the practice generally to offenses for which persons convicted in the *cours d'assises* had in most instances received misdemeanor punishments. As before World War I, this was especially applicable to white-collar crimes. The admission of working-class men to juries in 1908 had scarcely altered the lenient behavior of the panels toward these offenses. In the dozen years following World War I, acquittal rates for white-collar felonies remained high (about two-fifths to three-fifths of all those tried, except for those prosecuted for counterfeiting, whose acquittal rate was about one-third).[17] Juries still found extenuating circumstances for the overwhelming majority of white-collar criminals they convicted,[18] and again, except in counterfeiting cases, eight- to nine-tenths still received misdemeanor sentences.[19]

It was therefore hardly surprising that the movement to correctionalize white-collar offenses, already so evident well before World War I, was now carried further. The annual average number of persons tried for fraud

The Triumph of Experts over Jurors

declined from 118 in 1909–13 to 72 in the era 1919–31. Trials for other white-collar crimes had almost ceased in the *cours d'assises*.[20]

As a result of the further progress of correctionalization, jury trials had become almost a rarity in France by the post–World War I era. Of course, the sharp drop in cases tried by the *cours d'assises* during the war was due primarily to the unsettled conditions during the conflict. The mobilization of many magistrates, the entry of many potential delinquents into the armed forces (where their offenses were the purview of military rather than civilian tribunals), and the occupation of much of northeastern France by the enemy reduced the number of cases the courts had to or could try.[21]

In the dozen years following the war, the number of persons tried by the *cours d'assises* rose somewhat, but the annual average of 2,185 remained well below prewar figures (see Table 2.6). Part of the decline can be attributed to the overall decrease in the number of prosecutions after 1921. However, the proportional drop in cases in the *cours d'assises* (from 3,541 in 1921 to 1,512 in 1931, a big decrease of 57.3 percent) far exceeded the decline in the *tribunaux correctionnels* (from 279,216 in 1921 to 254,830 in 1931, or a reduction of only 8.7 percent).[22] As before the war, contemporaries attributed the proportionately greater decrease in the number of *cours d'assises* cases primarily to an increasing resort to correctionalization.[23] Less than 1 percent of criminal defendants were now being tried by juries (see Table 5.1). By 1930, correctionalization had proceeded so far that André Toulemon, an attorney at the Paris *cour d'appel*, declared it a threat to the very existence of the French jury system.[24]

The trend was not unique to France in this era: even in the United States, the proportion of criminal cases that went to jury trial was in sharp decline. In at least one way, the Progressive penal reformers did undermine trial by jury, though they had not intended it. According to David J. Rothman, the introduction of probation encouraged plea bargaining as persons under indictment sought to avoid jail terms by pleading guilty in return for a sentence of probation. By the 1920s and 1930s, plea bargaining "flourished" in the United States.[25] In 1945, of all felony prosecutions not dismissed in the United States, 75 percent of those charged pleaded guilty, 10 percent were tried by the judge, and only 15 percent were tried by a jury.[26] Plea bargaining had, in the words of one modern scholar, "triumphed" over a "vanishing jury." Persons with the power and interest to pursue plea bargaining did so for some of the same reasons their counterparts pursued correctionalization in France: it provided a much more efficient and less costly means of adjudicating cases than did jury trial, prosecutors used it to win more cases, defendants cooperated in the procedure to avoid the harsher sentences they would have received if convicted by a jury, and judges could better handle heavy case loads.[27] Again, the thesis that correctionalization was a form of vertical charge bargaining may mean that a not totally dissimilar process occurred in both France and the United States.

Another threat, according to some contemporary jurists, was that public support of the jury system continued to decline in France after World War I. Several jurists claimed that by the 1920s, not only magistrates but also many politicians, journalists, and ordinary French citizens had become outraged at the frequent and "scandalous" acquittals in the *cours d'assises*.[28] If Toulemon is to be believed, this had led to the loss of popular support for the jury system. Once again, scarcely anyone proposed the outright abolition of trial by jury. But it was only because "the French honor the jury as the Romans in their decadence adored their gods, always idolizing them, but bringing them fewer and fewer offerings and having little respect for their oracles."[29]

Perhaps this had a lot to do with a renewed and intensified outpouring of publications critical of the jury system in the years around 1930. Some journals, such as *Le Cri de Paris* and *Le Matin*, in 1928 launched a campaign that repeated the prewar charges against the panels. This was followed by a major *enquête* on the jury system in *Le Temps* in August–October 1929.[30]

The press campaign was followed by the publication in 1930 of Toulemon's book, *La Question du jury*, which received considerable attention. Toulemon was another jury critic whose arguments reflected the influence of the Positivist school. Not only were jurors incompetent and too lenient, but the system itself was outmoded and ran counter to modernity's increasing specialization of functions, which was a sign of the progress of civilization. Correctionalization was partly a manifestation of this movement, which would lead to a justice carried out by "men specialized in the function of judging, professional magistrates who do not decide on the basis of impression, but who make use of science and experience." Like so many other critics of the jury system, however, Toulemon did not call for its total abolition but instead for the introduction of *échevinage*.[31] By 1931, the anti-jury campaign had become so intense that Romanian jurist Thomas Dragu (whose impassioned defense of the system was published in Paris) could write that it was in France "that the sharpest and at the same time most steadfast campaign against the jury has been recently carried out."[32]

Yet the immediate objective of the jury reformers before 1932—passing a law allowing juries to vote with judges in determining punishment—seemed to extend jurors' power. It was a reform clearly aimed at reducing what the juries' critics believed was an unacceptably high acquittal rate.

The Triumph of Experts over Jurors

Major supporters of the reform in the Parliament, such as M. D. Bonnevay and André Lebert, argued that "scandalous acquittals" resulted from jurors' fears of excessively harsh punishments in certain cases and that these acquittals could be avoided if jurors deliberated with judges in determining the penalty (including the application of suspended sentences).[33] Evidently, the penal reforms already enacted had not gone far enough to completely satisfy jurors. Parole was limited by the fact that the decree regulating its use was not issued until 1958. Suspended sentences could be imposed only by the judges,[34] and they did so sparingly: little more than 7 percent of all persons convicted in the *cours d'assises* in the dozen years following World War I had their sentences suspended.[35] A law allowing juries to vote with judges in determining punishment, Lebert claimed, was desired by public opinion, the majority of magistrates who had practiced in the *cours d'assises*, and the juries themselves.[36]

With so much powerful support behind it, the proposal was finally enacted into law by the Chamber of Deputies on March 5, 1932. It stipulated that henceforth the twelve jurors, though still solely responsible for determining guilt or innocence (on which they voted separately), were to deliberate with the three judges in determining punishment (including whether to suspend the sentence), which had to be approved by at least eight of the fifteen.[37]

Although the enactment of the law was followed by a significant one-fourth decline in the acquittal rate in the *cours d'assises*—from 34.3 percent from 1919 through 1931 to 26.1 percent from 1932 through 1938 (see Table 2.1)—it is uncertain to what extent it was actually responsible for the decrease. The rate of exonerations had already begun to drop in the half-dozen or so years preceding passage of the law.[38] Furthermore, the magistrates responsible for the prosecution and investigation of crimes continued to be increasingly selective in determining which cases went to trial: the proportion of reported cases dropped by the prosecutors and *juges d'instruction* before trial in either the *cours d'assises* or *tribunaux correctionnels* rose from 61.5 percent in 1926–30 to 62.4 percent in 1931–35 and to 66.1 percent in 1936–40.[39] These factors at least suggest that the 1932 reform was not wholly responsible for the decline of acquittals.

But the law appeared to have at least one important effect on penalties: the proportion of persons convicted in the *cours d'assises* whose sentences were suspended rose sharply from 7.5 percent in the years 1919–31 to 17.7 percent in 1932–38 (the *Compte général* for 1939 was never published).[40] Less clear was the impact of the law on the death penalty. The average annual number of death sentences dropped sharply from thirty-two in 1919–31 to

The Triumph of Experts over Jurors

twenty in 1932–38.[41] But juries were already free to reject the death penalty before the law of 1932 through findings of extenuating circumstances for persons they convicted of capital crimes. In fact, one can regard the quarter-century from about 1906 to 1931 as an era marked by a temporary reversal in the long decline of capital punishment in France. The 1932 reform was followed during the next six years by only slight decreases in the proportions of convicts sentenced to hard labor terms of either life or less and by slight increases in the proportions sentenced to imprisonment for five years or more and also those sentenced to five years or less (see Table 2.3).

The evidence therefore suggests that by the post–World War I years, a reluctance to impose the punishments provided by law was just one—and apparently far from the most important—cause of the high acquittal rate in the *cours d'assises*. Even after the passage of the law of 1932, the conviction rate remained below what it was to be in jury trials in American federal criminal courts in the 1980s and 1990s (though the fact that by these decades, plea bargains, which resulted in only a small proportion of cases going to trial in the United States, may make comparisons with interwar France questionable)[42] and even slightly below what it had been in France during the Second Empire and the earliest years of the Third Republic. It remained far below the conviction rate in the *tribunaux correctionnels* (see Tables 2.1 and 2.2).

The juries' critics maintained that the acquittal rate was still relatively high in the *cours d'assises* because jurors were left uncertain of the guilt of at least some defendants due to the confusion caused by the almost total lack of rules of evidence.[43] The traditional difficulties this caused for jurors were aggravated in the twentieth century by the increasing resort to expert testimony on the mental state of criminal defendants.[44] Jurors needed guidance from experienced judges in weighing muddled and often contradictory evidence. The full implementation of *échevinage* was seen as a means by which this guidance could be provided. For this reason, it was recommended in the years around 1930 by such prominent jurists as A. Henry, Toulemon, and Henri Donnedieu de Vabres.[45] The law of 1932 was seen by jury reformers as simply a first step to a fusion of jury and judges.[46]

According to the reformers, this fusion was also made necessary by the fact that the 1932 act had reduced the power of magistrates too much: not only did the jury alone still determine the verdict, but judges, whose traditional role was to decide punishment, were now greatly outvoted in this matter by jurors. Therefore, according to Françoise Lombard, law manuals and commentaries after 1932 continually returned to the theme of the "magistrat dépouillé. . . . In short, from 1932 on, the strategy of the professionals

The Triumph of Experts over Jurors

consisted of using the democratic argument to show how magistrates are given insufficient power in the judging of criminals."[47]

What is more, liberals no longer mounted a vigorous defense of the independent jury system, a system that in the nineteenth century seemed to them to be the "palladium of liberty." As Bernard Schnapper has noted, after World War I the champions of the jury system seemed to have lost heart for the struggle, "as if sincerely democratic jurists were themselves also convinced of the necessity of reform."[48]

Perhaps this was in part due to the lessening role of juries in the protection of political and press freedoms. Nineteenth-century French liberals saw a strong and independent jury system as essential to the protection of the people's liberties largely because the panels of citizen-judges, representing popular sovereignty and free to defy the government, acquitted many persons accused of political and press offenses. This was particularly true during the July Monarchy and the Second Republic, when the government prosecuted many dissenters. But the argument that the jury system protected freedom of speech and press was subsequently undermined by the sharp decline in the number of persons tried by the *cours d'assises* for political and press offenses, from an annual average of 359 in the years 1831–51, to 60 in 1871–1913, to 4 in 1919–28.[49] Moreover, by the post–World War I period, the hostility between magistrates and politicians had been reduced.[50]

A more important reason seems to have been the wave of bad press concerning juries, especially after World War I. Not only had much of the press turned against the juries, but the jury system was seen as anachronistic within juristic and criminological circles. By 1929, Donnedieu de Vabres, a Paris law professor and one of the most prominent liberal jurists in France, could write, "Today, the institution of the jury is beaten and battered by the most advanced of the modernists: those who want to replace a justice of 'impression' with a truly rational and scientific one."[51] He agreed that under *échevinage*, jury and judges could work together to prevent "serious errors." Magistrates would not exercise undue influence over jurors, for the latter would greatly outnumber the former. Besides, there was no more reason to fear the ascendancy of judges over the jury than that of influential jurors over their colleagues. Whenever a juror voluntarily accepts "the advice of one more enlightened than he, why regret it and appear more royalist than the king?"[52]

The pressure from jurists and magistrates to institute *échevinage* was strong enough for the government to appoint a commission headed by one of the country's most important magistrates, Paul Matter, *procureur général* of the *cour de cassation*, to draw up a plan of reform that would propose a complete collaboration of judges and jury. The commission met from 1934 to 1938, when it delivered to the Chambre des députés a proposal to fully implement *échevinage*.[53] The outbreak of World War II kept the Parliament of the Third Republic from ever debating the proposal.

But in November 1941, the Vichy regime finally enacted a law implementing it. The regime's authorities calculated that for political reasons, some semblance of the jury system should be kept, but it had to be adapted to an authoritarian order. Vichy officials, particularly Minister of Justice J. Barthélemy—a leading authority on constitutional law and one of Marshal Pétain's chief juridical advisors[54]—seized upon the antidemocratic implications of the Matter Commission's proposal, which had lain dormant in ministerial cartons since 1938.[55] Vichyites were very critical of juries because of the "uncertainty" of their verdicts, their lack of severity, and the slowness of trials in the *cours d'assises*, all of which frustrated a regime that sought quick and exemplary justice to intimidate its opponents. The authorities realized, however, that it was dangerous to break entirely from the jury system, because it was an element of tradition to which the French remained attached, and it was one of the foundations of legality and of political legitimacy. The new law on the jury was in keeping with the Vichy government's policy of respecting juridical and judicial forms as much as the defense of the regime's antidemocratic order allowed. As Barthélemy put it, the 1941 reform did not abolish the jury but was meant to "remove its venom." The jury was marginalized rather than eliminated outright.[56]

The 1941 law was well designed to achieve this marginalization. Not only were judges and jury to deliberate and vote together in determining both guilt and innocence, but the number of lay jurors was reduced from twelve to six. Moreover, the office of jury foreman was abolished, and the *président* of the *cour d'assises* took over his function of directing the panel's deliberations. Magistrates were also now given a monopoly in the drawing up of the annual jury lists. Cantonal jury lists were to be composed by the *juges de paix* alone. The *arrondissement* lists were drawn up by the *président* of the local *tribunal civil* and all the *juges de paix* of the *arrondissement*, following the verification of the cantonal lists by the *procureur de la République* mentioning which persons fulfilled "the conditions of aptitude" for jury service.[57] Meanwhile, the regime further marginalized juries by sending more and more cases (especially those of a political nature) that had normally come under the purview of the *cours d'assises* to exceptional tribunals.[58]

France's democratic post–World War II regimes kept the new system of *échevinage*, though it was slightly modified in favor of lay jurors. An ordinance of 1945 raised their number to seven. The Fifth Republic's *Code*

The Triumph of Experts over Jurors

de procedure pénale of 1958 added two more lay jurors, and conviction now required eight of twelve votes (that is, at least five of the nine jurors).[59] Moreover, an ordinance of 1944 abolished the Vichy law's provision giving magistrates complete authority to draw up the annual jury lists and returned to the system of 1872, except that now women were admitted to the panels.[60] The old system was finally replaced in 1980 by the selection of jury session lists by lot from electoral lists.[61] But the system of *échevinage*, in which the three judges of the *cour d'assises* deliberate and vote with the jurors on both verdict and penalty, remained intact.

In the opinion of a number of jurists and historians, the system meant the practical abolition of the jury in France because its independence had been destroyed.[62] Statistics on jury verdicts suggest that *échevinage* at least gave the judges more influence over jurors, for its introduction was followed by a sharp decline in the acquittal rate in the *cours d'assises*. In general, during the two decades following the enactment of the 1941 law, the acquittal rate was only about one-tenth of persons tried. This was about equal to the acquittal rate in the *tribunaux correctionnels* (see Tables 2.1 and 2.2).

Échevinage was not the only possible explanation for the decline in acquittals after 1941. For one thing, the fact that from this date to 1952,[63] the *parquets, juges d'instruction*, and *chambres des mises en accusation* prosecuted or indicted a smaller proportion of alleged criminals than in the 1930s presumably meant that fewer of the weaker cases now went to trial. But the decrease was too modest for this to have been a major factor.[64] For jurist Louis Hugueney, "the general opinion" was that the decline in acquittals was due largely to the severe limitations the 1941 law placed on peremptory challenges to jurors, giving defense attorneys far less of a chance to dismiss jurors likely to convict. One problem with Hugueney's logic, however, was that the 1941 law allowed the prosecution the same limited number of peremptory challenges (three out of a session list of eighteen). The prosecution gained no greater advantage than it had enjoyed under the original *Code d'instruction criminelle* in force before 1941, when peremptory challenges, though allowed in a larger number of cases (two-thirds of thirty-six jurors on the session list as opposed to a total of six, or one-third, of eighteen after 1941, the other six being eliminated by lot only), were also equally allotted between defense and prosecution.[65]

The new Code of Criminal Procedure introduced in late 1958 even further disadvantaged the prosecution. It allowed the accused to challenge peremptorily as many as five jurors from the session list of twenty-seven, but counsel for the prosecution was allowed no more than four such challenges.[66] It is true that this reform was followed by a modest rise in the acquittal rate, from 7.9 percent in 1957–58 to 12.5 percent in 1959–63. But the latter figure was still much lower than it had been in 1932–41 and was only slightly more than two percentage points above what it had been in 1945–52 (see Table 2.1).

Therefore, neither of the above factors seems to have equaled the effect of *échevinage* in raising the conviction rate. Part of this was due to simple arithmetic, at least from 1941 through 1958. The law of 1941 required a majority vote of five of nine to obtain a conviction. This meant that if all three judges voted for conviction, the agreement of only two of the six jurors was necessary to condemn the defendant. Under the law of 1945, the three judges still needed the assent of less than half (three) of the seven jurors for conviction. After the revision of the Code of Criminal Procedure at the end of 1958, which of course required the assent of an actual majority of five jurors for conviction, the acquittal rate rose modestly, though it is not certain whether and to what extent this was the cause, or to what extent it was due to the new rule on summary challenges. Yet it is hard to imagine how, under *échevinage*, the professional judges could not have continued to exert considerable influence on the decisions of the lay jurors. Since the judges who acted alone in the *tribunaux correctionnels* were so strongly inclined to convict accused persons, and since magistrates had for so long complained about the jurors' "indulgence," it seems reasonable to assume that judges who deliberated with juries often exerted their influence in favor of conviction, though this influence must have been limited to some extent by the jurors' continuing to vote by secret ballot, as they had done since 1835.[67]

Yet according to the great attorney Maurice Garçon, the *président* of the *cours d'assises*, accompanied by two junior magistrates, possessed a prestige and experience that overwhelmed jurors and deprived them of their effective independence. The *président* also came into the jury chamber armed with the accused person's dossier, and he was in a position to abuse his authority (which in Garçon's opinion often favored the prosecution) by raising unexpected or unforeseen arguments that the defense had not been able to address during trial.[68] Robert Vouin was not so distrustful of judges, but he agreed that the system of *échevinage* at least restored the influence that the *président* of the *cour d'assises* lost with the 1881 abolition of the *résumé*.[69]

Less certain is the extent to which the judges influenced the jurors in respect to punishment. There was temporary movement toward somewhat more severity during the years just following World War II. The proportion of people convicted in the *cours d'assises* who received misdemeanor penalties dropped from 57.9 percent in 1932–38 to 47.4 percent in 1945–52. The proportion condemned to hard labor terms of less than life rose from 14.3

The Triumph of Experts over Jurors

percent to 23.3 percent, and for life terms the figure rose from 3.7 percent to 5.1 percent (see Table 2.3). The reasons for the trend are not clear. Judges may have been harsher than jurors when it came to convicting people, but (as already shown) this was not necessarily true when it came to punishment. Both magistrates and jurors may have been reacting with greater firmness when confronted by a sharp rise in crime during the first postwar years.[70]

Most dramatic was the temporary resurgence of the death penalty: the annual average number of death sentences imposed by the *cours d'assises* rose from twenty in 1932–38 to fifty-four in 1945–51. The death sentences imposed on some Vichyite collaborators did not seem to have contributed significantly to this number, since the *collabos* were generally tried by courts-martial, emergency tribunals, and a High Court created in 1944 to deal with those who had participated directly in the Vichy government.[71] The sharp rise in death sentences handed out in the *cours d'assises* rather appears to have been part of a movement toward sterner punishments for nonpolitical offenders during the high crime years of the immediate post–World War II era.

But after 1951, there was a very sharp decline in death sentences. The annual average dropped to only twelve from 1952 through 1964.[72] There had been ups and downs in the number of death sentences since the early nineteenth century. However, the final decline that began in 1952 would end with formal abolition in 1981.[73] The decrease in death sentences was soon followed by some movement toward leniency with regard to other penalties, including the abolition of hard labor sentences in 1960 (see Table 2.3). This trend occurred during an era when declining crime rates weakened the arguments of "hard-liners" and strengthened those of penal reformers who favored greater leniency.[74]

Échevinage therefore seems to have resulted in more convictions but not necessarily in harsher punishments. Yet not every politician or jurist in postwar France was happy with the system. In 1951, J. Isorni introduced before the National Assembly a proposal to repeal the law of 1941 and return to the system of 1932.[75] In 1955, Maurice Garçon announced his support of this measure. According to Garçon, the jury was a "just and liberal" institution. But this meant it was incompatible with authoritarian government, and "in servile imitation of the dictatorships, the government of Vichy took a fatal blow against a jury guilty of being independent, of protecting citizens against arbitrariness and of yielding poorly to suggested convictions. . . . [T]he law of November 25, 1941, a law of rare hypocrisy, took a fatal blow against the institution; one dared not say that one purely and simply suppressed the jurors, for fear possibly of stirring up opinion, but one reduced them very easily to impotence. They were kept only for form's sake." The law of 1941 had done "what Louis XVIII, Charles X, Louis-Philippe and Napoleon III had not dared to attempt."[76]

But Isorni and Garçon did not prevail. There was a relative lack of protest against the system of *échevinage* in postwar France. Part of the reason, according to Lombard and Schnapper, was that because of correctionalization, so few cases were now tried by the *cours d'assises* that the jury system no longer seemed important to most of the French.[77] Moreover, the long-standing and vehement criticisms of the jury system evidently had had their effect on public opinion. In 1955, liberal Paris law professor Robert Vouin claimed that *échevinage* was "very clearly desired by popular sentiment." Echoing André Gide's statement of four decades earlier, Vouin added: "If he perceives creakings in the judicial machine, the average Frenchman naturally blames the incompetence and the interpretation of the jury. . . . [H]e senses in the association of the court and the jury a guarantee of justice."[78] Since Vouin was a strong supporter of *échevinage*, his claim may have been exaggerated. But in 1962, American jurist George W. Pugh wrote that the "institution of the jury . . . is viewed with considerable skepticism by the French."[79] At the very least, there was no great outpouring of public sentiment in France demanding a return to an independent jury system, a fact that even Garçon had to admit.[80]

Several of the nation's prominent jurists also defended the system of *échevinage* from Garçon's assertion that it was the creation of the authoritarian and collaborationist Vichy regime. Vouin noted that the reform of 1941 was not really *vichyssoise* but stemmed directly from the proposal developed by the Matter Commission from 1934 to 1938 and had the backing of great liberal jurists.[81] Appeals court judge Gabriel Dupin de Beyssat made the same point, stating that Garçon's assertions "make litter of the most elementary true history. Their inaccuracy and their excess demonstrate . . . that passion and bias blind the most subtle minds." Again, *échevinage*, though implemented by the Vichy regime, was conceived during the Third Republic and was approved by major liberal jurists.[82]

One of these, Donnedieu de Vabres, was particularly important in the movement to retain *échevinage*: in the early years of the Fourth Republic, he headed a commission to propose reforms in the Code of Criminal Procedure, a commission that in 1949 recommended the continuation of *échevinage*.[83] Donnedieu de Vabres's fellow Paris law professor Louis Hugueney favored *échevinage* for another reason: his hope that it would reverse the correctionalization movement. In 1945, he wrote that those who wanted to preserve the democratic principle of lay participation in the administration of justice should support the retention of *échevinage*: "The law of November 25 [1941] provides a major solution to the crisis of the jury. Eroded by legal and judicial correctionalization, the *cour d'assises* was like a person dying of consumption. A drastic remedy was necessary to save it."[84] Hugueney's younger colleague, Vouin, added that the system of *échevinage* was a necessary substitute for the *président's résumé*.[85] Furthermore, under the system of *échevinage*, the judgments of the *cours d'assises* had improved, for they were less often overturned by the *cour de cassation* than had been the case before 1941.[86]

Yet the debate between Garçon and the defenders of *échevinage* went deeper than arguments over recent history, correctionalization, the need for a substitute for the *résumé*, or *cour de cassation* decisions. It also went to the very heart of the jury's role. Garçon, in terms that recall those of Adhemar Esmein, held that juries represent public opinion. It is true that "crime is an attack on morality," but morality changes over time. Jurors are sensitive to these changes. The role of the juror is different from that of the professional magistrate. The latter is concerned only with the material fact and if and how it falls under the letter of the law. The juror, however, "judges a question of responsibility. He must not only ascertain if the accused has committed the crime, but still yet is he guilty . . . that is to say, in the name of public opinion, sovereign arbiter of morals, he has the arbitrary right to alleviate or absolve." Jurors are "sometimes inclined to censure the laws," to "judge the value of the basis of the law." Their verdicts thereby open the way to legislative reforms.[87]

Garçon cited the example of bigamy. Under the Napoleonic *Code pénal*, the punishment for this crime was hard labor. But by the end of the nineteenth century, the penalty appeared excessive. The definition of the "legitimate family" was becoming looser. The legalization of divorce and of remarriage between accomplices in adultery and the legitimation of children born as a result of adulterous unions made bigamy appear as a less serious offense than it had once been. Hence, jurors very often found extenuating circumstances for those they convicted of the crime or acquitted them outright, because even the minimum sentence of two years' imprisonment, which the culprits could still have received, seemed too harsh. Such verdicts led to a law of 1933 that reduced bigamy to a misdemeanor punishable by six months' to three years' imprisonment. Jury decisions had thus brought the law into line with public opinion. The jury was also the "solid guardian of our liberties" because it had so often resisted government pressures in the trial of crimes of opinion.[88]

The Triumph of Experts over Jurors

Vouin saw the role of the jury differently: it was obligated to judge on the basis of the letter of the law alone. "The jury was not created to express the reactions of public opinion, but to assure to all citizens the benefit of judgment by their peers. It is the law, not opinion directed by the press, which is the expression of the general will."[89]

Nor could an ever-more scientific justice be competently imposed by citizen-judges unguided by the professional magistrates.[90] The increasing resort to expert testimony after World War II was therefore another reason put forth in favor of the retention of *échevinage*. In 1971, Dupin de Beyssat wrote:

> The manifest incompetence and the supreme inexperience of the jury are already unfortunate in ordinary cases, but they become scandalous when the proceedings involve the assessment of delicate expert evaluations or raise complex juridical or technical questions. . . . The magistrates are there to clarify and to aid the jurors. . . . [T]heir profession being to judge, they acquire an efficacious experience of men and of things. . . . Their decisions are more coherent because they keep in memory those they have already made in similar cases. It is not at all the same with the juror, who judges only one time and therefore has no experience and cannot recall a case similar to the one he is trying. Thus, one should not be astonished at the incoherent verdicts and the absence of regularity in the administration of criminal justice.

Dupin de Beyssat added:

> From day to day, judicial action is being perfected and the magistrates are entrusted with new means to better know the man and the crime: psychiatric evaluation, medical-psychological examination, personality investigation. . . . And the nostalgics of the jury would want the final decision to belong, in the most serious cases, to amateurs who cannot have knowledge of the dossier before trial and cannot any longer during the deliberation, where the law opposes it![91]

Dupin de Beyssat's criticisms of the jury system seem to sum up those of his fellow magistrates of twentieth-century France. *Échevinage* was a necessary reform. Yet even at that, there were still enough instances of jury bias to make correctionalization "irregular itself but justifiable in fact."[92]

Moreover, any opposition to *échevinage* that might have come from the numerous attorneys in Parliament was sidestepped in 1945, when the system was continued by an ordinance that did not require consultation of the legislature. Besides, according to Lombard, despite the supposed domi-

The Triumph of Experts over Jurors

nance of the legislative branch under the Fourth Republic's constitution, more and more power came to rest in the hands of the *fonctionnaires* of the *haute administration*, the experts or technocrats of the executive branch. The adoption and retention of the system of *échevinage* was part of the triumph of *fonctionnaires* over elected officials.[93]

The introduction of *échevinage* did not even realize Hugueney's hope that it would reverse the long-standing movement toward correctionalization.[94] Indeed, the decline in jury trials continued after World War II. From 1945 through 1952, the annual average number of persons tried by the *cours d'assises* remained below 2,000. In the years from 1957 through 1963, it only slightly exceeded 1,000 (see Table 2.6). To some extent, the decline was due to the legal downgrading of a number of felonies to misdemeanors, including bigamy in 1933, bribery and misappropriation of funds in 1943, and forgery and fraudulent bankruptcy in 1958.[95] But since few persons were any longer tried for these crimes in the *cours d'assises* (as already shown in the white-collar cases), the effect must have been small.

Correctionalization therefore remained a largely extralegal process. Magistrates could not resist a procedure that still held for them so many advantages. These included cheaper and quicker justice (especially since prosecutors who correctionalized cases could send them directly to the *tribunaux correctionnels* without further pretrial review or the more formal procedures of trial by jury), the desire to make sure the *cours d'assises* were not burdened with too many cases (some offenses labeled as felonies under the 1810 *Code pénal* were no longer considered serious), avoidance of the inconsistencies of punishment in the *cours d'assises*, and the expectation that in many instances the judges and juries would grant the felons they convicted sentences appropriate for misdemeanors.[96] However, as in the years around 1900, correctionalization was in some cases also carried out in the spirit of the movement for leniency in punishment, a movement that at least resumed after the early 1950s. In the post–World War II era, prosecutors correctionalized some cases because they believed "a felony conviction or sentence would be excessive under the particular circumstances or in light of the defendant's prior record."[97]

In fact, the decline of the jury system in France was part of a broader European pattern. During "the nineteenth century the jury was the flag of the liberal movement." In the course of that century, it was introduced in many European countries.[98] But in the twentieth century, it (or at least the "classic" jury composed of laymen alone) was abandoned or sharply curbed in most countries of continental Europe, replaced by either trial by professional judges alone or by systems of *échevinage*, as in France and Germany.

The Triumph of Experts over Jurors

By 1984, the independent criminal jury made up exclusively of laymen could be found on the Continent only in Belgium and in parts of Switzerland. Even in England, the grand jury had been abolished and the civil jury practically so.[99] The United States remains the great redoubt of the jury system, with grand juries, criminal trial juries, and civil juries all continuing to operate, though plea bargains and out-of-court settlements keep many cases from going to the panels.

The reasons for the decline of the jury system in other countries of continental Europe appear to have not been completely unrelated to the reasons for its decline in France. European jurist R. C. Van Caenegem cites the jury system's "exorbitant cost" as one reason, though he adds that "the question as to why the cost of the jury procedure, borne in the course of many centuries, suddenly became so unbearable in our own time remains open."[100] Another reason was the rise of a justice by experts, growing out of the development of criminology. In 1967, a colloquium was held at Louvain, Belgium, in which most of the eminent European criminalists present took a position against the very principle of the jury system. One of them, Professor Paul-Em Trousse, *conseiller* of the Cour de cassation de Bruxelles, called for the abandonment of the jury system and its replacement by a specialized magistrature very knowledgeable not only in penal law but also in criminology, sociology, psychology, and psychiatry. The result would be a better informed and more humane justice. Another participant, Professor Jean Graven, president of the Cour de cassation de Genève, claimed that the time had come to return to trial by professional judges because people had lost confidence in the jury.[101] Again, all this may be connected to the broader theme of the rise of government by experts or by the knowledgeable, with its perhaps antidemocratic implications, fulfilling, in part, the dreams of Plato and the comte de Saint-Simon.

By the post–World War II era, the jury system, once a subject of so much passionate debate among the French, had been reduced to insignificance. In the end, there was surprisingly little protest. So long as some form of the jury survived, even with the loss of its independence and with jurisdiction over very few cases, the French were satisfied that, at least symbolically, this gain of their great Revolution had not been lost.[102] In 1987, Schnapper wrote that in France, "the jury is no longer but a venerable and exquisitely outmoded institution. It has ceased to be the object of political debate; it has gained in serenity and in peace, a peace which resembles that of the cemetery."[103]

The Triumph of Experts over Jurors

CONCLUSION

In France, jurors were supposed to answer a series of questions concerning the "facts" of a case and leave "law" (penalty) to the judges. Yet for a century and a half, juries frequently resorted to nullification. Sometimes this was nullification of the law itself, as in political cases and in certain "routine" felony cases where social norms conflicted with the letter of the law. But far more common was sanction nullification. A broad analysis based on both contemporary sources and the writings of modern historians shows that there were a number of basic transitions in the authorities' long fight against jury sanction nullification. First, the panels were granted legal means of mitigating penalties through the law of 1832 on extenuating circumstances. This reform was only partially successful at ending the juries' frequent recourse to extralegal sanction nullification. The state then resorted to the tactic of shifting many cases away from the juries of the *cours d'assises* to the judges of the *tribunaux correctionnels* through the process of "correctionalization." However, the authorities remained unhappy with what they saw as too many acquittals among the cases still tried by juries. Politicians and jurists believed that the most important reason for high acquittal rates was the continued resistance of jurymen to what they feared would be excessive punishments imposed by the judges even following findings of extenuating circumstances. The Parliament responded by enacting the law of 1932, giving jurors a predominant say in determining penalties. But even this reform did not reduce acquittals much. In 1941, the government finally managed to "tame" the juries by placing them under the direct supervision of the judges in the system of *échevinage*. Nonetheless, through sanction nullification, juries had by this time done much to transform the penal justice system of France.

The core of the transformation was the movement away from a criminal justice system meant to try the crime to one that tried the criminal. Critics of the juries often interpreted the panels' behavior in this regard as biased, especially in the late nineteenth and early twentieth centuries. It was also frequently assumed that jurors were biased because of who they were. Jurists, especially magistrates, held that the "bad composition" of juries explained their weaknesses. One judge, Louis Proal, spoke for his colleagues when he claimed that the "merit of the jury depends on its composition."[1] Magistrates asserted repeatedly that the justice of the juries was defective because too many jurors were ignorant or uneducated or were in some fashion incompetent, and they were chosen through a politicized process. It was hardly surprising that magistrates, along with conservative or authoritarian politicians, claimed that the way to reform justice in the *cours d'assises* was to reform the composition of the juries.

Late-twentieth-century historians have repeated the accusation that jurors handed down the kinds of verdicts they did because of who they were. But these scholars tend to see class and gender as more important than "incompetence." Such historians believe that juries were much harsher toward thieves than toward violent criminals because the panels were almost exclusively bourgeois in composition, at least before 1908. They acquitted a far higher proportion of accused women than of accused men because before 1944, jurors were all males, and they were frequently gallant toward female defendants or saw them as less criminally responsible than men.

But jury composition was hardly the only reason for bias. There were also the types of evidence that jurors were allowed to consider and the ways this evidence was presented. There is good reason to believe that the almost total lack of rules of evidence led to many acquittals. In the near absence of such rules, jurors must have often been befuddled or overwhelmed in trying to determine on their own the relevance of testimony or how to weigh muddled and often contradictory evidence. This would have contributed to doubts about proof. Before 1881, the only guidance for jurors in respect to the evidence was provided by the *président*'s *résumé*. It may have been more than coincidence that the acquittal rate rose following the *résumé*'s abolition. In 1955, British law professor C. J. Hamson claimed that in France, it was "probably the mal-presentation of evidence which is largely responsible for the numerous reforms, proposed and made in the past and now brought forward, on the subject of the constitution and the function of the jury."[2] The ultimate response was not to borrow the strict rules of evidence that prevailed in Anglo-American courts—the result of centuries of tradition, practice, and statutes[3]—but to place jurors under the "expert" guidance of judges in the system of *échevinage*.

The fact that pretrial confessions were also, without restrictions, included in the evidence presented at trials in a nation where plea bargaining was not allowed and the defendant therefore still had to be tried helps to explain the higher rate of acquittals for violent crimes than for theft. As William Savitt shows, at least for the Côte d'Or in the mid-nineteenth century, thieves far more often confessed than did persons accused of violent crimes. The importance of evidentiary considerations in the deliberations of jurors is also attested to by the fact that in general, the crimes most difficult to prove, such as infanticide, abortion, and arson, were the ones that most often resulted in acquittal.

Nonetheless, these evidentiary factors still do not explain the sharp differentials in acquittal rates between men and women and between recidivists and first-time offenders. What critics of the juries saw as "bias" was more than anything else a trial of the person rather than of the crime. The behavior of the panels may have seemed irrational to many jurists and criminologists, but jurors were at least in part responding to the person and not to the offense.

The way evidence was presented in trials facilitated jury-based individualization. *Présidents* and witnesses could and often did speak at length about the personality and past history of accused persons and with virtually no restrictions. This must have conveyed to jurors the idea that the person of the accused was as much on trial as the crime he or she may have committed, that character was a crucial issue in judging. When this was combined with the system of "moral proofs" and the theatrical nature of trials in the *cours d'assises*, the temptation to see the individual as much as or more than the crime he or she was charged with must have often been irresistible. From the beginning, jurors seem to have frequently acquitted or convicted, or downgraded the charges, or (after 1832) found extenuating circumstances, in accordance with their pre-scientific notions of individualization relating to the moral character and/or honor of the accused, with the circumstances of the crime, and with the justice of the punishment. Then, at least in many cases, a significant shift in the nature of individualization occurred in the late nineteenth century when the development and popularization of scientific criminology, with its concepts of diminished responsibility (or in some cases, no responsibility) for certain criminals influenced jurors to judge even more on the basis of the person rather than of the crime.

It is true that evidence about the defendant's character or personality may have been helpful in determining the sentence, imposed by the judges before 1932 and predominantly by the jurors after that date.[4] It may also have been relevant in helping jurors to determine whether they should find extenuating circumstances for the persons they convicted. But it was all evidence presented to the jury before it arrived at its verdict, and therefore jurors could hardly believe it was irrelevant to findings of guilt or innocence, since it was admissible during trial.

Prejudicial or "subjective" evidence of this kind could be refuted at

Conclusion

length by defendants,[5] but those with a criminal past stood little chance of acquittal. Here, juries could really be tough. As already noted, from 1826 through 1870, conviction rates for recidivists tried in the *cours d'assises* were much higher than the conviction rates for nonrecidivists. Even Savitt admits that the "one clear prejudice" of nineteenth-century French juries was their strong proclivity to convict recidivists (though he neglects to mention the other "clear prejudice" of gender).[6] In this instance, the statement that in France, "one judges the man, not the facts" seems to be supported by the evidence. Character counted not only in sentencing but also in the verdict.

In fact, the high conviction rate for recidivists tried by the juries evidently reflected the widespread fear of recidivists among "honest folk," the same fear that resulted in the Parliament's passage of the Relegation Law of 1885. Significantly, during the parliamentary debates over the act, its defenders made a sharp distinction between the "habitual," "incorrigible," or "professional" criminals and the "accidental" criminals. "Accidental" criminals commit their crimes because they are subject to the influence of "strong, but temporary emotions," or a "moment of anger" or "weakness," whereas recidivists are "habitual" criminals who commit their crimes coldly and willfully. They are incurable and characterized by "natural perversity."[7]

Here, the behavior of juries anticipated the changes in penal law that by the end of the nineteenth century drew a sharp distinction between recidivists and first-time offenders. Long before 1885, the panels apparently thought the "habitual criminal" was deserving of harsh treatment and the "accidental" criminal of "indulgence." Recidivists were a real danger to society and therefore must be excluded. First-time offenders were much more likely to be "accidental" criminals, or had not yet proven themselves otherwise. They were a much lesser danger to society and could probably be freed and not commit a crime again, especially if the defendant had broken the law out of "passion."[8] Leniency for first-time offenders was eventually legalized through the law of 1885 on parole and the one of 1891 on suspended sentences.

French jurors were not alone in making the distinction: twentieth-century American juries were also much more likely to convict defendants they knew or suspected had a prior criminal record. According to Harry Kalven Jr. and Hans Zeisel, this was presumably because jurors believed that "as a matter of human experience it is especially unlikely that a person with no prior record will commit a serious crime."[9] But in the United States, a defendant's prior criminal record could be introduced by prosecutors during trials only "to identify the defendant as the author of the current offense, to establish motive or intent, or to show lack of mistake or accident," or, when

Conclusion

the defendant took the stand, to impeach his or her credibility as a witness.[10] In French trials, the defendant's previous criminal record was always admissible[11] and regularly noted, although by the 1990s, U.S. courts had so broadened the admissibility of "prior crimes" evidence as to make American and French practices "less dissimilar than they once were."[12] Still, during the nineteenth century, American and French trials were more dissimilar in this respect, to the greater prejudice of the recidivist defendants in France.

The prejudice against recidivists was part of a broader pattern of jury bias in France based above all on the perceptions of the dangerousness of accused persons and the appropriateness of the punishments. The recidivist, the assassin, and the thief were evidently seen as cold-blooded, calculating, or "habitual" criminals who might commit their crimes again if freed. But the first-time offender, the female, and the *criminel(le) passionel(le)* were apparently "accidental" criminals who had momentarily lost control of themselves and could probably be reintegrated into lawful society following acquittal or a short sentence. Again, character counted. This was yet another way in which French juries of the nineteenth and twentieth centuries seem to have acted much like the panels of eighteenth-century England, whose decisions were strongly influenced by the character of a defendant, at least when it came to jury devices for leniency.[13] And as in eighteenth-century England, these considerations could not be disentangled from issues related to punishment. Juries found means to moderate punishments they may have found excessive for certain crimes and for certain culprits. Lawmakers repeatedly revised penal laws to take into account the supposed sentiments of jurors.

Yet the leaders of the Revolution, when they introduced trial by jury, did not foresee that on the felony level, it would change a criminal justice system meant to try the crime into one that tried the man (or woman), not unlike that which existed in eighteenth-century England. They wanted a "classical" system of justice in which only the "facts" were judged and punishments were rigidly fixed so that persons convicted of the same crimes always received the same penalties. Very soon, juries found ways to modify this system. They did so through outright acquittals and also, before 1832, by refusing to find aggravating circumstances in the commission of many crimes where the evidence seemed clearly to show aggravation. After 1832, the panels did the same when they found extenuating circumstances in many cases where the extenuating circumstances probably did not exist. French juries ignored the truth in such instances in order to achieve mercy in punishment, just as English juries ignored the truth for the same reason in the eighteenth century.

Conclusion

Jury nullification of sanctions did not, however, satisfy Positivist champions of the "individualization of punishment." Positivists criticized jury-based individualization as ad hoc and ineffective. Juries were not sophisticated enough to implement the individualization of punishment as a "scientific" process that focused on the characteristics of individuals to determine what caused them to commit their crimes or to devise the appropriate punishment (or treatment) necessary for the reform of the offender.

Sometimes juries did seem to decide cases in accordance with Positivist ideas of the individualization of punishment. An example was the high conviction rate for recidivists. Positivists also drew a sharp distinction between repeat and first-time offenders. But jurors and Positivists judged on different bases. Juries saw recidivists as morally worse than first-time offenders, whereas Positivists saw recidivists as afflicted with an incurable illness, and they should therefore be permanently segregated from the rest of society. The influence on jurors of popularized notions derived from criminal anthropology may have been more evident in other cases by the *fin de siècle*. For example, traditional male gallantry combined with new "scientific" ideas of female criminal irresponsibility resulted in sharply rising acquittal rates for accused women. But Raymond Saleilles and other Positivists still held that juries carried out individualization poorly. Even when Positivists conceded that juries should continue to determine guilt or innocence, they believed that more "scientific" means must be found to determine the punishment of the individual offender, and that required experts trained in the new science of criminology.

The juries' instincts would eventually be taken over more professionally by the bench, most notably through correctionalization and the implementation of *échevinage*. The former, like jury sanction nullification itself, was often carried out in an extralegal fashion. Indeed, there is often some disjunction between how a justice system is supposed to operate and how it really operates. In the United States, trial by jury is guaranteed by the Constitution. Yet nearly nine of every ten persons convicted and sentenced in U.S. district courts from 1980 through 1994 had pleaded guilty or nolo contendere and were therefore tried by neither court nor jury.[14] Similarly in France, correctionalization was carried out with the cooperation of defendants.

This suited the French state just fine. As shown repeatedly, magistrates were careful to limit correctionalization to the kinds of *crimes* that in most instances were punished with mere misdemeanor penalties. Thus, the government argued that juries had already come to treat these crimes as de facto misdemeanors, and hence it made sense to try them in the *tribunaux cor-*

rectionnels. In France through correctionalization, and in the United States through plea bargaining, the state is relieved of much of the expense and trouble of jury trials, along with the potential for a clogging of the proceedings of the courts that use juries.

Correctionalization and plea bargaining greatly reduced the proportion of criminal cases decided by juries in France and the United States. In the former country, the independence of the panels was effectively destroyed by the implementation of *échevinage* in 1941. This also meant the effective end of jury nullification in France. Yet for a century and a half, jury sanction nullification had been an important means by which community-based norms (or at least nongovernmental ones) were injected into the criminal justice system. The authorities ultimately brought an end to this situation through a deceptive compromise: jurors were given a predominant voice in determining punishment, but only for the few cases that they still tried and under the supervision of judges. An institution imported into France during the Revolution as an expression of the sovereignty of the people had been effectively marginalized in favor of a justice by professionals. But this was not before juries had altered the criminal justice system in a way the men of the Revolution had never intended.

Conclusion

NOTES

Introduction

1. Thompson, *Making of the English Working Class*, 19, 80, 165, 467–68, 671, 720, 723; Paul Finkelman, "Politics, the Press, and the Law: The Trial of John Peter Zenger," in Belknap, *American Political Trials*, 25–44; Finkelman, "The Treason Trial of Costner Hamway," in Belknap, 77–95; Steven R. Boyd, "Political Choice—Political Justice: The Case of the Pennsylvania Loyalists," in Belknap, 45, 49, 53; Allen, "Political Trials by Jury," 223–28; Pierre-André Lecocq and Joel Bourgeois, "Jurys et liberté de la presse: La presse devant les jurys du Nord de l'an X à 1851," in Martinage and Royer, *Les destinées du jury criminel*, 215–16, 223–24, 228.

2. Green, *Verdict According to Conscience*, xiii.

3. Ibid., xviii–xx.

4. Ibid., 3.

5. Ibid., xiii, xviii–xix.

6. Ibid., 351, 356–57, 363.

7. Ibid., 363–64.

8. Innes and Styles, "Crime Wave," 381–84.

9. Ibid., 384–86.

10. Ibid., 386–87.

11. Ibid., 387, 401–2.

12. Green, *Verdict According to Conscience*, xiii, xviii, 26–30, 32, 35, 46, 52, 64, 98–99, 105–7, 127–28, 147, 149, 276, 280, 295, 356–57; Beattie, *Crime and the Courts*, 415, 419–21, 419n, 424–25, 430–32, 439–43; King, *Crime, Justice, and Discretion*, 234; Langbein, *Origins of Adversary Criminal Trial*, 58–59, 336.

13. Green, *Verdict According to Conscience*, 380.

14. Interestingly, where in England legal reforms inspired by Enlightenment ideas of equal penalties for persons convicted of the same crimes and of certainty of punishment in place of harshness of punishment (Green, *Verdict According to Conscience*, 365; Beattie, *Crime and the Courts*, 421) brought about an important reduction of the jury's role as mitigator of penalties, they had an opposite effect in France. The French Revolution and Napoleon brought in a system of penal law based on Enlightenment or Beccarian notions of certain and rigidly fixed punishments equally applicable to all offenders convicted of the same crimes. But French juries resisted this system of punishments. Just why they behaved differently from English juries in this regard is not clear, and the question merits investigation in some future study.

15. Woloch, *New Regime*, 361.

16. Ministère de la Justice, *Compte général de l'administration de la justice criminelle*, 1850, xxxv (hereafter referred to as *Compte général*).

17. Garner, "Criminal Procedure in France," 280.

18. See, for example, Allen, "Political Trials by Jury," 223–38; Berenson, *Trial of Madame*

Caillaux; Savitt, "Villainous Verdicts?"; Harris, "Melodrama, Hysteria and Feminine Crimes of Passion"; Vallaud, "Le crime d'infanticide"; and Donovan, "Infanticide and the Juries" and "Abortion, the Law, and the Juries."

19. At least two works deal broadly with the history of the jury and of jury behavior in France during the nineteenth and early twentieth centuries: Donovan, "Justice Unblind"; and Bernard Schnapper, "Le Jury français," in Schioppa, *Trial Jury*, 165–239. However, neither of these attempts a comprehensive study of the influence of the jury on the evolution of punishment.

20. Schnapper, "Le Jury français," 238.

21. Beattie, *Crime and the Courts*, 388; King, *Crime, Justice, and Discretion*, 244; J. M. Beattie, "London Juries in the 1690s," in Cockburn and Green, *Twelve Good Men and True*, 238; P. J. R. King, "Illiterate Plebeians, Easily Misled: Jury Composition, Experience, and Behavior in Essex, 1735–1815," in Cockburn and Green, 261, 266; Douglas Hay, "The Class Composition of the Palladium of Liberty: Trial Jurors in the Eighteenth Century," in Cockburn and Green, 310–11, 315, 335–36, 338, 340, 342–43, 349.

22. King, "Illiterate Plebeians, Easily Misled," 302, and *Crime, Justice, and Discretion*, 244; Hay, "Class Composition," 311, 350–51.

23. Douglas Hay, "Property, Authority and the Criminal Law," in Hay et al., *Albion's Fatal Tree*, 43, 51, 57.

24. J.-C. Farcy, "Les juges de paix et la politique au XIXe siècle," in Petit, *Une justice de proximité*, 143–63; Martin, *Crime and Criminal Justice*, 191–233; M. Perrot, "Delinquency and the Penitentiary System in Nineteenth Century France," in Forster and Ranum, *Deviants and the Abandoned*, 4:222.

25. Lallemand, *Le Recrutement des juges*, 88, 150, 152; Martin, *Crime and Criminal Justice*, 192; Royer et al., *Juges et notables*, 13–16, 140, 143–44.

26. Martin, *Crime and Criminal Justice*, 195.

27. Royer et al., *Juges et notables*, 307, 311, 314.

28. Ibid., 132, 265–66; Ensor, *Courts and Judges*, 40–43; Martin, *Crime and Criminal Justice*, 195–233.

29. Martin, *Crime and Criminal Justice*, 232, 232n.

30. As shall be shown, when juries tried *délits politiques et de presse*, the conviction rate was very low (about one-third from 1831 through 1851, two-fifths in the 1870s, and barely over half from 1880 though 1913). The rate was much higher when these crimes were tried only by the judges of the *tribunaux correctionnels*. Of the 1,721 persons tried for *délits politiques et de presse* by the *tribunaux correctionnels* from 1826 through 1830, 1,045 (60.7 percent) were convicted and 676 (39.3 percent) were acquitted. This figure does not include the sixteen persons tried for these offenses by the juries in late 1830, eight of whom were acquitted. Of the 21,661 tried by the *tribunaux correctionnels* from 1852 through 1870, 18,825 (87.1 percent) were convicted and 2,786 (12.9 percent) were acquitted. *Compte général*, 1826, Table 74, p. 110; 1827, Table 82, p. 121; 1828, Table 91, p. 139; 1829, Table 92, p. 141; 1830, Table 1, p. 2, and Table 68, p. 115; 1852, Table 72, p. 111; 1853, Table 72, p. 113; 1854–57, Table 74, p. 115; 1858–59, Table 72, p. 113; 1860, Table 70, p. 111; 1861–62, Table 70, p. 113; 1864–69, Table 67, p. 113; 1870, Table 62, p. 105.

31. Collingham, *July Monarchy*, 170; Collins, *Government and the Newspaper Press*, 67, 76–77, 79, 82, 95–97; Lecocq and Bourgeois, "Jurys et liberté de la presse," 216, 226–29; Merriman, *Agony of the Republic*, 33–36, 38.

32. Unlike the case with ordinary felonies, the *Compte général*'s tables for *délits politiques et de presse* did not include information on the occupations of persons charged with these offenses, although we may infer that those tried for press crimes would most often have occupations linked to writing or publishing. In France, political prisoners in general were regarded as "high-status offenders," and from the early 1830s they were granted special privileges (e.g., the right to wear clothing of their own choice, choice of their own doctor, dispensation from forced labor, etc.) that ordinary prisoners were denied. Whitman, *Harsh Justice*, 121–23.

33. Loubet, *La Justice criminelle*, 66; Toulemon, *La Question du jury*, 104–5.

34. Garner, "Criminal Procedure in France," 257–58.

35. Cruppi, *La Cour d'assises*, 5; Frase, "Comparative Criminal Justice," 630–31.

36. Toulemon, *La Question du jury*, 86; Cruppi, *La Cour d'assises*, 5.

37. Berenson, *Trial of Madame Caillaux*, 5–6.

38. *Code d'instruction criminelle*, Articles 310 and 312.

39. Ibid., Article 313; Garner, "Criminal Procedure in France," 261–62, 262n; Coudert, "French Criminal Procedure," 334; Martin, *Crime and Criminal Justice*, 178; Cruppi, *La Cour d'assises*, 73.

40. *Code d'instruction criminelle*, Article 319; Garner, "Criminal Procedure in France," 265.

41. Coudert, "French Criminal Procedure," 335; Garner, "Criminal Procedure in France," 262–65; Martin, *Crime and Criminal Justice*, 179; Hamson, "Prosecution of the Accused," 274.

42. Coudert, "French Criminal Procedure," 335; Garner, "Criminal Procedure in France," 268–70; Cruppi, *La Cour d'assises*, 82; Martin, *Crime and Criminal Justice*, 180.

43. Pugh, "Administration of Criminal Justice in France," 25.

44. Donnedieu de Vabres, *La Justice pénale*, 133.

45. Coudert, "French Criminal Procedure," 335; Garner, "Criminal Procedure in France," 271.

46. Pugh, "Administration of Criminal Justice in France," 26.

47. Ibid.; Tarde, *Penal Philosophy*, 440.

48. Berenson, *Trial of Madame Caillaux*, 5.

49. Loubat, "Programme minimum de réformes pénales [2]," 457.

50. Garner, "Criminal Procedure in France," 264, 263–67; Coudert, "French Criminal Procedure," 339; Pinon, "La réforme de la procedure criminelle," 76–77.

51. Beer, "Ce qu'est le jury criminel," 487–91.

52. Donovan, "Justice Unblind," 90.

53. *Code d'instruction criminelle*, Article 342; Garner, "Criminal Procedure in France," 272–73.

54. Cruppi, *La Cour d'assises*, 32, 169; Esmein, *History of Continental Criminal Procedure*, 563; Saleilles, *Individualization of Punishment*, 97; Gineste, *Essai sur l'histoire et l'organisation du jury criminel*, 176, 176n.

55. Pugh, "Administration of Criminal Justice in France," 10.

56. Saleilles, *Individualization of Punishment*, 10.

57. Ibid., 10, 75–76.

58. Davidovitch, "Criminalité et répression," 35.

59. Merriman, *Police Stories*, 7–8, 15–17, 29, 32, 37, 39, 41–42, 50, 53–54, 70, 75–76,

185–86; Payne, *Police State*, 212–13, 235, 245–46, 286; Martin, *Crime and Criminal Justice*, 42–44.

60. Savitt, "Villainous Verdicts?," 1047.

61. *Code d'instruction criminelle*, Article 345; Berenson, *Trial of Madame Caillaux*, 35.

62. Schnapper, "Le Jury français," 165.

63. Beattie, *Crime and the Courts*, 315.

64. Ibid., 424–25; Green, *Verdict According to Conscience*, 127–28, 276, 295; Langbein, *Origins of Adversary Criminal Trial*, 58–59.

65. Moore, *Jury*, 125.

66. Langbein, *Origins of Adversary Criminal Trial*, 321, 330.

Chapter 1

1. Martin, *Crime and Criminal Justice*, 126–27.

2. Dawson, *History of Lay Judges*, 4, 37–42, 60–63.

3. Ibid., 120.

4. Ibid., 44–47, 121–22, 299.

5. Langbein, *Torture and the Law of Proof*, 4–10.

6. Martin, *Crime and Criminal Justice*, 128–31; Coudert, "French Criminal Procedure," 330; Esmein, *History of Continental Criminal Procedure*, 218, 220, 224–25, 227, 409; Woloch, *New Regime*, 357.

7. Dawson, *History of Lay Judges*, 52–53, 56, 69–70, 76, 87, 94–95, 102–13.

8. Van Caenegem, *Judges, Legislators and Professors*, 36–37.

9. Green, *Verdict According to Conscience*, 3; Langbein, *Torture and the Law of Proof*, 9.

10. Coudert, "French Criminal Procedure," 328–29.

11. Robinson, *Everyday Life in Ancient Greece*, 57–59; Stone, *Trial of Socrates*, 181, 186; Finley, *Aspects of Antiquity*, 60–61.

12. Dawson, *History of Lay Judges*, 12, 16–18, 35–39.

13. Kalven and Zeisel, *American Jury*, 14n.

14. Dawson, *History of Lay Judges*, 120–21.

15. Levy, *Palladium of Justice*, 6–8, 13.

16. Dawson, *History of Lay Judges*, 121; Roger D. Groot, "The Early-Thirteenth-Century Criminal Jury," in Cockburn and Green, *Twelve Good Men and True*, 5.

17. Groot, "Early-Thirteenth-Century Criminal Jury," 3, 18–19, 25, 34–35.

18. Dawson, *History of Lay Judges*, 117–18, 293, 299.

19. Green, *Verdict According to Conscience*, 14, 16, 26–27, 52, 108; Cockburn and Green, *Twelve Good Men and True*.

20. Ibid., 105; Edward Powell, "Jury Trial at Goal Delivery in the Late Middle Ages: The Midland Circuit, 1400–1429," in Cockburn and Green, *Twelve Good Men and True*, 78–116; Langbein, *Origins of Adversary Criminal Trial*, 64.

21. Van Caenegem, *Judges, Legislators and Professors*, 37.

22. Langbein, *Torture and the Law of Proof*, 27–60, 64–69. Langbein's findings on the decline in the use of torture before the Enlightenment campaign against the practice have been confirmed by Andrews, *Law, Magistracy, and Crime in Old Regime Paris*, 1:442, 446–47, 454–61, 463–64, 466–67, 471.

23. Esmein, *History of Continental Criminal Procedure*, 369; Pierre Charles Ranouil, "L'intime conviction," in Martinage and Royer, *Les destinées du jury criminel*, 89.

24. Montesquieu, *L'Esprit des lois*, book 6, ch. 3, quoted in Esmein, *History of Continental Criminal Procedure*, 369.

25. Esmein, *History of Continental Criminal Procedure*, 401, 408.

26. The work and the debates in the Constituent Assembly on the jury have been described and analyzed by Antonio Padoa Schioppa, "La guiria all'Assemblea Constiuente francese," in Schioppa, *Trial Jury in England, France, Germany*, 75–163.

27. Esmein, *History of Continental Criminal Procedure*, 420.

28. Allen, "Political Trials by Jury," 222.

29. Gineste, *Essai sur l'histoire et l'organisation du jury criminel*, 55–56; Woloch, *New Regime*, 302; Assemblée Nationale Constituante: Séance du avril 6, 1790, in Mavidal and Laurent, *Archives Parlementaires* (hereafter referred to as *AP*), 12:550–58.

30. Assemblée Nationale Constituante: Séance du avril 30, 1790, *AP*, 15:343.

31. Assemblée Nationale Constituante: Séance du novembre 27, 1790, *AP*, 21:42–72.

32. F. Lombard, *Les Jurés*, 144–46, 150; Bernard Schnapper, "De l'origine sociale des jurés," in Martinage and Royer, *Les destinées du jury criminel*, 115.

33. Royer, *Histoire de la justice*, 284, 303, 310.

34. Soulas, *Le Recrutement du jury*, 284.

35. Quoted in Gineste, *Essai sur l'histoire et l'organisation du jury criminel*, 73.

36. Berenson, *Trial of Madame Caillaux*, 39.

37. Assemblée Nationale Constituante: Séance du novembre 27, 1790, *AP*, 21:59.

38. Ranouil, "L'intime conviction," 90; Esmein, *History of Continental Criminal Procedure*, 424; Royer, *Histoire de la justice*, 291.

39. Ranouil, "L'intime conviction," 86.

40. Assemblée Nationale Constituante: Séance du mars 29, 1790, *AP*, 12:435.

41. Ranouil, "L'intime conviction," 86.

42. Ibid., 89.

43. Savitt, "Villainous Verdicts?," 1032n.

44. Allen, *Les tribunaux criminels*, 40.

45. Ibid.; Esmein, *History of Continental Criminal Procedure*, 620.

46. Allen, "Political Trials by Jury," 222.

47. Woloch, *New Regime*, 357.

48. *Code d'instruction criminelle*, Article 336; Berenson, *Trial of Madame Caillaux*, 38–39; Garner, "Criminal Procedure in France," 272.

49. Quoted in Cruppi, *La Cour d'assises*, 35.

50. Esmein, *History of Continental Criminal Procedure*, 416.

51. Assemblée Nationale Constituante: Séance du novembre 27, 1790, *AP*, 21:59.

52. Woloch, *New Regime*, 361.

53. The number of questions can vary greatly with the nature and the complexity of the case. Garner, "Criminal Procedure in France," 273, 273n.

54. Woloch, *New Regime*, 357.

55. Garner, "Criminal Procedure in France," 269–70.

56. Berenson, *Trial of Madame Caillaux*, 38–39.

57. Hamson, "Prosecution of the Accused," 280.

58. Garner, "Criminal Procedure in France," 278–80.

59. Soulas, *Le Recrutement du jury*, 135.

60. Assemblée Nationale Constituante: Séance du avril 6, 1790, *AP*, 12:574–79.

61. Soulas, *Le Recrutement du jury*, 35, 107.

62. Constitution of 1791, Titre III, Section II.7, in Roberts and Comb, *French Revolution Documents*, 1:351–52.

63. Soulas, *Le Recrutement du jury*, 35, 38.

64. Guibourg, *Le jury criminel*, 36; Esmein, *History of Continental Criminal Procedure*, 413n, 414; Royer, *Histoire de la justice*, 371n.

65. Esmein, *History of Continental Criminal Procedure*, 410–11.

66. Ibid., 411–12; Woloch, *New Regime*, 357–58.

67. Gineste, *Essai sur l'histoire et organisation du jury criminel*, 57; Soulas, *Le Recrutement du jury*, 36.

68. Woloch, *New Regime*, 358–59; Martin, *Crime and Criminal Justice*, 137.

69. Esmein, *History of Continental Criminal Procedure*, 413–14, 418.

70. Ibid., 415.

71. Ibid., 417; Woloch, *New Regime*, 361.

72. Woloch, *New Regime*, 361.

73. Martin, *Crime and Criminal Justice*, 138.

74. Woloch, *New Regime*, 362–63.

75. Soulas, *Le Recrutement du jury*, 107.

76. F. Lombard, *Les Jurés*, 147.

77. Woloch, *New Regime*, 364.

78. Allen, "Political Trials by Jury," 222–28.

79. Woloch, *New Regime*, 364–65.

80. Soulas, *Le Recrutement du jury*, 36–37; Woloch, *New Regime*, 364.

81. Allen, "Political Trials by Jury," 224–25.

82. Woloch, *New Regime*, 366; Lucas, "Rules of the Game in Local Politics," 359–60.

83. Woloch, *New Regime*, 366–67; Allen, "Political Trials by Jury," 223–26.

84. Allen, "Political Trials by Jury," 225–26, 228.

85. Constitution of the Year III, Titre IV.35, in Roberts and Hardman, *French Revolution Documents*, 2:342–43; Soulas, *Le Recrutement du jury*, 38, 107; Bernard Schnapper, "Le Jury français," in Schioppa, *Trial Jury*, 167.

86. Woloch, *New Regime*, 368–69; Allen, *Les tribunaux criminels*, 59–60.

87. Wright, *Between the Guillotine and Liberty*, 34–35; Esmein, *History of Continental Criminal Procedure*, 447, 449–50; Brown, "Bonaparte's 'Booted Justice,'" 120.

88. Brown, "Bonaparte's 'Booted Justice,'" 120; Woloch, *New Regime*, 367.

89. Woloch, *New Regime*, 370–73.

90. Ibid., 361–62; Savitt, "Villainous Verdicts?," 1030.

91. Garner, "Criminal Procedure in France," 273; Woloch, *New Regime*, 361.

92. Allen, *Les tribunaux criminels*, 71–72; Woloch, *New Regime*, 365, 370, 372–73, 378.

93. Woloch, *New Regime*, 102, 367.

94. Brown, *Ending the French Revolution*, 152–53, 159–71, 213–16, 221–33, and "Bonaparte's 'Booted Justice,'" 121.

95. Schnapper, "Le Jury français," 167–68; Woloch, *New Regime*, 362.

96. Brown, "Bonaparte's 'Booted Justice,'" 121–22, and *Ending the French Revolution*, 316–24.

97. Esmein, *History of Continental Criminal Procedure*, 454, 517–18; Bouget, "Une juridiction d'exception"; Gilles Landron, "Les tribunaux criminels spéciaux contre les

tribunaux criminels avec jury (France, an IX-1811)," in Rousseaux, Dupont-Bouchat, and Vael, *Révolutions et justice pénale en Europe*, 189–98; Allen, *Les tribunaux criminels*, 257–66.

98. Brown, "Bonaparte's 'Booted Justice,'" 130n.

99. Esmein, *History of Continental Criminal Procedure*, 456; Wright, *Between the Guillotine and Liberty*, 37.

100. Bérenger, 16 Pluviose, *Arch. Parl.*, 301–2, cited in Esmein, *History of Continental Criminal Procedure*, 461.

101. Esmein, *History of Continental Criminal Procedure*, 459–60.

102. Brown, "Bonaparte's 'Booted Justice,'" 126.

103. Wright, *Between the Guillotine and Liberty*, 37.

104. "Procès-verbaux du Conseil d'État. Séance du 16 prairial an XII (5 juin 1804)," in Locre, *La législation civile*, 24:11.

105. Woloch, *New Regime*, 367–68.

106. Esmein, *History of Continental Criminal Procedure*, 465, 479.

107. Ibid., 467, 472.

108. Tribunaux d'appel, *Observations des tribunaux d'appel sur le projet de code criminel*, Observations du tribunal d'appel séant a Pau, 2:16–17; Orléans, 2:12; Nancy, 2:2, 4. The observations of each *tribunal d'appel* are separately paginated.

109. Ibid., Aix, 1:10, 12; Bourges, 2:3; Metz, 1:18–19; Nancy, 2:2–6; Pau, 2:17; Orléans, 2:12, 15; Toulouse, 2:2–3; Caen, 2:3; Nîmes, 2:7–9.

110. *Code pénal*, Articles 1, 6–10; Coudert, "French Criminal Procedure," 331, 333–34, 337; Wright, *Between the Guillotine and Liberty*, 39.

111. *Code d'instruction criminelle*, Articles 351 and 352; Schnapper, "Le Jury français," 179; Garner, "Criminal Procedure in France," 281. In 1800, under Napoleon, the *tribunal de cassation* was renamed the *cour de cassation*.

112. Royer, *Histoire de la justice*, 425–26; Esmein, *History of Continental Criminal Procedure*, 437–38, 440.

113. Gineste, *Essai sur l'histoire et l'organisation du jury criminel*, 58–59; Woloch, *New Regime*, 376.

114. Martin, *Crime and Criminal Justice*, 146–47; Coudert, "French Criminal Procedure," 332–33; Garner, "Criminal Procedure in France," 256–60.

115. Martin, *Crime and Criminal Justice*, 143.

116. Ibid.; Coudert, "French Criminal Procedure," 330–32.

117. Woloch, *New Regime*, 376.

118. Martin, *Crime and Criminal Justice*, 194; Hamson, "Prosecution of the Accused," 279.

119. Martin, *Crime and Criminal Justice*, 143; Woloch, *New Regime*, 362; Esmein, *History of Continental Criminal Procedure*, 533.

120. "Procès-verbaux du Conseil d'État. Séance du 16 prairial an XII (5 juin 1804)," in Locre, *La législation civile*, 24:46.

121. Soulas, *Le Recrutement du jury*, 38–39; Woloch, *New Regime*, 377.

122. *Code d'instruction criminelle*, Article 382.

123. Th. Riboud, "Rapport sur le Titre II du Livre II du Code d'instruction criminelle," in France, *Code d'instruction criminelle*, 112; Section de législation du Conseil d'État, "Projet d'avis" (juin 25 et 28, 1811), cited in Bourdon, *Napoleon au Conseil d'État*, 75.

124. *Code d'instruction criminelle*, Article 387.

125. Corbes, "La Cour d'assises des Côtes-du-Nord," 305.

126. P. J. R. King, "Illiterate Plebeians, Easily Misled: Jury Composition, Experience, and Behavior in Essex, 1735–1815," in Cockburn and Green, *Twelve Good Men and True*, 288–89; J. M. Beattie, "London Juries in the 1690s," in Cockburn and Green, 234.

127. *Code d'instruction criminelle*, Articles 387, 399–401.

128. Wright, *Between the Guillotine and Liberty*, 40.

129. Trebutien, *Cours élémentaire de droit criminel*, 2:348.

130. Gineste, *Essai sur l'histoire et l'organisation du jury criminel*, 176; Cruppi, *La Cour d'assises*, 32.

131. *Code d'instruction criminelle*, Article 342.

132. Ranouil, "L'intime conviction," 86; Esmein, *History of Continental Criminal Procedure*, 516.

133. Cruppi, *La Cour d'assises*, 31, 33; Esmein, *History of Continental Criminal Procedure*, 630; Beer, "Ce qu'est le jury criminel," 487–91; commentary by Henri Bergson in Prud'hon, *Le Jury criminel*, 128.

134. *Moniteur*, Jan. 4, 1791, quoted in Esmein, *History of Continental Criminal Procedure*, 422.

135. Savitt, "Villainous Verdicts?," 1032n.

136. Garner, "Criminal Procedure in France," 274; Beer, "Ce qu'est le jury criminel," 499–500; commentary by M. l'Avocat général Mornet in Prud'hon, *Le Jury criminel*, 62; Pinon, "La réforme de la procedure criminelle," 80–81; Mimin, *Le Concours du jury*, 9, 19, 22–23, 28; Guyho, *Les Jurés "maîtres de la peine,"* 23, 29; Donnedieu de Vabres, *La Justice pénale*, 128.

137. *Code d'instruction criminelle*, Article 342.

138. Schaefer, *Theories in Criminology*, 106–9; Clarence Ray Jeffrey, "The Historical Development of Criminology," in Manheim, *Pioneers in Criminology*, 366–67.

139. Harris, *Murders and Madness*, 4–5; Leps, *Apprehending the Criminal*, 17.

140. Nye, *Crime, Madness, and Politics*, 23–25; Corbes, "La Cour d'assises des Côtes-du-Nord," 324.

141. See the comments of Councilor of State Berlier in "Procès-verbaux du Conseil d'État. Séance du 16 prairial an XII (5 juin 1804)," in Locre, *La législation civile*, 24:45.

Chapter 2

1. Trebutien, *Cours élémentaire de droit criminel*, 2:348; "Appendice du Titre II du Livre II du Code d'instruction criminelle, formant la troisième loi de ce code, ou Loi du 2 mai 1827, relative a l'Organisation du jury," in Locre, *La législation civile*, 26:4–5.

2. The Constitutional Charter of 1814, Article 40, in Stewart, *Restoration Era*, 114.

3. Stewart, *Restoration Era*, 19, 165.

4. Collingham, *July Monarchy*, 70–71.

5. From 1828 through 1848, a total of 4,391,234 persons were inscribed on the annual jury lists. Of these, 3,976,443 (90.5 percent) were electors and 414,792 (9.4 percent) were non-electors. *Compte général*, 1828, Table 148, p. 239; 1829, Table 151, p. 243; 1830, Table 130, p. 219; 1831, Table 139, p. 229; 1832, Table 142, p. 239; 1833, Table 149, p. 249; 1834, Table 145, p. 245; 1835, Table 148, p. 249; 1836, Table 152, p. 251; 1837–38, Table 151, p. 251; 1839–41, Table 152, p. 249; 1842–48, Table 153, p. 257.

6. Collingham, *July Monarchy*, 73.

7. F. Lombard, *Les Jurés*, 203.

8. Marie-Renée Santucci, "Être ou ne pas Être juré au XIXeme siècle," in Martinage and Royer, *Les destinées du jury criminel*, 165, 169.

9. Bernard Schnapper, "De l'origine sociale des jurés," in Martinage and Royer, *Les destinées du jury criminel*, 120, 133.

10. Ibid., 119.

11. According to Marie-Renée Santucci's analysis of jury session lists in the Herault, the average juror in the department was 49 years old during the Restoration and 50.1 years old during the July Monarchy. From the jury session lists in the Deux-Sevres, Indre, and Sarthe at the end of the July Monarchy in 1847 and early 1848, Bernard Schnapper has calculated the age of the average juror in those departments at 49 years and 3 months. Santucci, "Être ou ne pas Être juré au XIXeme siècle," 166; Schnapper, "De l'origine sociale des jurés," 121.

12. Claverie, "De la difficulté de faire un citoyen," 148–49; Pourcher, "Des assises de grace?," 170, 172; Bernard Schnapper, "Le Jury français," in Schioppa, *Trial Jury*, 192n, 202.

13. F. Lombard, *Les Jurés*, 197; Claverie, "De la difficulté de faire un citoyen," 149, 151, 161; Pourcher, "Des assises de grace?," 170–71.

14. Schnapper, "Le Jury français," 184, 184n, 189.

15. F. Lombard, *Les Jurés*, 187, 189–90.

16. "Appendice du Titre II du Livre II du Code d'instruction criminelle," in Locre, *La législation civile*, 26:7–8.

17. "Procès-verbal de la Chambre des Pairs. Séance du 29 decembre 1826," in Locre, *La législation civile*, 26:11.

18. "Appendice du Titre II du Livre II du Code d'instruction criminelle," in Locre, *La législation civile*, 26:4–5.

19. Schnapper, "Le Jury français," 185.

20. Collingham, *July Monarchy*, 170.

21. F. Lombard, *Les Jurés*, 204–5.

22. Furet, *Revolutionary France*, 351.

23. Ibid., 326–64; Collingham, *July Monarchy*, 55–68, 116–42; Cobban, *History of Modern France*, 2:94–97; Wolf, *France*, 71–90.

24. Cobban, *History of Modern France*, 2:110; Collingham, *July Monarchy*, 76, 80.

25. Garraud, *Traité théorique*, 1:203.

26. Dalloz et al., *Code pénal annoté*, 289–90, 294–95.

27. The Constitutional Charter of 1814, Articles 63 and 65, in Stewart, *Restoration Era*, 115.

28. P. Lombard, *La Justice des bien-pensants*, 125–26; Schnapper, "Le Jury français," 183.

29. "Loi sur les juridictions prévôtales 20–27 decembre 1815," in Cahen and Mathiez, *Les lois françaises*, 24–25.

30. Ibid., 25; P. Lombard, *La Justice des bien-pensants*, 126–27.

31. Schnapper, "Le Jury français," 183.

32. Ibid., 183, 183n.

33. Stewart, *Restoration Era*, 44.

34. Schnapper, "Le Jury français," 183, 183n.

35. "Charte constitutionnelle de 1830," Article 69 (1), in Cahen and Mathiez, *Les lois françaises*, 69.

36. F. Lombard, *Les Jurés*, 197; Schnapper, "Le Jury français," 182–83, 186–87.

37. Wright, *Between the Guillotine and Liberty*, 63. Wright cites as a contemporary source in this regard Alphonse Bérenger, *De la répression pénale, de ses formes et des ses effets* (Paris: Cosse, 1855), 1:216.

38. Corbes, "La Cour d'assises des Côtes-du-Nord," 309n; *Compte général*, 1850, xxxv (source of quote); 1860, xxxviii.

39. Beattie, *Crime and the Courts*, 424–25; Green, *Verdict According to Conscience*, 295; Langbein, *Origins of Adversary Criminal Trial*, 58.

40. Garner, "Criminal Procedure in France," 279–80; Schnapper, "Le Jury français," 187.

41. Wright, *Between the Guillotine and Liberty*, 168.

42. From 1825 through 1831, a total of 3,546 persons were tried for capital crimes. Of these, 1,767 (49.8 percent) were convicted, and 1,779 (50.2 percent) were acquitted. Capital crimes included *assassinat* (premeditated homicide), poisoning, parricide, infanticide (through 1901), and arson of an inhabited structure. Excluded is *meurtre* (unpremeditated homicide) accompanied by another felony or misdemeanor. Though this crime was punishable by death, the *Compte général*'s Table 1 on acquittals and convictions for crimes against persons does not allow us to distinguish between conviction and acquittal rates for this offense and for all other cases of unpremeditated homicide, which were punishable by life at hard labor. In any case, trials for unpremeditated homicide accompanied by another felony or misdemeanor constituted only a rather small number of *meurtre* cases, if one judges by the few convictions in the *Compte général*'s Table 6, which deals only with the actual condemnations according to the decisions of juries. *Compte général*, 1825–31, Tables 1 and 2, pp. 2–3.

43. Schnapper, "Le Jury français," 187; F. Lombard, *Les Jurés*, 194; Corbes, "La Cour d'assises des Côtes-du-Nord," 316; Savitt, "Villainous Verdicts?," 1035; Dupin de Beyssat, *Le Jury criminel*, 11; Chatagnier, *De l'Infanticide*, 87; Vallaud, "Le crime d'infanticide," 479.

44. Saleilles, *Individualization of Punishment*, 11; Chatagnier, *De l'Infanticide*, 23; F. Lombard, *Les Jurés*, 225–26.

45. From 1980 through 1994, juries in U.S. federal courts handed down verdicts on 77,195 criminal defendants. Of these, they convicted 62,759 (81.2 percent) and acquitted only 14,536 (18.8 percent). Maguire and Pastore, *Bureau of Justice Statistics*, Table 5.27, p. 460. Comparable nationwide data on jury verdicts in state courts are unavailable.

46. From 1831 (when the *Compte général* first included figures on unprosecuted cases) through 1835, 52,937 (or 20.1 percent) of the total of 263,610 reported cases were either filed away without further action by the public prosecutors' offices or dropped before trial following investigation by the *juges d'instruction*, and 210,673 (79.9 percent) were tried in either the *cours d'assises* or the *tribunaux correctionnels*. The proportion tried declined steadily thereafter. According to André Davidovitch's calculations, it had dropped to an annual average of 60.1 percent in the years 1851–55, to 48.7 percent in 1871–75, to 38.3 percent in 1896–1900. Ministère de l'Economie et des Finances, *Annuaire statistique*, 161, 164; Davidovitch, "Criminalité et répression," 35.

47. Martin, *Crime and Criminal Justice*, 246–47.

48. Esmein, *History of Continental Criminal Procedure*, 531–32; Wright, *Between the Guillotine and Liberty*, 63; F. Lombard, *Les Jurés*, 226; Chatagnier, *De l'Infanticide*, 24; Vallaud, "Le crime d'infanticide," 479; Andre Laingui, "La sanction pénale dans le droit Français du XVIIIe et XIXe siècle," in Recueils de la Société Jean Bodin pour l'histoire comparative des institutions, *La peine*, 185.

49. Dalloz et al., *Code pénal annoté*, 916.

50. Corbes, "La Cour d'assises des Côtes-du-Nord," 326.

51. *Compte général*, 1860, xxxviii; Saleilles, *Individualization of Punishment*, 75–76; Savitt, "Villainous Verdicts?," 1035–36; Laingui, "La sanction pénale," 185–86; Gouda and Smith, "Famine, Crime, and Gender," 61.

52. *Code pénal*, Article 64.

53. Nye, *Crime, Madness, and Politics*, 28–31, 111–12.

54. Gouda and Smith, "Famine, Crime, and Gender," 61.

55. Green, *Verdict According to Conscience*, 356.

56. Wiener, *Reconstructing the Criminal*, 47–49, 61–62, 65, 78, 83, 91, 105–6.

57. Ibid., 88.

58. *Compte général*, 1850, xxxv.

59. From 1826 through 1831, there were a total of 21,643 accusations (charges) resulting in guilty verdicts in the *cours d'assises*. Of these, there was a full verdict for 11,670 (53.9 percent) of the cases. In 2,111 cases (9.8 percent) the charges were reduced to lesser felonies, and in 7,862 cases (36.3 percent), they were reduced to misdemeanors. Since the data from the relevant table of the *Compte général* from which these figures are derived refer to number of accusations resulting in guilty verdicts, not number of persons convicted (e.g., two persons may be tried together on the same charge), the number of guilty verdicts mentioned in this note will differ somewhat from the number of persons convicted in Table 2.1 of this book and in other tables based on numbers of persons and not charges. *Compte général*, 1826, Table 106, p. 175; 1827, Table 130, p. 209; 1828, Table 152, p. 247; 1829, Table 155, p. 251; 1830, Table 134, p. 227; 1831, Table 142, p. 235.

60. From 1832 through 1847, 62,339 charges resulted in guilty verdicts in the *cours d'assises*. Of these, 41,790 (67.0 percent) resulted in full guilty verdicts, 7,900 (12.7 percent) were reduced to lesser felonies, and 12,649 (20.3 percent) were reduced to misdemeanors. *Compte général*, 1832, Table 145, p. 245; 1833–47, Table 4, p. 7.

61. Savitt, "Villainous Verdicts?," 1036.

62. "Loi du 9 Septembre 1835 sur le jury," in Cahen and Mathiez, *Les lois françaises*, 72.

63. Dupin de Beyssat, *Le Jury criminel*, 12; Mimin, *Le Concours du jury*, 28.

64. Extenuating circumstances were found for 38,142 (68.8 percent) of the 55,464 persons convicted of *crimes* in the *cours d'assises* from 1834 through 1847. *Compte général*, 1834–35, Table 6, p. 15, and Table 7, p. 17; 1836–47, Table 6, p. 13, and Table 7, p. 15.

65. When a jury convicted someone of a *délit* in place of the felony charge, it was for the judges of the court, not the jury, to decide on extenuating circumstances, as would be the case for *délits* tried in the *tribunaux correctionnels*. Dalloz et al., *Code pénal annoté*, 924; *Compte général*, 1890, xii.

66. From 1834 through 1847, 40,500 persons convicted in the *cours d'assises* were sentenced to misdemeanor penalties. Of these, 27,958 (69.0 percent) were found guilty of *crimes* with extenuating circumstances. The remaining 12,542 (31.0 percent) were con-

victed of misdemeanors. *Compte général*, 1834–35, Table 2, p. 3, and Table 7, p. 17; 1836–47, Table 2, p. 3, and Table 7, p. 15.

67. From 1834 through 1847, 20,990 of the persons for whom the juries had found extenuating circumstances were eligible to have their sentences reduced by two degrees. Of these, 13,981 (66.6 percent) had their penalties so reduced, and 7,009 (33.4 percent) had their penalties reduced by one degree. There was little change thereafter. After 1923, the *Compte général* discontinued its tables on extenuating circumstances. *Compte général*, 1834–35, Table 7, p. 17; 1836–60, Table 7, p. 15; 1861–70, Table 7, p. 17; 1871–73, Table 7, p. 19; 1874–85, Table 8, p. 27; 1886–1909, Table 8, p. 21; 1910–13 and 1919–20, Table 8, p. 23; 1921–23, Table 6, p. 19.

68. Beattie, *Crime and the Courts*, 430–32.

69. According to Beattie, judges and juries in eighteenth-century England usually worked at arriving at verdicts both found acceptable. Ibid., 425–28.

70. In the years from 1825 through 1831, a total of 838 persons were sentenced to death in the *cours d'assises*. The number was 773 from 1832 through 1847. *Compte général*, 1825–47, Table 2, p. 3.

71. Wright, *Between the Guillotine and Liberty*, 168.

72. They accounted for only 113 (or 12.1 percent) of the 838 death sentences from 1825 through 1831. *Compte général*, 1825, Tables 1 and 2, pp. 2–3; 1826–27, Table 12, p. 21; 1828–31, Table 7, p. 13.

73. Of the 3,262 persons convicted of capital crimes in the *cours d'assises* from 1834 through 1847, 633 (19.4 percent) were sentenced to death, and extenuating circumstances were found for 2,629 (80.6 percent). *Compte général*, 1834–35, Table 6, p. 15, and Table 7, p. 17; 1836–47, Table 6, p. 13, and Table 7, p. 15.

74. Savey-Casard, *La peine de mort*, 59–74, 81; Wright, *Between the Guillotine and Liberty*, 168.

75. Savey-Casard, *La peine de mort*, 83.

76. Ibid., 87–88, 90–96.

77. Ibid., 101.

78. The conviction rate had risen to 54.5 percent (1,244 of the total of 2,283) of those tried from 1832 through 1835, and the number acquitted was 1,039 (45.5 percent). The 62.5 percent conviction rate for the years 1836–47 represented 4,949 persons convicted from a total of 7,913 persons tried for capital crimes. The number acquitted was 2,964 (37.5 percent). *Compte général*, 1832–47, Tables 1 and 2, pp. 2–3.

79. To such an extent was this true that until 1832, persons convicted of parricide had their right hand cut off immediately before being guillotined. Even after this date, they were led to the scaffold with their heads covered with a black veil. Corbes, "La Cour d'assises des Côtes-du-Nord," 313–14.

80. The French penal code stated that an attempted crime was to be regarded as the same as the accomplished crime, and both received the same penalty. *Code pénal*, Article 2 (1).

81. Extenuating circumstances were found for 91 (64.1 percent) of the 142 persons convicted of parricide from 1834 through 1847. During the same years, 1,385 were convicted of premeditated murder, and extenuating circumstances were found for 944 (68.2 percent). Extenuating circumstances were found for 138 (75.8 percent) of the 182 persons found guilty of unpremeditated homicide accompanied by another crime or misde-

meanor. The figures for poisoning are 280 (84.6 percent) of 331 and for arson of inhabited structures 471 (85.8 percent) of 549. *Compte général*, 1834–35, Table 6, pp. 12–14, and Table 7, pp. 16–17; 1836–47, Table 6, pp. 12–13, and Table 7, pp. 14–15.

82. *Code pénal*, Articles 300 and 302.

83. Donovan, "Infanticide and the Juries," 169, 174–75.

84. McLaren, "Abortion in France," 466.

85. Hufton, *Poor of Eighteenth-Century France*, 321–22.

86. Chatagnier, *De l'Infanticide*, 247–48.

87. McMillan, *Housewife or Harlot*, 62–69.

88. Fuchs, *Poor and Pregnant*, 211, 214–15.

89. Brouardel, *L'infanticide*, 2–3; Tardieu, *Étude médico-légale sur l'infanticide*, 10.

90. Vallaud, "Le crime d'infanticide," 475–76, 488–89.

91. Fuchs, *Poor and Pregnant*, 214–15.

92. The 47.7 percent acquittal rate for infanticide represents 377 of the total of 791 persons tried for the crime from 1825 through 1847. The number convicted was 414 (52.3 percent). From 1825 through 1831, 2,061 (48.1 percent) of the 4,287 persons tried for all other intentional homicides were acquitted. The number convicted was 2,226 (51.9 percent). *Compte général*, 1825–31, Table 1, p. 2.

93. This was so for several reasons. For one thing, since the bodies of dead infants decay more quickly than the bodies of adults, this meant that it was more difficult for forensic doctors to find the physical traces of homicides on the cadavers of babies than on other cadavers, especially since the former were generally not examined until about eight to fifteen days after they had died. Prosecutors in infanticide cases also had to prove that the accused women had actually been pregnant and had given birth and that their allegedly murdered infants had not been stillborn. These requirements presented major problems of evidence that were not found in the investigations of other homicides. Moreover, suffocation was by far the most common cause of death in infanticide cases, and this left no outward signs of violence. Chatagnier, *De l'Infanticide*, 24–25, 69, 106–8, 111, 113–14, 122–24, 128; Tardieu, *Étude médico-légale sur l'infanticide*, 12–13, 16–18, 20, 43, 45, 78, 98, 101, 103, 117, 201, 205, 217.

94. Vallaud, "Le crime d'infanticide," 479.

95. From 1826 through 1831, 336 persons were tried for infanticide and convicted. Of these, only 109 (32.4 percent) were actually convicted of the infanticide charge. Another 227 (67.6 percent) were found guilty of lesser crimes. From 1826 through 1830, 181 persons were convicted in the *cours d'assises* of negligent homicide of a newborn (*homicide par imprudence d'un enfant nouveau-né*). In none of these cases would this be an original or full charge for someone tried in the *cours d'assises*, since it was a *délit*. Nearly all or most of those convicted of negligent homicide of a newborn in the *cours d'assises* must have been tried for infanticide but were found guilty of the lesser offense instead. After 1830, the *Compte général* did not distinguish the negligent homicide of a newborn from other negligent homicides in its tables on persons convicted in the *cours d'assises*. But if one makes the assumption that all 181 persons convicted of negligent homicide of a newborn in the *cours d'assises* from 1826 through 1830 were actually tried for infanticide, this meant that 62.6 percent of the 289 persons charged with infanticide and convicted during those years were found guilty of the lesser offense. It also meant that conviction on the negligent homicide of a newborn charge accounted for 95.8 percent of all 189 convictions on

reduced charges for persons tried for infanticide from 1826 through 1830. *Compte général*, 1826–27, Table 1, p. 2, and Table 9, p. 16; 1828–31, Table 1, p. 2, and Table 4, p. 8. Moreover, a perusal of the 103 cases of infanticide reported on by the *Gazette des Tribunaux* from December 27, 1825, to April 24, 1829, shows that only 27 of the accused were convicted of the serious capital crime. Those convicted of lesser offenses numbered 20, 17 of whom were found guilty of negligent homicide of a newborn; 56 of the accused were acquitted outright. Donovan, "Infanticide and the Juries," 174n.

96. Vallaud, "Le crime d'infanticide," 479, 493n; Fuchs, *Poor and Pregnant*, 203; Schnapper, "Le Jury français," 187.

97. Wiener, *Reconstructing the Criminal*, 81.

98. Of the 414 persons convicted of infanticide from 1825 through 1831, 21 (5.1 percent) received the death sentence. Another 112 (27.1 percent) were sentenced to a life of hard labor. In addition, 6 (1.4 percent) were sentenced to more than five years in prison and 274 (66.2 percent) to five years or less. One (0.2 percent) received some other punishment. *Compte général*, 1825–31, Table 1, p. 2.

99. The 47.7 percent rate of jury downcharging represented 679 of the total of 1,423 persons tried for infanticide and convicted from 1832 through 1847. Juries convicted 744 (52.3 percent) on the original infanticide charge. *Compte général*, 1832, Table 1, p. 2, and Table 4, p. 10; 1833–35, Table 1, p. 2, and Table 6, p. 14; 1836–47, Table 1, p. 2, and Table 6, p. 13.

100. The 96.4 percent figure represents 670 persons from among the total of 695 convicted of infanticide from 1834 through 1847, a number that excludes children under the age of sixteen sent to houses of correction until they reached the age of twenty-one and for whom extenuating circumstances were inapplicable. *Compte général*, 1834–35, Table 6, p. 14, and Table 7, p. 17; 1836, Table 6, p. 13, and Table 7, p. 14; 1837–47, Table 6, p. 13, and Table 7, p. 15.

101. From 1832 through 1847, only 26 (1.8 percent) of the 1,423 persons convicted of infanticide received the death sentence. During the same period, 126 (8.9 percent) were sentenced to life at hard labor, 601 (42.2 percent) were sentenced to hard labor for terms of less than life, 57 (4.0 percent) received sentences of more than five years in prison, and 613 (43.1 percent) were punished with prison terms of five years or less. *Compte général*, 1832–47, Table 1, p. 2.

102. Martin, *Crime and Criminal Justice*, 8.

103. From 1825 through 1831, 4,926 (68.4 percent) of the 7,200 persons tried for *vol domestique* were convicted, and 2,274 (31.6 percent) were acquitted. Among the 24,234 people tried in the *cours d'assises* for all other thefts, 16,892 (69.7 percent) were convicted, and 7,342 (30.3 percent) were acquitted. From 1832 through 1847, 11,974 (69.9 percent) of the 17,142 persons tried for *vol domestique* were convicted, and 5,168 (30.1 percent) were acquitted. The figures for all other thefts were 36,676 (74.8 percent) convicted and 12,357 (25.2 percent) acquitted among a total of 49,033. *Compte général*, 1825–47, Table 2, p. 3.

104. Extenuating circumstances were found for 6,123 (80.9 percent) of the 7,570 persons convicted of *vol domestique* from 1834 through 1847. The same was true for 16,236 (60.3 percent) of the 26,912 persons convicted of all other aggravated thefts. *Compte général*, 1834–35, Table 6, p. 15, and Table 7, p. 17; 1836–47, Table 6, p. 13, and Table 7, p. 15.

105. Cruppi, *La Cour d'assises*, 323.

106. Tarde, *Penal Philosophy*, 444; Dragu, *Juges-citoyens ou juges de métier?*, 59. See also

the statements of an unnamed *président* of the *cours d'assises* of the Ardèche in his report to the Ministry of Justice on the court's second trimestrial session of 1833, quoted in Pourcher, "Des assises de grace?," 172.

107. Donovan, "Justice Unblind," 92–94; Perrot, "Délinquance et système pénitentiaire," 76; Pourcher, "Des assises de grace?," 172.

108. Savitt, "Villainous Verdicts?," 1047–48.

109. Ibid., 1049–50.

110. Ibid., 1053–54, 1060–61.

111. The 64.8 percent of persons convicted of aggravated thefts for whom extenuating circumstances were found represented 22,359 of the total of 34,482 found guilty of the crimes from 1834 through 1847. The 77.9 percent rate of findings of extenuating circumstances for assault resulting in the victim's incapacity to work for more than twenty days represented 896 of the total of 1,150 convicted of that crime from 1834 through 1847. The 72.6 percent figure for manslaughter is based on 722 of the total of 994 convicted. *Compte général*, 1834–35, Table 6, pp. 13, 15, and Table 7, pp. 16–17; 1836–47, Table 6, pp. 12–13, and Table 7, pp. 14–15.

112. The figures for 1825–31 for theft are 21,818 (69.4 percent) convicted, 9,616 (30.6 percent) acquitted among a total of 31,434 tried. For intentional homicides, with infanticide excluded but including *assassinat* (premeditated murder), *meurtre* (unpremeditated murder), *empoisonnement* (poisoning), and parricide, the figures are 2,226 (51.9 percent) convicted and 2,061 (48.1 percent) acquitted among a total of 4,287. In the years from 1832 through 1847, the figures for theft are 48,650 (73.5 percent) convicted and 17,525 (26.5 percent) acquitted among a total of 66,175 tried. For intentional homicides, the totals for these years are 5,963 (65.4 percent) convicted and 3,158 (34.6 percent) acquitted among the total of 9,121 tried. *Compte général*, 1825–47, Tables 1 and 2, pp. 2–3.

113. Savitt, "Villainous Verdicts?," 1053–54; *Compte général*, 1882, xv.

114. Nye, *Masculinity and Male Codes of Honor*, 33, 133–34.

115. Ibid., 129–30, 133, 145.

116. Ibid., 134.

117. No duelists were tried for murder in 1836. *Compte général*, 1837, Table 66, p. 98; 1838–39, Table 67, p. 101; 1840, Table 66, p. 98, and Table 67, p. 101; 1841, Table 67, p. 101; 1842, Table 66, p. 98, and Table 67, p. 101; 1843, Table 66, p. 98, and Table 67, p. 101; 1844—no duelists tried; 1845–46, Table 67, p. 101; 1847, Table 66, p. 98.

118. Nye, *Masculinity and Male Codes of Honor*, 146.

119. The complete figures for persons tried for assault and wounding of a parent or guardian in the years 1825–31 are 293 (50.1 percent) convicted and 292 (49.9 percent) acquitted among the total of 585 charged. From 1832 through 1847, they are 849 (62.7 percent) convicted and 504 (37.3 percent) acquitted among the total of 1,353 tried. *Compte général*, 1825–47, Table 1, p. 2.

120. The figures for persons tried for arson in the years 1825–31 are 188 (25.1 percent) convicted and 562 (74.9 percent) acquitted among the total of 750 charged. From 1832 through 1847, they are 1,214 (42.8 percent) convicted and 1,622 (57.2 percent) acquitted among the total of 2,836 tried. For destruction of property, the figures for the years 1825–31 are 32 (14.8 percent) convicted and 184 (85.2 percent) acquitted among the total 216 charged. From 1832 through 1847, they are 49 (19.8 percent) convicted and 198 (80.2 percent) acquitted among a total of 247 charged. *Compte général*, 1825–47, Table 2, p. 3.

121. Persons tried for the pillaging of grains or harvests accounted for 1,073 of the total of 1,553 persons tried for pillaging from 1825 through 1847. *Compte général*, 1825–47, Table 2, p. 3.

122. The overwhelming majority (1,025 or 95.5 percent) of the total of 1,073 persons tried for the pillaging of grains and harvests from 1825 through 1847 were prosecuted during years of hunger (1828–32, 1839–40, and 1846–47). *Compte général*, 1825–47, Table 2, p. 3.

123. The figures for persons tried for pillaging in the years 1825–31 are 70 (23.0 percent) convicted and 234 (77.0 percent) acquitted among the total of 304 persons charged. From 1832 through 1847, they are 410 (32.8 percent) convicted and 839 (67.2 percent) acquitted among a total of 1,259 charged. *Compte général*, 1825–47, Table 2, p. 3.

124. Beattie, *Crime and the Courts*, 321–22, 405–6.

125. Ibid., 378–79, 387–88, 410–11.

126. From 1833 through 1847, 13,476 persons were tried for white-collar crimes in the *cours d'assises*. Among these, the *Compte général*'s cross-tabulations by crime and occupational category show that 5,302 (or 39.3 percent) belonged to categories that can be described as bourgeois. During the same years, 112,047 persons were tried for all crimes, of whom 13,056 (11.7 percent) were bourgeois. *Compte général*, 1833, Table 21, p. 41; 1834–35, Table 22, p. 43; 1836–47, Table 22, p. 41.

127. Hard labor sentences were provided by the *Code pénal* for all cases of felony fraud save fraud in a private document, which was punished by *réclusion* (more than five years in prison). Hard labor sentences were also provided for fraudulent bankruptcy, extortion of titles and signatures, counterfeiting, and cases of official corruption except offering or accepting bribes. *Compte général*, 1834, Table 7, p. 16; 1846, Table 7, pp. 14–15.

128. Whitman, *Harsh Justice*, 101–4, 114, 117, 122.

129. Of the total of 57,600 persons tried in the *cours d'assises* for white-collar crimes from 1825 through 1913 and 1919 through 1931, not less than 35,215 (or 61.1 percent) were charged with fraud. *Compte général*, 1825–60, Table 2, p. 3; 1861–1909, Table 2, p. 5; 1910–13 and 1919–23, Table 2, p. 7; 1924–31, Table 1, p. 7.

130. From 1825 through 1831, 2,820 persons were tried for fraud in the *cours d'assises*, of whom 1,525 (54.1 percent) were convicted and 1,295 (45.9 percent) were acquitted. From 1832 through 1847, 9,227 persons were tried for the crime, of whom 5,301 (57.5 percent) were found guilty and 3,926 (42.5 percent) were acquitted. For fraudulent bankruptcy, the figures for 1825–31 were 695 persons tried, 312 (44.9 percent) convicted, and 383 (55.1 percent) acquitted. From 1832 through 1847, 1,999 persons were tried for the crime, of whom 737 (36.9 percent) were convicted and 1,262 (63.1 percent) were acquitted. For extortion of titles and signatures, 191 persons were tried for the crime from 1825 through 1831, of whom 78 (40.8 percent) were convicted and 113 (59.2 percent) were acquitted. From 1832 through 1847, 563 persons were tried for the crime, of whom 246 (43.7 percent) were convicted and 317 (56.3 percent) were acquitted. *Compte général*, 1825–47, Table 2, p. 3.

131. From 1834 through 1847, extenuating circumstances were found for 3,744 (79.4 percent) of the 4,713 persons convicted of felony fraud in the *cours d'assises*. Extenuating circumstances were found for 484 (84.0 percent) of the 576 people convicted of fraudulent bankruptcy and for 168 (78.5 percent) of the 214 persons found guilty of the extortion

of titles and signatures. *Compte général*, 1834–35, Table 6, pp. 12–14, and Table 7, p. 16; 1836–47, Table 6, p. 12, and Table 7, p. 14.

132. Of the 1,525 persons convicted of fraud in the *cours d'assises* from 1825 through 1831, 51 (3.3 percent) were sentenced to hard labor for life, 722 (47.3 percent) were sentenced to terms of hard labor for less than life, 655 (43.0 percent) were given prison terms of more than five years, 87 (5.7 percent) were sentenced to five years or less in prison, and 10 (0.7 percent) received some other penalty. Of the 5,301 convicted from 1832 through 1847, 7 (0.1 percent) were sentenced to hard labor for life, 606 (11.4 percent) were sentenced to terms of hard labor for less than life, 1,039 (19.6 percent) received prison terms of more than five years, 3,642 (68.7 percent) were sentenced to five years or less in prison, and 7 (0.1 percent) were given some other penalty. From 1825 through 1831, 209 (67.0 percent) of persons convicted of fraudulent bankruptcy were sentenced to hard labor for terms of less than life, 4 (1.3 percent) were sentenced to prison terms of more than five years, and 99 (31.7 percent) were sentenced to five years or less in prison. From 1832 through 1847, only 102 (13.8 percent) were sentenced to hard labor, 95 (12.9 percent) were sentenced to more than five years in prison, and 540 (73.3 percent) to five years or less. Of the 78 persons convicted of the extortion of titles and signatures from 1825 through 1831, 56 (71.8 percent) were sentenced to terms of hard labor, 3 (3.8 percent) to more than five years in prison, and 19 (24.4 percent) to five years or less in prison. From 1832 through 1847, of the 246 persons convicted of the crime, 56 (22.8 percent) were sentenced to hard labor, 44 (17.9 percent) to more than five years in prison, and 146 (59.3 percent) to five years or less in prison. *Compte général*, 1825–47, Table 2, p. 3.

133. Martin, *Crime and Criminal Justice*, 7.

134. The 63.1 percent acquittal rate represents 241 of the 382 persons tried for counterfeiting from 1825 through 1831. The convicted numbered 141 (36.9 percent). *Compte général*, 1825–31, Table 2, p. 3.

135. Of the 123 persons tried for counterfeiting and convicted from 1826 through 1831, 74 (60.2 percent) were found guilty of the full charge and 49 (39.8 percent) were convicted of a lesser offense. This had much to do with the fact that only 69 (48.9 percent) of the 141 convicted from 1825 through 1831 received the death sentence. *Compte général*, 1826–27, Table 2, p. 3, and Table 9, p. 16; 1828–31, Table 2, p. 3, and Table 4, p. 8.

136. *Compte général*, 1850, xxxvi.

137. From 1832 through 1847, 933 (59.0 percent) of the 1,582 persons tried for counterfeiting were convicted. *Compte général*, 1832–47, Table 2, p. 3.

138. Of the 839 persons convicted of counterfeiting (a figure that excludes children sentenced to houses of correction until the age of twenty-one) from 1834 through 1847, extenuating circumstances were found for 633 (82.5 percent). *Compte général*, 1834–35, Table 6, p. 13, and Table 7, p. 16; 1836–47, Table 6, p. 12, and Table 7, p. 14.

139. From 1832 through 1847, among the total of 933 persons convicted of counterfeiting, 7 (0.8 percent) were sentenced to death (all in 1832), 125 (13.4 percent) were sentenced to hard labor for life, 181 (19.4 percent) to terms of hard labor for less than life, 462 (49.5 percent) to more than five years in prison, 151 (16.2 percent) to five years or less in prison, and 7 (0.8 percent) to some other penalty. *Compte général*, 1832–47, Table 2, p. 3.

140. Of the total of 933 persons tried for counterfeiting and convicted from 1832

through 1847, 846 (90.7 percent) were found guilty of this crime, and 87 (9.3 percent) were convicted for lesser offenses. *Compte général*, 1832, Table 2, p. 3, and Table 4, p. 10; 1833–35, Table 2, p. 3, and Table 6, p. 13; 1836–47, Table 2, p. 3, and Table 6, p. 12.

141. From 1825 through 1853, 187 persons were tried for all crimes of official corruption except bribery, of whom 82 (43.9 percent) were convicted and 105 (56.1 percent) were acquitted. *Compte général*, 1825–53, Table 2, p. 3.

142. Extenuating circumstances were found for 43 (84.3 percent) of the 51 persons found guilty of felony-level crimes of official corruption other than bribery from 1834 through 1853. *Compte général*, 1834–35, Table 6, p. 13, and Table 7, p. 16; 1836–53, Table 6, pp. 12–13, and Table 7, pp. 14–15.

143. Among the 82 persons convicted of all crimes of official corruption except bribery from 1825 through 1853, 16 (19.5 percent) were sentenced to hard labor terms of less than life, 12 (14.6 percent) received prison terms of more than five years, and 54 (65.9 percent) were sentenced to prison terms of five years or less. *Compte général*, 1825–53, Table 2, p. 3.

144. Of the 253 persons tried for offering or accepting bribes from 1825 through 1831, 57 (22.5 percent) were convicted and 196 (77.5 percent) were acquitted. Of the 404 tried from 1832 through 1847, 74 (18.3 percent) were convicted and 330 (81.7 percent) were acquitted. *Compte général*, 1825–47, Table 2, p. 3.

145. Before 1832, these crimes were punished with more than five years' imprisonment or *au carcan* (to be put in shackles). Between 1825 and 1831, the overwhelming majority (51 or 91.2 percent) of the 57 persons convicted of bribery were sentenced to either punishment. The penalty of *au carcan* was abolished in 1832, and thereafter *réclusion* and *dégradation civique* (loss of civil rights) were the penalties provided in the penal code. Of the 97 persons convicted of offering or accepting bribes from 1832 through 1847, one (1.0 percent, in 1832) was sentenced *au carcan*, 4 (4.1 percent) to loss of civil rights, 6 (6.2 percent) to more than five years in prison, and 86 (88.7 percent) to five years or less in prison. *Compte général*, 1832–53, Table 2, p. 3.

146. Of the 72 persons convicted of offering or accepting bribes from 1834 through 1847, 65 (90.3 percent) were granted extenuating circumstances. *Compte général*, 1834–35 — no convictions; 1836–47, Table 6, p. 12, and Table 7, p. 14.

147. Schnapper, "Le Jury français," 187–88.

148. *Compte général*, 1880, ix; 1910, ix.

149. Legoyt, "Documents communs a divers pays," 86; Garraud, *Traité théorique*, 1:33–34; Yvernes, "La Justice en France," 303; Tarde, *Penal Philosophy*, 443; Beer, "Ce qu'est le jury criminel," 496n; Toulemon, *La Question du jury*, 83–84; *Compte général*, 1880, ix.

150. In England and the United States in the nineteenth and twentieth centuries, criminal justice administrators also increasingly sought to avoid jury trial, and for some of the same reasons as in France. In London and New York City during the nineteenth century, a growing number of criminal cases were disposed of in summary (i.e., nonjury) proceedings. Moreover, plea bargaining in felony cases expanded dramatically in England and America during the nineteenth and twentieth centuries. Caseload pressures and the increasing complexity of criminal trials contributed to the trend. Although in England, criminal justice administrators resorted to summary proceedings in part to escape the evidentiary difficulties associated with the country's system of private prosecution in

felony cases, they and their counterparts in the United States, as in France, also wished to dispose of cases without jury trial in order to obtain cheap and speedy justice and to get more convictions. Criminal suspects often cooperated in order to avoid pretrial detention and obtain more lenient sentences. Smith, "Emergence of Public Prosecution in London" and "Plea Bargaining and the Eclipse of the Jury."

151. Schnapper, "Le Jury français," 205–6.

152. Davidovitch, "Criminalité et répression," 37; Martin, *Crime and Criminal Justice*, 145–46, 175; Coudert, "French Criminal Procedure," 334.

153. *Compte général*, 1880, ix, lix; Toulemon, *La Question du jury*, 84.

154. Davidovitch, "Criminalité et répression," 37; Coudert, "French Criminal Procedure," 333–34; Frase, "Comparative Criminal Justice," 622, 625, 625n.

155. Pourcher, "Des assises de grace?," 170, 172–73; Claverie, "De la difficulté de faire un citoyen," 144–45, 148–49, 162; Pierre-André Lecocq and Joel Bourgeois, "Jurys et liberté de la presse: La presse devant les jurys du Nord de l'an X à 1851," in Martinage and Royer, *Les destinées du jury criminel*, 219–20; Schnapper, "Le Jury français," 191–92, 192n, 202.

156. Schnapper, "Le Jury français," 201–2; Pourcher, "Des assises de grace?," 168.

157. Schnapper, "Le Jury français," 181–82, 190, 193–94; Van Caenegem, *Judges, Legislators and Professors*, 37–38; Lecocq and Bourgeois, "Jurys et liberté de la presse," 221.

158. Collins, *Government and the Newspaper Press*, 60.

159. The exact number was 1,038. *Compte général*, 1831, Table 60, p. 95.

160. The total number of persons tried for *délits politiques et de presse* was 1,721 from 1826 through 1830. From 1831 through 1835, it was 3,204. *Compte général*, 1826, Table 74, p. 110; 1827, Table 82, p. 121; 1828, Table 91, p. 139; 1829, Table 92, p. 141; 1830, Table 68, p. 115; 1831, Tables 63–64, pp. 98–99; 1832, Tables 66–67, pp. 102–3; 1833, Tables 71–72, pp. 110–11; 1834, Tables 68–69, pp. 106–7; 1835, Tables 72–73, pp. 112–13.

161. Cobban, *History of Modern France*, 2:97.

162. Collins, *Government and the Newspaper Press*, 74.

163. Of the 3,204 persons tried for political and press misdemeanors by the juries of the *cours d'assises* from 1831 through 1835, 885 (27.6 percent) were convicted and 2,319 (72.4 percent) were acquitted. *Compte général*, 1831, Tables 63–64, pp. 98–99; 1832, Tables 66–67, pp. 102–3; 1833, Tables 71–72, pp. 110–11; 1834, Tables 68–69, pp. 106–7; 1835, Tables 72–73, pp. 112–13.

164. The acquittal rate for persons tried in the *cours d'assises* for *rébellion* was already very high during the last years of the Bourbon Restoration. From 1825 through 1830, 1,177 persons were tried for the crime, of whom 312 (26.5 percent) were convicted and 865 (73.5 percent) were acquitted. From 1831 through 1835, 1,454 persons were tried for *rébellion* in the *cours d'assises*, of whom 312 (21.5 percent) were convicted and 1,142 (78.5 percent) were acquitted. Very few persons were tried for *crimes politiques* during the years 1825–30, but 1,216 were tried from 1831 through 1835. Of these, 375 (30.8 percent) were convicted and 841 (69.2 percent) were acquitted. *Compte général*, 1825–35, Table 1, p. 2.

165. Of the 264 persons tried for *crimes politiques* in connection with the "Troubles de l'ouest" in 1832, 179 (67.8 percent) were acquitted. Of the 56 persons tried for their participation in the rue des Prouvaires incident, 30 (53.6 percent) were acquitted, as were 180 (70.3 percent) of the 256 persons tried in connection with the "Affaires des 5 et 6 juin" in Paris. In the case of the 35 persons tried in connection with the "Troubles de Lyon,"

28 (80.0 percent) were found not guilty. In most years, however, the *Compte général*'s statistics do not indicate the political persuasion of persons prosecuted for any of the categories of political or press offenses. *Compte général*, 1832, Table 19, pp. 38–40.

166. Collingham, *July Monarchy*, 170; Collins, *Government and the Newspaper Press*, 82.

167. Corbes, "La Cour d'assises des Côtes-du-Nord," 318–23.

168. Schnapper, "Le Jury français," 188; Collingham, *July Monarchy*, 147.

169. P. Lombard, *La Justice des bien-pensants*, 261–62; F. Lombard, *Les Jurés*, 197–98; Collingham, *July Monarchy*, 165–67.

170. "Loi du 9 Septembre 1835 sur le Jury," in Cahen and Mathiez, *Les lois françaises*, 72.

171. Collingham, *July Monarchy*, 165.

172. "Loi du 9 Septembre 1835 sur le Jury," in Cahen and Mathiez, *Les lois françaises*, 72.

173. "Loi du 9 Septembre 1835 sur les crimes, délits et contraventions de presse," in Cahen and Mathiez, *Les lois françaises*, 70–71.

174. From 1836 through 1847, 933 persons were tried in the *cours d'assises* for *délits politiques et de presse*. Of these, 292 (31.1 percent) were convicted and 641 (68.7 percent) were acquitted. *Compte général*, 1836, Tables 74–75, pp. 112–13; 1837–47, Table 73, p. 110.

175. Of the 335 persons tried for *crimes politiques* from 1836 through 1847, 131 (39.1 percent) were convicted and 204 (60.9 percent) were acquitted. Of the 1,113 persons tried for *rébellion* during the same years, 302 (27.1 percent) were convicted and 811 (72.9 percent) were acquitted. *Compte général*, 1836–47, Table 1, p. 2.

176. Collins, *Government and the Newspaper Press*, 97.

177. Martin, *Crime and Criminal Justice*, 143, 195; N. Martin (du Nord), août 16, 1842, to MM Les Procureurs généraux pres les cours royales, in *Recueil officiel des instructions et circulaires du Ministère de la justice*, 2:22.

178. Royer, *Histoire de la justice*, 522n; F. Lombard, *Les Jurés*, 226; Schnapper, "Le Jury français," 205; Martin, *Crime and Criminal Justice*, 175.

179. Toulemon, *La Question du jury*, 85.

Chapter 3

1. Savey-Casard, *La peine de mort*, 105–6; Wright, *Between the Guillotine and Liberty*, 84.

2. In 1836, 4 of the 10 persons convicted of *crimes politiques* were sentenced to death. Not one of the 121 persons convicted of these crimes from 1837 through 1847 was condemned to the guillotine. *Compte général*, 1836–47, Table 1, p. 2.

3. Bernard Schnapper, "Le Jury français," in Schioppa, *Trial Jury*, 195.

4. Quoted in Loubet, *La Justice criminelle*, 191.

5. F. Lombard, *Les Jurés*, 212.

6. E. Leroux, Séance du juillet 28, 1848, *Moniteur Universal* 1er août 1848, quoted in F. Lombard, *Les Jurés*, 212–13.

7. Forsyth, *History of Trial by Jury*, 302; Trebutien, *Cours élémentaire de droit criminel*, 2:348; Loubet, *La Justice criminelle*, 191; Soulas, *Le Recrutement du jury*, 43–44; Bernard Schnapper, "De l'origine sociale des jurés," in Martinage and Royer, *Les destinées du jury criminel*, 119; F. Lombard, *Les Jurés*, 213; Gineste, *Essai sur l'histoire et l'organisation du jury criminel*, 123–24.

8. Forsyth, *History of Trial by Jury*, 302; Gineste, *Essai sur l'histoire et l'organisation du jury criminel*, 91; Nouguier, *La Cour d'assises*, 1:492–93.

9. Guibourg, *Le jury criminel*, 23–25; Trebutien, *Cours élémentaire de droit criminel*, 2:346; Schnapper, "Le Jury français," 235.

10. Schnapper, "Le Jury français," 197.

11. Ibid., 198–99.

12. From 1849 through 1853, 625,470 persons were inscribed on the annual jury lists. Of these, 51,539 (8.2 percent) were workers, 87,926 (14.1 percent) were peasants, 49,396 (7.9 percent) were civil servants, 111,931 (17.9 percent) were merchants and manufacturers, 70,295 (11.2 percent) belonged to the liberal professions, and 254,383 (40.7 percent) were *propriétaires* and *rentiers*. *Compte général*, 1849, Table 148, p. 255; 1850, Table 149, p. 255; 1851, Table 147, p. 259; 1852, Table 141, p. 353; 1853, Table 139, p. 255.

13. According to Schnapper, the proportion of *propriétaires* and *rentiers* in the Sarthe, Deux-Sevres, and Indre declined from 50.1 percent in 1847–48 to 39.9 percent in 1848–53. The total he defines as "notables" (which included mayors and notaries along with *propriétaires* and *rentiers*) declined from 80 percent to 57 percent. The *gens du people* (farmers, employees, and workers), almost absent from the lists before, now accounted for 12 percent. If one adds to these those Schnapper labels as belonging to the "classe moyenne" (merchants, innkeepers, artisans, etc.), one comes to a figure of 43.5 percent—three times higher than in the preceding period. Schnapper, "De l'origine sociale des jurés," 125, 134, 136.

14. According to Marie-Renée Santucci, the average juror in the Herault during the Second Republic was 48.5 years old. Schnapper has calculated that the average juror in the Deux-Sevres, Indre, and Sarthe from 1848 to 1853 was 47 years and 15 days old. Santucci, "Être ou ne pas Être juré au XIXeme siècle," in Martinage and Royer, *Les destinées du jury criminel*, 166; Schnapper, "De l'origine sociale des jurés," 126.

15. Schnapper, "Le Jury français," 197–98.

16. *Compte général*, 1847–48, Table 2, p. 3.

17. Merriman, *Agony of the Republic*, 30–32, 55.

18. Of the 225 persons tried in 1848 for *délits politiques et de presse*, 157 (69.8 percent) were acquitted. The same held true for 126 (55.8 percent) of the 226 persons accused of *crimes politiques* and 136 (72.0 percent) of the 189 tried for *rébellion*. *Compte général*, 1848, Table 1, p. 2, and Table 73, p. 110.

19. Howard Machin, "The Prefects and Political Repression: February 1848 to December 1851," in Price, *Revolution and Reaction*, 280, 286–87; Collins, *Government and the Newspaper Press*, 110.

20. The number of persons tried for *délits politiques et de presse* rose to 1,137 in 1849 and to 1,162 in 1850. *Compte général*, 1849–50, Table 73, p. 110.

21. Of the 2,299 persons tried in the *cours d'assises* for *délits politiques et de presse* in the years 1849–50, 802 (34.9 percent) were convicted and 1,497 (65.1 percent) were acquitted. Of the 361 persons tried during these years for *crimes politiques*, 93 (25.8 percent) were convicted and 268 (74.2 percent) were acquitted. Among the 344 persons tried for *rébellion*, 58 (16.9 percent) were convicted and 286 (83.1 percent) were acquitted. *Compte général*, 1849–50, Table 1, p. 2, and Table 73, p. 110.

22. Machin, "Prefects and Political Repression," 287.

23. Merriman, *Agony of the Republic*, 135–36.

24. Schnapper, "Le Jury français," 200.

25. Merriman, *Agony of the Republic*, 110–16.

26. In 1851, 879 persons were tried in the *cours d'assises* for *délits politiques et de presse*, of whom 300 (34.1 percent) were convicted and 579 (65.9 percent) were acquitted. In the same year, 31 persons were tried for *crimes politiques*, of whom 9 (29.0 percent) were convicted and 22 (71.0 percent) were acquitted. The number of persons tried for *rébellion* was 49, of whom 9 (18.4 percent) were convicted and 40 (81.6 percent) were acquitted. *Compte général*, 1851, Table 1, p. 2, and Table 73, p. 110.

27. The conviction rate rose from 58.5 percent in 1848, to 60.3 percent in 1849, to 62.6 percent in 1850, to 66.7 percent in 1851. *Compte général*, 1848–51, Table 2, p. 3.

28. Schnapper, "Le Jury français," 200–204, and "De l'origine sociale des jurés," 116, 124, 125n.

29. Schnapper, "Le Jury français," 203.

30. Ibid.

31. Quoted in F. Lombard, *Les Jurés*, 227.

32. Payne, *Police State*, 49–50; Schnapper, "Le Jury français," 204–5; Royer, *Histoire de la justice*, 516; F. Lombard, *Les Jurés*, 224; Garraud, *Traité théorique*, 1:201.

33. Payne, *Police State*, 64–65; Royer, *Histoire de la justice*, 509–10.

34. Payne, *Police State*, 65.

35. Royer, *Histoire de la justice*, 509–10; P. Lombard, *La Justice des bien-pensants*, 319.

36. Schnapper, "Le Jury français," 208; F. Lombard, *Les Jurés*, 224–25.

37. Guibourg, *Le jury criminel*, 40; Schnapper, "De l'origine sociale des jurés," 127; Zeldin, *France 1848–1945*, 1:527.

38. Soulas, *Le Recrutement du jury*, 45.

39. The annual departmental list was to be composed of 2,000 names in the department of the Seine, 500 in departments of more than 300,000 people, 400 in departments of between 200,000 and 300,000 people, and 300 in departments of less than 200,000. Nouguier, *La Cour d'assises*, 1:422–26.

40. Ibid., 1:439–40; Trebutien, *Cours élémentaire de droit criminel*, 2:346; Royer, *Histoire de la justice*, 516–17; Schnapper, "Le Jury français," 207.

41. Nouguier, *La Cour d'assises*, 1:439, 443, 485–86, 490–91.

42. Ibid., 1:496; Gineste, *Essai sur l'histoire et l'organisation du jury criminel*, 91; Trebutien, *Cours élémentaire de droit criminel*, 2:346.

43. Schnapper, "De l'origine sociale des jurés," 128; Royer, *Histoire de la justice*, 517.

44. From 1854 (again, the annual jury list for each year was composed in the fall of the preceding year, so that the list for 1854 was drawn up in the autumn of 1853) through 1870, 723,796 persons were inscribed on the annual jury lists. Of these, 11,517 (1.6 percent) were workers or artisans, 48,476 (6.7 percent) were peasants, 92,088 (12.7 percent) were civil servants, 120,751 (16.7 percent) were merchants and manufacturers, 107,951 (14.9 percent) belonged to the liberal professions, and 343,013 (47.4 percent) were *propriétaires* and *rentiers*. *Compte général*, 1854, Table 139, p. 251; 1855, Table 135, p. 251; 1856–57, Table 137, p. 251; 1858–59, Table 135, p. 249; 1860, Table 133, p. 247; 1861–62, Table 131, p. 249; 1863, Table 134, p. 255; 1864, Table 131, p. 253; 1865–69, Table 132, p. 253; 1870, Table 101, p. 203.

45. The proportion of *propriétaires* on the jury session lists in the Deux-Sevres, Indre, and Sarthe rose from 39.9 percent in 1848–53 to 54.2 percent in 1854–60; the latter figure was even higher than in 1847–48. If one adds to the number their "allies" the notaries, the figure increases to 58.8 percent—virtually the same as the 59 percent during the last year of

the July Monarchy. Those jurors Schnapper labels as belonging to the "classes moyennes et populaires" declined sharply from 43.5 percent in 1848–53 to 17.7 percent in 1854–60. Peasants and wage-earners dropped from 12 percent to only 3.9 percent of the total. Santucci's analysis of jury session lists in the department of the Herault shows that the juries there also after 1853 strongly resembled those of the July Monarchy in socioeconomic composition. Schnapper, "De l'origine sociale des jurés," 125, 128, 134, 136; Santucci, "Être ou ne pas Être juré au XIXeme siècle," 149.

46. [Ministre de la Justice] Abbatucci, août 26, 1853, à MM Les Procureurs généraux, in *Recueil officiel des instructions et circulaires du Ministère de la justice*, 2:244.

47. Schnapper, "De l'origine sociale des jurés," 128.

48. [Ministre de la Justice] Abbatucci, janvier 26, 1857, à MM Les Procureurs généraux, in *Recueil officiel des instructions et circulaires du Ministère de la justice*, 2:366.

49. Soulas, *Le Recrutement du jury*, 47.

50. Schnapper, "Le Jury français," 206–7, 207n.

51. *Compte général*, 1860, xxix.

52. Ibid.

53. From 1831 through 1835, the average annual number of cases filed away by the *parquets* without further action was 34,643 (13.1 percent) of the total of 263,610 reported cases of felonies and misdemeanors. From 1846 through 1850, the number was 87,005 (25.4 percent) of the total of 342,575 reported cases. From 1861 through 1865, the average annual number of cases filed away without further action by the *parquets* was 119,393, or 38.3 percent of the total of 311,160 reported felonies and misdemeanors. From 1866 through 1870, it was 138,588 (43.1 percent) of 321,616 cases. Ministère de l'Economie et des Finances, *Annuaire statistique*, 161, 164.

54. Merriman, *Police Stories*, 7–8, 15–17, 29, 32, 37, 39, 41–42, 50, 53–54, 70, 75–76, 185–86; Payne, *Police State*, 212–13, 235, 245–46, 286; Martin, *Crime and Criminal Justice*, 42–44.

55. Schnapper, *Voies nouvelles*, 327–30; Nye, *Crime, Madness, and Politics*, 75; Wright, *Between the Guillotine and Liberty*, 50, 58–59, 75, 98; *Compte général*, 1868, xviii.

56. In respect to precise numbers, recidivists made up 6,831 (15.8 percent) of the 43,254 persons tried in the *cours d'assises* from 1826 through 1831. From 1832 through 1847, they made up 27,069 (22.5 percent) of the total of 120,258 persons tried. The number of recidivists in 1848 was 1,725, or 23.5 percent of the total of 7,352 accused persons. The figure for 1849–53 was 10,824 recidivists (or 30.3 percent of the total of 35,669 accused persons), and for 1854–70 it was 31,826 (37.4 percent of the total of 85,079 persons tried). *Compte général*, 1826, Table 2, p. 3, and Tables 69–71, pp. 100–102; 1827, Table 2, p. 3, and Table 70, p. 98; 1828, Table 2, p. 3, and Table 76, p. 112; 1829, Table 2, p. 3, and Table 77, p. 114; 1830, Table 2, p. 3, and Table 69, p. 94; 1831, Table 2, p. 3, and Table 94, p. 157; 1832, Table 2, p. 3, and Table 96, p. 161; 1833, Table 2, p. 3, and Table 101, p. 169; 1834, Table 2, p. 3, and Table 98, p. 165; 1835, Table 2, p. 3, and Table 102, p. 171; 1836, Table 2, p. 3, and Table 111, pp. 182–83; 1837–38, Table 2, p. 3, and Table 103, p. 169; 1839–48, Table 2, p. 3, and Table 105, p. 171; 1849–50, Table 2, p. 3, and Table 106, p. 167; 1851, Table 2, p. 3, p. 167; 1852, Table 2, p. 3, and Table 109, p. 167; 1853, Table 2, p. 3, and Table 108, p. 169; 1854, Table 2, p. 3, and Table 110, p. 171; 1855, Table 2, p. 3, and Table 110, p. 174; 1856, Table 2, p. 3, and Table 110, p. 173; 1857, Table 2, p. 3, and Table 111, p. 174; 1858–59, Table 2, p. 3, and Table 109, p. 172; 1860, Table 2, p. 3, and Table 105, p. 168; 1861–62, Table 2, p. 5, and

Table 105, p. 170; 1863, Table 2, p. 5, and Table 107, p. 173; 1864–69, Table 2, p. 5, and Table 104, p. 171; 1870, Table 2, p. 5, and Table 72, p. 139.

57. *Compte général*, 1852, xviii, xviiin; 1853, xxi; 1854, xxiii; 1855, xxiii; 1857, xxvii; 1858, xvii; 1860, lxii, lxiin; 1865, xxviii.

58. Garner, "Criminal Procedure in France," 264.

59. After 1870, the *Compte général*'s tables on recidivists contain data only on those who were convicted, making it impossible thereafter to calculate conviction and acquittal rates for repeat offenders.

60. Beattie, *Crime and the Courts*, 429, 436, 440–43, 448.

61. The conviction rate for all persons tried in the *cours d'assises* rose from 64.4 percent from 1832 through 1847 to 75.8 percent from 1854 through 1870. As already mentioned, the proportion among all persons tried who had previously been convicted of a felony or misdemeanor rose from 22.5 percent to 37.4 percent. Among all persons convicted, the proportion of recidivists increased from 29.4 percent in the years 1832–47 to 43.4 percent in 1854–70. That's an increase of 14 percentage points. If we then multiply the ratio of .14 by the total number (28,013) of recidivists among convicted persons in 1854–70, it shows that if in the latter period the proportion of recidivists among convicted persons had remained the same as in 1832–47, there would have been 3,922 fewer convictions. Therefore, if the proportion of recidivists had not changed, there would have been a total of 60,557 convicted persons instead of 64,479 among all those tried in the *cours d'assises*. The total conviction rate would be 71.2 percent, or 4.6 percentage points below the rate of 75.8 percent actually recorded. The overall conviction rate would have risen by 6.9 percentage points from 1832–47 to 1854–70 instead of by 11.5 points. Therefore, about four-tenths of the rise in the conviction rate from 1832–47 to 1854–70 was due to the increase in the proportion of recidivists among all accused persons.

62. Of the 147,506 persons tried for theft in the *cours d'assises* from 1826 through 1870, 51,264 (34.8 percent) were recidivists. For persons accused of premeditated murder, the figure was 3,026 (24.8 percent) of the total of 12,209; for unpremeditated murder, it was 1,622 (18.7 percent) of 8,671 persons tried; for assaults, it was 2,143 (17.8 percent) of 12,030 persons tried; and for manslaughter, it was 648 (12.3 percent) among the total of 5,259. *Compte général*, 1826, Tables 1–2, pp. 2–3, and Tables 69–71, pp. 100–102; 1827, Tables 1–2, pp. 2–3, and Tables 72–75, pp. 104–7; 1828, Tables 1–2, pp. 2–3, and Tables 87–89, pp. 130–32; 1829, Tables 1–2, pp. 2–3, and Tables 88–90, pp. 133–35; 1830, Tables 1–2, pp. 2–3, and Table 66, pp. 108–9; 1831, Tables 1–2, pp. 2–3, and Table 101, pp. 168–69; 1832, Tables 1–2, pp. 2–3, and Table 103, pp. 172–73; 1833, Tables 1–2, pp. 2–3, and Table 108, pp. 180–81; 1834, Tables 1–2, pp. 2–3, and Table 105, pp. 176–75; 1835, Tables 1–2, pp. 2–3, and Table 109, pp. 182–83; 1836, Tables 1–2, pp. 2–3, and Table 111, pp. 182–83; 1837–38, Tables 1–2, pp. 2–3, and Table 110, pp. 180–81; 1839–48, Tables 1–2, pp. 2–3, and Table 112, pp. 182–83; 1849–50, Tables 1–2, pp. 2–3, and Table 113, pp. 176–77; 1851, Tables 1–2, pp. 2–3, and Table 114, pp. 176–77; 1852, Tables 1–2 and Table 110, pp. 168–71; 1853, Tables 1–2, pp. 2–3, and Table 109, pp. 170–73; 1854, Tables 1–2, pp. 2–3, and Table 111, pp. 172–75; 1855, Tables 1–2, pp. 2–3, and Table 109, pp. 170–73; 1856–57, Tables 1–2, pp. 2–3, and Table 110, pp. 170–73; 1858–59, Tables 1–2, pp. 2–3, and Table 108, pp. 168–71; 1860, Tables 1–2, pp. 2–3, and Table 104, pp. 164–67; 1861–62, Tables 1–2, pp. 4–5, and Table 104, pp. 166–69; 1863, Tables 1–2, pp. 4–5, and Table 107, pp. 172–73; 1864–69, Tables 1–2, pp. 4–5, and Table 104, pp. 170–71; 1870, Tables 1–2, pp. 4–5, and Table 72, pp. 138–39.

63. *Compte général*, 1865, xvi; 1868, ix; 1877, x; 1878, xi; 1879, x; 1881, xii; 1882, xv; 1883, x; 1884, x; 1885, xi; 1886, xii; 1887, xiv; 1889, xi; 1900, xxxi–xxxii; 1902, xi.

64. Ibid., 1882, xv; 1887, xiv.

65. Vigarello, *History of Rape*, 30–36, 38, 40–42, 45, 47–49, 54, 57, 61–65, 67, 71–72, 75–78, 130–31; Corbes, "La Cour d'assises des Côtes-du-Nord," 325–26; Dalloz et al., *Code pénal annoté*, 502; Garçon, *Code pénal annoté*, 1:852, 875.

66. Priscilla Robertson, "Home as a Nest: Middle Class Childhood in Nineteenth-Century Europe," in deMause, *History of Childhood*, 426–28; Heywood, *Childhood in Nineteenth-Century France*, 229, 264–65; Donzelot, *Policing of Families*, 30; Fuchs, "Crimes against Children," 239–40, 253–56.

67. Duvergier, *Code pénal annoté*, 464n.

68. Garçon, *Code pénal annoté*, 1:844, 849, 852; Duvergier, *Code pénal annoté*, 53; Garraud and Bernard, "Des attentats a la pudeur et des viols," 402; Thoinot, *Medicolegal Aspects of Moral Offenses*, 7; *Compte général*, 1880, xl.

69. *Compte général*, 1825–60, Table 1, p. 2; 1861–65, Table 1, p. 4; Toutain, *La population de la France*, 54–55.

70. From 1825 through 1850, a total of 6,770 persons were tried for child molestation in the *cours d'assises*, or an average of 260 per year. From 1851 through 1880, 21,937 persons were tried for child molestation, an average of 731 per year. The figure then dropped to a total of 16,571 from 1881 through 1913, or an average of 502 per year. *Compte général*, 1825–60, Table 1, p. 2; 1861–1909, Table 1, p. 4; 1910–13, Table 1, p. 6.

71. Corbin, *Women for Hire*, 320.

72. From 1825 through 1831, 901 persons were tried for the rape and indecent assault of minors, of whom 564 (62.6 percent) were convicted and 337 (37.4 percent) were acquitted. From 1832 through 1847, a total of 4,486 were tried, of whom 3,310 (73.8 percent) were convicted and 1,176 (26.2 percent) were acquitted. In 1848, 366 were tried, with 251 (68.6 percent) convicted and 115 (31.4 percent) acquitted. The figures for 1849–54 are 2,623 (75.7 percent) convicted and 840 (24.3 percent) acquitted among the total of 3,463 tried. From 1855 through 1862, a total of 5,556 were tried, of whom 4,642 (83.5 percent) were convicted and 914 (16.5 percent) were acquitted. *Compte général*, 1825–60, Table 1, p. 2; 1861–62, Table 1, p. 4.

73. From 1855 through 1862, a total of 2,956 persons were tried for the rape and violent or aggravated indecent assault of minors under the age of fifteen, of whom 2,511 (84.9 percent) were convicted and 445 (15.1 percent) were acquitted. From 1863 through 1870, 2,581 persons were tried for these crimes, of whom 2,194 (85.0 percent) were convicted and 387 (15.0 percent) were acquitted. As for persons tried for the nonviolent indecent assault of children under the age of eleven, 2,600 were tried from 1855 through 1862, of whom 2,131 (82.0 percent) were convicted and 469 (18.0 percent) were acquitted. Then, from 1863 through 1870, 3,570 persons were tried for the nonviolent indecent assault of children under the age of thirteen. Of these, 2,849 (79.8 percent) were convicted and 721 (20.2 percent) were acquitted. *Compte général*, 1855–60, Table 1, p. 2; 1861–70, Table 1, p. 4.

74. The annual average number of persons tried for the rape and indecent assault of adults rose modestly from 173 per year from 1825 through 1830 to a peak of 234 in the years 1851–55. Thereafter, it declined, reaching only 153 in the years 1866–70. As for convictions and acquittals, of the 1,153 persons tried from 1825 through 1831, only 551 (47.8

percent) were convicted and 602 (52.2 percent) were acquitted. By the years 1855–62, convictions had risen to 1,153 (64.9 percent) of the total of 1,777 persons tried, with acquittals numbering 624 (35.1 percent). From 1863 through 1870, among the total of 1,355 tried, 903 (66.6 percent) were convicted and 452 (33.4 percent) were acquitted. *Compte général*, 1825–60, Table 1, p. 2; 1861–70, Table 1, p. 4.

75. From 1855 through 1870, 1,456 (80.4 percent) of the 1,812 persons convicted of the rape and indecent assault of adults were granted extenuating circumstances. The figure was 2,169 (68.5 percent) of the 3,167 persons tried for the rape and violent or aggravated indecent assault of children under the age of fifteen. *Compte général*, 1855–60, Table 6, pp. 12–13, and Table 7, pp. 14–15; 1861–70, Table 6, pp. 14–15, and Table 7, pp. 16–17.

76. Vigarello, *History of Rape*, 141–42, 148–51, 201.

77. Extenuating circumstances were found for 14,376 (69.3 percent) of the 20,743 persons convicted of felonies in the *cours d'assises* from 1849 through 1853. They were found for 43,689 (73.3 percent) of 59,630 convicted felons from 1854 through 1870. *Compte général*, 1849–60, Table 6, p. 13, and Table 7, p. 15; 1861–70, Table 6, p. 15, and Table 7, p. 17.

78. F. Lombard, *Les Jurés*, 224.

79. Garraud, *Traité théorique*, 1:33–34.

80. Martin, *Crime and Criminal Justice*, 143, 155; F. Lombard, *Les Jurés*, 227; Esmein, *History of Continental Criminal Procedure*, 541.

81. Legoyt, "Documents communs a divers pays," 86; *Compte général*, 1880, ix.

82. *Compte général*, 1850, xxxix; 1860, xxxv.

83. During the intervening period of 1848–53, of the 22,499 *accusations* resulting in guilty verdicts in the *cours d'assises*, conviction on the most serious charge had been rendered in 16,803 (74.6 percent) of the cases, 2,901 (12.9 percent) had been reduced to lesser felonies, and 2,795 (12.4 percent) had been reduced to misdemeanors. Of the 54,088 charges resulting in guilty verdicts from 1854 through 1870, conviction on the most serious charge had been rendered in 44,204 (81.7 percent) of the cases, 6,054 (11.2 percent) had been reduced to lesser felonies, and 3,830 (7.1 percent) had been reduced to misdemeanors. *Compte général*, 1848–60, Table 4, p. 7; 1861–70, Table 4, p. 9.

84. In 1848, extenuating circumstances were found for 202 of the 238 persons convicted of capital crimes (84.6 percent). For 1849–53, the figure is 1,431 of the total of 1,665 convicted, and for 1854–62, it is 2,909 of 3,328 convicted. Juries found extenuating circumstances for 2,435 of the 2,563 persons convicted of capital crimes from 1863 through 1870. *Compte général*, 1848–60, Table 6, p. 13, and Table 7, p. 15; 1861–70, Table 6, p. 15, and Table 7, p. 17.

85. In 1848, 36 persons were sentenced to death. The number was 234 from 1849 through 1853 (an annual average of 47), 422 from 1854 through 1862 (again an annual average of 47), and 128 (or an annual average of 16) from 1863 through 1870. *Compte général*, 1848–60, Table 2, p. 3; 1861–70, Table 2, p. 5.

86. Vallaud, "Le crime d'infanticide," 480.

87. Donovan, "Infanticide and the Juries," 167.

88. From 1854 through 1862, before the correctionalization of some infanticide cases in 1863, 2,159 persons were tried for the crime, of whom 1,478 (68.5 percent) were convicted and 681 (31.5 percent) were acquitted. The law of 1863 made almost no difference for the persons still tried in the *cours d'assises*. Of the 1,740 persons brought before these courts for infanticide from 1863 through 1870, 1,177 (67.6 percent) were convicted and

563 (32.4 percent) were acquitted. *Compte général*, 1854–60, Table 1, p. 2; 1861–70, Table 1, p. 4.

89. From 1849 through 1853, 442 (67.9 percent) of the 651 persons convicted of infanticide were sentenced to five to twenty years of hard labor. The figure was 1,106 (74.8 percent) of the 1,478 persons convicted from 1855 through 1862 and 971 (82.5 percent) of 1,177 convicted from 1863–70. *Compte général*, 1849–60, Table 1, p. 2; 1861–70, Table 1, p. 4.

90. *Compte général*, 1850, xxxix; 1860, xxxiv.

91. Ibid., 1859, vii.

92. Of the 414 persons convicted of *rébellion* in the *cours d'assises* from 1825 through 1831, 287 (69.3 percent) received *peines correctionnelles*. From 1832 through 1847, the figure was 481 (93.9 percent) of 512. From 1848 through 1863, misdemeanor penalties were meted out to 176 (88.4 percent) of the 92 persons convicted of *rébellion*. In respect to assaults resulting in the shedding of blood of state officials or agents of public authority, 49 (71.0 percent) of the 69 persons convicted of this crime in the years 1830–31 (before 1830 it was not mentioned as a separate offense in the *Compte général*'s tables) were sentenced to *peines correctionnelles*. The same was true of 469 (86.5 percent) of 542 convicted from 1832 through 1847 and of 200 (78.1 percent) of 256 found guilty from 1848 through 1862. *Compte général*, 1825–60, Table 1, p. 2; 1861–62, Table 1, p. 4.

93. The average annual number of persons tried for crimes against public order in the *cours d'assises* dropped from 126 in 1842–54 to 26 in 1855–62. *Compte général*, 1842–60, Table 1, p. 2; 1861–62, Table 1, p. 4.

94. From 1825 through 1831, 8,499 (39.0 percent) of the 21,818 persons convicted of theft in the *cours d'assises* were punished with prison terms of five years or less. From 1832 through 1847, these misdemeanor penalties were handed out to 29,716 (61.1 percent) of the total of 48,646 convicted. *Compte général*, 1825–47, Table 2, p. 3.

95. The exact averages were 4,369 per year from 1825 through 1841, 3,567 from 1842 through 1854, and 2,251 from 1855 through 1862. *Compte général*, 1842–60, Table 2, p. 3; 1861–62, Table 2, p. 5.

96. *Compte général*, 1858, viii.

97. The 50.4 percent figure represented 9,282 of the 18,416 persons convicted of theft in the *cours d'assises* from 1854 through 1862. *Compte général*, 1854–60, Table 2, p. 3; 1861–62, Table 2, p. 5.

98. From 1832 through 1853, 5,736 persons were tried for assault of a non-parent resulting in the incapacity to work for more than twenty days, among whom 2,741 (47.8 percent) were convicted and 2,995 (52.2 percent) were acquitted. *Compte général*, 1832–53, Table 1, p. 2.

99. Of the 2,782 persons convicted in the *cours d'assises* of assault of a non-parent from 1832 through 1853, 2,523 (90.7 percent) were sentenced to prison terms of five years or less. *Compte général*, 1832–53, Table 1, p. 2.

100. From 1854 through 1862, 666 persons were tried for assault of a non-parent, of whom 415 (62.3 percent) were convicted and 251 (37.7 percent) were acquitted. Among the 415 convicted, 355 (85.5 percent) were sentenced to prison terms of five years or less. *Compte général*, 1854–60, Table 1, p. 2; 1861–62, Table 1, p. 4.

101. From 1827 (when the *Compte général*'s table on full and reduced charges first mentions *accusations* by specific crime) through 1831, a total of 580 charges of assault of a non-

parent resulted in conviction in the *cours d'assises*. In 407 (70.2 percent) of the cases, the charge was reduced to a misdemeanor. The same was true for 879 (49.9 percent) among the total of 1,796 convictions from 1832 trough 1847, 32 (46.4 percent) of 69 in 1848, 155 (38.2 percent) of 406 from 1849 through 1853, and 120 (31.9 percent) of 376 from 1854 through 1863. *Compte général*, 1827, Table 130, p. 208; 1828, Table 152, p. 246; 1829, Table 155, p. 250; 1830, Table 134, p. 226; 1831, Table 142, p. 234; 1832, Table 145, p. 244; 1833–60, Table 4, p. 6; 1861–63, Table 4, p. 8.

102. The average was 334 in 1825–31, 201 in 1842–54, and 73 in 1855–62. *Compte général*, 1825–60, Table 1, p. 2; 1861–62, Table 1, p. 4.

103. *Compte général*, 1861, x. The *Compte général* for 1861 was published in 1863, when Delangle included this statement in the introduction.

104. Garraud, *Traité théorique*, 1:34; Toulemon, *La Question du jury*, 85; *Compte général*, 1880, ix, xiv, xviii.

Chapter 4

1. Bernard Schnapper, "Le Jury français," in Schioppa, *Trial Jury*, 209.

2. Ibid., 212; Royer, *Histoire de la justice*, 546n.

3. "Décret remettant provisoirement en vigueur le décret du 7 août 1848 sur le jury," *Journal officiel de la République Français* (hereafter referred to as *JO*), octobre 15, 1870, 1639.

4. Martin, *Crime and Criminal Justice*, 175.

5. Ibid.

6. *JO*, juin 11, 1872, 3918–19.

7. Guibourg, *Le jury criminel*, 36–37; Donovan, "Changing Composition of Juries," 261; *JO*, juin 11, 1872, 3919–20; juillet 11, 1872, 4729.

8. *JO*, juillet 11, 1872, 4726.

9. Ibid., 4726–29.

10. The *Compte général* for 1871 does not include a table on the occupations of persons included in the annual jury lists. It does include such a table (for the last time) in the volume for 1872. The number of men inscribed on the jury lists for that year is 123,882. Of these, 55,562 were *propriétaires* and *rentiers* living from the incomes from their properties or investments. This meant that they made up 44.9 percent of all persons inscribed, only slightly below the figure of 47.4 percent in the years 1854–70. Persons from the liberal professions numbered 12,486 in 1872 (or 10.1 percent, compared to 14.9 percent in 1854–70). Merchants and manufacturers numbered 24,261 (19.6 percent, compared to 16.7 percent in 1854–70) and civil servants 8,292 (6.7 percent, compared to 12.7 percent in 1854–70). In the two categories that can be considered non-bourgeois, workers and artisans saw their representation increase from 1.6 percent in 1854–70 to 4.9 percent (numbering 6,045) in 1872, and peasants went from 6.7 percent to 13.9 percent (or 17,236 persons). *Compte général*, 1872, Table 103, p. 209.

11. *JO*, août 2, 1872, 5305–6; novembre 15, 1872, 6999, 7004–6; novembre 16, 1872, 7030–32; novembre 21, 1872, 7156–57.

12. *JO*, novembre 21, 1872, 7157.

13. Ibid., 7159–61.

14. *JO*, novembre 15, 1872, 7005; novembre 16, 1872, 7030.

15. *JO*, novembre 15, 1872, 6999.

16. In the years 1871–72, 449 persons were tried for *délits politiques et de presse*, of whom 190 (42.3 percent) were convicted and 257 (57.7 percent) were acquitted. Trials in the *cours d'assises* for *crimes politiques* and *rébellion* were now so rare as to be statistically insignificant. *JO*, novembre 15, 1872, 7005; *Compte général*, 1871, Table 59, p. 96; 1872, Table 58, p. 102.

17. *JO*, novembre 16, 1872, 7032–33; novembre 21, 1872, 7161–63.

18. *JO*, août 2, 1872, 5305; novembre 15, 1872, 7000–7001; novembre 16, 1872, 7027–29, 7033–34.

19. *JO*, novembre 22, 1872, 7187.

20. *JO*, juin 11, 1872, 3919; novembre 16, 1872, 7033.

21. The new law retained the provision exempting from jury duty those "who have need of their daily and manual labor" and the absolute ban on domestics and persons who had ever been convicted of vagabondage and mendicity. Again, jurors were not compensated. Partie officielle: "Loi sur le jury," *JO*, novembre 24, 1872, 7241.

22. Quoted in Soulas, *Le Recrutement du jury*, 102.

23. *Compte général*, 1875, xi; 1880, xxxviii.

24. From 1873 through 1875, 173 persons were tried in the *cours d'assises* for *délits politiques et de presse*, of whom 76 (43.9 percent) were convicted and 97 (56.1 percent) were acquitted. *Compte général*, 1873, Table 58, p. 102; 1874, Table 37, p. 82; 1875, Table 34, p. 74.

25. Schnapper, "Le Jury français," 212.

26. From 1876 through 1878, 46 persons were tried in the *cours d'assises* for *délits politiques et de presse*, of whom 20 (43.5 percent) were convicted and 26 (56.5 percent) were acquitted. *Compte général*, 1876–78, Tables 33 and 34, p. 73.

27. Wolf, *France*, 374–75.

28. Schnapper, "Le Jury français," 213–14.

29. Garner, "Criminal Procedure in France," 264.

30. F. Lombard, *Les Jurés*, 255.

31. Schnapper, "Le Jury français," 223–25.

32. L. Gambetta, *Discours et plaidoiries*, ed. J. Reinach (Paris, 1883), 9:408, cited in Schnapper, "Le Jury français," 224.

33. Nord, *Republican Moment*, 126, 137.

34. Schnapper, "Le Jury français," 223–24.

35. Martin, *Crime and Criminal Justice*, 191.

36. Ibid., 196; F. Lombard, *Les Jurés*, 252; Royer, *Histoire de la justice*, 573–600.

37. Royer, *Histoire de la justice*, 577; Martin, *Crime and Criminal Justice*, 196.

38. Cruppi, *La Cour d'assises*, 22–23; Gineste, *Essai sur l'histoire et l'organisation du jury criminel*, 133–34; Loubet, *La Justice criminelle*, 81, 197–98; Beer, "Ce qu'est le jury criminel," 493; Gide, *Recollections of the Assize Court*, 7.

39. Loubet, *La Justice criminelle*, 195–96.

40. Gide, *Recollections of the Assize Court*, 121.

41. Goldstein, *Censorship of Political Caricature*, 226–32, 238–48.

42. From 1881 through 1893, 788 persons were tried for *délits politiques et de presse* in the *cours d'assises*, of whom 423 (53.7 percent) were convicted and 365 (46.3 percent) were acquitted. *Compte général*, 1881–85, Table 34, p. 77; 1886–88, Table 39, p. 55; 1889–93, Table 28, p. 51.

43. Soulas, *Le Recrutement du jury*, 108, 115.

44. Schnapper, "Le Jury français," 236.

45. The text of this circular (January 29, 1908) is published under the title "L'Inscription des ouvriers sur la liste annuelle du jury."

46. Guibourg, *Le jury criminel*, 23–25.

47. This report, which assessed the effects of the implementation of the 1908 circular and the laws compensating jurors, was addressed to the *garde des sceaux* ("Keeper of the Seals," a title for the minister of justice) and is summarized in the article "Le Jury criminel en 1909."

48. Schnapper, "Le Jury français," 237–38.

49. According to Christian Soulas, of the thirty-six jurors on the session list for the third trimester of 1933 in the department of Herault, fifteen were *propriétaires* (compared to often twenty or more before 1908), nine belonged to the urban middle class, six were "intellectuals," only five were *ouvriers*, and one was an *employé*. Edward Berenson found that among the twelve jurors who tried the famous case of Henriette Caillaux in 1914, there were seven tradesmen and artisans, two persons living on investments, two civil servants, and one architect. Soulas, *Le Recrutement du jury*, 133; Berenson, *Trial of Madame Caillaux*, 253–54n.

50. Schnapper, "Le Jury français," 165.

51. According to figures compiled by André Davidovitch, of the annual average number of 356,535 suspected criminal cases reported from 1876 through 1880, 213,178 (49.66 percent) were filed away in the public prosecutors' offices without further action, and 12,502 (3.65 percent) were dropped by the *juges d'instruction*. In the years 1901–5, an annual average of 496,485 cases were reported, of which 313,738 (62.52 percent) were filed away without further action by the prosecutors' offices, and 14,301 (2.88 percent) were dropped by the *juges d'instruction*. Davidovitch, "Criminalité et répression," 39–41.

52. During this era, the Sûreté Générale, an agency originally created in 1828 to oversee the activities of police *commissaires* charged with special duties, expanded. It eventually became the Sûreté Nationale, the equivalent of the U.S. Federal Bureau of Investigation. The number of personnel of the Sûreté Générale rose from 1,057 in 1880 to 1,647 in 1913. In the 1880s, Alphonse Bertillon worked at the Paris Sûreté to develop his system of *anthropometrie*, which used a series of physical measurements and photographs to identify individual criminals. In 1888, Bertillon took charge of a new permanent department, the Identité judiciaire. In the 1890s, Bertillon was one of the men who perfected fingerprinting, invented by Henry Faulds in 1880. It eventually replaced *anthropometrie*. Martin, *Crime and Criminal Justice*, 47–48, 53, 57, 79–81.

53. Ibid., 169–71.

54. Cruppi, *La Cour d'assises*, 141; Garner, "Criminal Procedure in France," 264, 271–72.

55. Garner, "Criminal Procedure in France," 266–67.

56. Martin, *Crime and Criminal Justice*, 191–233; Royer, *Histoire de la justice*, 573–600; Langbein, *Origins of Adversary Criminal Trial*, 81–82; Beattie, *Crime and the Courts*, 348.

57. Garner, "Criminal Procedure in France," 264; Coudert, "French Criminal Procedure," 335; Langbein, *Origins of Adversary Criminal Trial*, 338.

58. Garner, "Criminal Procedure in France," 267.

59. Beattie, *Crime and the Courts*, 342–43; Langbein, *Origins of Adversary Criminal Trial*, 321–22, 330.

60. Langbein, *Origins of Adversary Criminal Trial*, 323.

61. Garner, "Criminal Procedure in France," 263–67; Coudert, "French Criminal Procedure," 339; Pinon, "La réforme de la procedure criminelle," 76–77.

62. Robert Vouin, "La Cour d'assises française de 1808 à 1958," in Institut de droit comparé de l'Universite de Paris, *Problemes contemporains de procedure pénal*, 232.

63. Loubat, "Programme minimum de réformes pénales [2]," 457.

64. Garner, "Criminal Procedure in France," 271.

65. Ibid., 274; Pinon, "La réforme de la procedure criminelle," 80–81; commentary by M. l'Avocat général Mornet in Prud'hon, *Le Jury criminel*, 62; Beer, "Ce qu'est le jury criminel," 499–500; Mimin, *Le Concours du jury*, 9, 19, 22–23, 28; Guyho, *Les Jurés "maîtres de la peine,"* 22–23, 29; Donnedieu de Vabres, *La Justice pénale*, 128; *Compte général*, 1890, xi–xii; Summers, "Criminal Jury in France," 206.

66. Quoted in Guyho, *Les Jurés "maîtres de la peine,"* 27.

67. Garner, "Criminal Procedure in France," 273–74.

68. Guyho, *Les Jurés "maîtres de la peine,"* 22; Garner, "Criminal Procedure in France," 274.

69. Toulemon, *La Question du jury*, 259–60.

70. Garner, "Criminal Procedure in France," 273–74, 277; Pinon, "La réforme de la procedure criminelle," 80–81.

71. From 1873 through 1879, 3,579 persons were tried in the *cours d'assises* for the non-violent or non-aggravated indecent assault of children under the age of thirteen, of whom 2,870 (80.2 percent) were convicted and 709 (19.8 percent) were acquitted. From 1880 through 1893, 6,047 were tried, of whom 4,149 (68.6 percent) were convicted and 1,898 (31.4 percent) were acquitted. The figures for 1894–1908 are 4,108 tried, 2,822 (68.7 percent) convicted, and 1,286 (31.3 percent) acquitted. From 1909 through 1913, 1,236 were tried, of whom 869 (70.3 percent) were convicted and 367 (29.7 percent) were acquitted. From 1873 through 1879, extenuating circumstances were found for 2,448 (75.4 percent) of the 3,246 persons convicted of the felony charge of nonviolent or non-aggravated indecent assault of children. From 1880 through 1893, they were found for 3,718 (79.6 percent) of the 4,671 persons convicted of the felony charge, and from 1894 through 1908, the figure was 2,673 (83.3 percent) of 3,207 persons convicted. Extenuating circumstances were found for 841 (80.6 percent) of the 1,044 persons convicted from 1909 through 1913. Of the 2,870 persons tried for the nonviolent or non-aggravated indecent assault of children and convicted from 1873 through 1879, 2,196 (76.5 percent) were sentenced to prison terms of five years or less. Such punishments were handed down to 2,363 (83.7 percent) of the 2,822 persons convicted from 1894 through 1908. *Compte général*, 1873, Table 1, p. 4, Table 6, p. 14, and Table 8, p. 18; 1874–85, Table 1, p. 4, Table 7, p. 22, and Table 8, p. 26; 1886–1909, Table 1, p. 4, Table 7, p. 16, and Table 8, p. 20; 1910–13, Table 1, p. 6, Table 7, p. 18, and Table 8, p. 22.

72. From 1876 through 1880, 4,044 persons were tried in the *cours d'assises* for the rape and indecent assault of children, an average of 809 per year. Thereafter, the number dropped sharply. By the years 1911–13, when 1,190 persons were tried, the annual average was down to 397—less than half the figure for 1876–80. *Compte général*, 1873–1909, Table 1, p. 4; 1910–13, Table 1, p. 6.

73. According to Georges Vigarello, the correctionalization of sex crimes (including the rape and indecent assault of children) "became commonplace around 1870, to the

215

point where 50 percent of the sex offenses tried in the magistrates' courts [commonly as affronts to public decency] were assaults or rapes." Reports of sex crimes apparently rose, but more and more cases were sent to the *tribunaux correctionnels*, where trials for sex offenses increased between 1880 and 1900. In 1903, statistician Maurice Yvernes claimed that correctionalization had "without any doubt" played an "enormous" part in reducing trials for indecent assault in the *cours d'assises*. Vigarello, *History of Rape*, 158–59; Yvernes, "La Justice en France," 302.

74. Of the 1,314 persons convicted of the violent rape and violent indecent assault of minors from 1873 through 1879, 860 (65.4 percent) were granted extenuating circumstances. From 1880 through 1893, 1,547 were convicted and 1,078 (69.7 percent) were granted extenuating circumstances. From 1894 through 1908, the figures were 938 convicted and 733 (78.1 percent) granted extenuating circumstances. The proportion granted extenuating circumstances declined somewhat in the era from 1909 through 1913, however, to 214 (70.6 percent) of the 303 persons convicted. As for punishments, among the 1,963 persons tried for the violent rape and indecent assault of minors and convicted on either the full charge or on a lesser one from 1873 through 1879, 715 (36.4 percent) were sentenced to prison terms of five years or less. The proportion rose continuously thereafter, to 53.4 percent (311 of the total of 582) in the years 1909–13. *Compte général*, 1873, Table 1, p. 4, Table 6, pp. 14, 17, and Table 7, pp. 18–19; 1874–85, Table 1, p. 4, Table 7, pp. 22, 25, and Table 8, pp. 26–27; 1886–1909, Table 1, p. 4, Table 7, pp. 16, 19, and Table 8, pp. 20–21; 1910–13, Table 1, p. 6, Table 7, pp. 18, 21, and Table 8, pp. 22–23.

75. From 1873 through 1879, 2,283 persons were tried in the *cours d'assises* for the rape and violent or aggravated indecent assault of minors under the age of fifteen, of whom 1,963 (86.0 percent) were convicted and 320 (14.0 percent) were acquitted. From 1880 through 1893, 3,036 were tried, of whom 2,438 (80.3 percent) were convicted and 598 (19.7 percent) were acquitted. The figures for 1894–1908 were 2,087 tried, 1,630 (78.1 percent) convicted, and 457 (21.9 percent) acquitted. From 1909 through 1913, 736 were tried, of whom 582 (79.1 percent) were convicted and 154 (20.9 percent) were acquitted. *Compte général*, 1873–1909, Table 1, p. 4; 1910–13, Table 1, p. 6.

76. From 1873 trough 1879, when 86.0 percent of all persons tried for violent or aggravated child molestation were convicted, the conviction rate for persons charged with all other crimes in the *cours d'assises* was 78.9 percent (representing 24,283 persons among 30,766 tried). This was a gap of 7.1 percentage points. The gap widened continuously thereafter. By the period from 1909 through 1913, when 79.1 percent of all persons tried for violent or aggravated child molestation were convicted, the conviction rate for persons charged with all other crimes had dropped to 63.4 percent (or 9,447 persons among 14,892 tried). This was a gap of 15.7 percentage points. *Compte général*, 1873–1909, Tables 1 and 2, pp. 4–5; 1910–13, Tables 1 and 2, pp. 6–7.

77. Donovan, "Combatting the Sexual Abuse of Children," 82–84; Prevost, *De la prostitution des enfants*, 43, 46–48, 108, 136.

78. From 1873 through 1879, 963 persons were tried in the *cours d'assises* for the rape and indecent assault of adults, of whom 711 (73.8 percent) were convicted and 252 (26.2 percent) were acquitted. In the years 1880–93, 1,331 were tried, of whom 874 (65.7 percent) were convicted and 457 (34.3 percent) were acquitted. The figures for 1894–1908 were 1,081 tried, 682 (63.1 percent) convicted, and 399 (36.9 percent) acquitted. From 1909 through 1913, 302 were tried, of whom 200 (66.2 percent) were convicted and 102

(33.8 percent) were acquitted. *Compte général*, 1873–1909, Table 1, p. 4; 1910–13, Table 1, p. 6.

79. Extenuating circumstances were found for 1,282 (78.7 percent) of the 1,628 persons convicted of the rape and indecent assault of adults from 1880 through 1913. *Compte général*, 1880–85, Table 7, pp. 22, 25, and Table 8, pp. 26–27; 1886–1909, Table 7, pp. 16, 19, and Table 8, pp. 20–21; 1910–13, Table 7, pp. 18, 21, and Table 8, pp. 22–23.

80. Of the 711 persons tried in the *cours d'assises* for the rape and indecent assault of adults and convicted from 1873 through 1879, 376 (52.9 percent) were sentenced to prison terms of five years or less. From 1880 through 1893, such sentences were handed out to 516 (63.3 percent) of convicted persons. The figure dropped slightly to 59.1 percent (403 of 682) from 1894 through 1908. Among the 200 convicted from 1909 through 1913, 120 (60.0 percent) were sentenced to prison terms of five years or less. *Compte général*, 1873–1909, Table 1, p. 4; 1910–13, Table 1, p. 6.

81. The total number was 610 from 1876 through 1880, or an annual average of 122. From 1911 through 1913, it was 173, or an annual average of 58. *Compte général*, 1876–80, Table 1, p. 4; 1911–13, Table 1, p. 6.

82. Vigarello, *History of Rape*, 158–59.

83. Cruppi, *La Cour d'assises*, 59–60; Berenson, *Trial of Madame Caillaux*, 28–40; Harris, *Murders and Madness*, 117.

84. Berenson, *Trial of Madame Caillaux*, 39.

85. Schaefer, *Theories in Criminology*, 106–9, 271; Manheim, *Pioneers in Criminology*, 16; Clarence Ray Jeffrey, "The Historical Development of Criminology," in Manheim, *Pioneers in Criminology*, 366–67.

86. Wright, *Between the Guillotine and Liberty*, 110–11; Saleilles, *Individualization of Punishment*, 18.

87. Alexander Fontana, "The Intermittences of Rationality," in Foucault, *I, Pierre Rivière*, 276–77, 281, 287; Schaefer, *Theories in Criminology*, 117.

88. Wright, *Between the Guillotine and Liberty*, 115–24.

89. Ibid., 176; Nye, *Crime, Madness, and Politics*, 97–131.

90. Wiener, *Reconstructing the Criminal*, 159–71, 173, 187, 217, 224, 226–32, 235–40, 257–63, 271–72, 284, 308–10, 313–23, 325–29, 335–36, 341–42, 352, 355, 371, 374, 379–80.

91. Green, "Freedom and Criminal Responsibility," 1918–43.

92. Berenson, *Trial of Madame Caillaux*, 19–20, 32, 36, 39–40.

93. Nye, *Crime, Madness, and Politics*, 28–29.

94. Cruppi, *La Cour d'assises*, 59, 60, quoted in Berenson, *Trial of Madame Caillaux*, 39–40. Bracketed aside is Berenson's.

95. From 1873 through 1913, a total of 158,273 persons were tried in the *cours d'assises*, of whom 134,238 (84.8 percent) were males and 24,035 (15.2 percent) were females. The proportion changed very little from one period to the next within this forty-year time frame. *Compte général*, 1873, Table 15, p. 34; 1874, Table 16, p. 42; 1875–78, Table 16, p. 40; 1879–85, Table 18, p. 42; 1886–89, Table 15, pp. 30–31; 1890–1909, Table 13, p. 27; 1910–13, Table 13, p. 29.

96. Donovan, "The Relationship between Migration and Criminality," 19–44; Nye, *Crime, Madness, and Politics*, 109–19; O'Brien, *Promise of Punishment*, 66–69.

97. Harris, "Melodrama, Hysteria and Feminine Crimes of Passion," 53.

98. From 1873 through 1879, 11,939 males were tried for theft in the *cours d'assises*, of

whom 10,449 (87.9 percent) were convicted and 1,440 (12.1 percent) were acquitted. Through the same period, 1,853 females were tried for theft, of whom 1,319 (71.2 percent) were convicted and 534 (28.8 percent) were acquitted. Then, from 1880 through 1913, 45,258 males were tried for theft, of whom 37,405 (82.6 percent) were convicted and 7,853 (17.4 percent) were acquitted. For females charged with theft, the figures were 4,884 tried, 2,587 (53.0 percent) convicted, and 2,297 (47.0 percent) acquitted. Therefore, from 1873 through 1879, the differential between the acquittal rate for men and the acquittal rate for women charged with theft was 16.7 percentage points in favor of the women. In the period 1880–1913, the differential had increased to 29.6 percentage points. As for fraud, from 1880 through 1913, 6,794 men were tried for the crime in the *cours d'assises*, of whom 4,053 (59.7 percent) were convicted and 2,741 (40.3 percent) were acquitted. Through the same period, 879 women were tried for fraud, of whom 349 (39.7 percent) were convicted and 530 (60.3 percent) were acquitted. *Compte général*, 1873, Table 11, p. 27; 1874, Table 12, p. 35; 1875–85, Table 13, p. 35; 1886–1909, Table 15, p. 31; 1910–13, Table 15, p. 33.

99. Reviews of the extensive late-nineteenth- and early-twentieth-century literature in France purporting to show that many or most female crimes were due to the psychological and biological weaknesses of women are provided in Barrows, *Distorting Mirrors*, 57–60, and O'Brien, *Promise of Punishment*, 64–69.

100. In 1910, Helie Courtis wrote: "The great and miraculous function of maternity, the necessity of maintaining the species, condemns the reproducing woman (*creatrice*) to an inferior degree of individual evolution and, by her lesser capacity for mental synthesis and her impulsiveness, places her between the adolescent and the adult." In 1897, Raymond de Ryckere wrote: "The normal woman has many characteristics which she shares with the savage and the child (irascibility, vengeance, jealousy, vanity . . .)." Helie Courtis, *Étude médico-légale des crimes passionnels*, thèse pour le doctorat en médecine, Toulouse, 1910, cited in Harris, "Melodrama, Hysteria and Feminine Crimes of Passion," 53; Ryckere, Review of *La femme criminelle*, 306.

101. Comments by Oscar Bloch in Société Générale des Prisons, "Seconde Séance du 28 juin 1913," 964; Granier, *La femme criminelle*, 442.

102. Harris, "Melodrama, Hysteria and Feminine Crimes of Passion," 48–49.

103. Macé, *Les femmes criminelles*, 235.

104. Harris, "Melodrama, Hysteria and Feminine Crimes of Passion," 49.

105. O'Brien, *Promise of Punishment*, 67–68; Vlamynck, "La délinquance au feminin," 685; Icard, *La femme pendant la periode menstruelle*, x, 9–10, 134–43, 145–56, 167; Granier, *La femme criminelle*, 44–46, 167; Vallaud, "Le crime d'infanticide," 484.

106. O'Brien, "Kleptomania Diagnosis," 68–71.

107. Of the total of 18,714 women tried in the *cours d'assises* from 1880 through 1913, 4,580 (24.5 percent) were charged with infanticide. It is impossible to tell from the judicial statistics how many women on the national level were tried for "crimes of passion," but 2,115 (11.3 percent of all women tried) were charged with some kind of intentional homicide other than infanticide. *Compte général*, 1880–85, Table 13, p. 34; 1886–1909, Table 15, p. 30; 1910–13, Table 15, p. 32.

108. Berenson, "Politics of Divorce," 38; Harris, "Melodrama, Hysteria and Feminine Crimes of Passion," 40–41.

109. O'Brien, *Promise of Punishment*, 64.

Notes to Pages 129–30

110. Commentary by Henri Bergson in Prud'hon, *Le Jury criminel*, 125.

111. According to Ruth Harris, the number of murders in Paris that could be described as crimes of passion rose from six in 1880 to thirty-five in 1910. *Crimes passionnels* never accounted for more than a third of murders committed by men, but it was the dominant form of murder committed by women in Paris. Five of six murders committed by women in 1881 were crimes of passion. In 1905, the figure was nine of eleven, and in 1910, all fourteen murders committed by women were crimes of passion. Harris, "Melodrama, Hysteria and Feminine Crimes of Passion," 35, 59n.

112. See, for instance, Hartman, *Victorian Murderesses*, 144, 166, 246, 267; Harris, "Melodrama, Hysteria and Feminine Crimes of Passion," 31, 33, 35, 38; and Donovan, "Justice Unblind," 94–95.

113. Proal, *Passion and Criminality*, 609–10.

114. Harris, *Murders and Madness*, 36.

115. *Le Temps*, May 13, 1912.

116. Harris, *Murders and Madness*, 233; Macé, *Les femmes criminelles*, 359–60.

117. Harris, *Murders and Madness*, 233–34.

118. Fuchs, *Poor and Pregnant*, 211, 213.

119. Vallaud, "Le crime d'infanticide," 484.

120. Fuchs, *Poor and Pregnant*, 211.

121. Of the 1,555 persons tried for infanticide in the *cours d'assises* from 1873 through 1879, 1,191 (76.6 percent) were convicted and 364 (23.4 percent) were acquitted. From 1880 through 1890, 2,117 persons were tried for infanticide, of whom 1,319 (62.3 percent) were convicted and 798 (37.7 percent) were acquitted. The figures for 1891–1901 were 1,476 tried, 837 (56.7 percent) convicted, and 639 (43.3 percent) acquitted. From 1902 through 1908, 677 persons were tried for infanticide, of whom 299 (44.2 percent) were convicted and 378 (55.8 percent) were acquitted. From 1909 through 1913, the figures were 481 tried, 191 (39.7 percent) convicted, and 290 (60.3 percent) acquitted. *Compte général*, 1873–1909, Table 1, p. 4; 1910–13, Table 1, p. 6.

122. Wiener, *Reconstructing the Criminal*, 269.

123. Granier, *La femme criminelle*, ix, 377, 436; Proal, *Passion and Criminality*, 612–13.

124. From 1826 through 1879, 13,004 women were tried in the *cours d'assises* for intentional homicides. Of these, 9,431 (72.5 percent) were charged with infanticide, and only 3,573 (27.5 percent) were charged with other intentional homicides. From 1880 through 1913, 6,695 women were tried for intentional homicides, of whom 4,580 (68.4 percent) were charged with infanticide and 2,115 (31.6 percent) were tried for other intentional homicides. *Compte général*, 1826–27, Table 4, p. 6; 1828–31, Table 8, p. 14; 1832, Table 8, p. 16; 1833, Table 10, p. 20; 1834–35, Table 11, p. 22; 1836–60, Table 11, p. 20; 1861–70, Table 11, p. 22; 1871–73, Table 11, p. 26; 1874, Table 12, p. 34; 1875–85, Table 13, p. 34; 1886–1909, Table 15, p. 30; 1910–13, Table 15, p. 32.

125. The average annual number of persons tried for infanticide in France dropped sharply from 219 in 1876–80 to 93 in 1906–10. Donovan, "Infanticide and the Juries," 159.

126. From 1873 through 1879, 1,191 persons were tried for infanticide and convicted. Of these, 1,025 (86.1 percent) were actually found guilty of infanticide and 166 (13.9 percent) were convicted of a lesser crime. From 1891 through 1901, 837 persons were tried for infanticide and convicted, 467 (55.8 percent) of whom were found guilty of the crime

and 370 (44.2 percent) of whom were convicted of a lesser offense. Extenuating circumstances were found for everyone convicted of infanticide itself in the 1891–1901 period. In the era from 1873 through 1879, 8 (0.7 percent) of the 1,191 convicts were sentenced to death, 22 (1.8 percent) were sentenced to hard labor for life, 979 (82.2 percent) were sentenced to five to twenty years of hard labor, 23 (1.9 percent) were given sentences of more than five years' imprisonment, 153 (12.8 percent) were given prison sentences of five years or less, and 6 (0.5 percent) received some other punishment. Of the 837 convicted from 1891 through 1901, none were sentenced to death or to hard labor for life, 462 (55.2 percent) were sentenced to five to twenty years of hard labor, 21 (2.5 percent) to prison terms of more than five years, 353 (42.4 percent) to prison terms of five years or less, and 1 (0.1 percent) to another penalty. *Compte général*, 1873, Table 1, p. 4, and Table 6, p. 16; 1874–79, Table 1, p. 4, and Table 7, p. 24; 1891–1901, Table 1, p. 4, Table 7, p. 18, and Table 8, p. 21; Loubat, "Programme minimum de réformes pénales [2]," 452.

127. Loubat, "Programme minimum de réformes pénales [2]," 452.

128. From 1891 through 1901, 1,476 persons were tried for infanticide, of whom 837 (56.7 percent) were convicted and 639 (43.3 percent) were acquitted. From 1902 through 1908, 677 persons were tried for infanticide, of whom 299 (44.2 percent) were convicted and 378 (55.8 percent) were acquitted. From 1909 through 1913, 481 persons were tried for the crime, of whom 191 (39.7 percent) were convicted and 290 (60.3 percent) were acquitted. *Compte général*, 1891–1909, Table 1, p. 4; 1910–13, Table 1, p. 6; Loubat, "Programme minimum de réformes pénales [2]," 452.

129. From 1902 through 1913, 366 persons were convicted of infanticide proper. Six of these were children under the age of sixteen sent to houses of correction until the age of twenty-one and for whom extenuating circumstances were inapplicable. Extenuating circumstances were found for 356 (98.9 percent) of the 360 convicts for whom extenuating circumstances were applicable. *Compte général*, 1902–9, Table 7, p. 18, and Table 8, p. 21; 1910–13, Table 7, p. 20, and Table 8, p. 23.

130. Of the 490 persons tried for infanticide in the *cours d'assises* and convicted from 1902 through 1913, 10 (2.0 percent) were sentenced to hard labor terms of five to twenty years, 40 (8.2 percent) were sentenced to prison terms of more than five years, 434 (88.6 percent) were punished with prison terms of five years or less, and 6 (1.2 percent) received some other punishment. *Compte général*, 1902–9, Table 1, p. 4; 1910–13, Table 1, p. 6.

131. Donovan, "Justice and Sexuality," 240.

132. Bidelman, *Pariahs Stand Up!*, 103.

133. Ibid., 73–75; Harsin, *Policing Prostitution*, 355; McMillan, *Housewife or Harlot*, 21, 23–24, 88–89.

134. Moses, *French Feminism*, 176, 206, 208, 222, 226.

135. Bidelman, *Pariah Stand Up!*, 57, 105; McMillan, *Housewife or Harlot*, 81.

136. Moses, *French Feminism*, 229.

137. Bidelman, *Pariahs Stand Up!*, 93.

138. Hartman, *Victorian Murderesses*, 144, 267; *Code pénal*, Article 324.

139. Donovan, "Justice and Sexuality," 239–40.

140. In 1878, M. Bérenger introduced one such proposal in the Senate. In 1883, another proposal to abrogate the ban on paternity suits was introduced in the Chamber of Deputies by G. Rivet. Vallaud, "Le crime d'infanticide," 496n.

141. At the opening of the twentieth century, appeals court judge Louis Proal wrote: "[W]hat is wanted is a modification of the Law forbidding inquiry into the question of paternity. This reform is demanded by MM. Lecointa, Bérenger, Beaune, Poiton, Beaudant, Rodière, Laurent, that is to say by magistrates and lawyers possessed of the practical spirit. . . . Our code is old-fashioned, it wants reforming." Proal, *Passion and Criminality*, 313.

142. Moses, *French Feminism*, 229–30.

143. Wiener, *Men of Blood*, 123–25.

144. Harris, "Melodrama, Hysteria and Feminine Crimes of Passion," 37; Weber, *France, Fin de Siècle*, 138; Nye, *Masculinity and Male Codes of Honor*, 172–215.

145. Hartman, *Victorian Murderesses*, 144, 267.

146. Harris, "Melodrama, Hysteria and Feminine Crimes of Passion," 57.

147. Wiener, *Men of Blood*, 27–30, 34–35, 37, 40–41, 43–46, 75, 123–25, 201–9, 214–15, 235–39.

148. From 1825 through 1830, an average of 118 persons were tried each year for infanticide and only 12 for abortion. From 1831 through 1890, the annual average number of persons tried for infanticide in each five-year period varied from 102 to 230, and the average for abortion varied from 14 to 88. In the years 1891–95, the annual average for abortion reached 102 (it was 157 for infanticide). As late as 1906–10, the annual average number of persons tried for infanticide (93) still well exceeded the number (73) tried for abortion. In the years 1911–13, the annual average number of persons tried for abortion (154) finally exceeded the number (101) tried for infanticide. *Compte général*, 1825–60, Table 1, p. 2; 1861–1909, Table 1, p. 4; 1910–13, Table 1, p. 6.

149. Bertillon, *La dépopulation de la France*, 243; Allemane, *L'avortement criminel*, 270–72; Spengler, *France Faces Depopulation*, 240n (this book was originally published in 1938).

150. From 1835 through 1913, 4,742 persons were tried for abortion. Of these, 1,932 (40.7 percent) were never married, 626 (13.2 percent) were widowed or divorced, 2,182 (46.0 percent) were married, and 2 (0.04 percent) were of unknown martial status. *Compte général*, 1835, Table 16, p. 32; 1836–60, Table 16, p. 30; 1861–70, Table 16, p. 32; 1871–73, Table 16, p. 36; 1874, Table 17, p. 44; 1875–78, Table 17, p. 42; 1879–85, Table 18, p. 44; 1886–1909, Table 18, p. 36; 1910–13, Table 18, p. 38.

151. Of the 4,742 persons tried for abortion from 1835 through 1913, 2,182 (46.0 percent) were married. The same was true for 2,055 (15.1 percent) of the 13,629 persons tried for infanticide. *Compte général*, 1835, Table 16, p. 32; 1836–60, Table 16, p. 30; 1861–70, Table 16, p. 32; 1871–73, Table 16, p. 36; 1874, Table 17, p. 44; 1875–78, Table 17, p. 42; 1879–85, Table 18, p. 44; 1886–1909, Table 18, p. 36; 1910–13, Table 18, p. 38.

152. From 1873 through 1879, extenuating circumstances were found for 42 (74.4 percent) of the 58 persons convicted for performing abortions. During the same years, extenuating circumstances were found for 165 (74.7 percent) of the 221 convicted *avortées*. From 1880 through 1913, 125 abortionists were convicted, and juries found extenuating circumstances for 116 (92.8 percent) of them. The same was found for 679 (87.5 percent) of the 776 convicted *avortées*. *Compte général*, 1873, Table 6, p. 14, and Table 7, p. 18; 1874–85, Table 7, p. 22, and Table 8, p. 26; 1886–1909, Table 7, p. 16, and Table 8, p. 20; 1910–1913, Table 7, p. 18, and Table 8, p. 22.

153. *Code pénal*, Articles 19, 21, 317.

154. Only 10 of the 125 abortionists convicted from 1880 through 1913 received penalties of hard labor. *Compte général*, 1880–85, Table 7, p. 22; 1886–1909, Table 7, p. 16; 1910–13, Table 7, p. 18.

155. Of the 423 people tried for abortion from 1873 through 1879, 269 (62.3 percent) were convicted and 163 (37.7 percent) were acquitted. Then, from 1880 through 1890, 596 persons were tried for abortion, of whom 240 (40.3 percent) were convicted and 356 (59.7 percent) were acquitted. The figures for 1891–1901 were 898 tried, 326 (36.3 percent) convicted, and 572 (63.7 percent) acquitted. From 1902 through 1908, 372 persons were tried for the crime, among whom 104 (28.0 percent) were convicted and 268 (72.0 percent) were acquitted. The number of persons tried for the crime from 1909 through 1913 was 641, of whom 216 (33.7 percent) were convicted and 425 (66.3 percent) were acquitted. *Compte général*, 1873–1909, Table 1, p. 4; 1910–13, Table 1, p. 6.

156. As in the case of infanticide, prosecutors in abortion cases had to convince the jury the accused woman had been pregnant. But in abortion cases, prosecutors faced the additional difficulty of proving that an abortion was intentional and not spontaneous. Also, the women who had undergone abortions rarely testified against abortionists, because *avortées* were not allowed any immunity if they agreed to testify against those who had performed the abortions. In addition, as in American law, French law recognized the confidentiality of patient-doctor relationships. This impeded the presentation of evidence against persons accused of the crime. Many abortions were performed by abortionists whose skill at their craft was less than satisfactory. In other cases, the women themselves induced (or attempted to induce) the acts. Therefore, a sizable proportion of all female admissions to the larger hospitals was because of injuries or infections from the operations or in order to have the doctors complete those the *avortées* had begun. Many of these women admitted their acts on condition of professional discretion. In most such instances, the doctors felt bound by the confidentiality of the doctor-patient relationship and would therefore refuse to testify in court against the women if they were prosecuted for the crime. Berthélemy, "Les mesures," 119–21, 124; Bertillon, *La dépopulation de la France*, 242; Allemane, *L'avortement criminel*, 108, 111–12; McLaren, "Abortion in France," 478–79.

157. Bertillon, *La dépopulation de la France*, 243; Allemane, *L'avortement criminel*, 270–72; Spengler, *France Faces Depopulation*, 240n.

158. Extenuating circumstances were found for 128 (61.0 percent) of the 210 persons convicted of abortion from 1834 through 1848. There was little variation for the periods from 1849 through 1879. Altogether, of the 1,117 persons convicted of abortion through these thirty years, juries found extenuating circumstances for 792 (70.9 percent) of them. Extenuating circumstances were found for 206 (82.7 percent) of the 249 persons convicted of abortion from 1880 through 1890. Between 1891 and 1913 (again, there was little variation in the periods within this time frame), the juries found extenuating circumstances for 589 (90.3 percent) of the 652 persons they convicted of abortion. *Compte général*, 1834–35, Table 6, p. 12, and Table 7, p. 16; 1836–60, Table 6, p. 12, and Table 7, p. 14; 1861–70, Table 6, p. 14, and Table 7, p. 16; 1871–73, Table 6, p. 14, and Table 7, p. 18; 1874–85, Table 7, p. 22, and Table 8, p. 26; 1886–1909, Table 7, p. 16, and Table 8, p. 20; 1910–13, Table 7, p. 18, and Table 8, p. 22.

159. Of the 320 persons tried in the *cours d'assises* for abortion and convicted from 1902 through 1913, 281 (87.8 percent) were sentenced to prison terms of five years or less. *Compte général*, 1902–9, Table 1, p. 4; 1910–13, Table 1, p. 6.

160. McManners, *Church and State in France*, 5–8, 11, 19, 32–33, 35–39, 44–50, 123–26, 149; Clark, *Position of Women in Contemporary France*, 178.

161. McLaren, "Abortion in France," 462–63, 466–70.

162. Spengler, *France Faces Depopulation*, 53; Bertillon, *La depopulation de la France*, 3, 67–69.

163. Bertillon, *La dépopulation de la France*, 102–57, 210–38; Lux, "Un crime que l'on ne punit plus," 671–72; Berthélemy, "Les mesures," 103.

164. McLaren, "Abortion in France," 466–72, 479.

165. Arcis, "La criminalité feminine," 949.

166. From 1831 through 1835, 387 cases of suspected criminal abortion were reported to the police. The number was 1,679 in the years 1851–55, 3,491 from 1891 through 1895, and 4,517 from 1906 through 1910. Donovan, "Abortion, the Law, and the Juries," 161.

167. In the introduction to the 1880 *Compte général*, the Ministry of Justice complained that "for a number of years abortive practices have been exercised with a scandalous skill." Jacques Lux added in 1908 that "this atrocious industry of the *faiseuses d'anges* ["Angel Makers"—a popular nineteenth-century French expression for abortionists] has developed in France with alarming rapidity." *Compte général*, 1880, xv; Lux, "Un crime que l'on ne punit plus," 671.

168. Dr. A. Brochard, *La verité sur les enfants trouvés* (Paris: E. Plon, 1876), 98–99, cited in McLaren, "Abortion in France," 466; Berthélemy, "Les mesures," 102; Brouardel, *L'avortement*, 43.

169. Maurice Ajam, *Monographie d'un jury d'assises* (Archives d'anthropologie criminelle, 1899), cited in Loubat, "Programme minimum de réformes pénales [2]," 450.

170. Spengler, *France Faces Depopulation*, 102; Bertillon, *La depopulation de la France*, 119–21, 141.

171. Spengler, *France Faces Depopulation*, 78–82; Bertillon, *La dépopulation de la France*, 102–7.

172. Of the 2,927 persons accused of abortion in France from 1833 through 1888, 828 (28.3 percent) were employed in agriculture (most of whom were undoubtedly peasants), 846 (28.9 percent) were workers, 252 (8.6 percent) were personal domestics, 60 (2 percent) were employed in hotels, restaurants, and inns, 717 (24.5 percent) were bourgeois, and 224 (7.7 percent) had no occupation or their occupation was unknown. *Compte général*, 1833, Table 21, p. 40; 1834–35, Table 22, p. 42; 1836–60, Table 22, p. 40; 1861–69, Table 22, p. 42; 1870, Table 18, p. 36; 1871, Table 18, p. 40; 1872–73, Table 20, p. 44; 1874, Table 21, p. 52; 1875–78, Table 21, p. 50; 1879–85, Table 22, p. 52; 1886–88, Table 21, p. 42.

173. As already shown in note 155, the acquittal rate for abortion slightly decreased from 72.0 percent in 1902–8 to 66.3 percent in 1909–13. The latter figure was, however, higher than it had been before 1901.

174. McLaren, "Abortion in France," 470.

175. From 1873 through 1879, 4,485 persons were tried for capital crimes in the *cours d'assises*, of whom 3,437 (76.6 percent) were convicted on either the capital charge or on some lesser one and 1,048 (23.4 percent) were acquitted. From 1880 through 1893, 8,859 were tried, of whom 5,927 (66.9 percent) were convicted and 2,932 (33.1 percent) were acquitted. The figures for 1894–1901 (before infanticide was made a noncapital crime) were 3,910 tried, 2,521 (64.5 percent) convicted, and 1,389 (35.5 percent) acquitted. From 1902

through 1908, 2,311 persons were tried for capital crimes, of whom 1,578 (68.3 percent) were convicted and 733 (31.7 percent) were acquitted. In the era from 1909 through 1913, 1,740 persons were tried, 1,095 (62.9 percent) of whom were convicted; 645 (37.1 percent) were acquitted. *Compte général*, 1873–1909, Tables 1 and 2, pp. 4–5; 1910–13, Tables 1 and 2, pp. 6–7.

176. In the years 1871–72, 47 (7.4 percent) of the total of 663 persons convicted of capital crimes were sentenced to death, and juries saved from the guillotine the other 586 (92.6 percent) through findings of extenuating circumstances. From 1873 through 1879, extenuating circumstances were found for 2,286 (91.9 percent) of the 2,448 persons convicted of capital crimes and 202 (8.1 percent) were sentenced to death. For the period 1880–93, the figures were 3,699 convicted, with extenuating circumstances for 3,282 (88.7 percent) and 417 (11.3 percent) sentenced to death. From 1894 through 1908, 2,306 persons were convicted of capital crimes, of whom 336 (14.6 percent) were sentenced to death and extenuating circumstances were found for 1,970 (85.4 percent). Among the 677 persons convicted of capital crimes from 1909 through 1913, 136 (20.1 percent) were sentenced to the guillotine and extenuating circumstances were found for 541 (79.9 percent). *Compte général*, 1871–73, Table 6, p. 17, and Table 7, p. 19; 1874–85, Table 7, p. 25, and Table 8, p. 27; 1886–1909, Table 7, p. 19, and Table 8, p. 21; 1910–13, Table 7, p. 21, and Table 8, p. 23.

177. *Compte général*, 1873–1909, Table 2, p. 5; 1910–13, Table 2, p. 7.

178. Nye, *Crime, Madness, and Politics*, 214, 279; Wright, *Between the Guillotine and Liberty*, 171–73.

179. Wright, *Between the Guillotine and Liberty*, 171.

180. From 1902 through 1905, the number of persons sentenced to death each year oscillated between nine and eighteen, and the proportion of these among all persons convicted of capital crimes varied from 8.7 percent to 14.2 percent. But in 1906, the figure jumped to 21.3 percent (or twenty-nine death sentences). It reached 26.3 percent (or forty-one death sentences) in 1907 and 32.0 percent (or forty-nine death sentences) in 1908, the very year the anti–capital punishment bill was defeated. Thereafter, from 1909 through 1913, death sentences leveled off at about one-fifth of all capital crime convictions. Nevertheless, this still remained above the figure from before 1906. *Compte général*, 1902–9, Table 7, p. 19, and Table 8, p. 21; 1910–13, Table 7, p. 21, and Table 8, p. 23.

181. Of the 313 persons sentenced to death from 1902 through 1913, 211 (67.4 percent) were convicted of premeditated homicide, 78 (24.9 percent) were convicted of unpremeditated murder accompanied by another felony or misdemeanor, 19 (6.1 percent) were found guilty of parricide, 3 (1.0 percent) were convicted of poisoning, 1 (0.3 percent) was found guilty of arson of an inhabited structure, and 1 (0.3 percent) was found guilty of violence and cruelty against children. *Compte général*, 1902–9, Table 12, p. 26; 1910–13, Table 12, p. 28.

182. Of the 211 persons condemned to death for premeditated murder from 1902 through 1913, 142 (67.3 percent) had killed in the commission of a robbery and 69 (32.7 percent) had some other motive. Of the 78 persons condemned to death for unpremeditated murder, 42 (53.8 percent) killed to steal and 36 (46.2 percent) murdered in the commission of some other felony or misdemeanor. *Compte général*, 1902–9, Table 12, p. 26; 1910–13, Table 12, p. 28.

183. Beattie, *Crime and the Courts*, 433–34.

Chapter 5

1. Weber, *France, Fin de Siècle*, 116.

2. "Loi tendant a réprimer les menées anarchistes," July 28–29, 1894, in Cahen and Mathiez, *Les lois françaises*, 225.

3. Of the total of 162 persons tried by the juries in 1894 for violating the law against *apologie de faits qualifié crimes*, 82 (50.6 percent) were acquitted. *Compte général*, 1894, Table 28, p. 51.

4. "Loi tendant a réprimer les menées anarchistes," July 28–29, 1894, in Cahen and Mathiez, *Les lois françaises*, 225–27; Bernard Schnapper, "Le Jury français," in Schioppa, *Trial Jury*, 215; Weber, *France, Fin de Siècle*, 115–16.

5. Schnapper, "Le Jury français," 215.

6. Weber, *France, Fin de Siècle*, 117.

7. Cahen and Mathiez, *Les lois françaises*, 225.

8. Schnapper, "Le Jury français," 212, 215.

9. *Compte général*, 1896, xiv.

10. From 1895 through 1913, 870 persons were tried in the *cours d'assises* for *délits politiques et de presse*, of whom 462 (53.1 percent) were convicted and 408 (46.9 percent) were acquitted. *Compte général*, 1895–1902, Table 28, p. 51; 1903–9, Table 27, p. 51; 1910–13, Table 27, p. 53.

11. According to André Davidovitch's calculations, the total number of persons tried by the *tribunaux correctionnels* averaged 194,836 per year from 1851 through 1855. In most of the five-year periods thereafter through 1913, the number was actually lower. In just a few periods (1891–95 and 1911–13), it was slightly higher than in 1851–55. Davidovitch, "Criminalité et répression," 35.

12. Cruppi, *La Cour d'assises*, 3–4; Garraud, *Traité théorique*, 1:33–34; Yvernes, "La Justice en France," 302.

13. Cruppi, *La Cour d'assises*, 3, 7.

14. Beer, "Ce qu'est le jury criminel," 496n; Tarde, *Penal Philosophy*, 443; Toulemon, *La Question du jury*, 83–84; Yvernes, "La Justice en France," 303.

15. *Compte général*, 1894, xi.

16. From 1909 through 1913, 7,670 *accusations* resulted in convictions in the *cours d'assises*. In 5,669 cases (73.9 percent), there was a full verdict. In 978 cases (12.8 percent), the charge was reduced to a lesser felony. In 1,023 cases (13.3 percent), the charge was reduced to a misdemeanor. *Compte général*, 1909, Table 5, p. 13; 1910–13, Table 5, p. 15.

17. From 1880 through 1913, a total of 44,773 persons convicted in the *cours d'assises* received *peines correctionnelles* of imprisonment for five years or less. Of these, 34,113 (76.2 percent) were convicted of felonies with extenuating circumstances. In 15,589 such cases, the felony would have been punished by prison terms of more than five years without extenuating circumstances and was automatically reduced to a *peine correctionnelle* when the jury found extenuating circumstances. In 10,660 other cases, the accused persons were convicted of misdemeanors. Altogether, 26,249 persons, or 58.6 percent of the total of 44,773, were sentenced to *peines correctionnelles* as a result of jury decisions. For 18,524 persons (or 41.4 percent of the total), *peines correctionnelles* were imposed by judicial discretion. These were persons granted extenuating circumstances for crimes punishable by hard labor for five years or more and whose sentences could be reduced to misdemeanor prison terms only if the judges used their discretion to lower the penalty by two degrees.

Compte général, 1880–85, Table 2, p. 5, and Table 8, p. 27; 1886–1909, Table 2, p. 5, and Table 8, p. 21; 1909–13, Table 2, p. 7, and Table 8, p. 23.

18. Yvernes, "La Justice en France," 302; *Compte général*, 1880, xiv; 1894, vi, ix, xi; 1900, vii–viii, xiv–xv.

19. From 1873 through 1879, 2,610 persons were tried in the *cours d'assises* for fraud, of whom 1,903 (72.9 percent) were convicted and 707 (27.1 percent) were acquitted. From 1880 through 1913, 7,673 were tried, of whom 4,402 (57.4 percent) were convicted and 3,271 (42.6 percent) were acquitted. As for fraudulent bankruptcy, from 1873 through 1879, 775 persons were tried, 458 (59.1 percent) were convicted, and 317 (40.9 percent) were acquitted. From 1880 through 1913, 1,875 persons were tried for the crime, of whom 856 (45.6 percent) were convicted and 1,019 (54.3 percent) were acquitted. From 1871 through 1879, 165 persons were tried for all crimes of official corruption except bribery, of whom 124 (75.2 percent) were convicted and 41 (24.8 percent) were acquitted. From 1880 through 1913, 509 persons were tried for these crimes, of whom 291 (57.2 percent) were convicted and 218 (42.8 percent) were acquitted. For counterfeiting and the extortion of titles and signatures, the declines in conviction rates were substantial but not as sharp. The conviction rate for extortion in 1871–79 was 52.3 percent (79 persons among the total of 151 tried), and from 1880 through 1913 it was 42.9 percent (165 among 385 tried). From 1873 through 1879, the conviction rate for counterfeiting was 71.7 percent (391 persons among the total of 545 persons tried), and from 1880 through 1913 it was 61.8 percent (2,667 among 4,317 tried). For bribery, the conviction rate in the years 1871 through 1879 was already very low (17.7 percent or 23 of 107 persons tried). From 1880 through 1913, it actually rose slightly to 20.0 percent (41 of 164 persons tried). *Compte général*, 1871–1909, Table 2, p. 5; 1910–13, Table 2, p. 7.

20. Among the 4,043 persons convicted of felony fraud from 1880 through 1913, juries found extenuating circumstances for 3,607 (89.1 percent). They were found for 621 (90.8 percent) of the 684 persons convicted of fraudulent bankruptcy. The juries found extenuating circumstances for 2,288 (90.3 percent) of the 2,534 persons they convicted of counterfeiting, 144 (91.7 percent) of the 157 they convicted of the extortion of titles and signatures, and 233 (95.1 percent) of the 245 persons found guilty of crimes of official corruption other than bribery. In respect to bribery, only 60 persons were convicted of this from 1880 through 1913 and 1919 through 1923 (the two periods are combined because of the small number of cases). Juries found extenuating circumstances for 38 (63.3 percent) of the convicts. *Compte général*, 1880–85, Table 7, pp. 22–25, and Table 8, pp. 26–27; 1886–95, Table 7, pp. 16–19, and Table 8, pp. 20–21; 1896–1909, Table 7, pp. 16–18, and Table 8, pp. 20–21; 1910–13, Table 7, pp. 18–20, and Table 8, pp. 22–23.

21. Of the 4,402 persons tried in the *cours d'assises* for fraud and convicted from 1880 through 1913, 3,403 (77.3 percent) were sentenced to prison terms of five years or less. The same penalties were handed out to 729 (85.2 percent) of the 856 persons tried for fraudulent bankruptcy and convicted. The figure was 250 (85.9 percent) among the 291 persons convicted of all crimes of official corruption except bribery, 145 (87.9 percent) among the 165 persons convicted for extortion, and 32 (78.0 percent) among the 41 persons tried for bribery and convicted. *Peines correctionnelles* were imposed on only 470 (17.6 percent) of persons tried for counterfeiting and convicted. *Compte général*, 1880–1909, Table 2, p. 5; 1910–13, Table 2, p. 7.

22. The annual average number of persons tried for fraud in the *cours d'assises* dropped

from a high of 577 from 1832 through 1847 to 118 from 1909 through 1913. Trials for fraudulent bankruptcy declined from a peak average of 134 per year from 1854 through 1870 to only 34 in 1909–13. For the extortion of titles and signatures, the decrease was from a high of 45 from 1849 through 1853 to 6 from 1894 through 1913. Trials for offering or accepting bribes declined from an annual average peak of 36 from 1825 through 1831 to 5 from 1894 through 1913. The number tried for all other cases of official corruption peaked at an annual average of 288 from 1880 through 1893 and declined to 221 in 1894–1913. Counterfeiting, the one major white-collar crime not susceptible to correctionalization, was an exception to the trend: the annual average number of persons tried for the crime in the *cours d'assises* rose sharply from 68 in 1873–79 to 110 in 1909–13. *Compte général*, 1825–60, Table 2, p. 3; 1861–1909, Table 2, p. 5; 1910–13, Table 2, p. 7; Yvernes, "La Justice en France," 302.

23. Leniency in sentencing also provided a justification for the correctionalization of fraudulent bankruptcy cases. *Compte général*, 1900, xv.

24. The number of persons tried for *escroquerie* in the *tribunaux correctionnels* rose more or less continuously from an annual average of 1,179 in 1826–41 to 4,180 in 1879–93, before declining somewhat to 3,329 in 1894–1913. Donovan, "Magistrates and Juries," 393.

25. Nye, *Crime, Madness, and Politics*, 95; Schnapper, *Voies nouvelles*, 346–47; Wright, *Between the Guillotine and Liberty*, 146–47.

26. Valle's statement came in response to G. Baron's protest against correctionalization in the Chambre des députés. Lalou, "Budget de la justice," 128.

27. Ibid.; Frase, "Comparative Criminal Justice," 630–31.

28. Bertillon, *La dépopulation de la France*, 9–61, 139–40, 180–92, 236–43, 247–50, 265–309; Spengler, *France Faces Depopulation*, 23, 62, 111–23, 126–28; Thomson, *Democracy in France*, 173n; Nye, *Crime, Madness, and Politics*, 167–68; McLaren, "Sex and Socialism," 477–87, 490–91, and "Abortion in France," 481–83.

29. The French birthrate dropped from 22.2 per 1,000 population from 1890 through 1900 (during the very decade repopulationism became a major organized movement) to 18.8 per 1,000 from 1911 through 1913, despite pro-natalist agitation. Estimates of the annual number of abortions in France by the late nineteenth and early twentieth centuries ranged from 150,000 to 500,000. Spengler, *France Faces Depopulation*, 53; McLaren, "Abortion in France," 479.

30. Allemane, *L'avortement criminel*, 113; Lux, "Un crime que l'on ne punit plus," 671.

31. Allemane, *L'avortement criminel*, 167; Berthélemy, "Les mesures," 104.

32. Berthélemy, "Les mesures," 105–14, 120–24, 127; Bertillon, *La depopulation de la France*, 242.

33. In early 1917, a Senator Cazeneuve introduced a bill before the French Senate that would correctionalize abortion because, in the words of a reporter for the *Revue pénitentiaire et de droit pénal*, in the *cours d'assises* "scandalous acquittals have too often roused public opinion." "La répression de l'avortement," 84.

34. According to Allemane, for example, making abortion a *délit* to be tried by the *tribunaux correctionnels* "would have, assuredly, excellent advantages; it would procure a more regular and less risky repression." Allemane, *L'avortement criminel*, 271.

35. Ibid., 275; "La répression de l'avortement," 83–84; Berthélemy, "Les mesures," 125–26.

36. According to Bertillon's estimate of 1911, France's leading politicians were either bachelors or married men who averaged only one to one-and-a-half children each. Bertillon, *La dépopulation de la France*, 138–40.

37. From 1901 through 1905, 250 persons were tried for abortion, an average of 50 per year. The total number rose to 365 in the years 1906–10, an average of 73 per year. From 1911 through 1913, the total number rose to 461, an average of 154 per year. *Compte général*, 1901–9, Table 1, p. 4; 1910–13, Table 1, p. 6.

38. Esmein, *History of Continental Criminal Procedure*, 562. See also the many complaints concerning the French juries by legal scholars, judges, lawyers, prosecutors, and other observers in the collection of opinions in Prud'hon, *Le Jury criminel*, 45–71, 113–29, 157–60. The *enquête* that produced this book followed an "acquittement tout a fait inattendu" by a Parisian jury (9, 161). For specifically magisterial criticisms of the juries in this period, see Cruppi, *La Cour d'assises*, 34; Guyho, *Les Jurés "maîtres de la peine,"* 12, 14–15, 18, 24; Loubat, "La Crise de la répression [I]," 462–63; Loubet, *La Justice criminelle*, 65–72; Proal, *Le Crime et la peine*, 453–55; and Tarde (included here because he was a former *juge d'instruction*), *Penal Philosophy*, 431–32, 439–45, 452–53, 460–61.

39. Louis Proal, a judge at the appeals court of Aix and previously a *juge d'instruction* and *procureur*, suggested in 1894 that crimes against morals, abortions, and most aggravated thefts (*vols qualifiés*) be removed from the jurisdiction of the *cours d'assises* and transferred to the *tribunaux correctionnels* (*Le Crime et la peine*, 457). William Loubat, a Lyons *procureur général*, questioned whether it was necessary for juries to judge thefts by domestics, innkeepers, and carters or crimes against morals, abortions, and counterfeiting. He also suggested that correctionalization be regulated rather than left to the whims of the *parquets*; "La Crise de la répression II," 23–24.

40. Loubet, *La Justice criminelle*, 69–72, 198; Tarde, *Penal Philosophy*, 440; Proal, *Passion and Criminality*, 292–94, 402, 578, 583–84, 615.

41. In 1914, an anonymous *magistrat de la cour d'appel* commented, "The intellectual level of the jury has been considerably lowered in recent years. . . . Many times, the foreman of the jury is replaced by a colleague because he is 'literally' incapable of reading the verdict. [Can a worker] understand, from his knowledge of the language, the difference between premeditation and provocation?" Prud'hon, *Le Jury criminel*, 68. In 1911, William Loubat also claimed to "have seen a jury foreman incapable of pronouncing the verdict because he could not read. . . . I have noticed on a jury session list the presence of an anarchist, an individual whose wife keeps a *maison de rendez-vous*, and two others who have been convicted, one for public indecency, the other for vagabondage." Loubat, "La Crise de la répression II," 24. See also Pinon, "La réforme de la procedure criminelle," 83; and commentary by President Tournade (who had presided over the *cour d'assises* of the Seine) in Prud'hon, *Le Jury criminel*, 73.

42. Soulas, *Le Recrutement du jury*, 80–81.

43. P. J. R. King, "Illiterate Plebeians, Easily Misled: Jury Composition, Experience, and Behavior in Essex, 1735–1815," in Cockburn and Green, *Twelve Good Men and True*, 257–58, 266–67, 273–74.

44. Ibid., 301; Beattie, *Crime and the Courts*, 378–79, 387–88; Douglas Hay, "The Class Composition of the Palladium of Liberty: Trial Jurors in the Eighteenth Century," in Cockburn and Green, *Twelve Good Men and True*, 330, 350.

45. King, "Illiterate Plebeians, Easily Misled," 255, 302–4.

46. Royer et al., *Juges et notables*, 13–16.

47. F. Lombard, *Les Jurés*, 262; Cruppi, *La Cour d'assises*, 21; Loubat, "Programme minimum de réformes pénales [2]," 453; Loubet, *La Justice criminelle*, 195–97.

48. F. Lombard, *Les Jurés*, 252, 261, 271, 303–4.

49. Royer, *Histoire de la justice*, 610–11; Royer et al., *Juges et notables*, 33–35, 45–48, 92–93, 265–67, 284; Martin, *Crime and Criminal Justice*, 197–98; Ensor, *Courts and Judges*, 40–43.

50. Royer et al., *Juges et notables*, 249, 281.

51. Ibid., 86–88, 307, 311, 314, 317–18; Martin, *Crime and Criminal Justice*, 195.

52. F. Lombard, *Les Jurés*, 261; Royer, *Histoire de la justice*, 617–20.

53. F. Lombard, *Les Jurés*, 210, 239–40, 261, 282–83.

54. Schnapper, "Le Jury français," 216; Gineste, *Essai sur l'histoire et l'organisation du jury criminel*, 70; Tarde, *Penal Philosophy*, 444; F. Lombard, *Les Jurés*, 274; Gide, *Recollections of the Assize Court*, 119.

55. Ferri's and Garafalo's arguments against the jury system are summarized in Dragu, *Juges-citoyens ou juges de métier?*, 11–13.

56. In 1890, a French edition of Garafalo's *Criminologie* was published, and the first French edition of Ferri's *Sociologie criminelle* appeared in 1893. Schnapper, "Le Jury français," 220.

57. Nye, *Crime, Madness, and Politics*, 106–7; Tarde, *Penal Philosophy*, 440–45, 453; Pinon, "La réforme de la procedure criminelle," 83.

58. Saleilles, *Individualization of Punishment*, xviii; Wright, *Between the Guillotine and Liberty*, 127.

59. Saleilles, *Individualization of Punishment*, 10–11, 97.

60. Ibid., 97–98, 233.

61. Ibid., 204, 207, 209–10; Whitman, *Harsh Justice*, 51–52.

62. Nye, *Crime, Madness, and Politics*, 83, 95; Wright, *Between the Guillotine and Liberty*, 143–46.

63. Wiener, *Reconstructing the Criminal*, 282–84, 342, 345, 347–48, 351, 354.

64. Nye, *Crime, Madness, and Politics*, 28, 95.

65. Schnapper, *Voies nouvelles*, 446–47; Wright, *Between the Guillotine and Liberty*, 146–47.

66. Rothman, *Conscience and Convenience*, 53–81.

67. Willrich, *City of Courts*, xxi–xxv, xxxiii, 56–60, 67–72, 74–79, 84–87, 89, 94–95, 97–100, 108–10, 112–14, 122–25, 242–46, 276.

68. Green, "Freedom and Criminal Responsibility," 1947–48, 1951, 1955, 1974–75.

69. Roscoe Pound, "Introduction to the English Version," in Saleilles, *Individualization of Punishment*, xvii.

70. In 1949, Jerome Frank wrote that "jury-made law is par excellence, capricious and arbitrary, yielding to the maximum in way of lack of uniformity, and of unknowability." Jerome Frank, *Courts on Trial* (Princeton: Princeton University Press, 1949), 132, quoted in Moore, *Jury*, 232. See also the quotes of other American jurists critical of juries on page 232 of Moore's book.

71. Garner, "Criminal Procedure in France," 276.

72. Rothman, *Conscience and Convenience*, 77–81, 427–30; Whitman, *Harsh Justice*, 193–94.

73. Green, "Freedom and Criminal Responsibility," 2002–7, 2013–22, 2039–40, 2048, 2052.

74. Frase, "Comparative Criminal Justice," 676; Moore, *Jury*, 144–45, 231, 255; Levy, *Palladium of Justice*, 69–105.

75. Cruppi, *La Cour d'assises*, 310.

76. Toulemon, *La Question du jury*, 279; Mimin, *Le Concours du jury*, 6–8; Cruppi, *La Cour d'assises*, 290–91, 308–10, 321–22, 326; F. Lombard, *Les Jurés*, 236; Guyho, *Les Jurés "maîtres de la peine,"* 29–30.

77. F. Lombard, *Les Jurés*, 260–63.

78. Cruppi, *La Cour d'assises*, 290–91, 321–22, 326–27.

79. Guyho, *Les Jurés "maîtres de la peine,"* 29–30.

80. Brissaud and Bechade-Labarthe, *Les Attributions nouvelles du jury criminel*, 12–20; Mimin, *La Concours du jury*, 23; Dupin de Beyssat, *Le Jury criminel*, 12; Garner, "Criminal Procedure in France," 277; Summers, "Criminal Jury in France," 206.

81. Summers, "Criminal Jury in France," 206.

82. Toulemon, *La Question du jury*, 283.

83. Commentary by Henri Robert in Prud'hon, *Le jury criminel*, 21.

84. Schnapper, "Le Jury français," 223–25.

85. Ibid., 223–24; Esmein, *History of Continental Criminal Procedure*, 564; Saleilles, *Individualization of Punishment*, 75–76.

86. Garner, "Criminal Procedure in France," 273–74, 277; F. Lombard, *Les Jurés*, 257–58.

Chapter 6

1. Zeldin, *France 1848–1945*, 2:1040–82.

2. One of the few examples is a fourteen-page chapter entitled "Ebb Tide 1918–1940" in Wright, *Between the Guillotine and Liberty*, 175–89.

3. Ibid., 175–79.

4. The annual average number of criminal cases reported to the public prosecutors' offices declined from 506,984 in the years 1919–20 to 493,978 in 1921–25. The number increased to 553,548 in 1926–30 and to 588,094 in 1931–35 before dropping slightly to 582,566 in 1936–40 (the figure for the last period, calculated by Davidovitch, excludes 1939, the data for which were not available). However, the proportion of cases that were brought to trial before the *cours d'assises* and *tribunaux correctionnels* declined from 212,948 (38.5 percent) in 1926–30, to 221,080 (37.6 percent) in 1931–35, to 197,300 (33.9 percent) in 1936–40. Davidovitch, "Criminalité et répression," 35, 40.

5. Wright, *Between the Guillotine and Liberty*, 178–79.

6. Brissaud and Bechade-Labarthe, *Les Attributions nouvelles du jury criminel*, 12–20; Mimin, *Le Concours du jury*, 23; Dupin de Beyssat, *Le Jury criminel*, 12.

7. Juries found extenuating circumstances for 5,631 (76.0 percent) of the 7,406 persons found guilty of *crimes* from 1919 through 1923. After 1923, the *Compte général*'s tables no longer allow one to clearly calculate grants of extenuating circumstances for persons who had actually been found guilty of felonies. *Compte général*, 1919–20, Table 7, p. 21, and Table 8, p. 23; 1921–23, Table 5, p. 17, and Table 6, p. 19.

8. From 1919 through 1931, a total of 419 persons were sentenced to death. From 1919 through 1923, a total of 745 persons were convicted of capital crimes, of whom 218

(29.3 percent) were sentenced to death and extenuating circumstances were found for the other 527 (70.7 percent). *Compte général*, 1919–20, Table 2, p. 7, Table 7, p. 21, and Table 8, p. 23; 1921–23, Table 2, p. 7, Table 5, p. 17, and Table 6, p. 19; 1924–31, Table 1, p. 7.

9. Spengler, *France Faces Depopulation*, 23.

10. From 1919 to 1923, a total of 1,494 persons were tried for abortion in the *cours d'assises*. *Compte général*, 1919–23, Table 1, p. 6.

11. Of the 1,494 persons tried for abortion in the *cours d'assises* from 1919 to 1923, 562 (37.6 percent) were convicted and 932 (62.4 percent) were acquitted. The acquittal rate had been 66.3 percent in the years 1909–13. *Compte général*, 1919–23, Table 1, p. 6.

12. Spengler, *France Faces Depopulation*, 127; Nye, *Crime, Madness, and Politics*, 168–69.

13. Thomson, *Democracy in France*, 185–86.

14. Spengler, *France Faces Depopulation*, 240n.

15. The 1,494 persons tried for abortion from 1919 through 1923 accounted for 10.7 percent of the total of 13,999 tried for all crimes in the *cours d'assises*. *Compte général*, 1919–23, Tables 1 and 2, pp. 6–7.

16. Donovan, "Abortion, the Law, and the Juries," 163–64, 173–74, 180–81.

17. From 1919 through 1931, 935 persons were tried for fraud in the *cours d'assises*, of whom 476 (50.9 percent) were convicted and 459 (49.1 percent) were acquitted. For fraudulent bankruptcy, the figures were 190 tried, 76 (40.0 percent) convicted, and 114 (60.0 percent) acquitted. As for persons accused of all crimes of official corruption except bribery, 160 were tried, of whom 92 (57.5 percent) were convicted and 68 (42.5 percent) were acquitted. During the same period, 130 persons were tried for offering or accepting bribes, of whom 37 (28.5 percent) were convicted and 93 (71.5 percent) were acquitted. The number of persons tried for extortion was only twelve, of whom six were convicted and six were acquitted. The number of persons tried for counterfeiting was 171, of whom 113 (66.1 percent) were convicted and 58 (33.9 percent) were acquitted. *Compte général*, 1919–23, Table 2, p. 7; 1924–31, Table 1, p. 7.

18. Among the 237 persons convicted of felony fraud from 1919 through 1923, extenuating circumstances were found for 216 (91.1 percent). Extenuating circumstances were found for 15 (83.3 percent) of the 18 persons convicted of fraudulent bankruptcy, 48 (82.8 percent) of the 58 convicted of counterfeiting, 21 (87.5 percent) of the 24 convicted of felonies of official corruption other than bribery, and for all three of the persons found guilty of the extortion of titles and signatures. *Compte général*, 1919–20, Table 7, pp. 18–20, and Table 8, pp. 22–23; 1921–23, Table 5, pp. 14–16, and Table 6, pp. 18–19.

19. Of the 475 persons tried for fraud in the *cours d'assises* and convicted from 1919 through 1931, 358 (75.4 percent) were sentenced to prison terms of five years or less. Such penalties were handed out to 62 (81.6 percent) of the 76 persons convicted of fraudulent bankruptcy, 78 (84.8 percent) of the 92 convicted of all crimes of official corruption except bribery, 31 (83.8 percent) of the 37 convicted of bribery, and all six of those found guilty of the extortion of titles and signatures. Among the 113 persons tried for counterfeiting and convicted, only 20 (17.7 percent) were sentenced to *peines correctionnelles*. *Compte général*, 1919–23, Table 2, p. 7; 1924–31, Table 1, p. 7.

20. From 1919 through 1931, the annual average number of persons tried for fraudulent bankruptcy was only sixteen. It was thirteen for counterfeiting, twelve for the extortion of titles and signatures, twelve also for cases of official corruption except bribery,

and ten for offering and accepting bribes. *Compte général*, 1919–23, Table 2, p. 7; 1924–31, Table 1, p. 7.

21. Royer, *Histoire de la justice*, 669, 672–74, 677, 679, 683n, 687, 689–92, 695.

22. *Compte général*, 1921, Table 2, p. 7, and Table 24, p. 61; 1931, Table 1, p. 7, and Table 19, p. 53.

23. Brissaud and Bechade-Labarthe, *Les Attributions nouvelles du jury criminel*, 4; Summers, "Criminal Jury in France," 205; Toulemon, *La Question du jury*, 9–10.

24. Toulemon, *La Question du jury*, 9.

25. Rothman, *Conscience and Convenience*, 98–100.

26. Kalven and Zeisel, *American Jury*, 17–18.

27. Fisher, *Plea Bargaining's Triumph*, 1–17, 40–42, 47–51, 55–58, 88–91, 104–9, 112–14, 121–25, 128–29, 136–37, 152–53, 155–56, 161–62, 167, 174–80, 196–202, 208, 220–24, 229–30.

28. Toulemon, *La Question du jury*, 3–7; Mimin, *Le Concours du jury*, 5–6.

29. Toulemon, *La Question du jury*, 4–5, 89–90, 182–83.

30. Bernard Schnapper, "Le Jury français," in Schioppa, *Trial Jury*, 232; Dragu, *Juges-citoyens ou juges de métier?*, 9.

31. Summers, "Criminal Jury in France," 202–3; Schnapper, "Le Jury français," 232; Dupin de Beyssat, *Le Jury criminel*, 18; Toulemon, *La Question du jury*, 10, 12, 82–84, 86, 183, 203, 264–66.

32. Dragu, *Juges-citoyens ou juges de métier?*, 9.

33. Brissaud and Bechade-Labarthe, *Les Attributions nouvelles du jury criminel*, 12–13.

34. Wright, *Between the Guillotine and Liberty*, 146–47.

35. Of the 18,657 persons convicted in the *cours d'assises* from 1919 through 1931, 1,390 (7.5 percent) had their sentences suspended. *Compte général*, 1919–20, Table 7, p. 21; 1921–23, Table 5, p. 7; 1924–31, Table 1, p. 7.

36. Lebert qtd. in Brissaud and Bechade-Labarthe, *Les attributions nouvelles du jury criminel*, 14–15.

37. Dupin de Beyssat, *Le Jury criminel*, 12; Summers, "Criminal Jury in France," 206; Brissaud and Bechade-Labarthe, *Les Attributions nouvelles du jury criminel*, 22–24; Garraud, *Précis de droit criminel*, 958, 974–75, 978, 1014–15.

38. In 1924, 2,100 persons were tried in the *cours d'assises*, of whom 1,313 (62.5 percent) were convicted and 787 (37.5 percent) were acquitted. The acquittal rate declined continuously from this year through 1930, when it reached 29.8 percent (or 468 persons among the total of 1,571 persons tried). In 1931, 1,512 persons were tried, of whom 1,004 (66.4 percent) were convicted and 508 (33.6 percent) were acquitted. *Compte général*, 1924–31, Table 1, p. 7.

39. Davidovitch, "Criminalité et répression," 35.

40. The figure of 17.7 percent represents 1,411 of the 7,989 persons convicted in the *cours d'assises* from 1932 through 1938. Ministère de l'Economie et des Finances, *Annuaire statistique*, 163.

41. From 1932 through 1938, 138 persons were sentenced to death. Ministère de l'Economie et des Finances, *Annuaire statistique*, 163.

42. From 1980 through 1994, nearly nine of every ten persons convicted and sentenced in U.S. district courts had pleaded guilty or nolo contendere and were therefore tried by neither court nor jury. Maguire and Pastore, *Bureau of Justice Statistics*, Table 5.27, p. 460.

43. Toulemon, *La Question du jury*, 82n, 266; Summers, "Criminal Jury in France," 202–3; Donnedieu de Vabres, *La Justice pénale*, 122–23.

44. Hamson, "Prosecution of the Accused," 274–75; Nye, *Crime, Madness, and Politics*, 111–12.

45. A. Henry, "La Loi du 5 mars 1932," *Revue Dalloz*, pt. 4 (1932): 129, cited in F. Lombard, *Les Jurés*, 274–75; Toulemon, *La Question du jury*, 262; Donnedieu de Vabres, *La Justice pénale*, 133–34.

46. F. Lombard, *Les Jurés*, 275–76; Schnapper, "Le Jury français," 233; Summers, "Criminal Jury in France," 208.

47. F. Lombard, *Les Jurés*, 275.

48. Schnapper, "Le Jury français," 233.

49. From 1831 through 1851, a total of 7,540 persons were tried for *délits politiques et de presse* in the *cours d'assises*. From 1871 through 1913, the number was 2,596, and from 1919 through 1928, it was only 38. The *Compte général*'s table on trials for political and press misdemeanors ceased after 1928, evidently because such trials had by this time become so rare. *Compte général*, 1831, Tables 63–64, pp. 98–99; 1832, Tables 66–67, pp. 102–3; 1833, Tables 71–72, pp. 110–11; 1834, Tables 68–69, pp. 106–7; 1835, Tables 72–73, pp. 112–13; 1836, Tables 74–75, pp. 112–13; 1837–51, Table 73, p. 51; 1871, Table 59, p. 96; 1872–73, Table 58, p. 102; 1874, Table 37, p. 82; 1875, Table 34, p. 74; 1876–78, Tables 33 and 34, p. 73; 1879–85, Table 34, p. 77; 1886–88, Table 39, p. 55; 1889–1902, Table 28, p. 51; 1903–9, Table 27, p. 51; 1910–13 and 1919–20, Table 27, p. 53; 1921–23, Table 23, p. 47; 1924–28, Table 18, p. 39.

50. F. Lombard, *Les Jurés*, 272.

51. Ibid., 272; Donnedieu de Vabres, *La Justice pénale*, 122.

52. Donnedieu de Vabres, *La Justice pénale*, 133–34.

53. F. Lombard, *Les Jurés*, 276; Dupin de Beyssat, *Le Jury criminel*, 13.

54. Werth, *France 1940–1955*, 193; Thomson, *Democracy in France*, 280n.

55. Dupin de Beyssat, *Le Jury criminel*, 13.

56. Alain Bancaud, "La cour d'assises pendant le régime de Vichy: une juridiction politiquement encombrante?," in Association française pour l'histoire de la justice, *La cour d'assises*, 53–58. Barthélemy's "venom" statement comes from a press communiqué of December 4, 1941, quoted on page 54 of Bancaud's article.

57. F. Lombard, *Les Jurés*, 276–77, 285–86; Dupin de Beyssat, *Le Jury criminel*, 12–13; Louis Hugueney, "La Loi du 25 novembre 1941 sur le jury," in Hugueney and Donnedieu de Vabres, eds., *Études de science criminelle et de droit comparé*, 22; Rousselet, *Histoire de la justice*, 115.

58. Bancaud, "La cour d'assises pendant le régime de Vichy," 55–55.

59. Dupin de Beyssat, *Le Jury criminel*, 13–14.

60. F. Lombard, *Les Jurés*, 286.

61. Schnapper, "Le Jury français," 238–39.

62. Ibid.; F. Lombard, *Les Jurés*, 277; Dupin de Beyssat, *Le Jury criminel*, 19; Garçon, "Faut-il modifier," 455, 469, 471–72.

63. After 1952, the judicial statistics do not make possible an accurate estimate of the proportion of all criminal cases dropped before trial.

64. According to figures compiled by Davidovitch, from 1931 through 1935 the *parquets* filed away, without prosecuting, an annual average of 347,935 (or 59.11 percent)

of 588,094 reported criminal cases of all kinds. This figure increased to 367,935 (63.16 percent) of 582,566 in 1936–40 and to 628,317 (66.77 percent) of 941,038 in 1941–45. It declined slightly to 568,513 (65.56 percent) of 867,160 in 1946–50. In 1952, it was 501,727 (69.85 percent) of 718,442 cases. The proportion of cases dropped by the *juges d'instruction* and *chambres des mises en accusation* fluctuated rather narrowly and unevenly, however, from an annual average of 19,367 (or 3.29 percent of all reported cases) in 1931–35, to 17,331 (2.97 percent) in 1936–40, 28,141 (2.99 percent) in 1941–45, 27,679 (3.19 percent) in 1946–50, and 20,883 (2.90 percent) in 1952. Davidovitch, "Criminalité et répression," 35.

65. Hugueney, "La Loi du 25 novembre 1941 sur le jury," 34–35.

66. Kock, *French Code of Criminal Procedure*, 109.

67. Animat, Deschamps, and Drevon, *Les Jurés*, 7; Hugueney, "La Loi du 25 novembre 1941 sur le jury," 23; Garner, "Criminal Procedure in France," 274.

68. Garçon, "Faut-il modifier," 470–71.

69. Robert Vouin, "La Cour d'assises française de 1808 à 1958," in Institut de droit comparé de l'Universite de Paris, *Problemes contemporains de procedure pénal*, 229, 232.

70. Wright, *Between the Guillotine and Liberty*, 192.

71. Werth, *France 1940–1955*, 259, 286–89.

72. From 1952 through 1964, a total of 158 persons were condemned to death in the *cours d'assises*. Ministère de l'Economie et des Finances, *Annuaire statistique*, 163.

73. From 1965 through 1980, 186 persons were sentenced to death in France, which was again an annual average of about twelve. There were no death sentences in 1981, the year capital punishment was finally abolished in France. Ministère de l'Economie, des Finances et du Budget, *Annuaire Rétrospectif*, 634.

74. Wright, *Between the Guillotine and Liberty*, 194–98.

75. F. Lombard, *Les Jurés*, 278.

76. Garçon, "Faut-il modifier," 469.

77. F. Lombard, *Les Jurés*, 267; Schnapper, "Le Jury français," 239.

78. Vouin, "La question du jury," 506.

79. Pugh, "Administration of Criminal Justice in France," 11.

80. Garçon, "Faut-il modifier," 471.

81. Vouin, "La question du jury," 503–4.

82. Dupin de Beyssat, *Le Jury criminel*, 13.

83. F. Lombard, *Les Jurés*, 278.

84. Hugueney, "La Loi du 25 novembre 1941 sur le jury," 35–36.

85. Vouin, "La Cour d'assises française de 1808 à 1958," 232.

86. Vouin, "La question du jury," 506.

87. Garçon, "Faut-il modifier," 457–58.

88. Ibid., 458–59.

89. Vouin, "La question du jury," 505.

90. Ibid., 506.

91. Dupin de Beyssat, *Le Jury criminel*, 20, 22.

92. Ibid., 20.

93. F. Lombard, *Les Jurés*, 280–83.

94. Frase, "Comparative Criminal Justice," 662; Pugh, "Administration of Criminal Justice," 11–12.

95. Frase, "Comparative Criminal Justice," 571–72n.

96. Ibid., 571, 622–25; Charles, *La Justice en France*, 85.

97. Frase, "Comparative Criminal Justice," 623.

98. Van Caenegem, *Judges, Legislators and Professors*, 37–38 (source of quote); Esmein, *History of Continental Criminal Procedure*, 571.

99. Van Caenegem, *Judges, Legislators and Professors*, 35–38; Dupin de Beyssat, *Le Jury criminel*, 15–16.

100. Van Caenegem, *Judges, Legislators and Professors*, 36.

101. Dupin de Beyssat, *Le Jury criminel*, 18.

102. Ibid., 22.

103. Schnapper, "Le Jury français," 239.

Conclusion

1. Proal, *Le Crime et la peine*, 456.

2. Hamson, "Prosecution of the Accused," 275.

3. Gineste, *Essai sur l'histoire et l'organisation du jury criminel*, 176n.

4. Pugh, "Administration of Criminal Justice in France," 25.

5. Hamson, "Prosecution of the Accused," 274; Berenson, *Trial of Madame Caillaux*, 5.

6. Savitt, "Villainous Verdicts?," 1050n.

7. Nye, *Crime, Madness, and Politics*, 84.

8. Commentary of Jean Appleton in Prud'hon, *Le Jury criminel*, 122.

9. Kalven and Zeisel, *American Jury*, 179–80.

10. Ibid., 145; Frase, "Comparative Criminal Justice," 681n.

11. Frase, "Comparative Criminal Justice," 677.

12. Ibid., 682. According to Kalven and Zeisel, in 59 percent of cases in which the defendant had a record in American criminal trials by jury of the mid-twentieth century, jurors knew about it, and in 41 percent of such cases they did not. Kalven and Zeisel, *American Jury*, 147.

13. Beattie, *Crime and the Courts*, 415, 429, 436, 443, 448; Langbein, *Origins of Adversary Criminal Trial*, 59.

14. Maguire and Pastore, *Bureau of Justice Statistics*, Table 5.27, p. 460.

BIBLIOGRAPHY

Official Publications

Code d'instruction criminelle, édition conformé a l'édition originale du Bulletin des lois,
suivi des Motifs exposé par des Conseillers d'État et des Rapports fait par la Commission
de la Legislation du Corps Législatif, sur chacune des lois qui composent le Code. Paris:
Imprimerie de Mame, Frères, 1810.

Code pénal. Paris: Imprimerie Royale, 1833.

Journal officiel de la République Français.

Ministère de la Justice. *Compte général de l'administration de la justice criminelle*, 1825–.
Paris: Imprimerie Nationale, 1827–.

Ministère de l'Economie, des Finances et du Budget. *Annuaire Rétrospectif de la France*
1948–1988. Paris: Institut National de la Statistique et des Études Économiques,
1990.

Ministère de l'Economie et des Finances. *Annuaire statistique de la France: Résumé*
rétrospectif. Paris: Institut National de la Statistique et des Études Économiques,
1966.

Recueil officiel des instructions et circulaires du Ministère de la justice. 3 vols. Paris:
Imprimerie Nationale, 1879–83.

Tribunaux d'appel. *Observations des tribunaux d'appel sur le projet de code criminel.* 2 vols.
Paris: Imprimerie Impériale, an XIII.

Books, Articles, and Dissertations

Allemane, Felix. *L'avortement criminel: Étude sociale, juridique et médico-légale.*
Carcassonne, n.p., 1911.

Allen, Robert. "Political Trials by Jury in the Côte d'Or, 1792–1800." *Proceedings of the*
Annual Meeting of the Western Society for French History 18 (1991): 222–30.

———. *Les tribunaux criminels sous la Révolution et l'Empire, 1792–1811.* Rennes: Presses
Universitaires de Rennes, 2005.

Andrews, Richard Mowery. *Law, Magistracy, and Crime in Old Regime Paris.* Vol. 1, *The*
System of Criminal Justice. Cambridge: Cambridge University Press, 1994.

Animat, M., M. F. Deschamps, and F. Drevon. *Les Jurés.* Paris: Presses Universitaires
de France, 1980.

Arcis, Paul. "La criminalité feminine." *Revue pénitentiaire et de droit pénal* 37 (1913):
945–51.

Association française pour l'histoire de la justice, ed. *La cour d'assises: Bilan d'un héritage*
démocratique. Paris: La Documentation française, 2001.

Barrows, Susanna. *Distorting Mirrors: Visions of the Crowd in Late Nineteenth-Century*
France. New Haven: Yale University Press, 1981.

Beattie, J. M. *Crime and the Courts in England 1600–1800.* Princeton: Princeton
University Press, 1986.

Beer, Henri. "Ce qu'est le jury criminel ce qu'il devrait être: notes et réflexions d'un juré." *Revue politique et parlementaire* 53 (1907): 483–509.

Belknap, Michael R., ed. *American Political Trials*. Westport, Conn.: Greenwood Press, 1994.

Berenson, Edward. "The Politics of Divorce in France of the Belle Epoque: The Case of Joseph and Henriette Caillaux." *American Historical Review* 93 (1988): 31–55.

——. *The Trial of Madame Caillaux*. Berkeley: University of California Press, 1992.

Berthélemy, H. "Les mesures propres à prevenir et à réprimer l'avortement criminel." *Revue pénitentiaire et de droit pénal* 41 (1917): 99–128.

Bertillon, Jacques. *La dépopulation de la France, ses consequences, ses causes, mesures a prendre pour la combattre*. Paris: Felix Alcan, 1911.

Bidelman, Patrick K. *Pariahs Stand Up! The Founding of the Liberal Feminist Movement in France, 1858–1889*. Westport, Conn.: Greenwood Press, 1982.

Bouget, Dominique. "Une juridiction d'exception: la tribunal spécial d'Indre-et-Loire (an IX-1811)." *Histoire de la Justice* 7 (1994): 89–116.

Bourdon, Jean, ed. *Napoleon au Conseil d'État: Notes et procès-verbaux inèdits de Jean-Guilaume Locre, Secrétaire Général du Conseil d'État*. Paris: Editions Berger-Levrault, 1963.

Brissaud, Jacques, and Jean Bechade-Labarthe. *Les Attributions nouvelles du jury criminel: Commentaire thèorique et pratique de la loi du 5 mars 1932*. Paris: A. Pedone, 1932.

Brouardel, Paul. *L'avortement*. Paris: J.-B. Baillière, 1901.

——. *L'infanticide*. Paris: J.-B. Baillière et Fils, 1897.

Brown, Howard G. "Bonaparte's 'Booted Justice' in Bas-Languedoc." *Proceedings of the Western Society for French History: Selected Papers of the Annual Meeting* 25 (1998): 120–30.

——. *Ending the French Revolution: Violence, Justice, and Repression from the Terror to Napoleon*. Charlottesville: University of Virginia Press, 2006.

Cahen, L., and A. Mathiez, eds. *Les lois françaises de 1815 à nos jours accompagnèes des documents les plus importants*. Paris: Felix Alcan, 1919.

Charles, Raymond. *La Justice en France*. Paris: Presses Universitaires de France, 1953.

Chatagnier, M. *De l'infanticide dans ses rapports avec la loi, la morale, la médecine légale et les mesures administratives*. Paris: Imprimerie Générale de Jurisprudence, 1855.

Clark, Frances I. *The Position of Women in Contemporary France*. London: P. S. King, 1937.

Claverie, Elisabeth. "De la difficulté de faire un citoyen. Les 'Acquittements scandaleux' du jury dans la France provinciale du début du XIXe siècle." *Études rurales* 96 (1984): 143–66.

Cobban, Alfred. *A History of Modern France*. Vol. 2, *1799–1871*. Hammondsworth, U.K.: Penguin Books, 1965.

Cockburn, J. S., and Thomas A. Green, eds. *Twelve Good Men and True: The Criminal Trial Jury in England, 1200–1880*. Princeton: Princeton University Press, 1988.

Collingham, H. A. C. *The July Monarchy: A Political History of France, 1830–1848*. London: Longman, 1988.

Collins, Irene. *The Government and the Newspaper Press in France, 1814–1881*. London: Oxford University Press, 1959.

Corbes, H. "La Cour d'assises des Côtes-du-Nord de 1811 à 1832." *Annales de Bretagne* 56 (1959): 305–27.

Corbin, Alain. *Women for Hire: Prostitution and Sexuality in France after 1850*. Translated by Alan Sheridan. Cambridge, Mass.: Harvard University Press, 1990.

Coudert, Frederic R. "French Criminal Procedure." *Yale Law Journal* 19 (1910): 326–40.

Cruppi, Jean. *La Cour d'assises*. Paris: Calmann Levy, 1898.

Dalloz, Edouard, et al. *Code pénal annoté et explique d'apres la jurisprudence et la doctrine*. Paris: Au Bureau de la Jurisprudence Générale, 1881.

Davidovitch, André. "Criminalité et répression France depuis un siècle (1851–1952)." *Revue française de sociologie* 2 (1961): 30–49.

Dawson, John P. *A History of Lay Judges*. Cambridge, Mass.: Harvard University Press, 1960.

deMause, Lloyd, ed. *The History of Childhood*. New York: Psychohistory Press, 1974.

Donnedieu de Vabres, H[enri]. *La Justice pénale d'aujourd'hui*. Paris: Armand Colin, 1929.

Donovan, James M. "Abortion, the Law, and the Juries in France, 1825–1913." *Criminal Justice History: An International Annual* 9 (1988): 157–88.

———. "The Changing Composition of Juries in France, 1791–1913." *Proceedings of the Western Society for French History: Selected Papers of the Annual Meeting* 23 (1996): 256–72.

———. "Combatting the Sexual Abuse of Children in France, 1825–1913." *Criminal Justice History: An International Annual* 15 (1994): 59–93.

———. "Infanticide and the Juries in France, 1825–1913." *Journal of Family History* 16 (1991): 157–76.

———. "Justice and Sexuality in Victorian Marseille, 1825–1885." *Journal of Social History* 21 (1987): 229–62.

———. "Justice Unblind: The Juries and the Criminal Classes in France, 1825–1914." *Journal of Social History* 15 (1981): 89–108.

———. "Magistrates and Juries in France, 1791–1952." *French Historical Studies* 22 (1999): 379–420.

———. "The Relationship between Migration and Criminality in Marseille, 1825–1880." Ph.D. diss., Syracuse University, 1982.

Donzelot, Jacques. *The Policing of Families*. Translated by Robert Hurley. New York: Pantheon Books, 1979.

Dragu, Thomas. *Juges-citoyens ou juges de métier? Essai sociologique de légitimation du jury*. Paris: M. Rivière, 1931.

Dupin de Beyssat, Gabriel. *Le Jury criminel, son histoire, ses problèmes*. Cour d'appel d'Orleans, Audience solonnelle de rentrée du 16 septembre 1971.

Duvergier, J. B. *Code pénal annoté*. Paris: A. Guyot, 1833.

Ensor, R. C. K. *Courts and Judges in France, Germany, and England*. London: Oxford University Press, 1933.

Esmein, Adhemar. *A History of Continental Criminal Procedure with Special Reference to France*. Translated by Rachel Szold Jastrow. Montclair, N.J.: Patterson Smith, 1968.

Finley, M. I. *Aspects of Antiquity: Discoveries and Controversies*. Hammondsworth, U.K.: Penguin Books, 1977.

Fisher, George. *Plea Bargaining's Triumph: A History of Plea Bargaining in America*. Stanford, Calif.: Stanford University Press, 2003.

Forster, R., and O. Ranum, eds. *Deviants and the Abandoned in French Society: Selections from the "Annales: Economiés, Sociétés, Civilisations,"* vol. 4. Translated by E. Forster and P. M. Ranum. Baltimore: Johns Hopkins University Press, 1978.

Forsyth, William. *History of Trial by Jury*. New York: Burt Franklin, 1971.

Foucault, Michel, ed. *I, Pierre Rivière, Having Slaughtered My Mother, My Sister, and My Brother* . . . Translated by Frank Jellinek. New York: Pantheon Books, 1975.

Frase, Richard S. "Comparative Criminal Justice as a Guide to American Law Reform: How the French Do It, How Can We Find Out, and Why Should We Care." *California Law Review* 78 (1990): 541–683.

Fuchs, Rachel Ginnis. "Crimes against Children in Nineteenth-Century France." *Law and Human Behavior* 6 (1982): 237–59.

———. *Poor and Pregnant in Paris: Strategies for Survival in the Nineteenth Century*. New Brunswick, N.J.: Rutgers University Press, 1992.

Furet, François. *Revolutionary France 1770–1880*. Translated by Antonia Nevill. Oxford: Blackwell, 1995.

Garçon, E. *Code pénal annoté*. 2 vols. Paris: J.-B. Sirey, 1901–6.

Garçon, Maurice. "Faut-il modifier la composition et les attributions du jury." *Revue de droit pénal et de criminologie* 35 (1955): 455–72.

Garner, James W. "Criminal Procedure in France." *Yale Law Journal* 25 (1916): 255–84.

Garraud, René. *Précis de droit criminel, contenant l'explication élémentaire de la partie du Code pénal, de Code d'instruction criminelle et des lois qui ont modifié ces deux codes*. Paris: Sirey, 1934.

———. *Traité théorique et pratique du droit pénal français*. 2 vols. Paris: L. Larose, 1898.

Garraud, René, and P. Bernard. "Des attentats a la pudeur et des viols sur les enfants (législation-statistique)." *Archives d'anthropologie criminelle et des sciences pénales* 1 (1886): 396–435.

Gide, André. *Recollections of the Assize Court*. Translated by Philip A. Watkins. London: Hutchinson and Co., n.d. [1913].

Gineste, Fernand. *Essai sur l'histoire et l'organisation du jury criminel en France et dans états modernes*. Castres: Imprimerie Abeilhou, 1896.

Goldstein, Robert Justin. *Censorship of Political Caricature in Nineteenth-Century France*. Kent, Ohio: Kent State University Press, 1989.

Gouda, Frances, and Peter H. Smith. "Famine, Crime, and Gender in Nineteenth-Century France: Explorations in Time-Series Analysis." *Historical Methods* 16 (1983): 59–73.

Granier, Camille. *La femme criminelle*. Paris: Octave Doin, 1906.

Green, Thomas A. "Freedom and Criminal Responsibility in the Age of Pound: An Essay in Criminal Justice." *Michigan Law Review* 93 (1995): 1915–2053.

———. *Verdict According to Conscience: Perspectives on the English Criminal Trial Jury 1200–1800*. Chicago: University of Chicago Press, 1985.

Guibourg, Léon. *Le jury criminel, son organization, son fonctionnement: Exposé pratique de la législation et de la jurisprudence réglant la formation du Jury et ses attributions*. Paris: Administration du Bulletin-commentaire des lois nouvelles et décrets, 1911.

Guyho, Corentin. *Les Jurés "maîtres de la peine."* Paris: A. Pedone, 1908.

Hamson, C. J. "The Prosecution of the Accused—English and French Legal Methods." *Criminal Law Review* 2 (1955): 272–82.

Harris, Ruth. "Melodrama, Hysteria and Feminine Crimes of Passion in the Fin-de-Siècle." *History Workshop Journal* 25 (1988): 31–63.

———. *Murders and Madness: Medicine, Law, and Society in the Fin de Siècle*. Oxford: Clarendon Press, 1989.

Harsin, Jill. *Policing Prostitution in Nineteenth-Century Paris*. Princeton: Princeton University Press, 1985.

Hartman, Mary. *Victorian Murderesses: A True History of Thirteen Respectable French and English Women Accused of Unspeakable Crimes*. New York: Schocken Books, 1977.

Hay, Douglas, et al. *Albion's Fatal Tree: Crime and Society in Eighteenth-Century England*. New York: Pantheon Books, 1975.

Heywood, Colin. *Childhood in Nineteenth-Century France: Work, Health and Education among the "Classes Populaires."* Cambridge: Cambridge University Press, 1988.

Hufton, Olwen H. *The Poor of Eighteenth-Century France*. Oxford: Clarendon Press, 1974.

Hugueney, Louis, and H. Donnedieu de Vabres, eds. *Études de science criminelle et de droit comparé: Études doctrinales et chroniques sur l'activite législatif et jurisprudentielle recente en matière de droit criminel*. Paris: Sirey, 1945.

Icard, Severin. *La femme pendant la periode menstruelle: Étude de psychologie morbide et de médecine légale*. Paris: Alcan, 1890.

Innes, Joanna, and John Styles. "The Crime Wave: Recent Writing on Crime and Criminal Justice in Eighteenth-Century England." *Journal of British Studies* 25 (1986): 380–435.

"L'Inscription des ouvriers sur la liste annuelle du jury." *Revue pénitentiaire* 32 (1908): 315–17.

Institut de droit comparé de l'Université de Paris, Travaux de la Section de droit pénal et de science criminelle IV. *Problemes contemporains de procédure pénal: Recueil d'études en hommage à M. Louis Hugueney*. Paris: Sirey, 1964.

"Le jury criminel en 1909." *Revue pénitentiaire* 33 (1909): 616–18.

Kalven, Harry, Jr., and Hans Zeisel. *The American Jury*. Boston: Little, Brown, 1966.

King, Peter. *Crime, Justice, and Discretion in England, 1740–1820*. New York: Oxford University Press, 2000.

Kock, Gerald L., trans. *The French Code of Criminal Procedure*. South Hackensack, N.J.: Fred B. Rothman, 1964.

Lallemand, Paul. *Le Recrutement des juges*. Paris: Domat-Montchrestien, 1936.

Lalou, Henri. "Budget de la justice." *Revue pénitentiaire* 29 (1905): 126–31.

Langbein, John H. *The Origins of Adversary Criminal Trial*. New York: Oxford University Press, 2003.

———. *Torture and the Law of Proof: Europe and England in the Ancien Régime*. Chicago: University of Chicago Press, 1977.

Legoyt, A. "Documents communs a divers pays: Justice criminelle." *Journal de la Société de statistique de Paris* 1 (1860): 84–88.

Leps, Marie Christine. *Apprehending the Criminal: The Production of Deviance in Nineteenth-Century Discourse*. Durham, N.C.: Duke University Press, 1992.

241

Levy, Leonard W. *The Palladium of Justice: Origins of Trial by Jury*. Chicago: Ivan R. Dee, 1999.

Locre, [Jean-Guillaume,] ed. *La législation civile, commerciale et criminelle de la France, ou commentaire et complément des codes français*. 31 vols. Paris: Treuttel et Wurtzm, 1827–32.

Lombard, Françoise. *Les Jurés: Justice representative et representations de la justice*. Paris: Editions l'Harmattan, 1993.

Lombard, Paul. *La Justice des bien-pensants 1799–1871*. Paris: Flammarion, 1995.

Loubat, William. "La Crise de la répression [I]." *Revue politique et parlementaire* 68 (1911): 434–68.

———. "La Crise de la répression II—Les Remèdes." *Revue politique et parlementaire* 69 (1911): 5–27.

———. "Programme minimum de réformes pénales [2]." *Revue politique et parlementaire* 74 (1913): 435–58.

Loubet, Louis. *La Justice criminelle en France étudiée principalement dans ses rapports avec l'institution et l'organisation du jury, le régime pénitentiare et l'enseignement primaire*. Paris: Laroze et Forcel, 1890.

Lucas, Colin. "The Rules of the Game in Local Politics under the Directory." *French Historical Studies* 16 (1989): 345–71.

Lux, Jacques. "Un crime que l'on ne punit plus." *Revue bleue*, 23 Mai 1908, 671–72.

Macé, G. *Les femmes criminelles*. Paris: Eugene Lasquelle, 1904.

Maguire, Kathleen, and Ann Pastore, eds. *Bureau of Justice Statistics Sourcebook of Criminal Justice Statistics 1994*. Washington, D.C.: USGPO, 1995.

Manheim, Hermann, ed. *Pioneers in Criminology*. New York: Quadrangle Books, 1960.

Martin, Benjamin F. *Crime and Criminal Justice under the Third Republic: The Shame of Marianne*. Baton Rouge: Louisiana State University Press, 1990.

Martinage, Renée, and Jean-Pierre Royer, eds. *Les destinées du jury criminel*. Lille: Hellemmes, 1990.

Mavidal, M. J., and M. E. Laurent, eds. *Archives Parlementaires de 1787 à 1860*. Vols. 12, 15, and 21. Paris: Paul Dupont, 1881–85.

McLaren, Angus. "Abortion in France: Women and the Regulation of Family Size, 1800–1914." *French Historical Studies* 7 (1978): 461–85.

———. "Sex and Socialism: The Opposition of the French Left to Birth Control in the Nineteenth Century." *Journal of the History of Ideas* 37 (1976): 475–92.

McManners, John. *Church and State in France, 1870–1914*. New York: Harper and Row, 1972.

McMillan, James F. *Housewife or Harlot: The Place of Women in French Society, 1870–1940*. New York: St. Martin's Press, 1981.

Merriman, John H. *The Agony of the Republic: The Repression of the Left in Revolutionary France, 1848–1851*. New York: Yale University Press, 1978.

———. *Police Stories: Building the French State, 1815–1851*. New York: Oxford University Press, 2006.

Mimin, Pierre. *Le Concours du jury a la détermination de la peine: Commentaire de la loi du 5 mars 1932*. Paris: Godde, 1933.

Moore, Lloyd E. *The Jury: Tool of Kings, Palladium of Liberty*. Cincinnati: Anderson Publishing Co., 1988.

Moses, Claire Goldberg. *French Feminism in the Nineteenth Century*. Albany: State
University of New York Press, 1984.

Nord, Philip. *The Republican Moment: Struggles for Democracy in Nineteenth-Century
France*. Cambridge, Mass.: Harvard University Press, 1995.

Nouguier, Charles. *La Cour d'assises, traité pratique*. 2 vols. Paris: Cosse et Marchal,
1860.

Nye, Robert A. *Crime, Madness, and Politics in Modern France: The Medical Concept of
National Decline*. Princeton: Princeton University Press, 1984.

——. *Masculinity and Male Codes of Honor in Modern France*. New York: Oxford
University Press, 1993.

O'Brien, Patricia. "The Kleptomania Diagnosis: Bourgeois Women and Theft in Late
Nineteenth-Century France." *Journal of Social History* 17 (1983): 65–77.

——. *The Promise of Punishment: Prisons in Nineteenth-Century France*. Princeton:
Princeton University Press, 1982.

Payne, Howard C. *The Police State of Louis Napoleon Bonaparte, 1851–1860*. Seattle:
University of Washington Press, 1966.

Perrot, Michelle. "Délinquance et système pénitentiare en France au XIX siècle."
Annales: Economies, Sociétés, Civilisations 30 (1975): 67–91.

Petit, J.-G., ed. *Une justice de proximité, la justice de paix (1790–1958)*. Paris: Presses
Universitaires de France, 2003.

Pinon, H. "La réforme de la procedure criminelle." *Revue politique et parlementaire* 66
(1910): 75–95.

Pourcher, Yves. "Des assises de grace? Le jury de la cour d'assises de la Lozère au XIX
siècle." *Études rurales* 96 (1984): 167–80.

Prevost, Eugene. *De la prostitution des enfants: Étude juridique et sociale (Loi du 11 avril
1908)*. Paris: Plon-Nourrit, 1909.

Price, Roger, ed. *Revolution and Reaction: 1848 and the Second French Republic*. London:
Croom Helm, 1975.

Proal, Louis. *Le Crime et la peine*. Paris: F. Alcan, 1894.

——. *Passion and Criminality in France: A Legal and Literary Study*. Translated by
A. R. Allinson. Paris: Charles Carrington, 1901.

Prud'hon, Pierre, ed. *Le Jury criminel*. Paris: E. Rey, 1914.

Pugh, George W. "Administration of Criminal Justice in France: An Introductory
Analysis." *Louisiana Law Review* 23 (1962): 1–28.

Recueils de la Société Jean Bodin pour l'histoire comparative des institutions.
La peine. Troisième partie-Europe depuis le XVIIIe siècle. Bruxelles: De Boeck
Wesmael, 1989.

"La répression de l'avortement." *Revue pénitentiare et de droit pénal* 41 (1917): 83–84.

Roberts, J. M., and R. C. Comb, eds. *French Revolution Documents*. Vol. 1. New York:
Barnes and Noble, 1966.

Roberts, J. M., and John Hardman, eds. *French Revolution Documents*. Vol. 2. Oxford:
Blackwell, 1973.

Robinson, C. R. *Everyday Life in Ancient Greece*. Westport, Conn.: Greenwood Press,
1978.

Rothman, David J. *Conscience and Convenience: The Asylum and Its Alternatives in
Progressive America*. New York: Aldine de Gruyter, 2002.

Rousseaux, Xavier, Marie-Sylvie Dupont-Bouchat, and Claude Vael, eds. *Révolutions et justice pénale en Europe: modeles français et traditions nationales*. Paris: L'Harmattan, 1999.

Rousselet, Marcel. *Histoire de la justice*. Paris: Presses Universitaires de France, 1968.

Royer, Jean-Pierre. *Histoire de la justice en France de la monarchie absolue à la République*. Paris: Presses Universitaires de France, 1995.

Royer, Jean-Pierre, et al. *Juges et notables au XIXe siècle*. Paris: Presses Universitaires de France, 1982.

Ryckere, Raymond de. Review of *La femme criminelle et la prostituée*, by C. Lombroso and G. Ferrero. *Archives d'anthropologie criminelle* 12 (1897): 301–21.

Saleilles, Raymond. *The Individualization of Punishment*. Translated by Rachel Szold Jastrow. Montclair, N.J.: Patterson Smith, 1968.

Savey-Casard, Paul. *La peine de mort: Esquisse historique et juridique*. Genève: Droz, 1968.

Savitt, William. "Villainous Verdicts? Rethinking the Nineteenth-Century French Jury." *Columbia Law Review* 96 (1996): 1019–61.

Schaefer, Stephen. *Theories in Criminology: Past and Present Philosophies of the Crime Problem*. New York: Random House, 1969.

Schioppa, Antonio Padoa, ed. *The Trial Jury in England, France, Germany, 1700–1900*. Berlin: Duncker and Humblot, 1987.

Schnapper, Bernard. *Voies nouvelles en histoire du droit: La justice, la famille, la répression pénale (XVI–XXeme siècles)*. Paris: Presses Universitaires de France, 1991.

Smith, Bruce P. "The Emergence of Public Prosecution in London, 1790–1850." *Yale Journal of Law and the Humanities* 18 (2006): 29–62.

———. "Plea Bargaining and the Eclipse of the Jury." *Annual Review of Law and Social Science* 1 (2005): 131–49.

Société Générale des Prisons. "Seconde Séance du 28 juin 1913." *Revue pénitentiare et de droit pénal* 37 (1913): 945–71.

Soulas, Christian. *Le Recrutement du jury*. Lyon: Bosc Frères, M. and L. Riou, Imprimeurs-Éditeurs, 1933.

Spengler, Joseph J. *France Faces Depopulation*. New York: Greenwood Press, 1968.

Stewart, John Hall. *The Restoration Era in France*. Princeton: D. Van Nostrand Company, 1968.

Stone, I. F. *The Trial of Socrates*. New York: Anchor Books, 1989.

Summers, Lionel Morgan. "The Criminal Jury in France and Its Recent Reform." *American Bar Association Comparative Law Bureau Bulletin for 1933*. Washington, D.C., 1933. 199–209.

Tarde, Gabriel de. *Penal Philosophy*. Translated by Rapelje Howell. Boston: Little, Brown, 1912.

Tardieu, Ambroise. *Étude médico-légale sur l'infanticide*. Paris: J.-B. Baillière et Fils, 1868.

Thoinot, L. *Medicolegal Aspects of Moral Offenses*. Translated by Arthur W. Weysse. Philadelphia: F. A. Davis Company, 1920.

Thompson, E. P. *The Making of the English Working Class*. New York: Vintage Books, 1966.

Thomson, David. *Democracy in France since 1870*. London: Oxford University Press, 1969.

Toulemon, André. *La Question du jury*. Paris: Sirey, 1930.

Toutain, J.-C. *La population de la France de 1700 à 1959*. Paris: Cahiers de l'Institut de Science Economique Appliquée, 1963.

Trebutien, E. *Cours élémentaire de droit criminel comprenant l'exposé et le commentaire des deux premiers livres du Code pénal, du Code d'instruction criminelle en entier, et des lois et décrets qui sont venus modifier ces codes*. 2 vols. Paris: Auguste Durand, 1854.

Vallaud, Dominique. "Le crime d'infanticide et l'indulgence des cours d'assises en France au XIX siècle." *Social Science Information* 21 (1982): 475–99.

Van Caenegem, R. C. *Judges, Legislators and Professors: Chapters in European Legal History*. Cambridge: Cambridge University Press, 1993.

Vigarello, Georges. *A History of Rape: Sexual Violence in France from the 16th to the 20th Century*. Translated by Jean Birrell. Cambridge, U.K.: Polity Press, 2001.

Vlamynck, Alain. "La délinquance au feminin: crimes et répression dans le Nord (1880–1913)." *Revue de Nord* 63 (1981): 676–702.

Vouin, Robert. "La question du jury." *Revue de science criminelle et de droit pénal comparé* 20 (1955): 503–7.

Weber, Eugen. *France, Fin de Siècle*. Cambridge, Mass.: Harvard University Press, 1986.

Werth, Alexander. *France 1940–1955*. Boston: Beacon Press, 1966.

Whitman, James Q. *Harsh Justice: Criminal Punishment and the Widening Divide between America and Europe*. Oxford: Oxford University Press, 2003.

Wiener, Martin J. *Men of Blood: Violence, Manliness and Criminal Justice in Victorian England*. Cambridge: Cambridge University Press, 2004.

———. *Reconstructing the Criminal: Culture, Law, and Policy in England, 1830–1914*. Cambridge: Cambridge University Press, 1990.

Willrich, Michael. *City of Courts: Socializing Justice in Progressive Era Chicago*. Cambridge: Cambridge University Press, 2003.

Wolf, John B. *France: 1814–1919, The Rise of a Liberal-Democratic Society*. New York: Harper Torchbooks, 1963.

Woloch, Isser. *The New Regime: Transformations of the French Civic Order, 1789–1820s*. New York: W. W. Norton, 1994.

Wright, Gordon. *Between the Guillotine and Liberty: Two Centuries of the Crime Problem in France*. New York: Oxford University Press, 1983.

Yvernes, Maurice. "La Justice en France de 1881 à 1900." *Journal de la Sociètè de statistique de Paris* 44 (1903): 297–316.

Zeldin, Theodore. *France, 1848–1945*. 2 vols. Oxford: Clarendon Press, 1973.

INDEX

Abortion: acquittal rates for, 16, 18, 129, 135–37, 138, 141, 146–47, 148, 161, 179, 222 (n. 155), 223 (n. 173); proof of, 16, 129, 136, 179, 222 (n. 156); and jury resistance to punishments, 17; and social norms, 18, 135, 137–38; persons tried for, 135–36, 147, 161, 221 (nn. 148, 150, 151), 223 (n. 172), 228 (n. 37), 231 (n. 10); abortionists distinguished from *avortées*, 136, 221 (n. 152); and juries finding extenuating circumstances, 136, 221 (n. 152), 222 (n. 158); sentencing for, 136–37, 222 (nn. 154, 159); prevalence of, 137–38, 146, 227 (n. 29); police reports of, 138, 223 (n. 166); and repopulationists, 146, 160; and correctionalization, 147, 160, 227 (nn. 33, 34)

Accused persons: rights of, 11, 38, 40, 42–43, 45, 120, 146; and *interrogatoires*, 13, 121–22; and inquisitorial criminal procedure, 23; and peremptory challenges, 34, 168–69; as recidivists, 98–100, 208 (n. 61); as bourgeois, 200 (n. 126). *See also* Character of accused persons

Acquittal rates: and law of 1832, 5, 18, 62–63, 72, 79, 100; for political cases, 9, 35–37, 40, 45, 51, 82, 83–84, 85, 90–92, 114, 116, 142, 166, 203 (n. 164), 204 (n. 174), 205 (nn. 18, 21), 206 (n. 26), 213 (nn. 16, 24, 26), 225 (n. 10); for infanticide, 16, 17, 68, 69, 72, 129, 132, 133, 135, 136, 137, 148, 179, 197 (n. 92), 198 (n. 99), 219 (n. 121), 220 (n. 128); and sanction nullification, 16, 18, 57, 59, 140; for abortion, 16, 18, 129, 135–37, 138, 141, 146–47, 148, 161, 179, 222 (n. 155), 223 (n. 173); for women, 18, 127, 129, 130, 134–35, 148, 178, 179, 182, 218 (n. 98); and harsh punishment,
35, 38, 46, 47, 80, 122–23, 124, 132, 136, 164, 165, 177; and jurors' interpretation of *question intentionnelle*, 36, 38; and judiciary's criticism of jury system, 37, 41, 45; for ordinary crimes, 37, 51; and inquisitorial system, 45; for violent crimes, 49, 70–71, 72, 75, 77, 108–9, 178, 199 (n. 112); for capital crimes, 57, 66, 72, 194 (n. 42), 196 (n. 78); for *vol domestique*, 69, 198 (n. 103); for property crimes, 70–71, 76–77, 178, 199 (nn. 112, 120), 200 (nn. 121, 122, 123); for white-collar crimes, 78, 80, 161, 200 (n. 130), 202 (nn. 141, 144), 231 (n. 17); and correctionalization, 86, 120, 143, 147, 148, 177; and criminal responsibility, 120, 125, 127; and abolition of *résumé*, 121–22; and evidence, 165, 178; and *échevinage*, 168

Adultery law, 133, 134, 135
Ajam, Maurice, 138
Alexandrine, Zelenine, 131
Allemane, Felix, 147, 227 (n. 34)
Allen, Robert, 36–37
American Institute of Criminal Law and Criminology (AICLC), 154
Anarchists, 118, 141–42
Anthropometrie, 214 (n. 52)
Anti-clerical laws, 117, 137
Anti-Jacobin reaction, 35, 36
Appeals court (*cour royale*), 29, 40–41, 52
Athens, 25, 26

Baron, G., 227 (n. 26)
Barrot, Odilon, 117
Barthélemy, J., 167
Barthou, Louis, 156
Beattie, J. M., 4, 196 (n. 69)

Index

individualization achieved by, 152, 154, 179; shifting attitudes toward, 155; uncertainty of, 167. *See also* Verdicts

Jury devices for leniency: and convictions downgraded to misdemeanors, 2, 3, 4, 49, 56–57, 62, 68, 79, 105, 143, 145, 149, 179, 195 (nn. 59, 60), 225 (nn. 16, 17); and sanction nullification, 2–3; and discretion in imposition of punishment, 4, 5–6, 12, 68; extralegal, 5, 49; and questions asked of juries, 5, 56–57; and aggravating circumstances, 5, 57, 62, 181; and partial verdicts, 5–6, 56–57; and fact-finding procedures, 6; and extenuating circumstances, 6, 8, 17, 18, 49, 51, 59, 61, 62, 63, 65, 80, 105, 110, 177, 181, 196 (nn. 67, 73); judicial statistics on, 62; and political cases, 88; and sentencing, 122–23; and criminological theories, 141, 151

Jury duty: as right, 6, 19, 88, 112, 113, 114

Jury independence: and political and press cases, 1, 8, 9; and correctionalization, 3; and *échevinage*, 11, 20, 80, 156, 157, 158, 168, 183; judges' destruction of, 48, 140, 141; and criminological theories, 158; and jury system as symbolic, 175

Jury leniency: and partial verdicts, 6; for first-time offenders, 8, 179, 180, 181, 182; criticism of, 10, 19, 23, 41, 51, 82, 141, 147, 148–49, 163; and acquittal rates, 35, 159, 163; causes of, 38, 68; and property cases, 69–70, 77; and white-collar crimes, 78–80, 161; and correctionalization, 85, 105, 108–9, 141, 160; and criminological theories, 111, 141; and women, 132, 133, 134; and *crimes passionnels*, 135, 181; and abortion, 136, 147. *See also* Jury devices for leniency

Jury lists: composition of, 6, 32–33, 34, 35, 37, 43–44, 50, 89, 91, 96, 112–14, 192 (n. 5); political abuse of, 8, 32, 33, 35, 37, 39, 44, 112, 114, 115, 117–18; judiciary's control of, 8, 113, 114, 149, 167, 168; prefect's control of, 51–53; and bourgeois

jurors, 90, 205 (nn. 12, 13); and Second Empire, 94–95, 97, 113–14, 115, 206 (n. 39); exclusions from, 114–15, 118, 213 (n. 21)

Jury nullification: in political cases, 1, 2, 4, 177; forms of, 2–3, 17; and modification of criminal justice system, 3; judges' response to, 141; and *échevinage*, 183. *See also* Sanction nullification

Jurys d'accusation (grand juries), 33, 36, 42

Jury selection process: government intrusion into, 8, 9, 96–97; debates on, 18; political nature of, 35–36, 39, 52–53, 114, 118, 149, 178; restrictions on, 88–89; and Second Empire, 94–97; and law of 1872, 113

Jury system: destruction of independence of, 3, 20, 158, 168, 170–71, 183; effect of regime changes on, 8, 9, 19, 33; decline of, 10–11, 35, 48, 157, 162, 174, 175; as "palladium of liberty," 11, 18, 41, 49, 51, 54, 84, 88, 166; liberals' abandonment of support for, 11, 158, 166; effect on criminal justice system, 11–12, 17, 23, 32, 48, 56, 105, 183; liberal support for, 18, 19, 20, 49, 82, 86, 111, 116–17, 141, 146, 156–57, 166, 174; political debates on, 18, 28; Napoleon's limits on, 23, 39–45, 87; subversion of, 34–35; criticism of, 37, 41, 146–55, 158, 163, 166, 175; paradox in history of, 49; reform of, 51–54, 92–93, 159, 163–67; *enquêtes* on, 92–93, 163, 228 (n. 38); Positivist critique of, 151, 153, 154, 158, 163; publications critical of, 163; decline in public support for, 163, 171; role in protection of political and press freedoms, 166, 172; marginalization of, 167; public opinion represented by, 172, 173; and judgment by peers, 173; costs of, 175

Jury trials: and democracy, 1; dynamics of influencing jury bias, 2; as essential right, 11, 19, 28, 29, 93, 111, 167; theatrical nature of, 12–14, 46, 179; effects on legal system, 16; newspaper accounts of, 16; Revolutionary-Napoleoenic era

Index